PRACTICE WORKBOOK

TRIGONOMETRY

+ guided practice questions

1500+ QUESTIONS YOU NEED TO KILL IN → **HIGH SCHOOL**

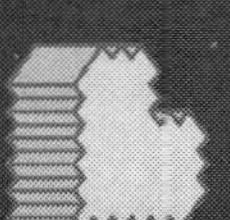

made by
Brain Hunter Prep
with love from New York

1. The Unit Circle page 4
   - Section 1.1: Understanding the Unit Circle page 4
   - Section 1.2: Converting degrees to radians page 11
   - Section 1.3: Converting radians to degrees page 16
   - Section 1.4: Basic Trig Review page 20
2. Trig Functions page 24
   - Section 2.1: Understanding the 6 Trig Functions page 24
   - Section 2.2: Finding Missing Sides & Angles page 47
   - Section 2.2: Quiz page 54
3. Special Angles page 68
   - Section 3.1: 30-60-90 & 45-45-90 Right Triangle page 68
   - Section 3.2: 30-60-90 & 45-45-90 Right Triangle (Advanced Problems) page 83
   - Section 3.2: Quiz page 86
4. Trig Functions for 0°, 30°, 45°, 60° and 90° page 90
   - Section 4: Quiz page 98
5. Trig Functions Quadrant II - IV page 102
   - Section 5.1: Reference Angle page 102
   - Section 5.2: Solving Trig Functions for Quadrants II, III, and IV page 110
   - Section 5.2: Quiz page 116
6. The Law of Sines & The Law of Cosines page 121
   - Section 6.1: The Law of Sines page 121
   - Section 6.1: Quiz page 124
   - Section 6.2: The Law of Cosines page 138
   - Section 6.2: Quiz page 146
7. Answer Key page 159

2
3
9
c2
a2+b2
(x+y)n=
√2
k<0
x/(x+2) − 8/(x+6) =
√3/2
BRAIN
HUNTER

Chapter 1
The Unit Circle

Section 1.1 Understanding the Unit Circle

The concept of the unit circle is fundamental to trigonometry, bridging the gap between the linear world of algebra and the cyclical patterns observed in trigonometry. At its core, the unit circle is a simple geometric shape - a circle with a radius of one - but its implications and applications in mathematics, and specifically in trigonometry, are profound.

Imagine a circle, centered at the origin of a coordinate plane, with a radius of exactly one unit. This circle is aptly named the **"unit circle."** While the idea might seem basic, as we journey around this circle, we will discover that **every point** on its circumference has a unique relationship to the angles it creates and the lengths of the sides of the triangles we can form inside the circle.

These relationships give rise to the fundamental trigonometric functions: sine, cosine, and tangent.

One of the primary reasons the unit circle is so invaluable is its ability to allow us to **define** trigonometric functions for **all real numbers**, not just specific angles.

In this chapter, you will explore how angles are measured, how they can be represented in both degrees and radians, and how every point on the circle corresponds to a unique set of trigonometric values.

QUICK FACTS AND LESSONS TO LEARN

Take a look at the diagram below. This is a Unit Circle. As you can see, the **radius** is 1 and the center is at the origin (0, 0).

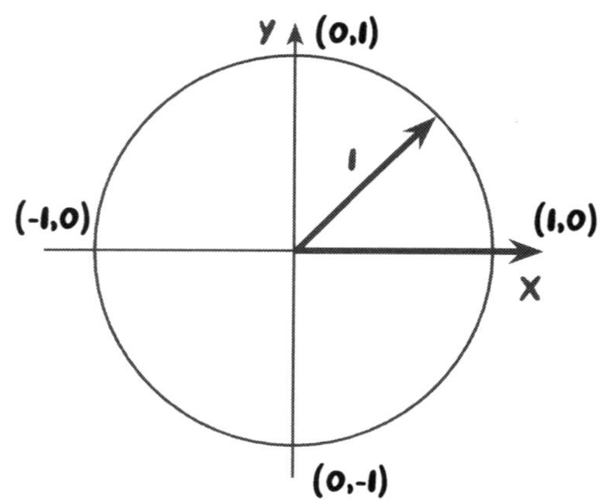

You know that a circle has **360°**.

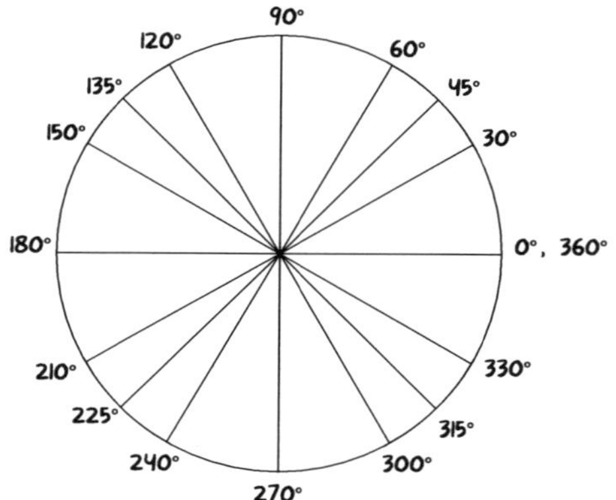

Chapter 1
The Unit Circle

What is the equation of a Unit Circle?

The general equation of any circle is $(x - a)^2 + (y - b)^2 = r^2$, where the center of the circle is the coordinates (a, b) and the radius is noted by the variable r.

Now that you know the general equation of any circle, can you find out the equation of a Unit Circle? **Remember**, a Unit Circle has a radius of 1 and the center is at the origin. Pause here and see if you can determine the equation of a Unit Circle with the given information.

Were you able to determine the equation of a Unit Circle? If not, let's go ahead and think this through together!

Step 1: I know the general equation of any circle is $(x - a)^2 + (y - b)^2 = r^2$

Step 2: I need to identify the variables a, b, and r. I know the variables a and b represent the coordinates (a, b). As we learned, the center of a Unit Circle is (0,0) so the variable a = 0 and b = 0. Finally, we know the radius of a Unit circle is 1. Let's plug the known variables.

Step 3: $(x - 0)^2 + (y - 0)^2 = 1^2$

Step 4: Simplify

Step 5: After we simply, we see that the **equation of a unit circle** is $x^2 + y^2 = 1$

The equation of a unit circle is $x^2 + y^2 = 1$

Arcs on the Unit Circle

When you hear the phrase "a piece of the pie," you can think of an arc as representing the crusty edge of that pie slice. In simple words, an arc is a segment or a portion of a circle's circumference.

Now, consider the unit circle, which is centered at the origin (0, 0) of a coordinate plane and has a radius of exactly one unit. Every point on this circle is exactly one unit away from the center.

When we talk about an angle formed in the unit circle, we generally refer to the angle formed between the x-axis and a line segment (or radius) drawn from the center of the circle to a point on the circle. As this line segment (or radius) sweeps or rotates from its initial position, it "cuts out" or delineates an arc on the circle. The size of this arc is directly related to the size of the angle.

Measuring Arcs

In trigonometry, one of the first skills you need to master as a student is to convert degrees to radians, and radians to degrees which you will practice in section 1.2.

Arcs on the unit circle can be measured in two common ways:

1) Degrees: This is the measurement you're most familiar with. A full circle contains **360°**, so if a radius of the unit circle rotates **90°** from the positive x-axis, the arc it sweeps out is $\frac{1}{4}$ of the circle's circumference.

2) Radians: This is a more "natural" way to measure angles when working in the context of circles, especially the unit circle. A **full circle** is **2π** radians.

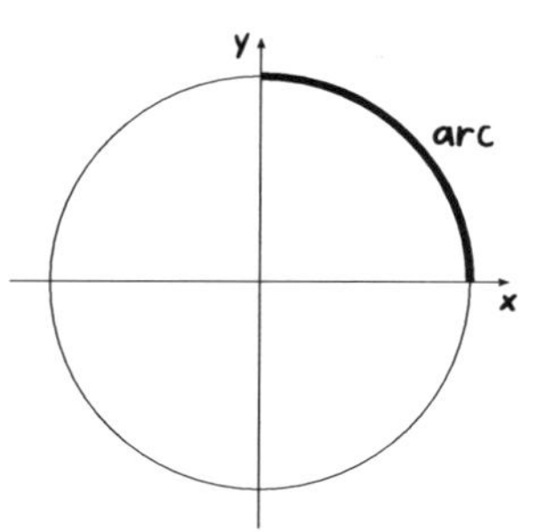

Now that you know in a full circle there are 2π radians, how many radians are in half a circle?

In half a circle, there are **π** radians, which is also 180°.

With this information, there are a few important facts that we can **conclude.**

π radians = 180° and 2π radians = 360°

Using this information, 1 Radian is equal to how many degrees?

How would you go about solving this problem?

We know **π** radians = 180°

To solve for 1 radian, we need to divide **π** on both sides.

$$\frac{\cancel{\pi}\text{ radians}}{\cancel{\pi}} = \frac{180°}{\pi}$$

We see that 1 radian = $\frac{180°}{\pi}$.

If you use a calculator and divide 180 degrees by **π**, **you will get approximately 57.2958...°**

You do **not** need to remember this information, but you **must know** that 1 radian= $\frac{180°}{\pi}$

Knowing this helps us to go from **radians to degrees** and **degrees to radians.**

Now that we know a few fundamental information of a Unit Circle, let's take a close look at the diagram below. This should make sense to you.

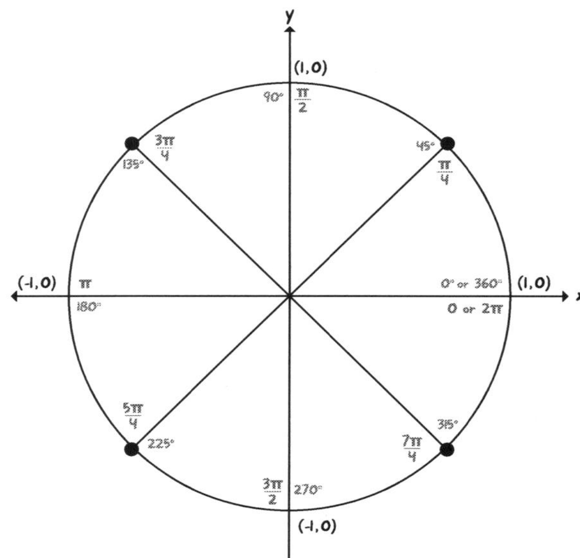

This is a Unit Circle diagram that is divided into 45° increments. We see at 360° that we have 2π radians. At the 180° position, we see π radians. This is information we already know.

How about 90°? What is the radian equivalent for 90°? Since π radians = 180°, we can just divide both sides by 2 to get $\frac{\pi}{2}$ = 90°.

How about 45°? What is the radian equivalent for 45°? Since π radians = 180°, we can just divide both sides by 4 to get $\frac{\pi}{4}$ = 45°.

Here is a chart below of common degrees and radian conversion.

Degrees	Radians
0	0
30	$\frac{\pi}{6}$
45	$\frac{\pi}{4}$
60	$\frac{\pi}{3}$
90	$\frac{\pi}{2}$
180	π
270	$\frac{3\pi}{2}$
360	2π

While you **do not need** to memorize this entire chart, it is helpful to remember a few of these to make your calculations faster. We can always find out the answer since we know that π radians = 180°.

On the next section, you will get to practice with many problems and you will see practice examples.

Before we end this section, let's talk about why radians is the preferred way to measure angles when dealing with Unit Circles.

* When dealing with calculus, especially differentiation and integration of trigonometric functions, radians provide more straightforward results.

* In the unit circle, for an angle measured in radians, the length of the subtended arc is numerically equal to the measure of the angle. This means, for small angles, the sine of the angle (in radians) is approximately equal to the angle itself, which is useful in linear approximations.

* Radians are the natural choice for Fourier Transforms, series expansions, and other advanced mathematical topics. They ensure consistency and elegance in mathematical expressions.

Don't worry about understanding why radians are the preferred way to measure angles instead of degrees. We included this because as learners, it's important to understand why we need to learn these topics and how they apply to real-life!

Up until now, you have always used degrees in your math classes. In trigonometry, we get introduced into the wonderful world of radians.

Section 1.1 Quiz

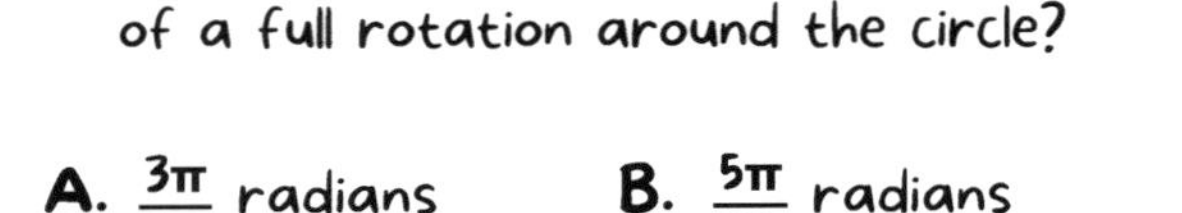

Let's reinforce what we have learned by answering the questions below.

1. What is the radius of a unit circle?

   A. 2 units **B.** 0.5 units
   C. 1 unit **D.** 10 units

2. How many degrees are equivalent to π radians?

   A. 90° **B.** 180°
   C. 270° **D.** 360°

3. Which angle measure is equivalent to one full rotation around the unit circle?

   A. 180° **B.** 270°
   C. π radians **D.** 2π radians

4. What is the relationship between degrees and radians?

   A. π radians = 180° **B.** 1 radian = 180°
   C. π radians = 90° **D.** 1 radian = 360°

5. If an angle in the unit circle is $\frac{\pi}{4}$ radians, how many degrees is this?

   A. 45° **B.** 90°
   C. 135° **D.** 180°

6. How many radians are in three-quarters of a full rotation around the circle?

   A. $\frac{3\pi}{4}$ radians **B.** $\frac{5\pi}{4}$ radians
   C. $\frac{3\pi}{2}$ radians **D.** $\frac{7\pi}{4}$ radians

7. Which of the following is an acute angle?

   A. π radians **B.** 2π radians
   C. $\frac{3\pi}{2}$ radians **D.** $\frac{\pi}{6}$ radians

8. Each radian is ________ degrees.

   A. $\frac{90}{\pi}$ **B.** 90
   C. $\frac{180}{\pi}$ **D.** 45

9. The equation of a unit of circle is ________.

   A. $x^2 + y^2 = 1$ **B.** $x^2 + y^2 = 0$
   C. $(x - a)^2 + (y - b)^2 = r^2$ **D.** $x + y = 1$

10. Which of the following is an obtuse angle?

    A. 30° **B.** $\frac{\pi}{4}$ radians
    C. $\frac{\pi}{3}$ radians **D.** 94°

Section 1.2 Converting degrees to radians

In the previous section, you learned that 1 radian = $\frac{180°}{\pi}$.

Memorize the following rules to convert between degrees and radians.

To convert degrees to radians, multiply by $\frac{\pi}{180°}$

To convert radians to degrees, multiply by $\frac{180°}{\pi}$

Let's quickly make sure we understand why we need to multiple by $\frac{\pi}{180}$ to convert degrees to radians. In section 1.1, we learned that 1 radian = $\frac{180°}{\pi}$.

In order to know how to convert **degrees** to **radians**, we we need to ask ourself **1° is equal to how many radians**?

We can manipulate the equation 1 radian = $\frac{180°}{\pi}$ to figure out how many radians are in 1° or **each degree**.

We want to manpiulate the equation so on the right side we have only 1°. Multiply π on both sides, and divide by 180 and you are left with $\frac{\pi}{180}$ = **1°** or each degree.

$$\pi \times 1 \text{ radian} = \frac{180°}{\cancel{\pi}} \times \cancel{\pi}$$

$$\frac{\pi}{180} = \frac{180^{\text{degrees}}}{180}$$

$$\frac{\pi}{180} = 1 \text{ degree}$$

Let's take a look at the following practice questions.

1. Convert 65° to radians.

Guided Explanation:

We know the rule "To convert degrees to radians, multiply by $\frac{\pi}{180}$".

$$65 \times \frac{\pi}{180} = \frac{65\pi}{180}$$

We can simplify this further by dividing the top and bottom by **5**.

$$\frac{65\pi \div 5}{180 \div 5} = \frac{13\pi}{36}$$

The answer is $\frac{13\pi}{36}$ radians.

2. Convert 40° to radians.

Guided Explanation:

We know the rule "To convert degrees to radians, multiply by $\frac{\pi}{180}$".

$$40 \times \frac{\pi}{180} = \frac{40\pi}{180}$$

We can simplify this further by dividing the top and bottom by **20**.

$$\frac{40\pi \div 20}{180 \div 20} = \frac{2\pi}{9}$$

The answer is $\frac{2\pi}{9}$ radians.

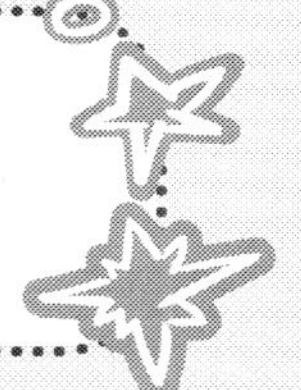

3. Convert 190° to radians.

Guided Explanation:

We know the rule "To convert degrees to radians, multiply by $\frac{\pi}{180}$".

$$190 \times \frac{\pi}{180} = \frac{190\pi}{180}$$

We can simplify this further by dividing the top and bottom by 10.

$$\frac{190\pi \div 10}{180 \div 10} = \frac{19\pi}{18}$$

The answer is $\frac{19\pi}{18}$ radians.

Recap: To successfully convert any given angle from degrees to radians, we must:

1. Multiply the given angle by π and divide by 180.
2. If the result is a fraction, always make sure the fraction is in its simplest/reduced form.

Now, complete the following problems on the next page and show all the work.

Section 1.2 Quiz

Directions: Convert the given angle from degrees to radians. If the result is a fraction, make sure the fraction is in its simplest/reduced form. Show your work.

1. 330°
2. 125°
3. 190°
4. 105°
5. 65°
6. 255°
7. 70°
8. 270°
9. 55°
10. 220°
11. 5°
12. 250°
13. 40°
14. 205°
15. 90°
16. 340°
17. 290°
18. 45°
19. 200°
20. 310°
21. 35°
22. 235°
23. 300°
24. 245°
25. 110°
26. 175°
27. 80°
28. 355°
29. 160°
30. 130°
31. 75°
32. 230°
33. 180°
34. 115°
35. 295°
36. 315°

37. 85°

38. 320°

39. 325°

40. 360°

41. 285°

42. 140°

43. 305°

44. 145°

45. 0°

46. 265°

47. 135°

48. 100°

49. 350°

50. 335°

51. 225°

52. 15°

53. 185°

54. 60°

55. 275°

56. 280°

57. 215°

58. 240°

59. 155°

60. 195°

61. 165°

62. 150°

63. 95°

64. 20°

65. 345°

66. 170°

67. 30°

68. 210°

69. 25°

70. 50°

71. 260°

72. 120°

Section 1.3 Converting radians to degrees

In the previous section, you had the opportunity to master converting degrees to radians. Section 1.3 is all about converting radians to degrees.

Let's recall our rule table.

To convert degrees to radians, multiply by $\frac{\pi}{180}$

To convert radians to degrees, multiply by $\frac{180°}{\pi}$

Let's take a look at the following practice questions.

1. Convert $\frac{11\pi}{18}$ radians to degrees.

Guided Explanation:

We know the rule "To convert radians to degrees, multiply by $\frac{180°}{\pi}$".

$$\frac{11\pi}{18} \times \frac{180°}{\pi} = \frac{1{,}980°\pi}{18\pi}$$

We can simplify this further. Notice that the π's cancel out because there is a π on the numerator and also on the denominator. We are only left with $\frac{1{,}980}{18}$ which gives us 110°.

The answer is 110°.

2. Convert $\frac{17\pi}{36\pi}$ radians to degrees.

Guided Explanation:

We know the rule "To convert radians to degrees, multiply by $\frac{180°}{\pi}$".

$$\frac{17\pi}{36} \times \frac{180°}{\pi} = \frac{3{,}060°\pi}{36\pi}$$

We can simplify this further. Notice that the π's cancel out because there is a π on the numerator and also on the denominator. We are only left with $\frac{3{,}060}{36}$ which gives us 85°.
The answer is 85°.

3. Convert $\frac{10\pi}{9}$ radians to degrees.

Guided Explanation:

We know the rule "To convert radians to degrees, multiply by $\frac{180°}{\pi}$".

$$\frac{10\pi}{9} \times \frac{180°}{\pi} = \frac{1{,}800°\pi}{9\pi}$$

We can simplify this further. Notice that the π's cancel out because there is a π on the numerator and also on the denominator. We are only left with $\frac{1{,}800}{9}$ which gives us 200°.

The answer is 200°.

Recap: To successfully convert any given angle from radians to degrees, we must:

Multiply the given radian by 180° and divide by π.

Now, complete the following problems on the next page and show all the work.

Section 1.3 Quiz

Directions: Convert the given angle from radians to degrees. Show your work.

1. $\frac{47\pi}{36}$
2. $\frac{3\pi}{2}$
3. $\frac{35\pi}{36}$
4. $\frac{\pi}{36}$
5. $\frac{59\pi}{36}$
6. $\frac{2\pi}{3}$
7. $\frac{19\pi}{12}$
8. $\frac{19\pi}{18}$
9. $\frac{25\pi}{18}$
10. $\frac{13\pi}{18}$
11. $\frac{13\pi}{36}$
12. $\frac{\pi}{4}$
13. $\frac{\pi}{6}$
14. $\frac{5\pi}{3}$
15. $\frac{5\pi}{36}$
16. $\frac{3\pi}{4}$
17. $\frac{43\pi}{36}$
18. $\frac{23\pi}{36}$
19. $\frac{53\pi}{36}$
20. $\frac{2\pi}{9}$
21. $\frac{35\pi}{18}$
22. $\frac{71\pi}{36}$
23. $\frac{\pi}{3}$
24. $\frac{\pi}{2}$
25. $\frac{29\pi}{18}$
26. $\frac{41\pi}{36}$
27. $\frac{17\pi}{18}$
28. $\frac{31\pi}{18}$
29. $\frac{\pi}{12}$
30. 2π
31. $\frac{5\pi}{6}$
32. $\frac{23\pi}{12}$
33. 0
34. $\frac{7\pi}{9}$
35. $\frac{49\pi}{36}$
36. $\frac{13\pi}{12}$

Section 1.3 Quiz

37. $\frac{7\pi}{6}$

38. $\frac{4\pi}{3}$

39. $\frac{17\pi}{12}$

40. $\frac{29\pi}{36}$

41. $\frac{17\pi}{36}$

42. $\frac{8\pi}{9}$

43. $\frac{16\pi}{9}$

44. $\frac{65\pi}{36}$

45. $\frac{4\pi}{9}$

46. π

47. $\frac{31\pi}{36}$

48. $\frac{5\pi}{4}$

49. $\frac{7\pi}{18}$

50. $\frac{61\pi}{36}$

51. $\frac{14\pi}{9}$

52. $\frac{55\pi}{36}$

53. $\frac{5\pi}{18}$

54. $\frac{37\pi}{36}$

55. $\frac{67\pi}{36}$

56. $\frac{10\pi}{9}$

57. $\frac{5\pi}{12}$

58. $\frac{\pi}{9}$

59. $\frac{13\pi}{9}$

60. $\frac{17\pi}{9}$

61. $\frac{11\pi}{12}$

62. $\frac{7\pi}{36}$

63. $\frac{11\pi}{6}$

64. $\frac{7\pi}{4}$

65. $\frac{25\pi}{36}$

66. $\frac{11\pi}{18}$

67. $\frac{\pi}{18}$

68. $\frac{5\pi}{9}$

69. $\frac{19\pi}{36}$

70. $\frac{11\pi}{36}$

71. $\frac{11\pi}{9}$

72. $\frac{23\pi}{18}$

73. $\frac{7\pi}{12}$

Section 1.4 Basic Trig Review

In the previous sections, you learned about the Unit Circle and how to convert degrees to radians **and** radians to degrees. In section 1.4, we will briefly review basic trigonometry concepts that you should already be familiar with and then we will practice plotting angles on the Unit Circle.

Basic Trigonometry Review

Types of Angles:

* Acute Angle: An angle smaller than 90°.

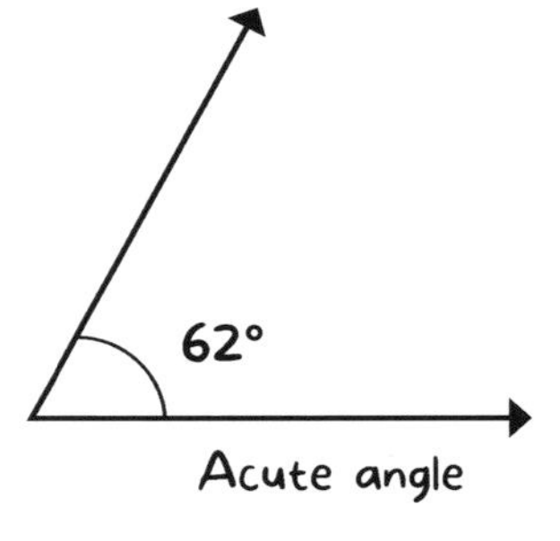

* Right Angle: An angle that is exactly 90°.

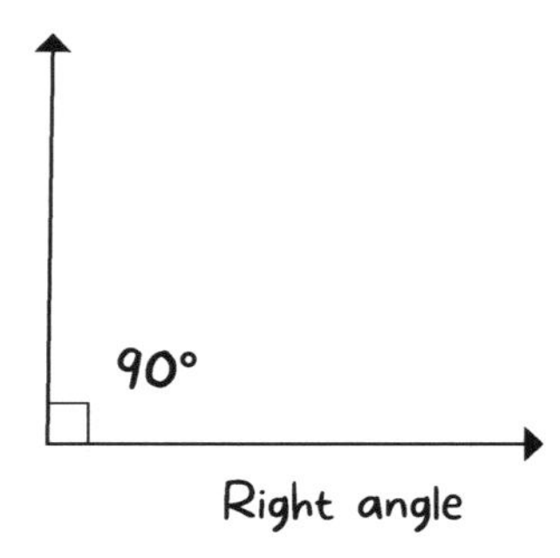

* Obtuse Angle: An angle between 90° and 180°.

Obtuse angle

Complementary and Supplementary Angles:

* Complementary Angles: Two angles that add up to 90°.

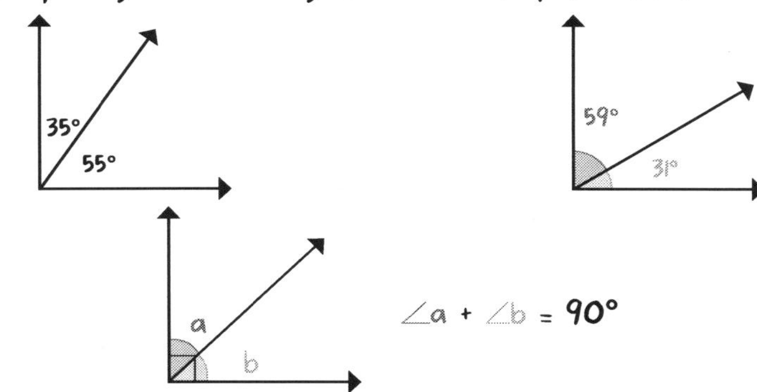

* Supplementary Angles: Two angles that add up to 180°.

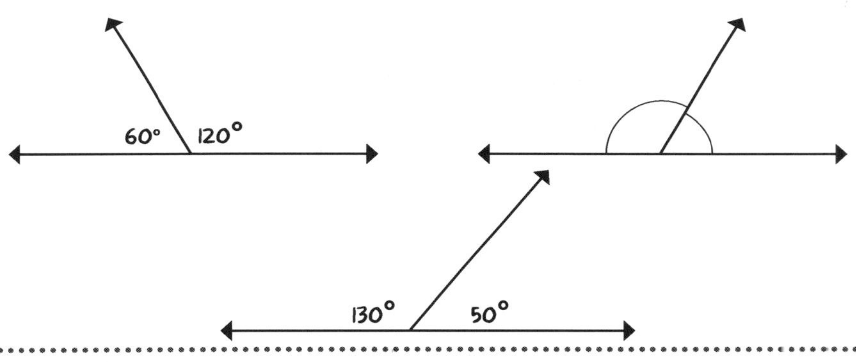

Triangle Facts

* The **sum** of the interior angles of any triangle is **always** 180°.
* A triangle with a 90° angle is termed a **right** triangle. The side facing this right angle is known as the **hypotenuse,** while the remaining two sides are referred to as the **legs.**

leg
hypotenuse
right angle
leg

Pythagorean Theorem:

* For a right triangle, the square of the length of the hypotenuse (the side opposite the right angle) is equal to the sum of the squares of the lengths of the other two sides.

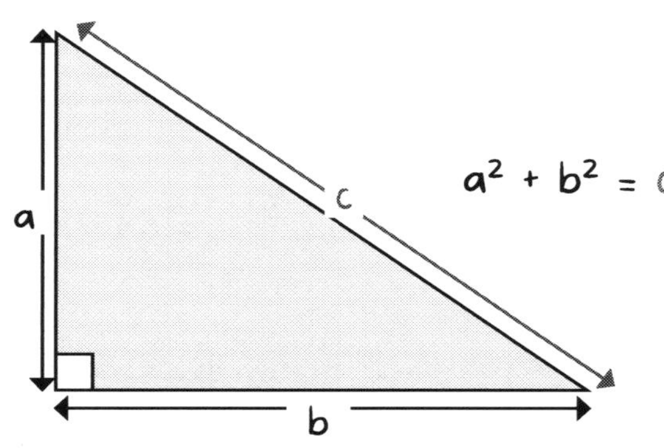

$$a^2 + b^2 = c^2$$

We can use the pythagorean theorem when we know two of the values, to solve for the unknown. Here are two examples:

$5^2 + 12^2 = c^2$

$25 + 144 = c^2$

$169 = c^2$

$c^2 = 169$

$c = \sqrt{169}$

$c = 13$

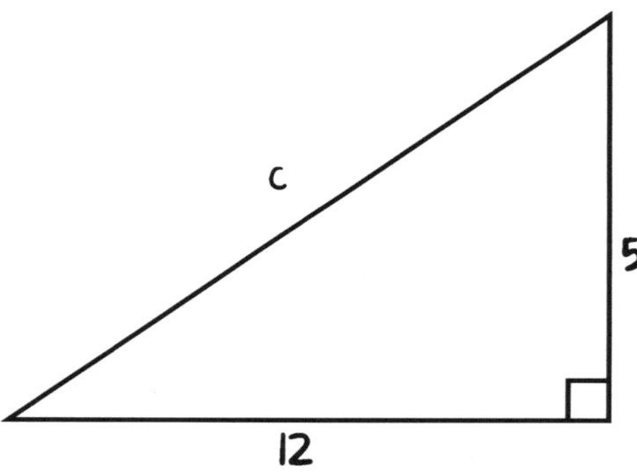

$20^2 = a^2 + 16^2$

$20^2 - 16^2 = a^2 + 16^2 - 16^2$

$400 - 256 = a^2$

$144 = a^2$

$\sqrt{144} = a$

$a = 12$

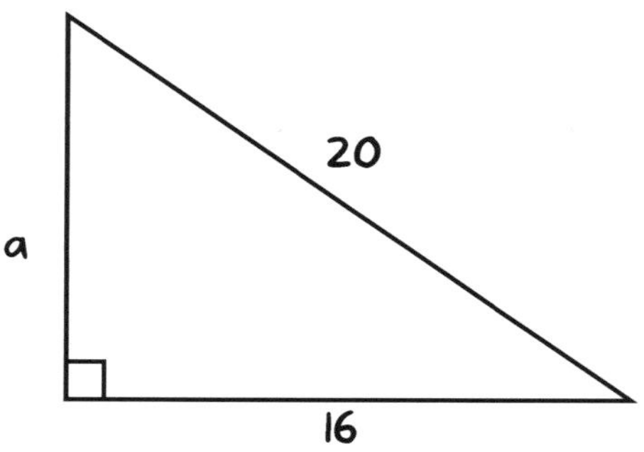

Fun Fact: The Greek Alphabet

Letters	Name	Letters	Name	Letters	Name
α	alpha	ι	iota	ρ	rho
β	beta	κ	kappa	σ	sigma
γ	gamma	λ	lambda	τ	tau
δ	delta	μ	mu	υ	upsilon
ε	epsilon	ν	nu	φ	phi
ζ	zeta	ξ	xi	χ	chi
η	eta	ο	omicron	ψ	psi
θ	theta	π	pi	ω	omega

Instead of using the angle notation $\angle A$ to denote an angle, you will often see the use of lowercase Greek letters to represent angles. You do **not** need to memorize this chart, but take a look at "theta" which is boxed on the diagram above. You will see this greek letter used often in the rest of this workbook, which will be used to represent angles.

This workbook does **not** contain practice problems to the above basic trigonometry review as you should already be comfortable with this material. These concepts are important to know because we will be building upon what we already know in Chapter 2.

Section 2.1 Understanding the 6 Trig Functions

Trigonometry is the branch of mathematics that deals with the relationships between the sides and angles of triangles, especially right triangles. Whether you're looking at the slope of a ramp, the height of a building, or trying to determine the distance across a river, the principles of trigonometry are at play.

In this section, you will learn about **sine, cosine,** and **tangent,** often referred to collectively as the "trigonometric ratios". Let's define the three terms.

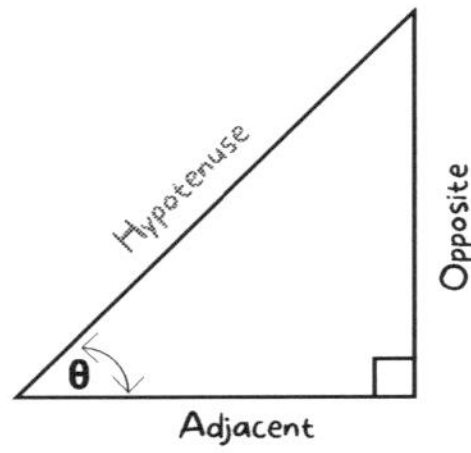

Right Traingle Diagram

1. Sine (sin):

For a given angle **θ** in a right triangle:

Sine is the ratio of the length of the side that is **opposite** this angle to the length of the **hypotenuse** (the side opposite the right angle).

Mathematically,

$$\sin(\theta) = \frac{\text{opposite}}{\text{hypotenuse}}$$

2. Cosine (cos):

For a given angle **θ** in a right triangle:

Cosine is the ratio of the length of the side that is **adjacent** to this angle (i.e., the side next to the angle but not the hypotenuse) to the length of the **hypotenuse.**

Mathematically,

$$\cos(\theta) = \frac{\text{adjacent}}{\text{hypotenuse}}$$

3. Tangent (tan):

For a given angle θ in a right triangle:

Tangent is the ratio of the **sine** of the angle to the **cosine** of the angle. It can also be understood as the ratio of the side opposite the angle to the side adjacent to it.

Mathematically,

$$\tan(\theta) = \frac{\sin(\theta)}{\cos(\theta)} = \frac{\text{opposite}}{\text{adjacent}}$$

You **must** remember the sin cos tan formulas for trigonometry. Fortunately, there is a great acronym to remember this.

Remember the mnemonic word SOHCAHTOA.

Another mnemonic that you may prefer is to remember the phrase 'Studying Our Homework Can Always Help To Obtain Achievement". We recommend remembering the word **SOHCAHTOA**.

SOH ⟶ $\sin(\theta) = \frac{\text{Opposite}}{\text{Hypotenuse}}$

CAH ⟶ $\cos(\theta) = \frac{\text{Adjacent}}{\text{Hypotenuse}}$

TOA ⟶ $\tan(\theta) = \frac{\text{Opposite}}{\text{Adjacent}}$

There are **three** other trig functions we must know, **cosecant (csc), secant (sec),** and **cotangent (cot).** These are the **reciprocolas** of the sin, cos, and tan functions. So it's actually pretty easy to remember!

Important Note:

Many students confuse and think cosecant is the reciprocal of sin and secant to be the reciprocal of cos, which is **NOT** true. Do not confuse these two up.

* Cosecant (csc) is the reciprocal of sin
* Secant (sec) is the reciprocal of cos
* Cotangent (cot) is the reciprocal of tan

$$\csc(\theta) = \frac{\text{hypotenuse}}{\text{opposite}}, \quad \sec(\theta) = \frac{\text{hypotenuse}}{\text{adjacent}}, \quad \cot(\theta) = \frac{\text{adjacent}}{\text{opposite}}$$

In section 2.1, we will get comfortable practicing questions to **identify the value** of the six trig functions.

Let's take a look at a few practice exercises.

Question 1: What is cos θ?

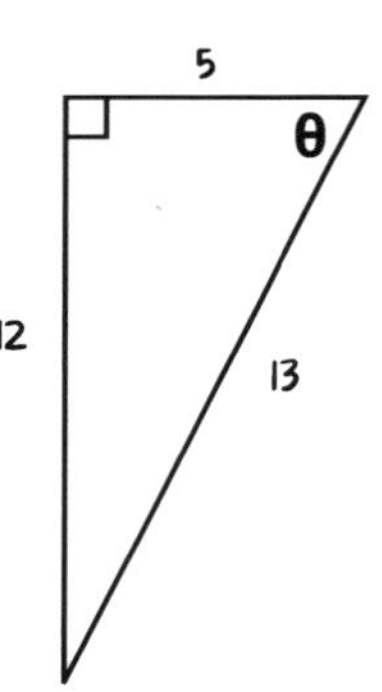

We have a right-sided triangle here with all **3** sides labeled with their lengths.

We know $\cos\theta = \frac{\text{adjacent}}{\text{hypotenuse}}$

Looking at **θ**, we can see **5** is adjacent and **13** is the hypotenuse.

So $\cos\theta = \frac{5}{13}$.

Question 2: What is tan θ?

We have a right-sided triangle here with all 3 sides labeled with their lengths.

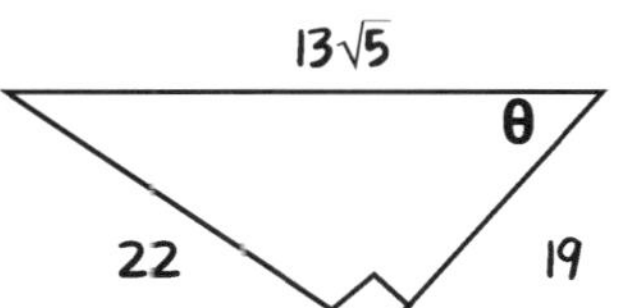

We know $\tan\theta = \dfrac{\text{opposite}}{\text{adjacent}}$

Looking at θ, we can see 22 is opposite and 19 is adjacent.

So $\tan\theta = \dfrac{22}{19}$.

Question 3: What is sin θ?

We have a right-sided triangle here with all 3 sides labeled with their lengths.

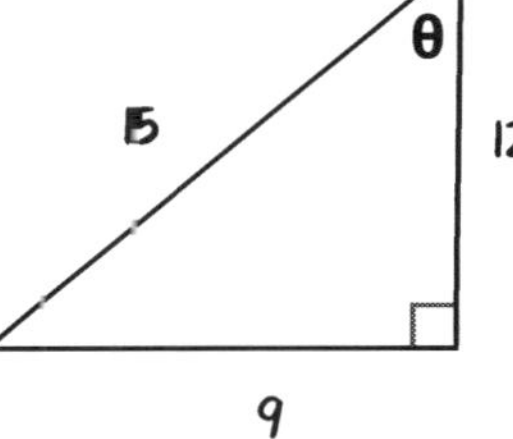

We know $\sin\theta = \dfrac{\text{opposite}}{\text{hypotenuse}}$

Looking at θ, we can see 9 is opposite and 15 is the hypotenuse.

So $\sin\theta = \dfrac{9}{15}$. **However**, we can actually simply this fraction further by dividing the numerator and denominator by 3 to get $\dfrac{3}{5}$.

So $\sin\theta = \dfrac{3}{5}$.

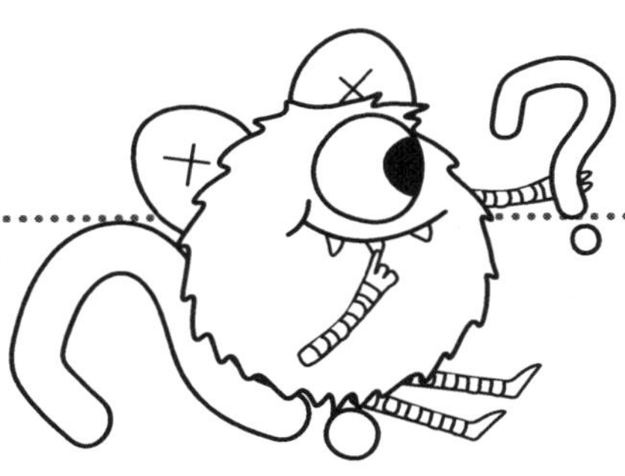

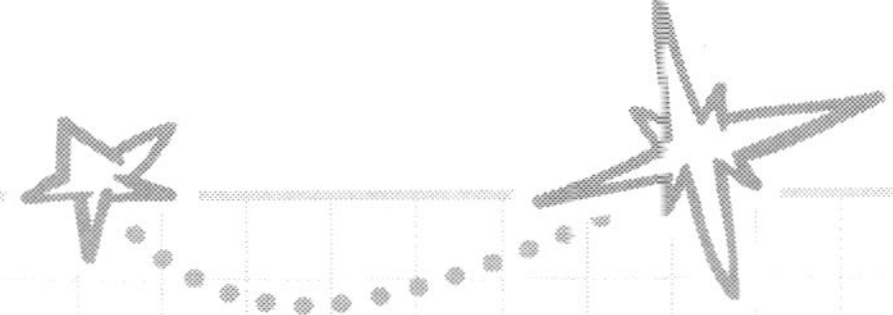

Question 4: What is $\cos\theta$?

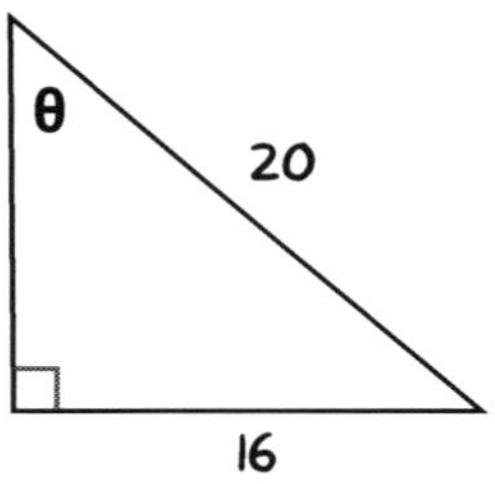

We have a right-sided triangle here with **2 sides** labeled.

We know $\cos\theta = \dfrac{\text{adjacent}}{\text{hypotenuse}}$

We do **not** know the adjacent value, because it was not provided in the diagram. How can we solve for this missing value?

Pythagorean Theorem!

We have $a^2 + 16^2 = 20^2$

$$a^2 + 256 = 400$$

$a^2 = 144$ (Now take the square root of both sides to get $a = 12$).

a = 12

Let's go ahead and relabel our right triangle.

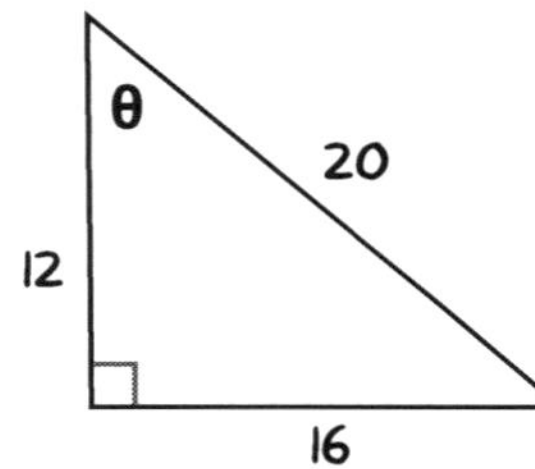

Now we know the adjacent value is 12 and the hypotenuse is 20.

So, $\cos\theta = \dfrac{12}{20}$. We can simplify this fraction by dividing the numerator and denominator by 4 to get $\dfrac{3}{5}$.

So $\cos\theta = \dfrac{3}{5}$.

Question 5: What is sin θ?

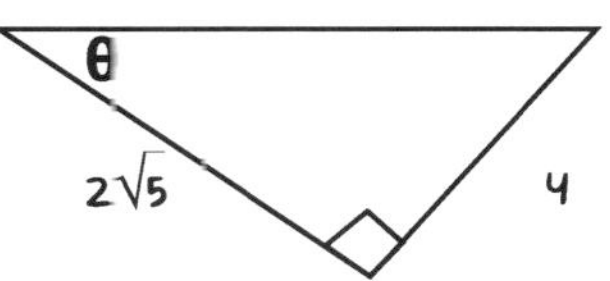

We have a right-sided triangle here with **2 sides** labeled.

We know $\sin\theta = \dfrac{\text{opposite}}{\text{hypotenuse}}$

We do **not** know the hypotenuse, because it was not provided in the diagram. How can we solve for this missing value?

Pythagorean Theorem!

We have $(2\sqrt{5})^2 + 4^2 = c^2$

$$4(5) + 16 = c^2$$

$$20 + 16 = c^2$$

$36 = c^2$ (Now take the square root of both sides to get $c = 6$).

Let's go ahead and relabel our right triangle.

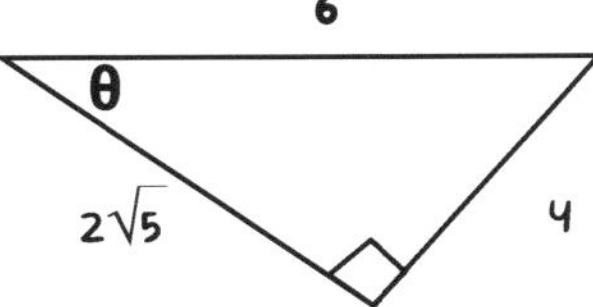

Now we know the opposite value is 4 and the hypotenuse is 6.

So, $\sin\theta = \dfrac{4}{6}$. We can simplify this fraction by dividing the numerator and denominator

by 2 to get $\dfrac{2}{3}$.

So $\sin\theta = \dfrac{2}{3}$.

Question 6: What is sec θ?

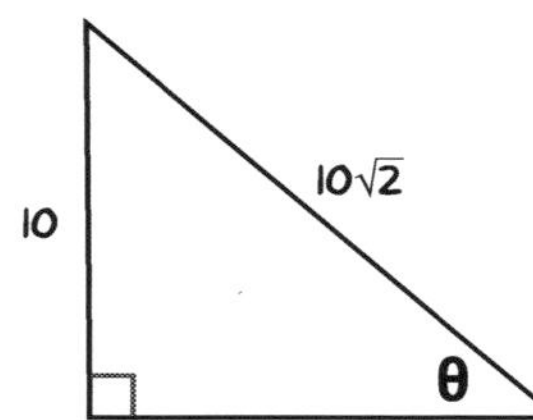

We have a right-sided triangle here with **2 sides** labeled.

We know $\sec \theta = \dfrac{\text{hypotenuse}}{\text{adjacent}}$

We know the value of the hypotenuse, but we **do not** know the adjacent value. How can we solve for this missing value?

Pythagorean Theorem!

We have $10^2 + b^2 = (10\sqrt{2})^2$

$$100 + b^2 = (100 \times 2)$$
$$100 + b^2 = 200$$

$b^2 = 100$ (Now take the square root of both sides to get $b = 10$).
Let's go ahead and relabel our right triangle.

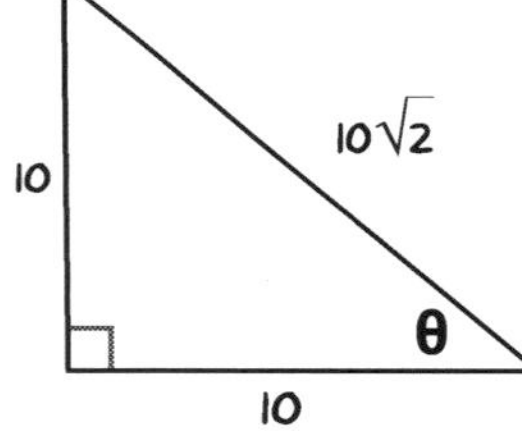

Now we know the adjacent value is 10 and the hypotenuse is $10\sqrt{2}$.

So, $\sec \theta = \dfrac{10\sqrt{2}}{10}$. We can simplify this. Notice the 10's cancel out and we are left with $\sqrt{2}$.

So $\sec \theta = \sqrt{2}$.

Question 7: What is cot θ?

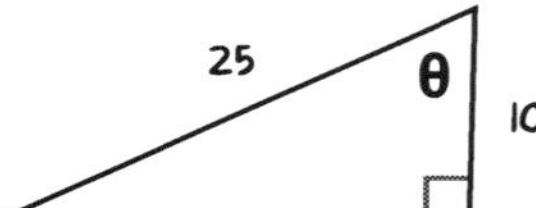

We have a right-sided triangle here with **2 sides** labeled.

We know $\cot \theta = \dfrac{\text{adjacent}}{\text{opposite}}$

We know the adjacent value, but we **do not** know the opposite value. How can we solve for this missing value?

Pythagorean Theorem !

We have $10^2 + b^2 = (25)^2$

$$100 + b^2 = 625$$

$b^2 = 525$ (Now take the square root of both sides to get $\sqrt{525}$.

We can simplify $\sqrt{525}$ to $\sqrt{25} \times \sqrt{21} \rightarrow 5\sqrt{21}$

Let's go ahead and relabel our right triangle.

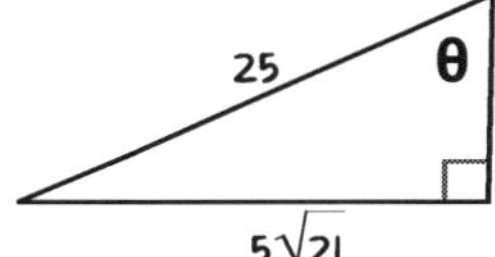

Now we know the adjacent value is 10 and the opposite is $5\sqrt{21}$.

So, $\cot\theta = \dfrac{10}{5\sqrt{21}}$.

This is an interesting situation! Whenever there is a radical in the denominator of a fraction, it must be rationalized. You should have covered this in math class last year before trigonometry. You can rationalize it by multiplying both the numerator and the denominator by that square root.

$$\frac{10}{5\sqrt{21}} \times \frac{5\sqrt{21}}{5\sqrt{21}} = \frac{\overset{2}{\cancel{50}}\sqrt{21}}{\cancel{25}\times 21} = \frac{2\sqrt{21}}{21}$$

So $\cot\theta = \dfrac{2\sqrt{21}}{21}$.

In order to successfully find the value of the trig functions, you must remember the six trig functions (sin, cos, tan, sec, csc, cot). You must be able to use the Pythagorean Theorem for some problems and in some cases, you must be comfortable rationalizing denominators when required like in question 7.

You are now ready to tackle practice problems to find the value of the trig function indicated.

Section 2.1 Quiz

Directions: Find the value of the trig function indicated. Use a separate piece of paper to show your work if needed. The triangles are not drawn to scale.

1. $\tan\theta$

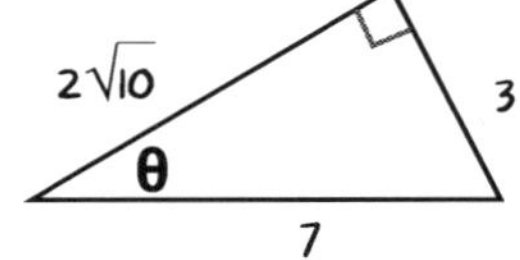

2. $\tan\theta$

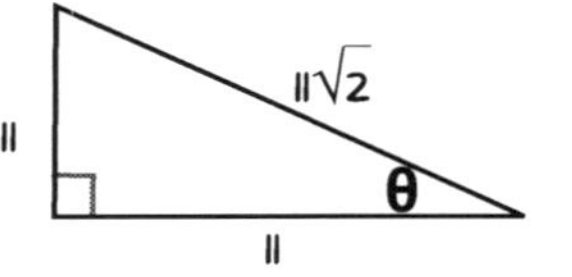

3. $\sec\theta$

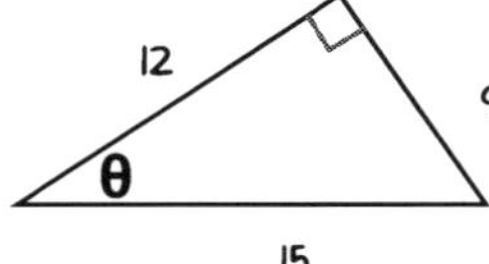

4. $\sec\theta$

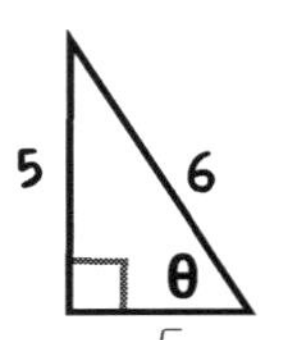

5. $\cot\theta$

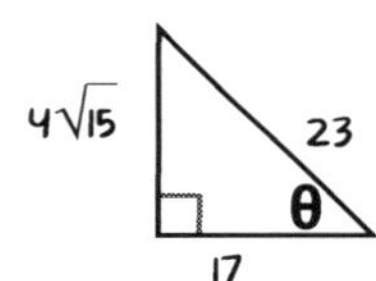

6. $\cos\theta$

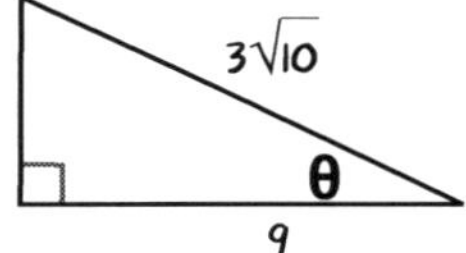

7. $\cot\theta$

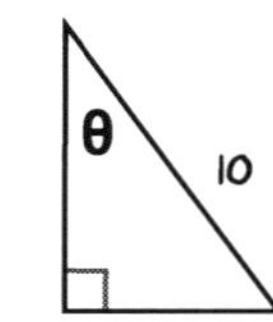

8. $\sec\theta$

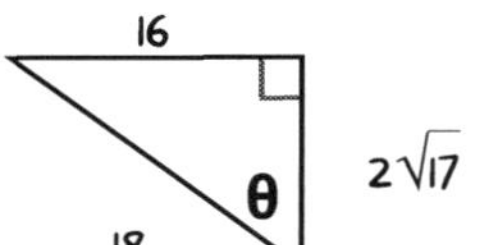

9. $\cos\theta$

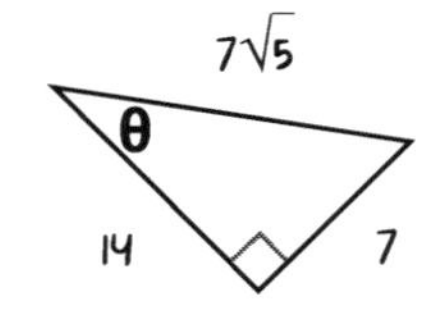

10. $\sec\theta$

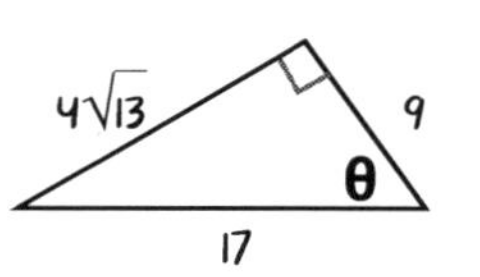

11. $\sec\theta$

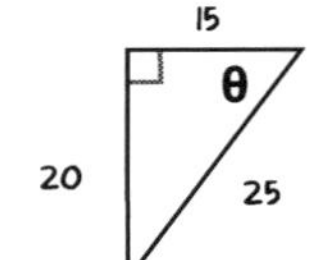

12. $\cot\theta$

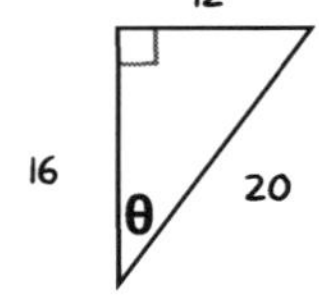

13. $\sin\theta$

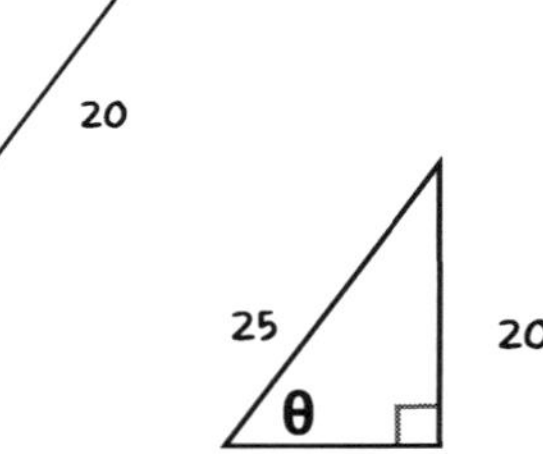

14. $\cos\theta$

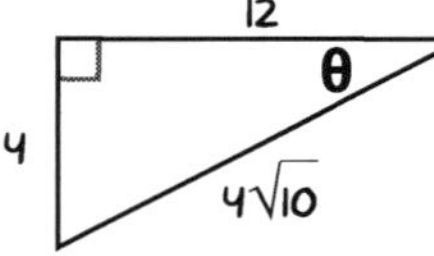

15. $\sec\theta$

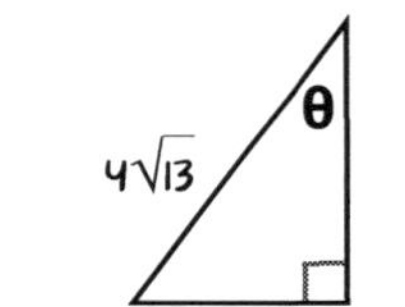

16. $\cot\theta$

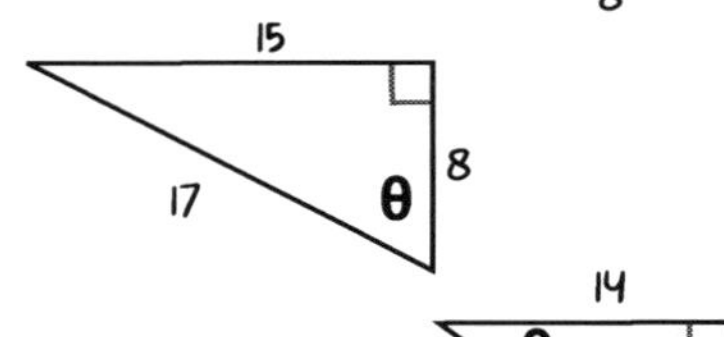

17. $\sec\theta$

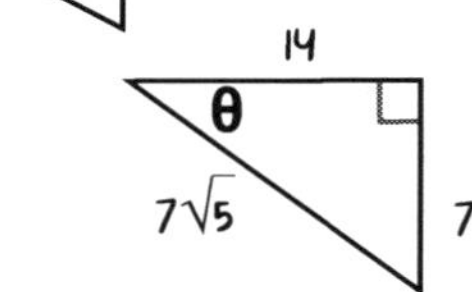

18. $\tan\theta$

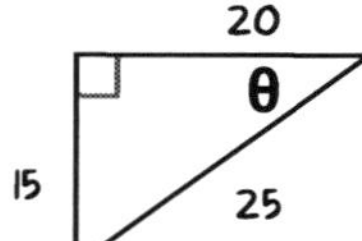

19. $\tan\theta$

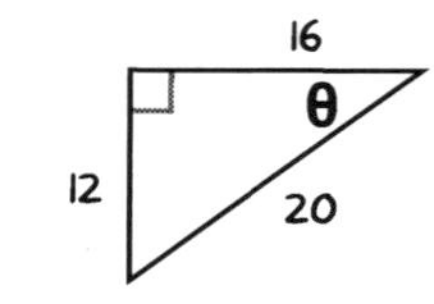

20. $\sec\theta$

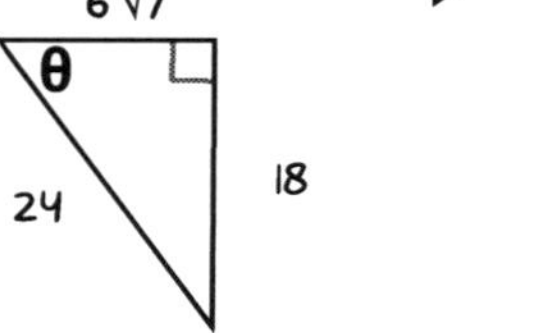

Section 2.1 Quiz

21. $\sin\theta$

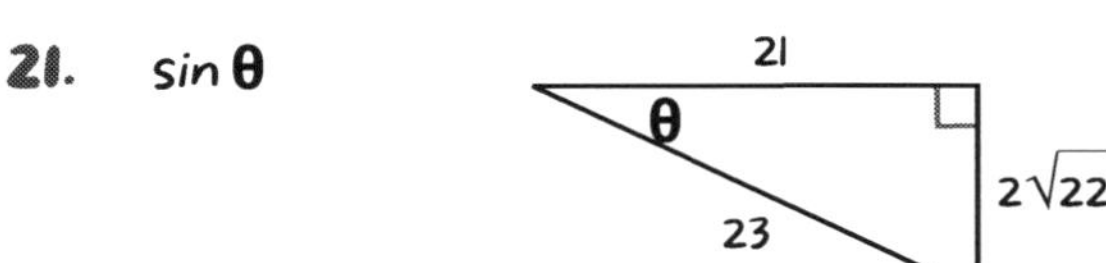

22. $\csc\theta$

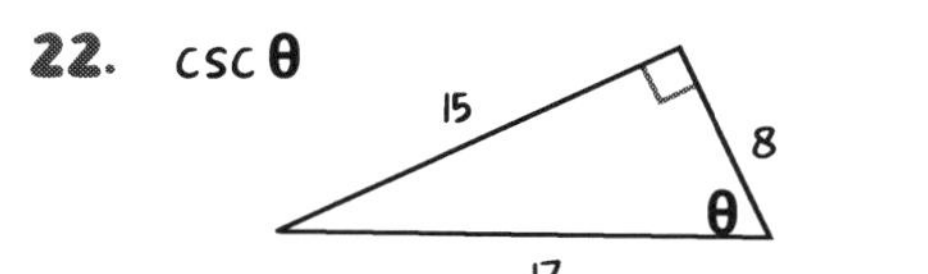

23. $\sec\theta$

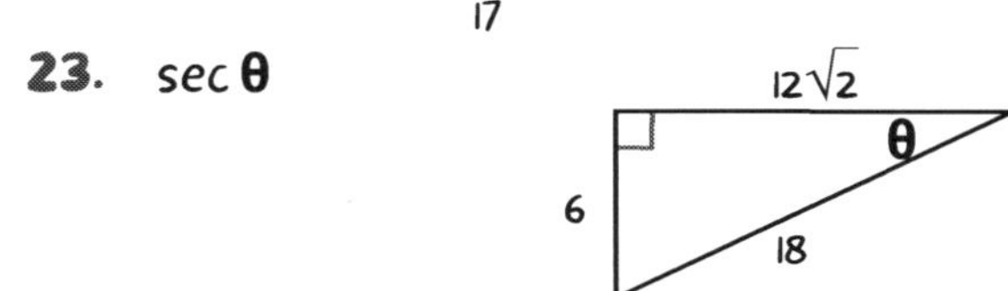

24. $\csc\theta$

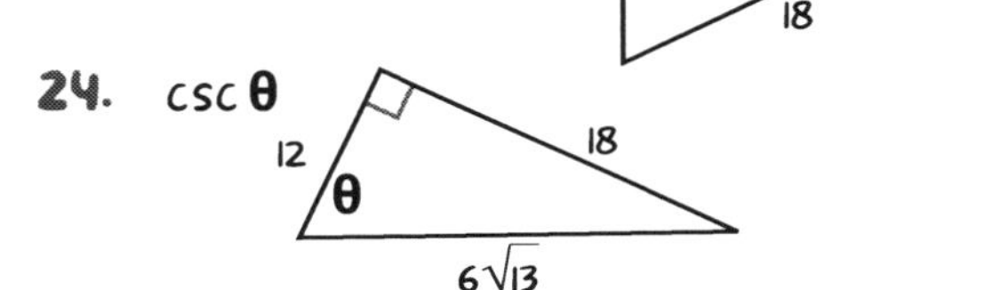

25. $\cot\theta$

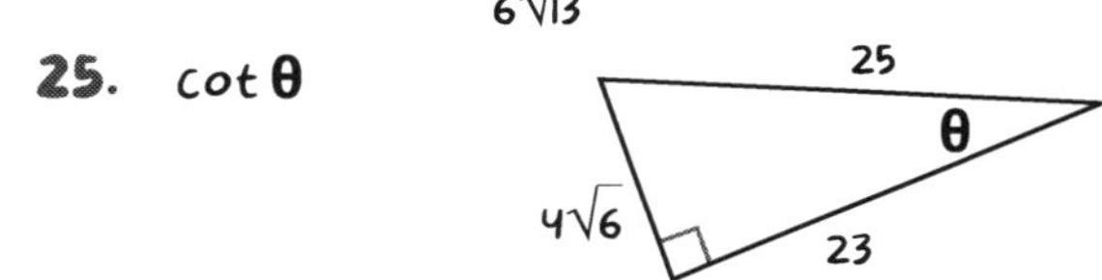

26. $\cos\theta$

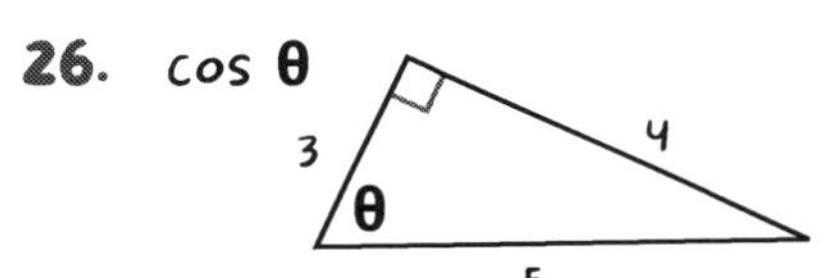

27. $\tan\theta$

28. $\tan\theta$

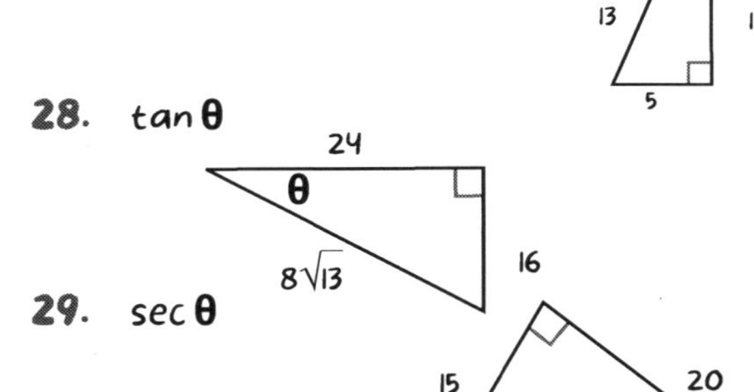

29. $\sec\theta$

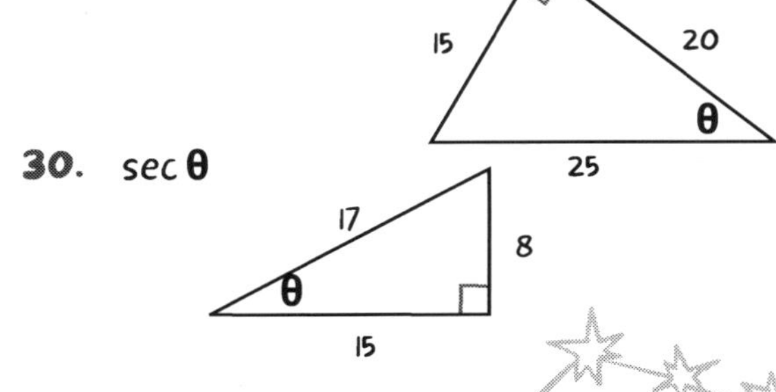

30. $\sec\theta$

31. $\tan\theta$

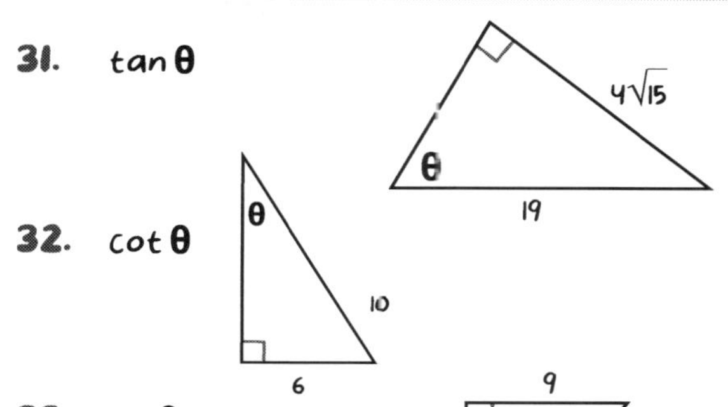

32. $\cot\theta$

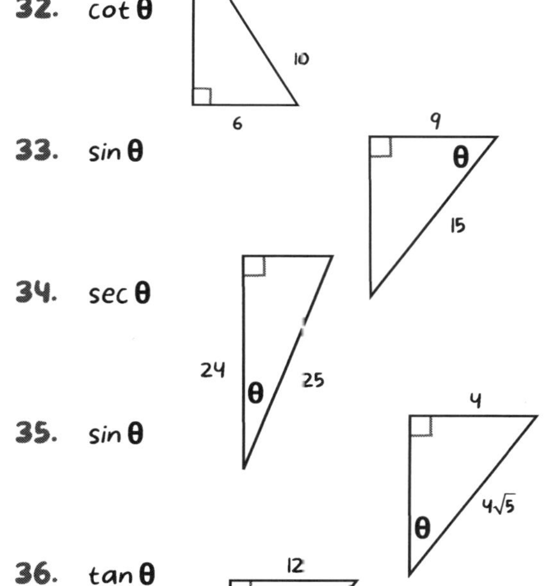

33. $\sin\theta$

34. $\sec\theta$

35. $\sin\theta$

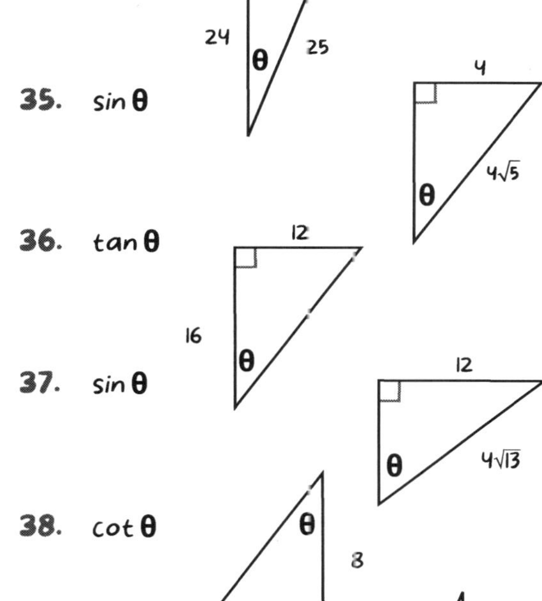

36. $\tan\theta$

37. $\sin\theta$

38. $\cot\theta$

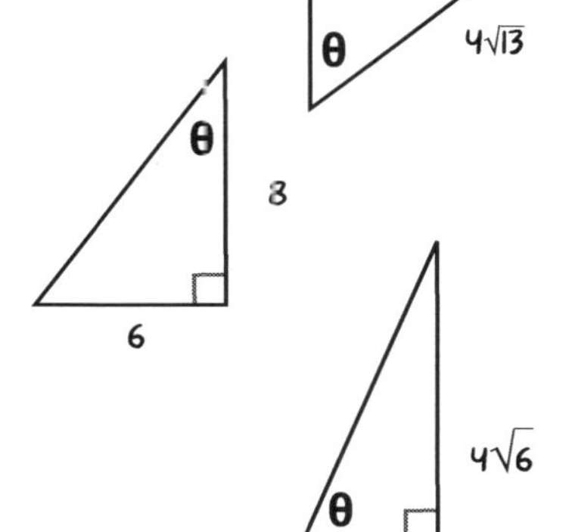

39. $\cos\theta$

40. $\sin\theta$

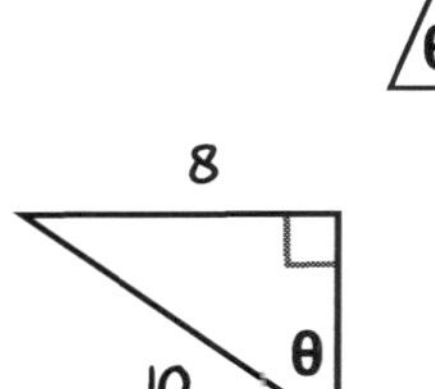

Section 2.1 Quiz

41. sec θ

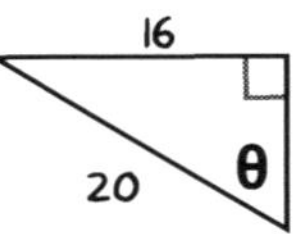

42. cos θ

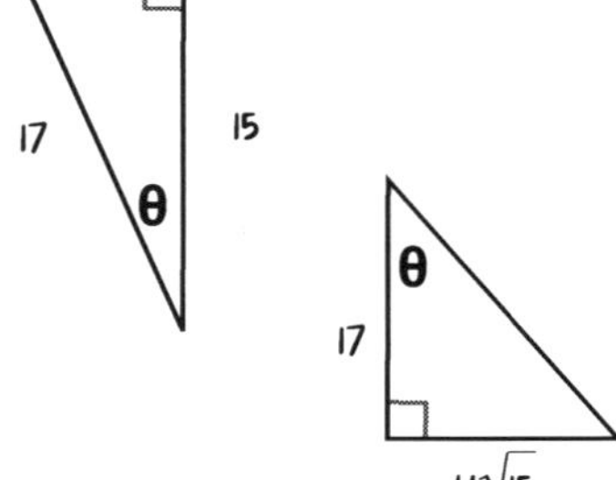

43. cot θ

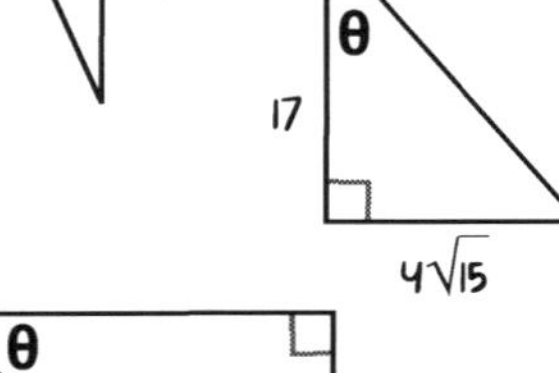

44. tan θ

θ
8
17

45. sin θ

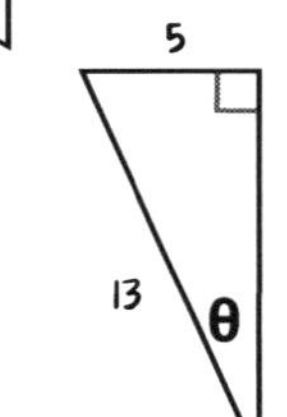

46. csc θ

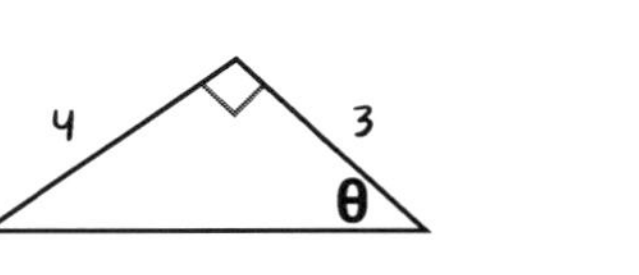

47. cos θ

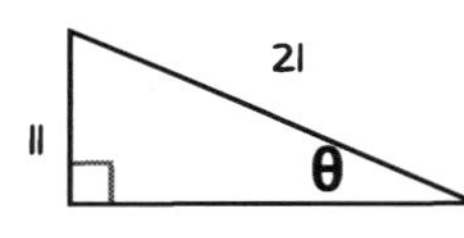

48. tan θ

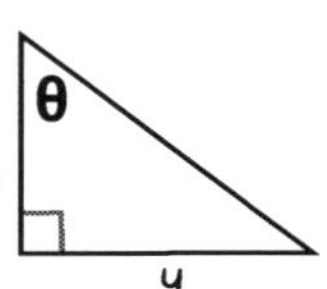

49. sin θ

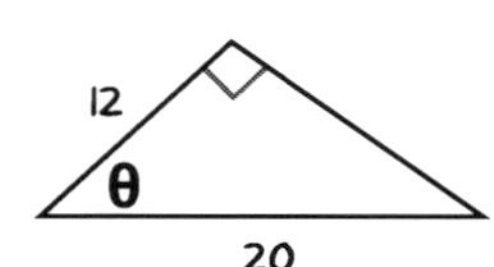
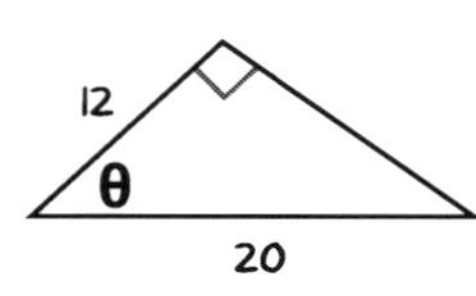

50. csc θ

θ
6
8

51. sin θ

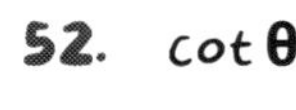

52. cot θ

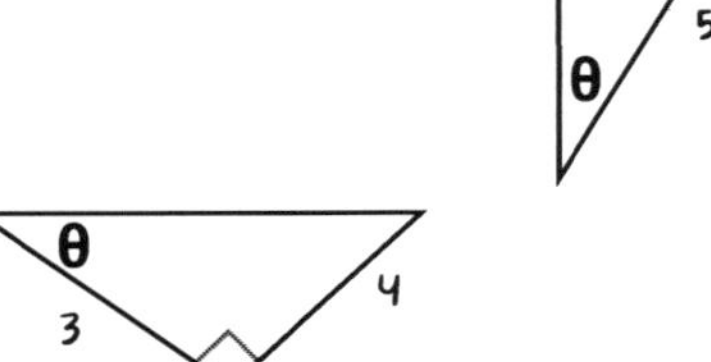

53. csc θ

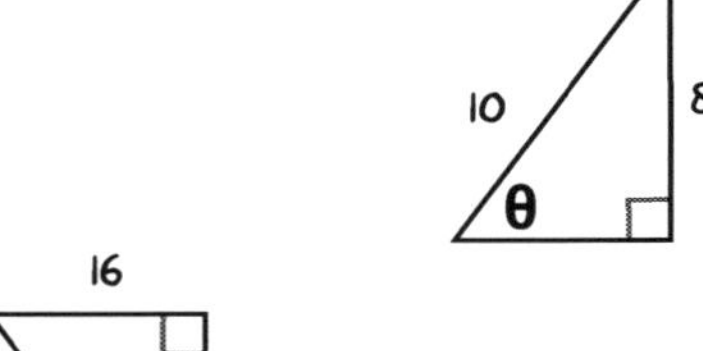

54. csc θ

16
24
θ

55. sec θ

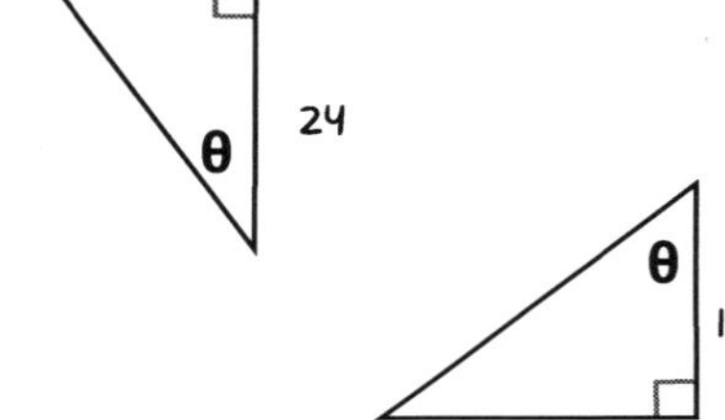

56. cos θ

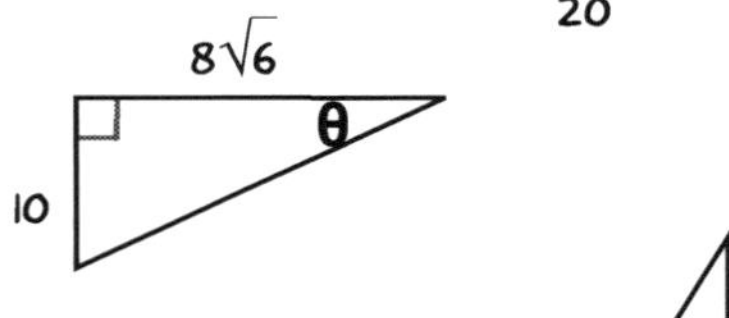

57. sin θ

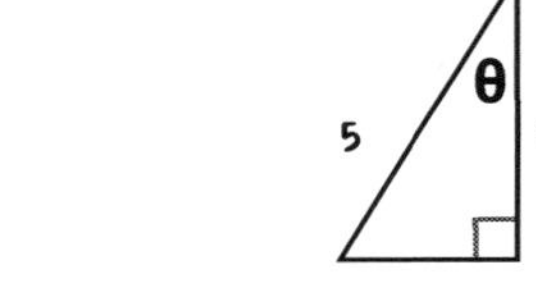

58. sec θ

25
θ
7

59. cot θ

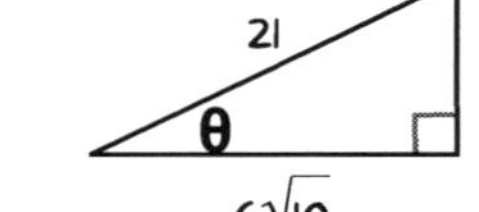

60. csc θ

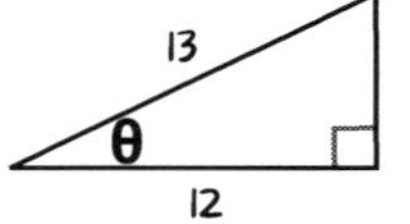
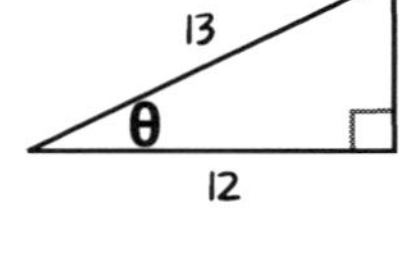

Section 2.1 Quiz

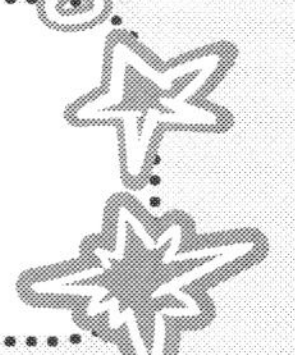

61. $\cot\theta$

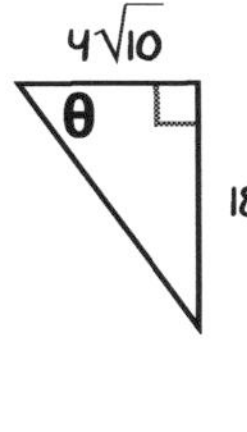

62. $\cot\theta$

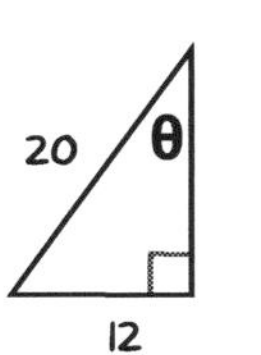

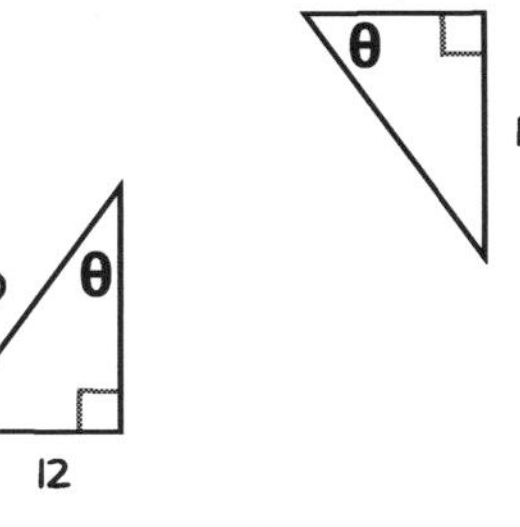

63. $\sin\theta$

64. $\sec\theta$

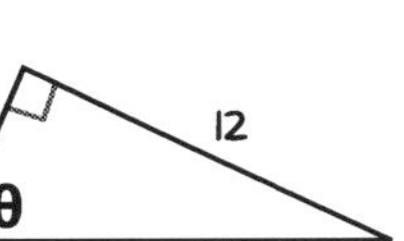

65. $\cos\theta$

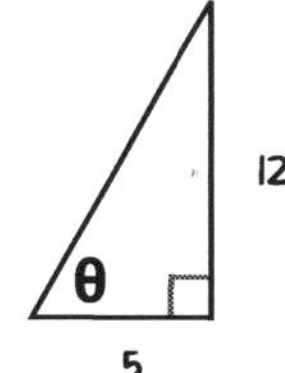

66. $\cot\theta$

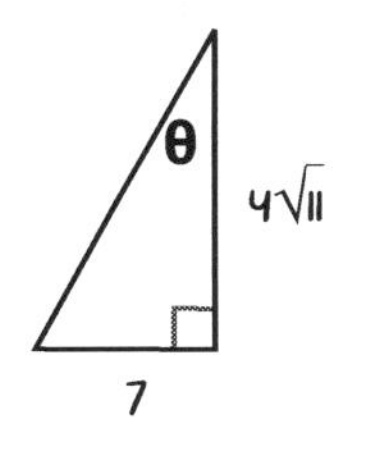

67. $\cot\theta$

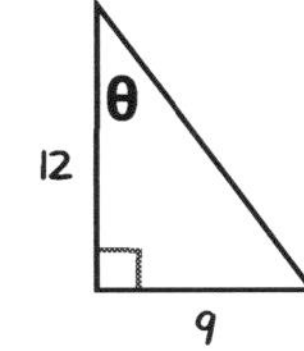

68. $\sec\theta$

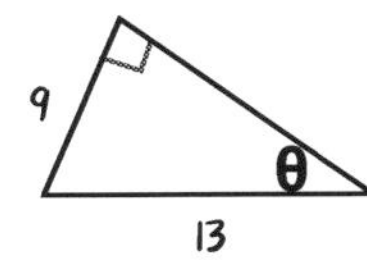

69. $\csc\theta$

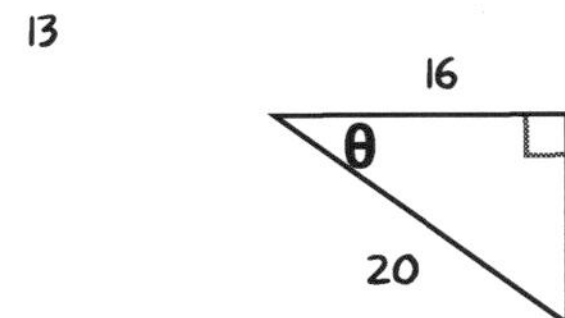

70. $\csc\theta$

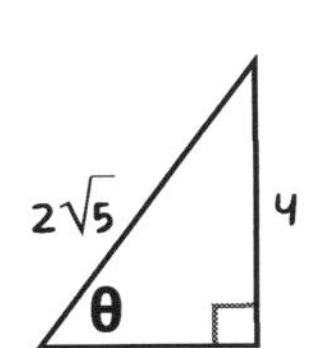

71. $\sin\theta$

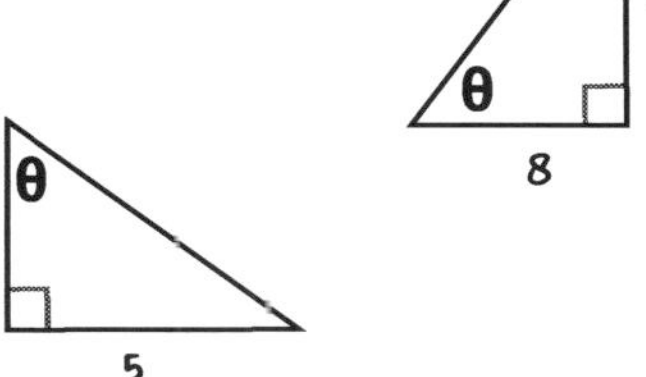

72. $\csc\theta$

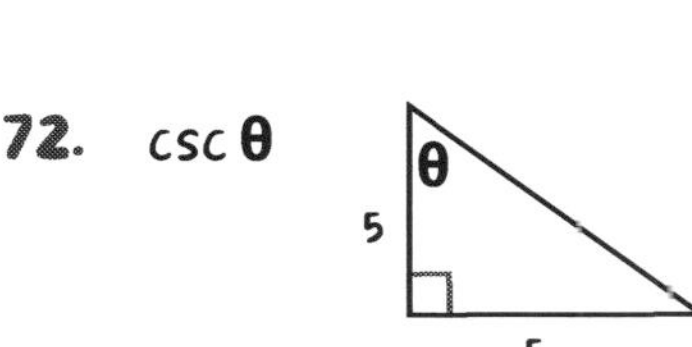

73. $\csc\theta$

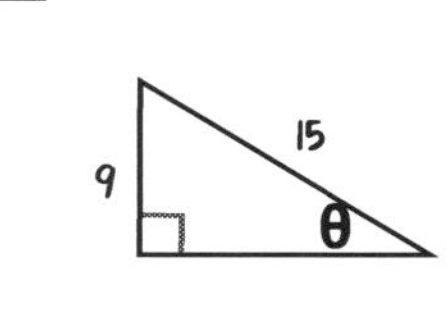

74. $\cot\theta$

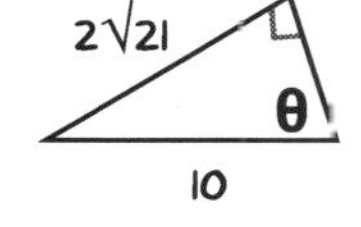

75. $\sec\theta$

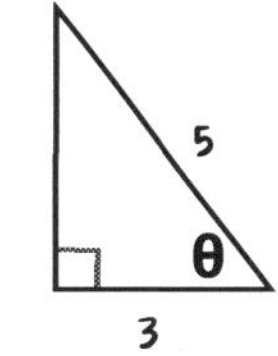

76. $\sin\theta$

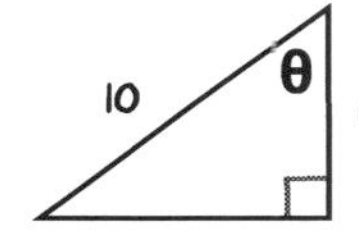

77. $\csc\theta$

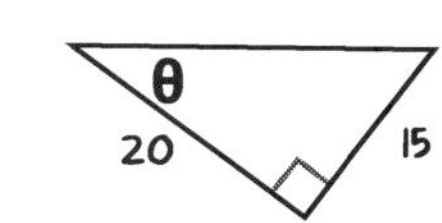

78. $\cos\theta$

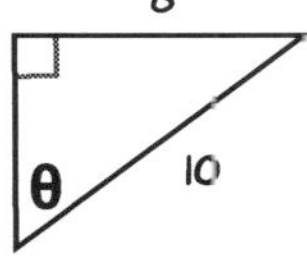

79. $\cot\theta$

80. $\tan\theta$

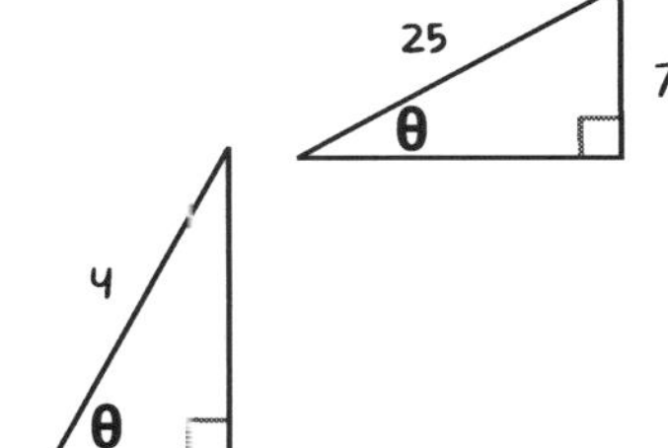

Section 2.1 Quiz

81. $\sin\theta$

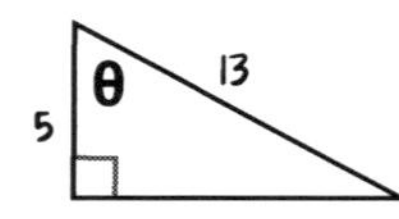

82. $\tan\theta$

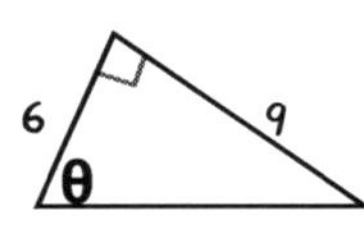

83. $\sin\theta$

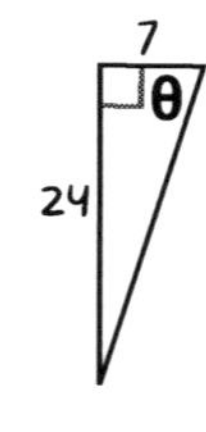

84. $\sin\theta$

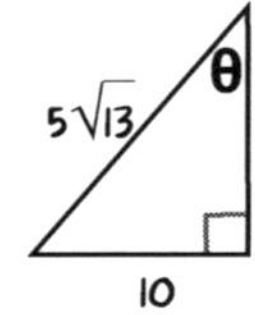

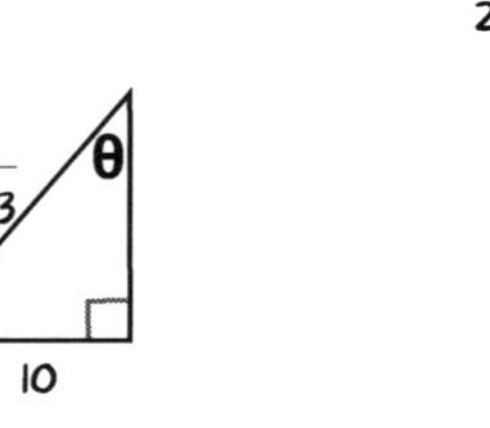

85. $\tan\theta$

86. $\sin\theta$

87. $\sec\theta$

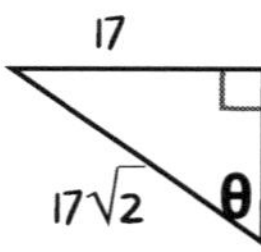

88. $\sin\theta$

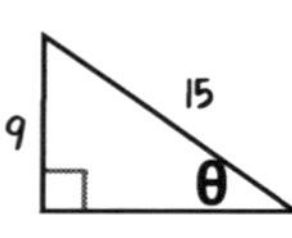

89. $\cot\theta$

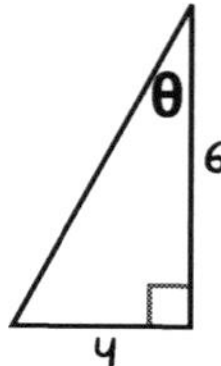

90. $\tan\theta$

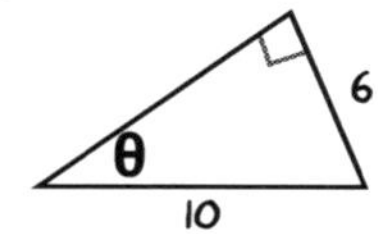

91. $\cos\theta$

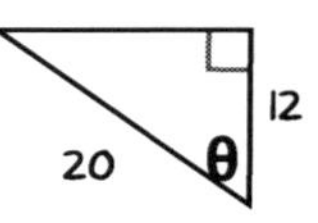

92. $\cos\theta$

93. $\sin\theta$

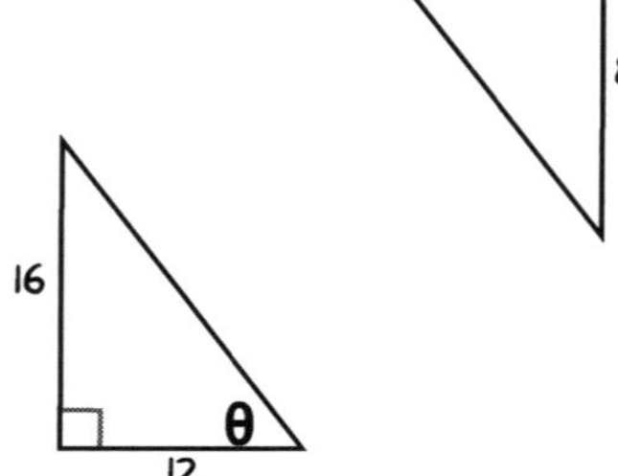

94. $\csc\theta$

95. $\sin\theta$

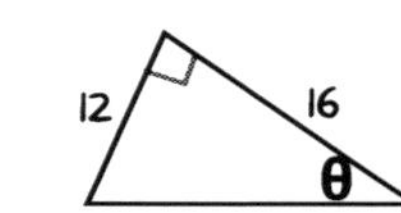

96. $\sec\theta$

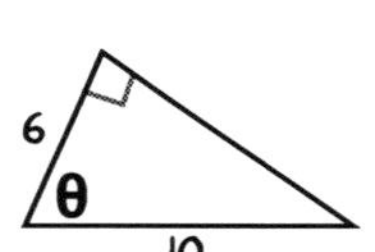

97. $\sec\theta$

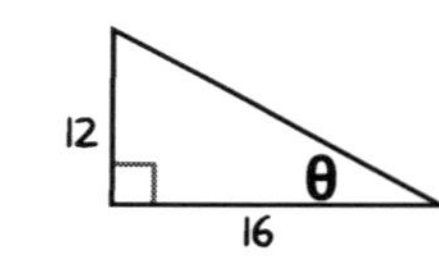

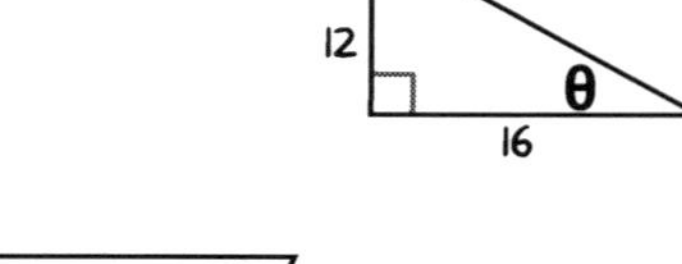

98. $\cos\theta$

99. $\sec\theta$

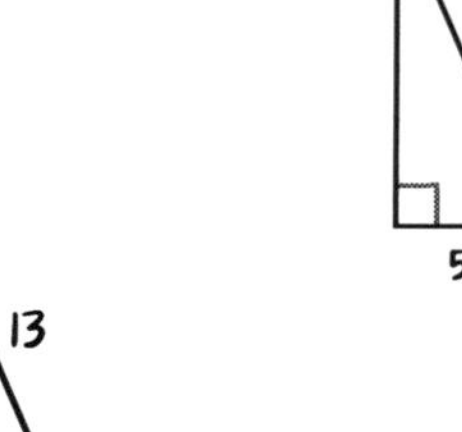

100. $\csc\theta$

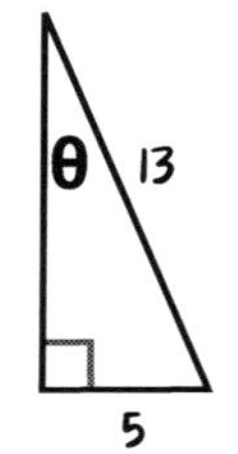

Section 2.1 Quiz

101. $\sin\theta$

102. $\tan\theta$

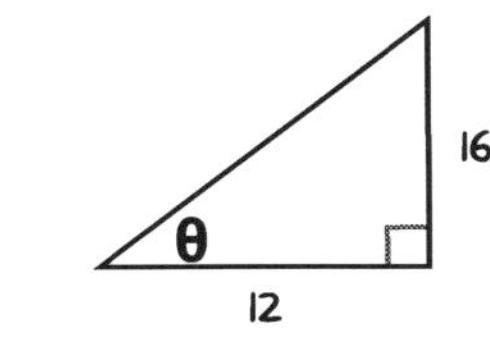

103. $\tan\theta$

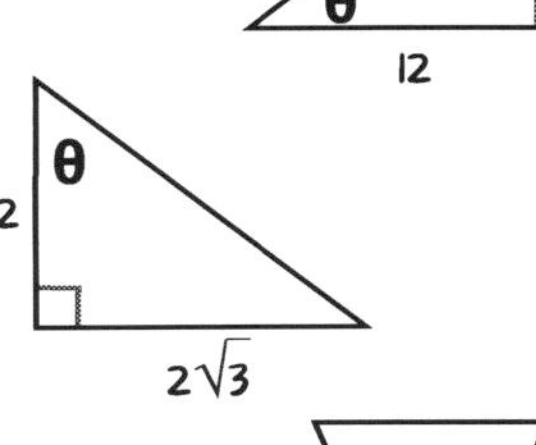

104. $\cot\theta$

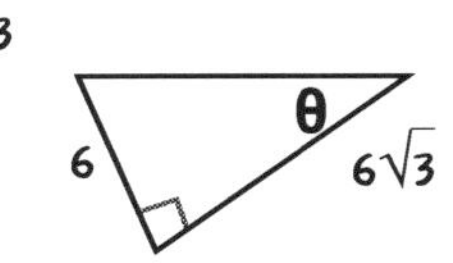

105. $\csc\theta$

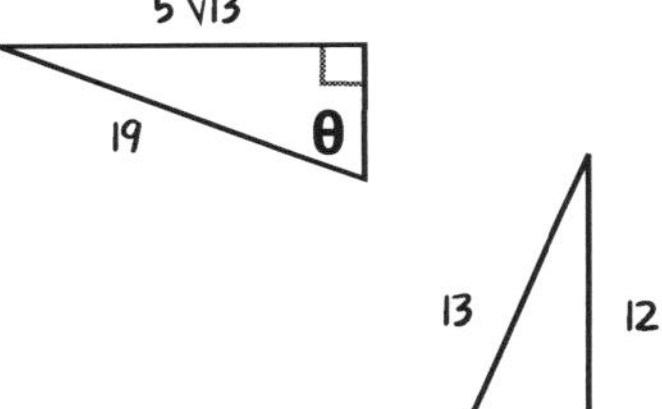

106. $\tan\theta$

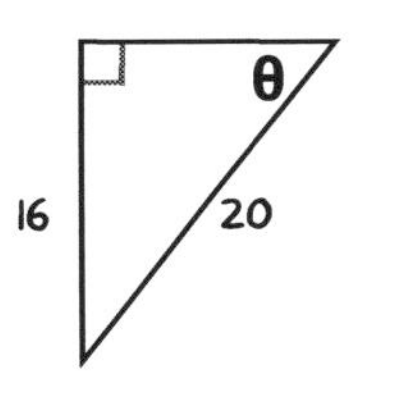

107. $\sin\theta$

108. $\csc\theta$

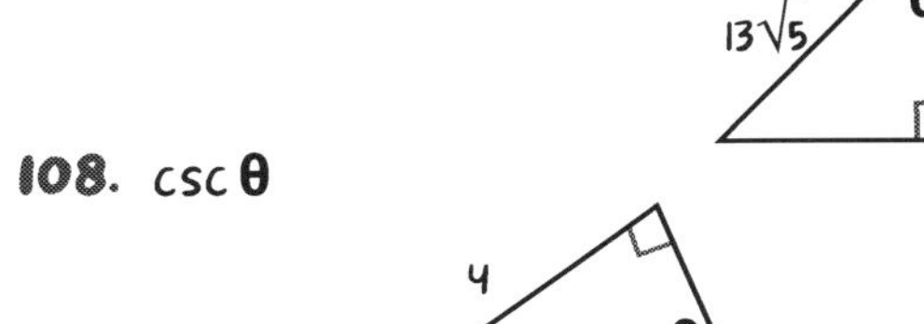

109. $\sin\theta$

110. $\sec\theta$

111. $\cos\theta$

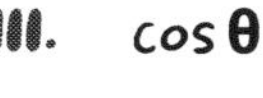

112. $\sin\theta$

113. $\tan\theta$

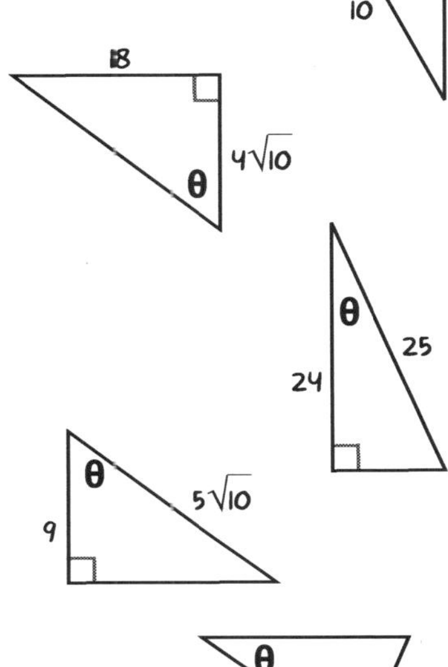

114. $\cos\theta$

115. $\csc\theta$

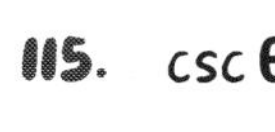

116. $\cot\theta$

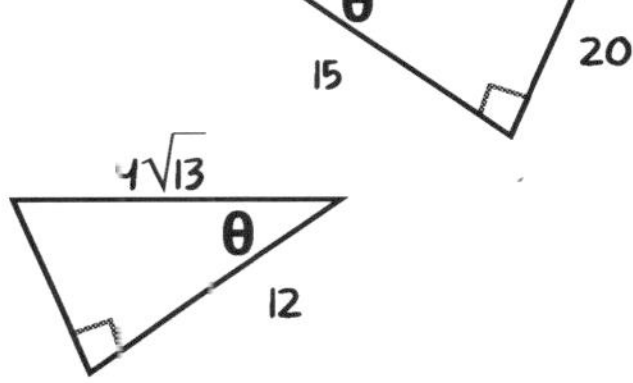

117. $\cos\theta$

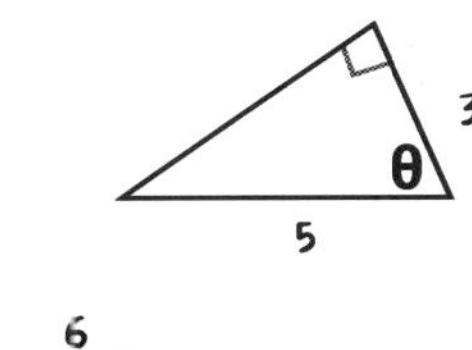

118. $\cot\theta$

119. $\cos\theta$

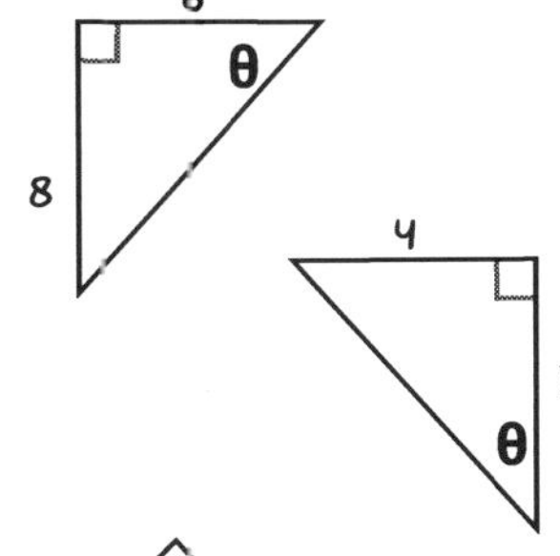

120. $\tan\theta$

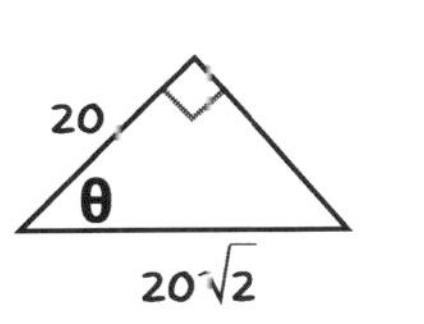

Section 2.1 Quiz

121. $\sec\theta$

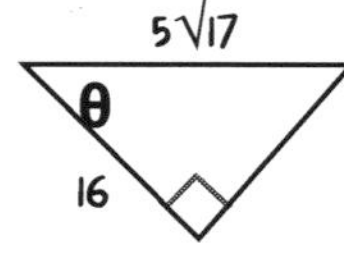

122. $\cot\theta$

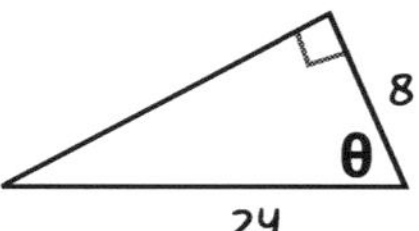

123. $\sec\theta$

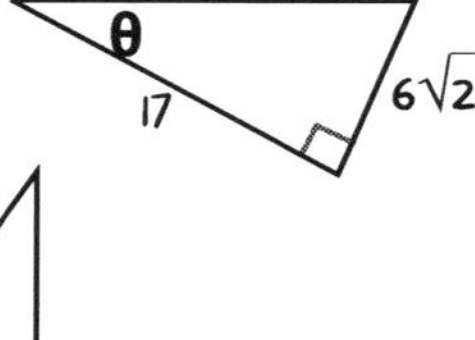

124. $\cot\theta$

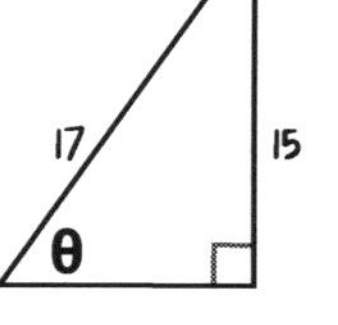

125. $\tan\theta$

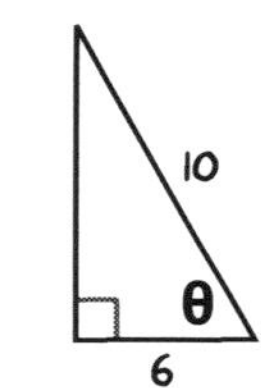

126. $\sec\theta$

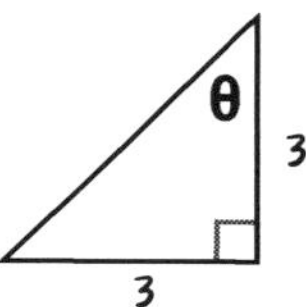

127. $\sec\theta$

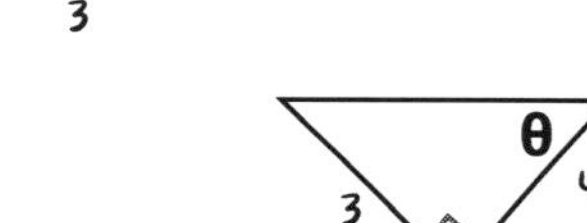

128. $\cot\theta$

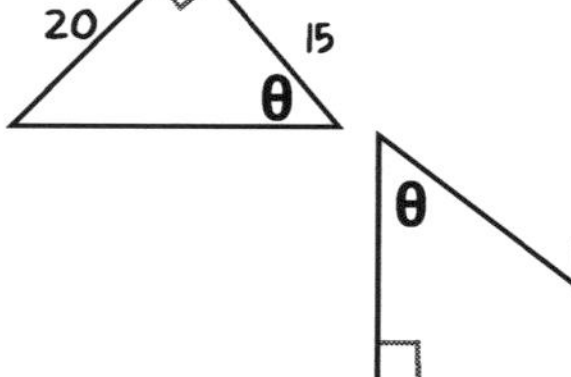

129. $\tan\theta$

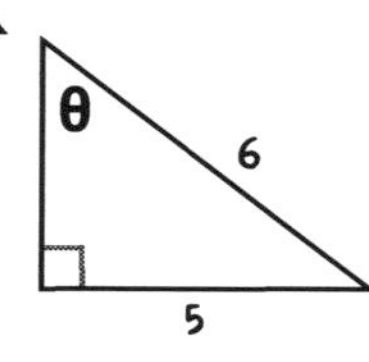

130. $\csc\theta$

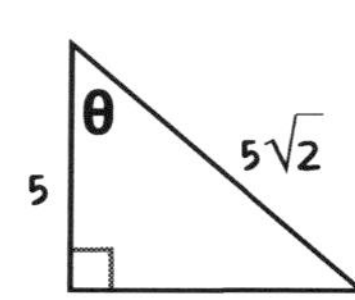

131. $\tan\theta$

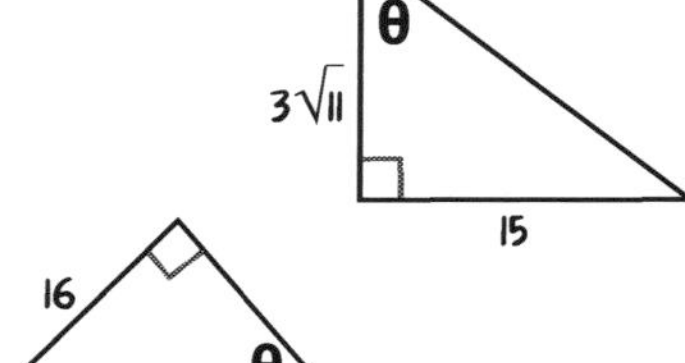

132. $\sec\theta$

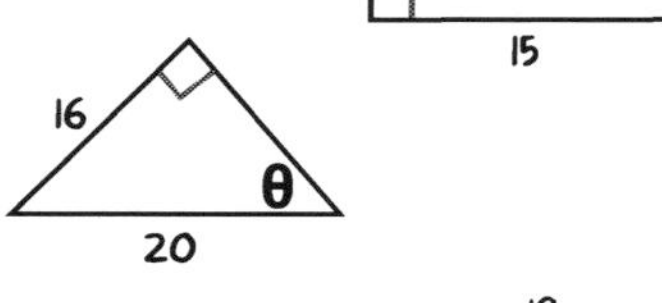

133. $\csc\theta$

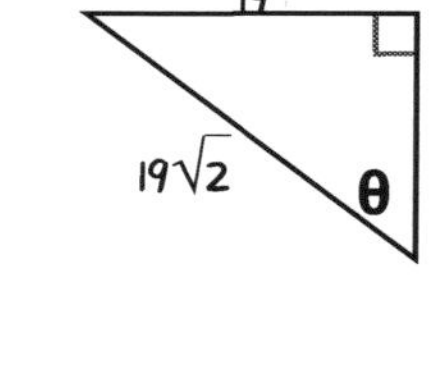

134. $\cot\theta$

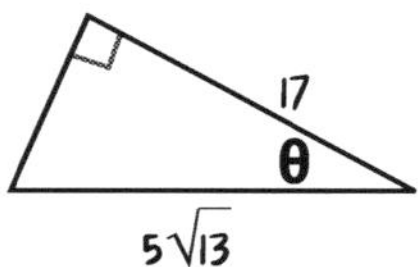

135. $\sec\theta$

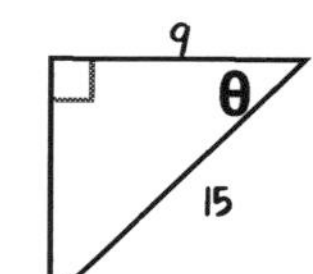

136. $\sec\theta$

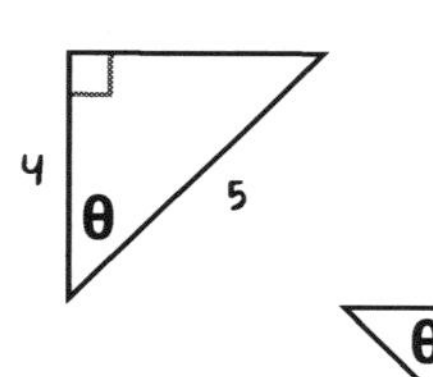

137. $\csc\theta$

θ
20
15

138. $\sin\theta$

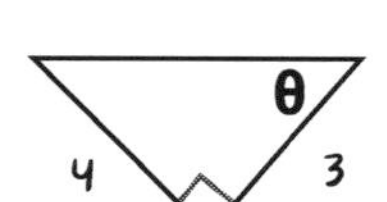

139. $\cos\theta$

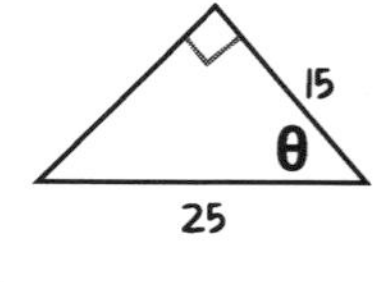

140. $\cos\theta$

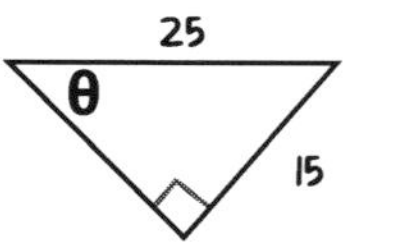

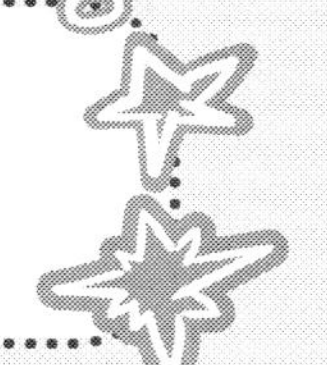

Section 2.1 Quiz

141. $\cos\theta$

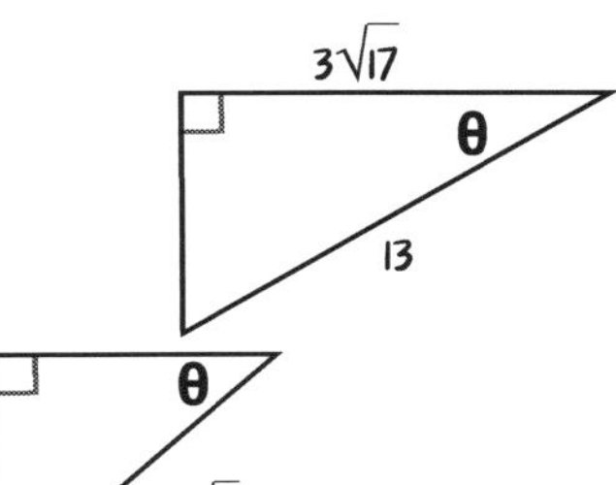

142. $\cot\theta$

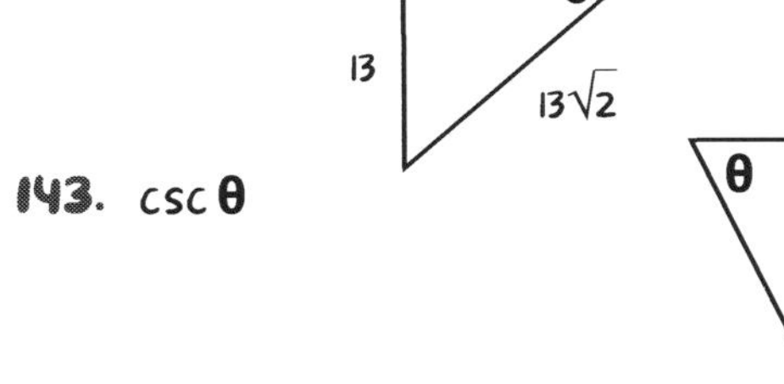

143. $\csc\theta$

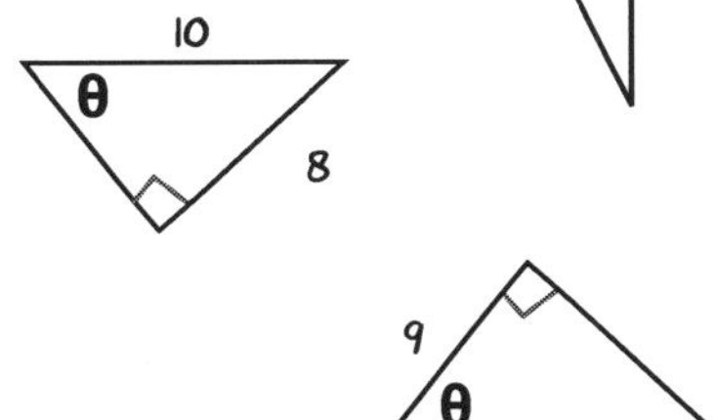

144. $\tan\theta$

145. $\cot\theta$

146. $\tan\theta$

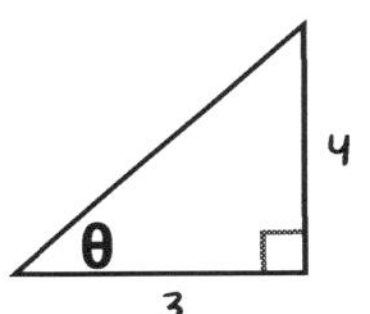

147. $\sin\theta$

148. $\sin\theta$

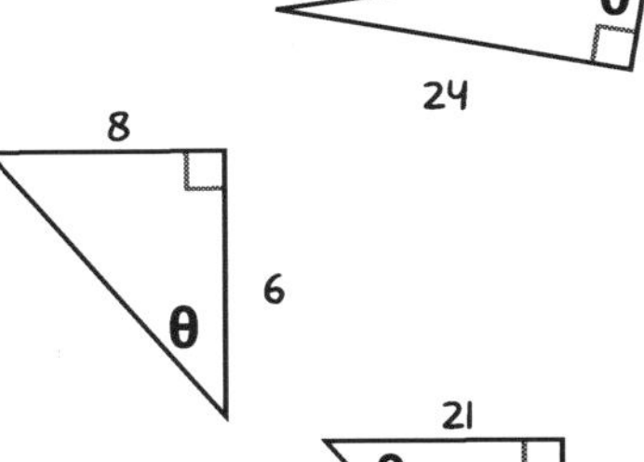

149. $\cos\theta$

150. $\cos\theta$

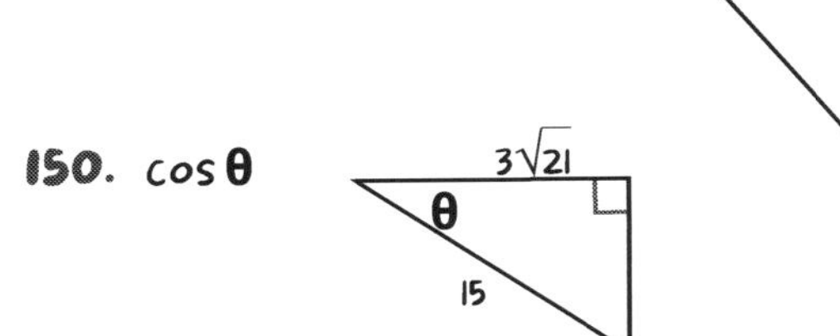

151. $\sec\theta$

152. $\cos\theta$

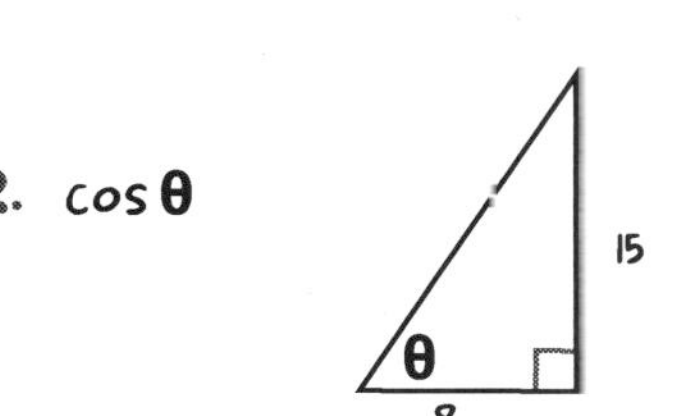

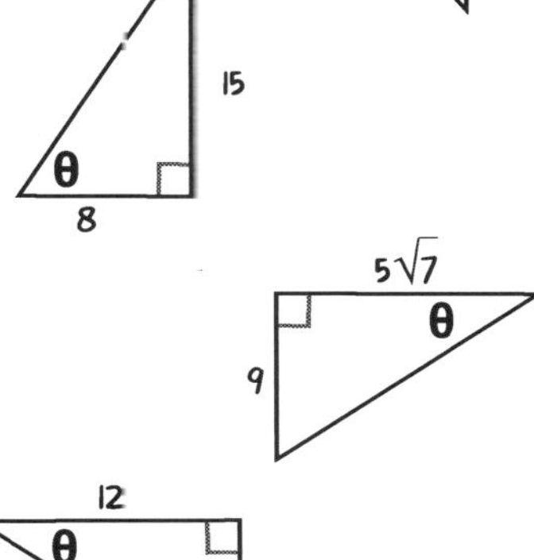

153. $\cot\theta$

154. $\sec\theta$

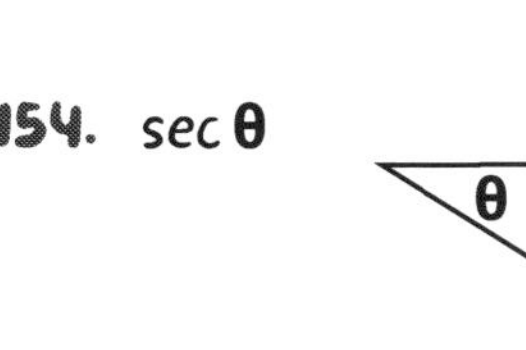

155. $\csc\theta$

156. $\sec\theta$

157. $\csc\theta$

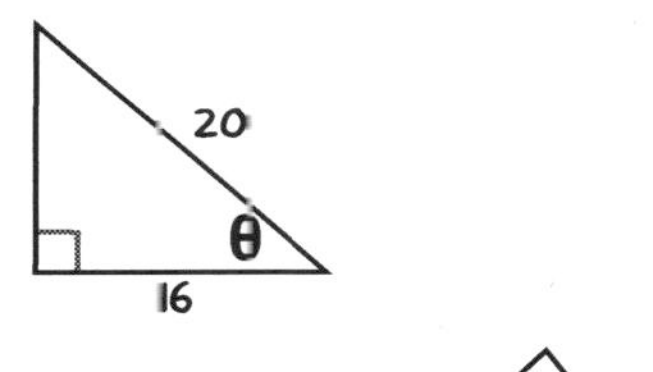

158. $\tan\theta$

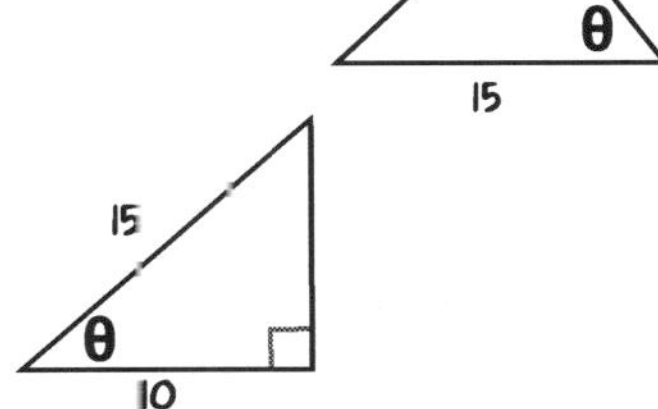

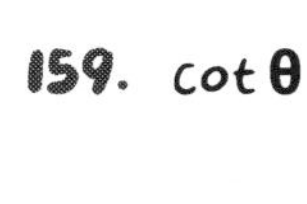

159. $\cot\theta$

160. $\sec\theta$

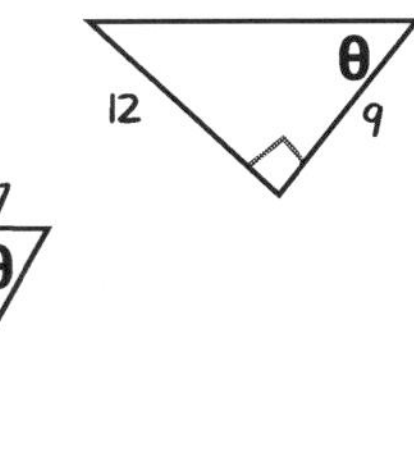

Section 2.1 Quiz

161. $\cos\theta$

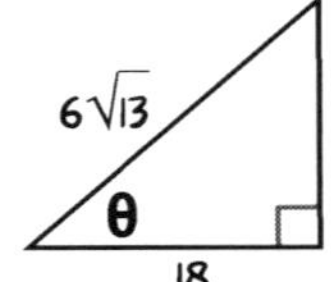

162. $\cos\theta$

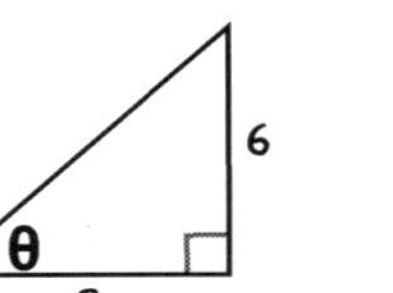

163. $\csc\theta$

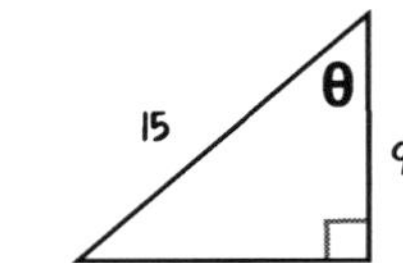

164. $\sec\theta$

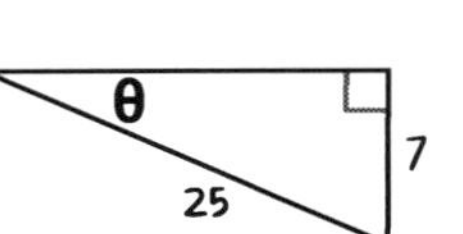

165. $\csc\theta$

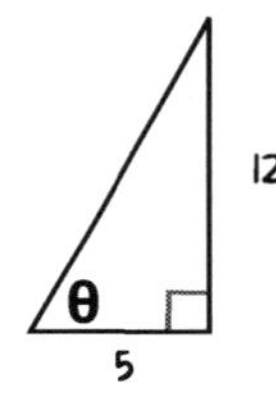

166. $\csc\theta$

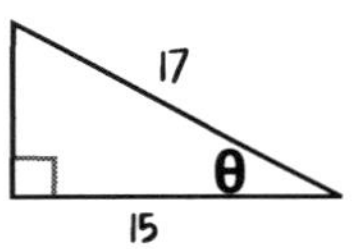

167. $\tan\theta$

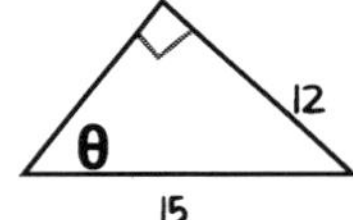

168. $\tan\theta$

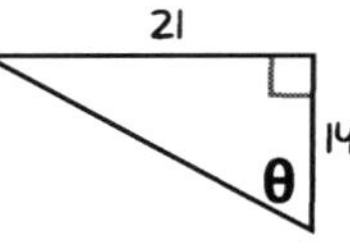

169. $\csc\theta$

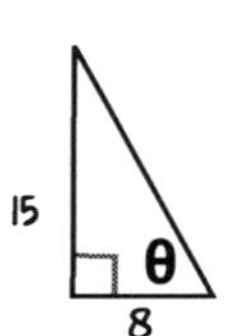

170. $\csc\theta$

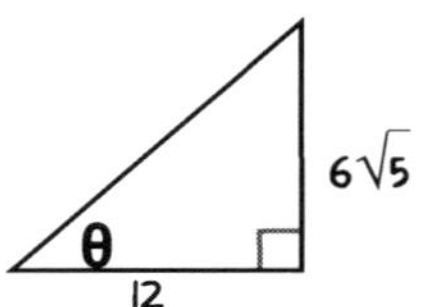

171. $\sec\theta$

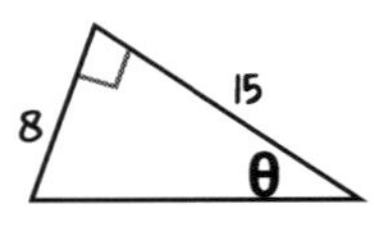

172. $\sin\theta$

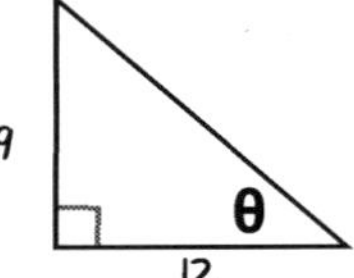

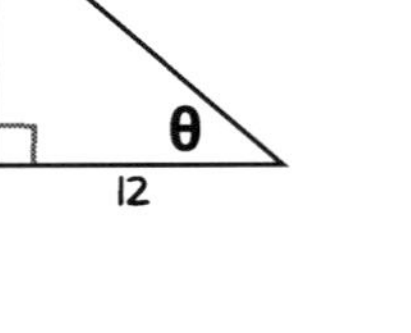

173. $\sin\theta$

25 θ 7

174. $\cot\theta$

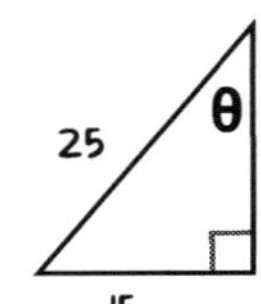

175. $\cot\theta$

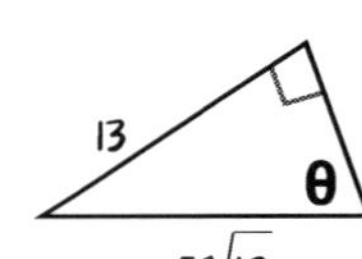

176. $\cot\theta$

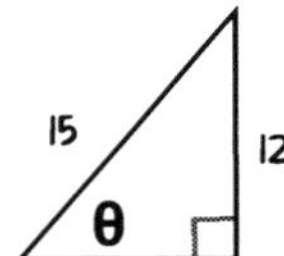

177. $\cot\theta$

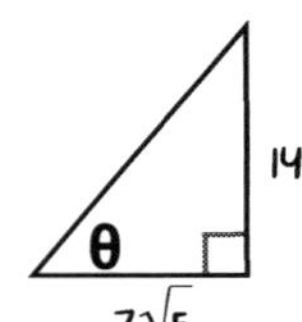

178. $\csc\theta$

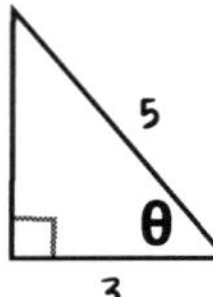

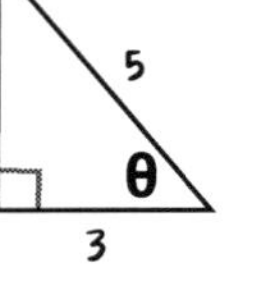

179. $\csc\theta$

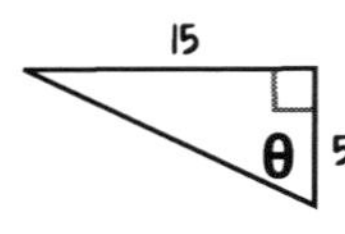

180. $\sin\theta$

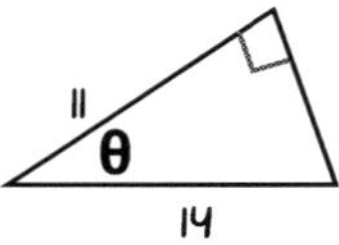

Section 2.1 Quiz

181. $\cos\theta$

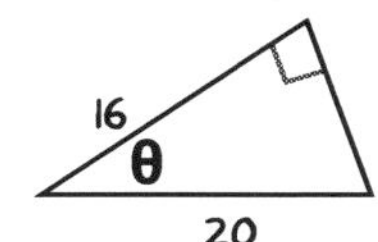

182. $\cos\theta$

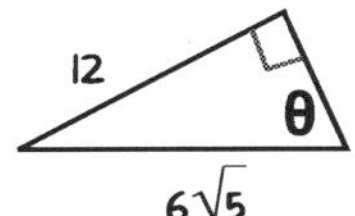

183. $\csc\theta$

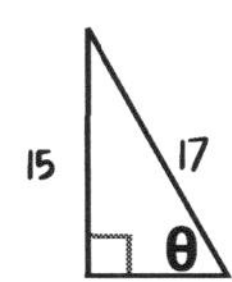

184. $\sec\theta$

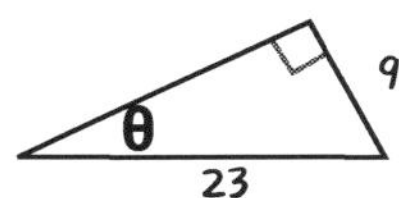

185. $\sin\theta$

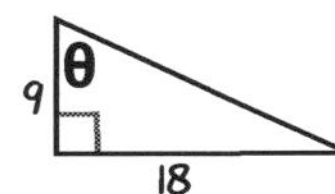

186. $\sec\theta$

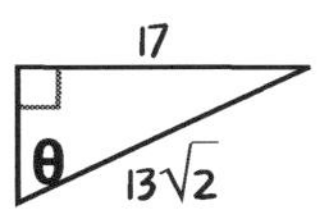

187. $\tan\theta$

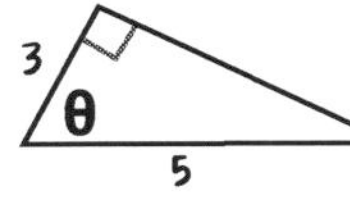

188. $\sin\theta$

189. $\cos\theta$

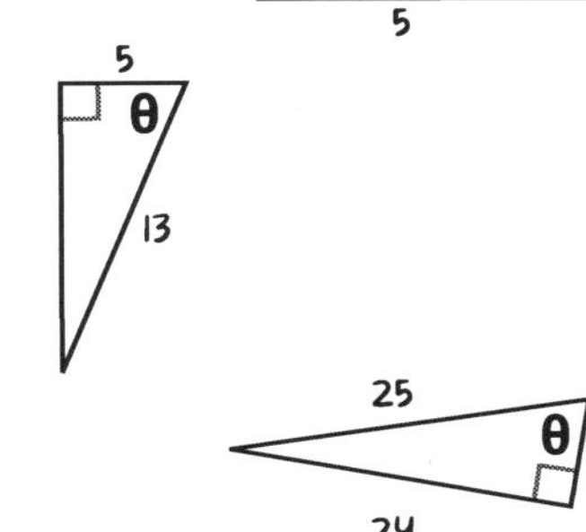

190. $\cot\theta$

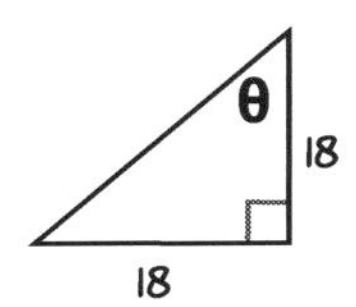

191. $\tan\theta$

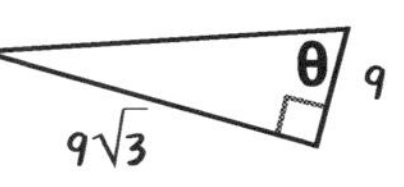

192. $\sin\theta$

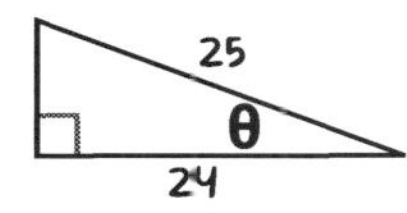

193. $\cos\theta$

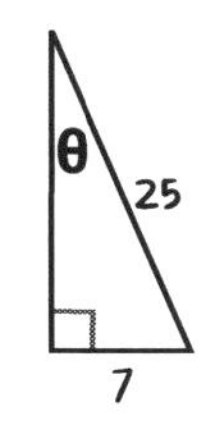

194. $\cos\theta$

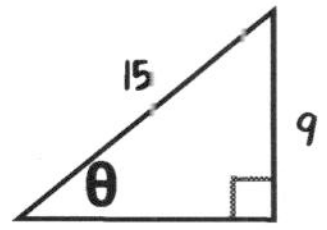

195. $\sin\theta$

196. $\cot\theta$

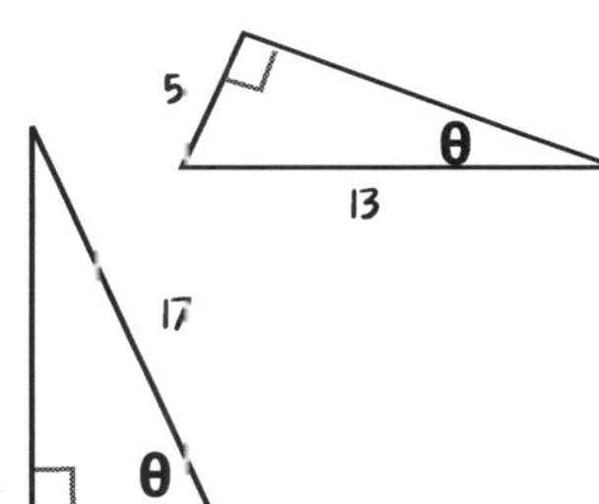

197. $\cot\theta$

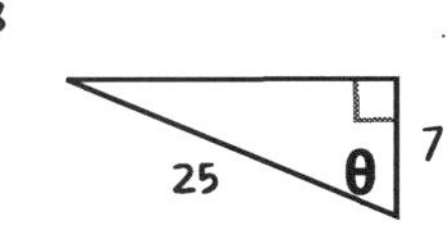

198. $\cot\theta$

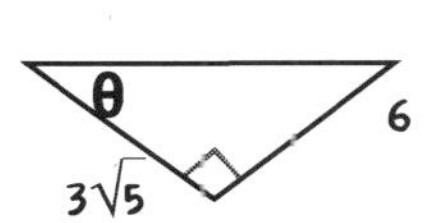

199. $\cot\theta$

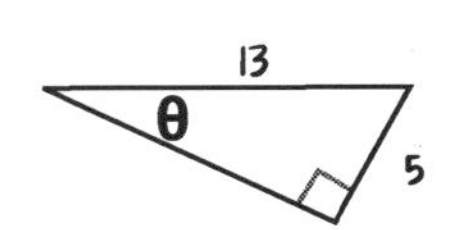

200. $\cos\theta$

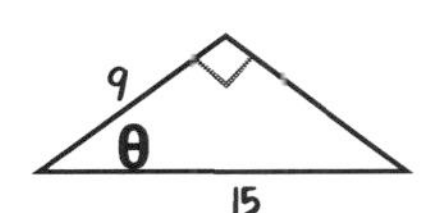

Section 2.1 Quiz

201. $\cot\theta$

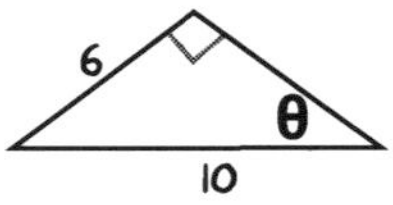

202. $\cos\theta$

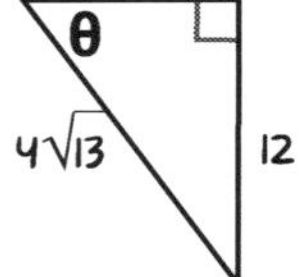

203. $\csc\theta$

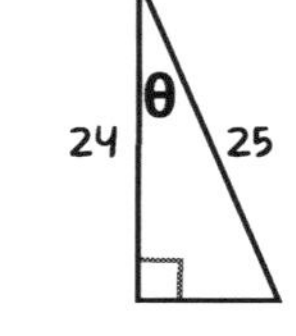

204. $\cos\theta$

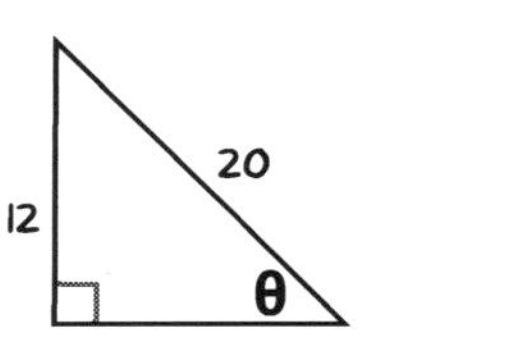

205. $\sec\theta$

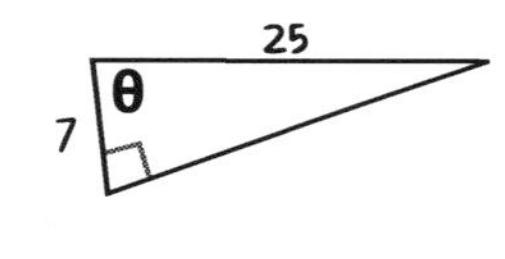

206. $\tan\theta$

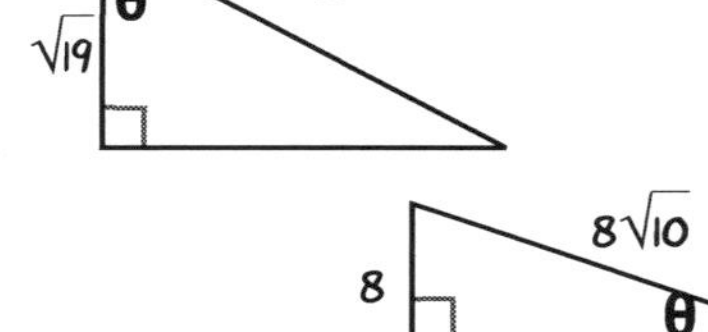

207. $\tan\theta$

(Triangle: 8, $8\sqrt{10}$, θ)

208. $\csc\theta$

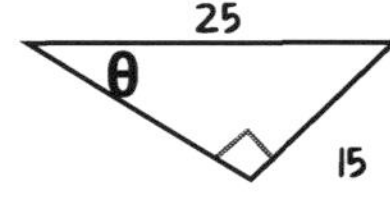

209. $\csc\theta$

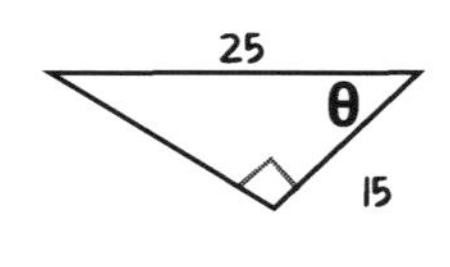

210. $\cot\theta$

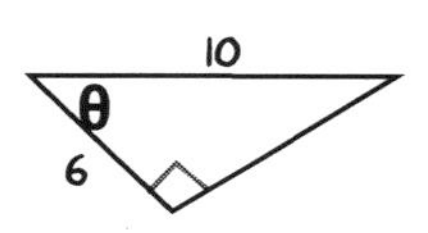

211. $\sin\theta$

(Triangle: 12, θ, 5)

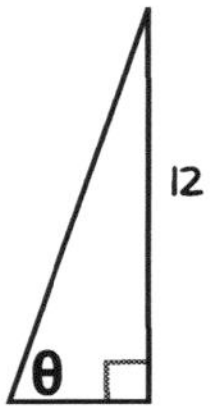

212. $\sec\theta$

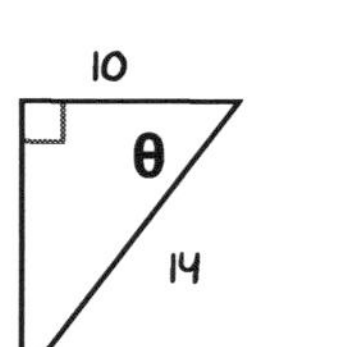

213. $\cos\theta$

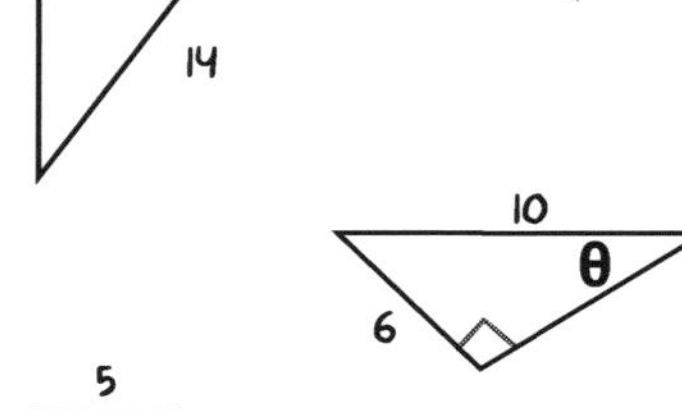

214. $\sec\theta$

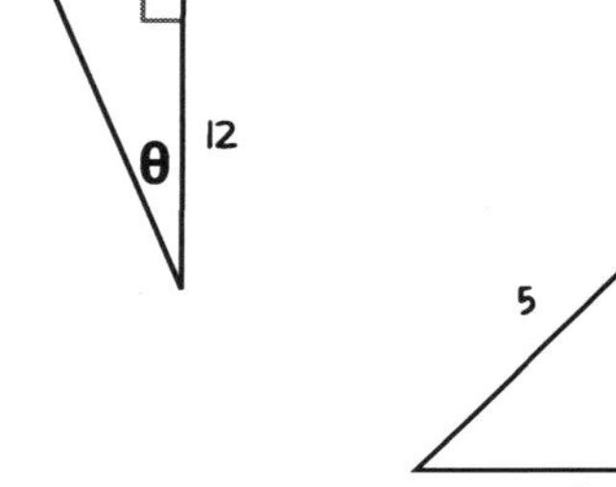

215. $\cos\theta$

216. $\csc\theta$

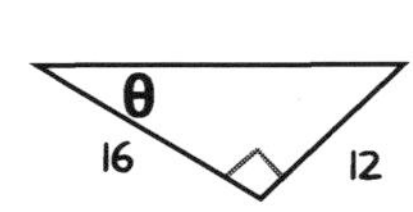

217. $\cos\theta$

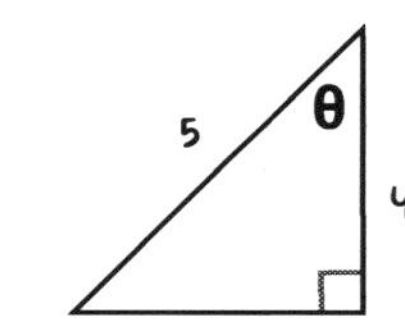

218. $\tan\theta$

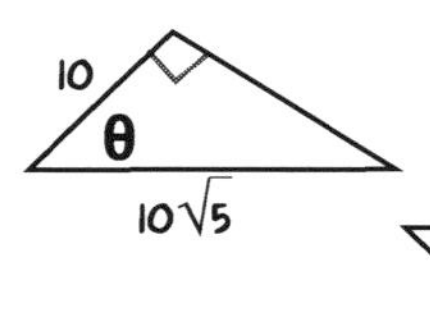

219. $\tan\theta$

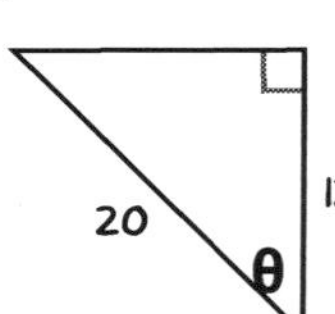

220. $\cos\theta$

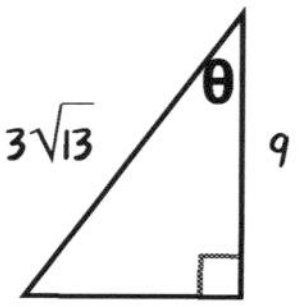

(Triangle: $3\sqrt{13}$, θ, 9)

Section 2.1 Quiz

221. $\sin\theta$

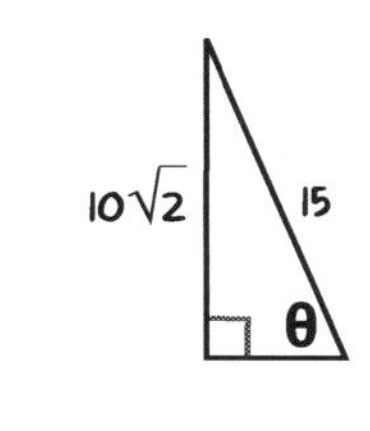

222. $\cot\theta$

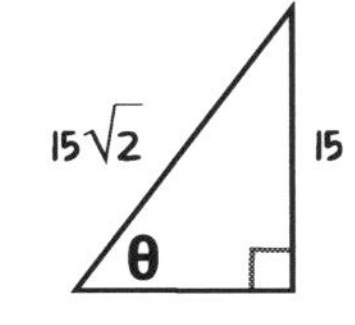

223. $\cos\theta$

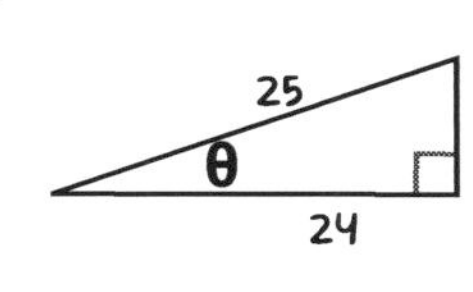

224. $\cot\theta$

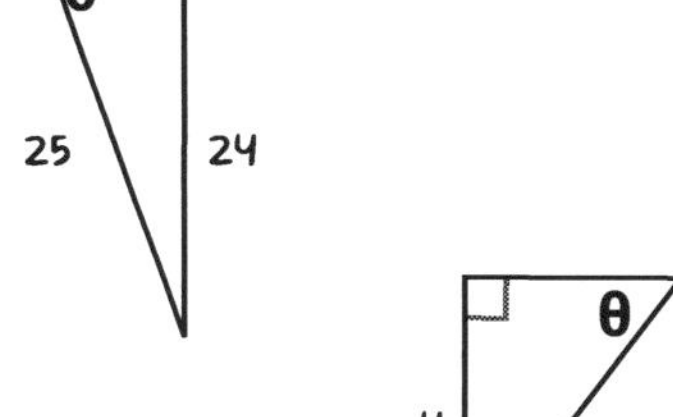

225. $\cos\theta$

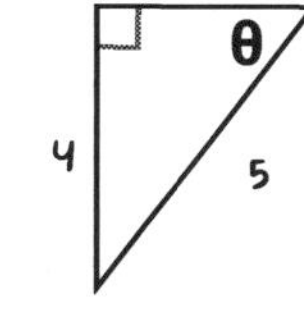

226. $\sec\theta$

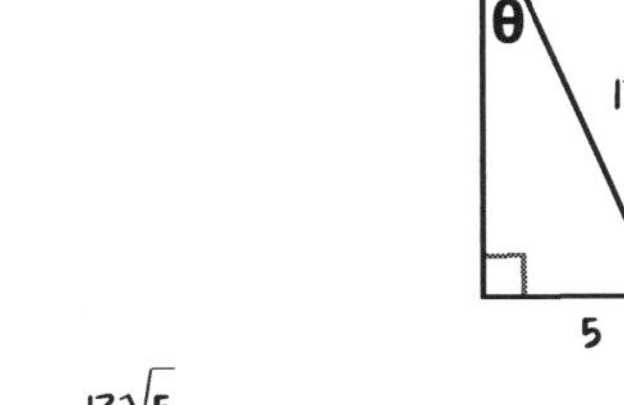

227. $\cos\theta$

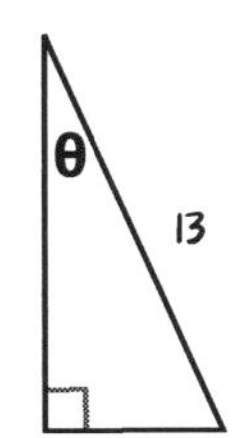

228. $\sec\theta$

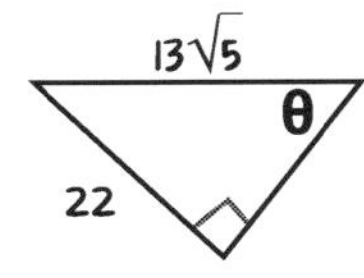

229. $\sin\theta$

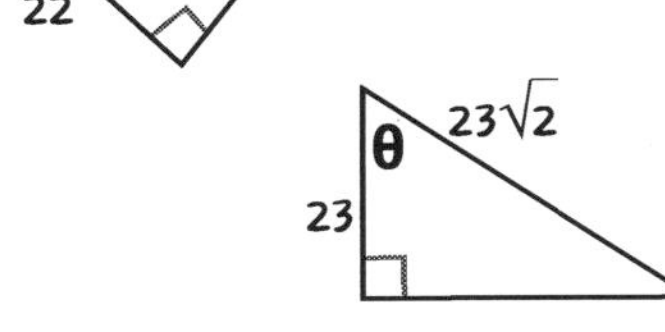

230. $\sec\theta$

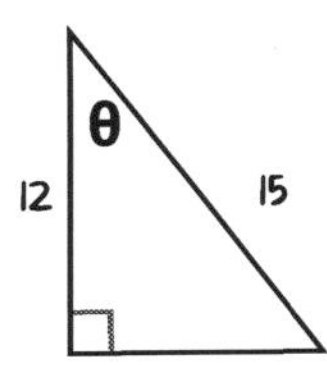

231. $\sin\theta$

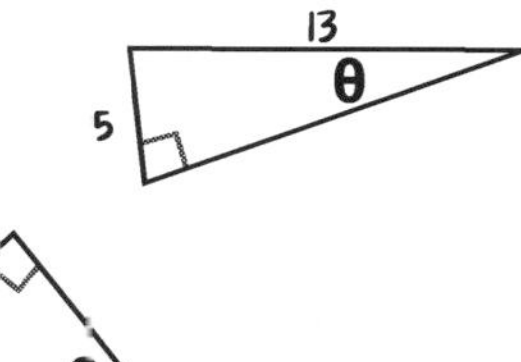

232. $\sin\theta$

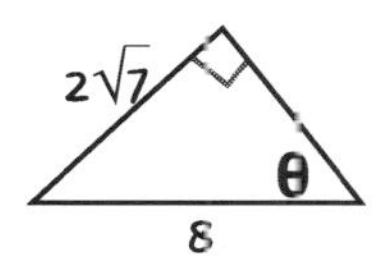

233. $\sin\theta$

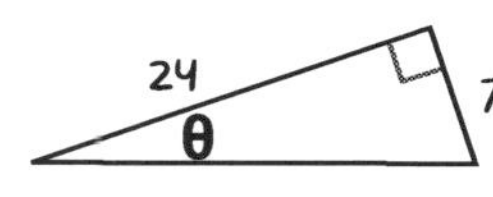

234. $\csc\theta$

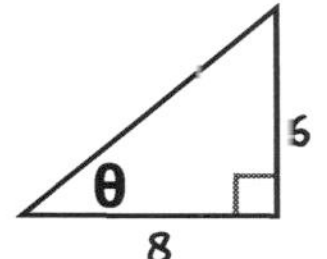

235. $\sin\theta$

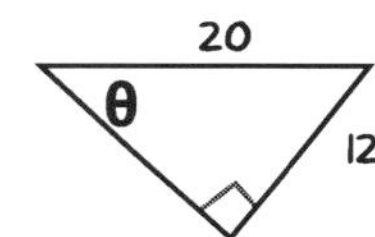

236. $\tan\theta$

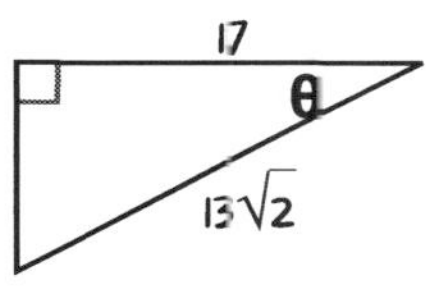

237. $\sin\theta$

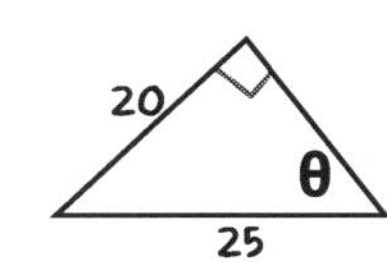

238. $\tan\theta$

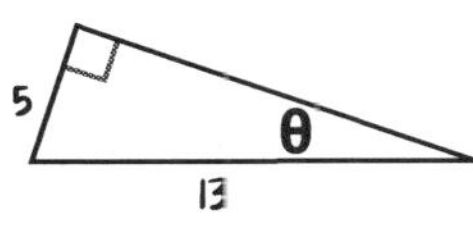

239. $\tan\theta$

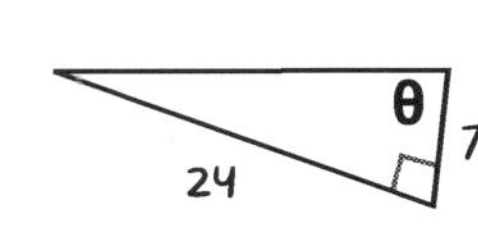

240. $\sin\theta$

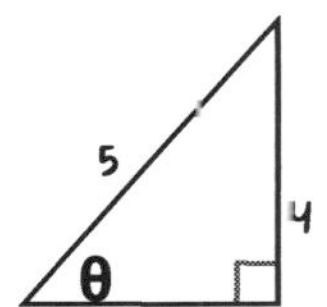

Section 2.1 Quiz

241. $\csc\theta$

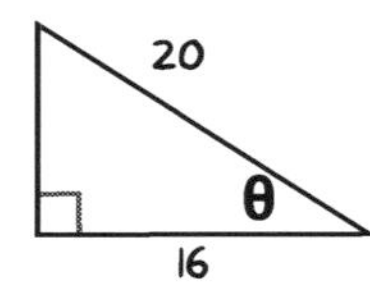

242. $\csc\theta$

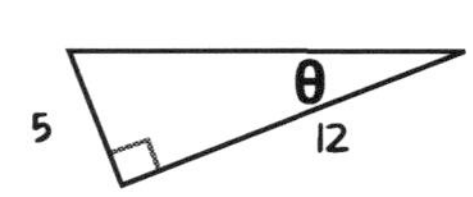

243. $\cot\theta$

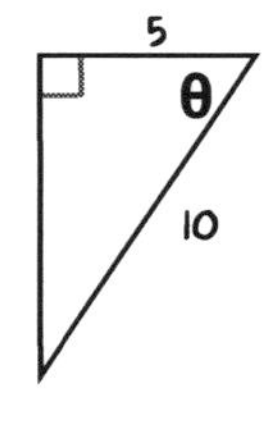

244. $\cos\theta$

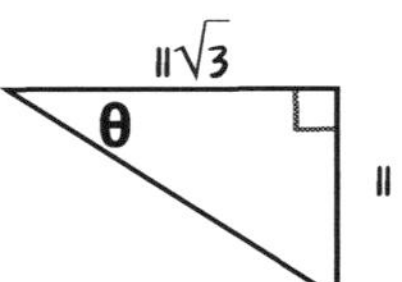

245. $\sec\theta$

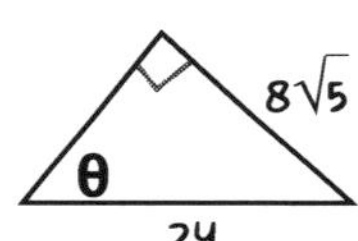

246. $\sin\theta$

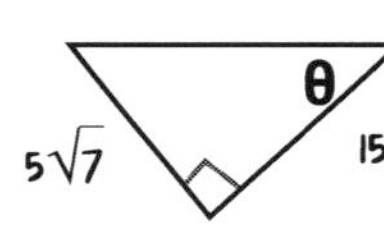

247. $\sec\theta$

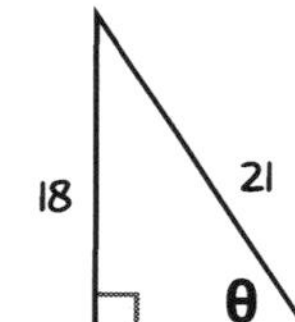

248. $\sec\theta$

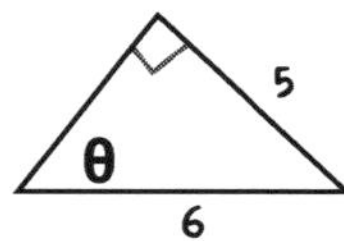

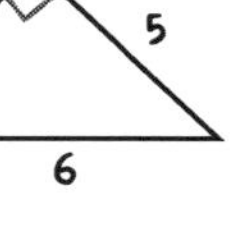

249. $\sin\theta$

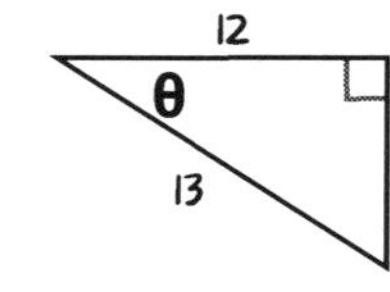

250. $\csc\theta$

251. $\cos\theta$

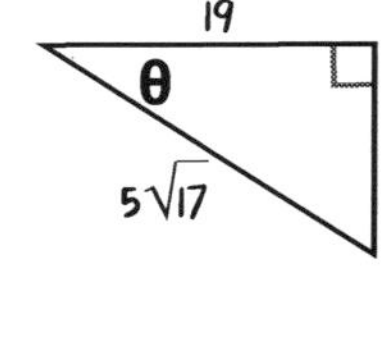

252. $\csc\theta$

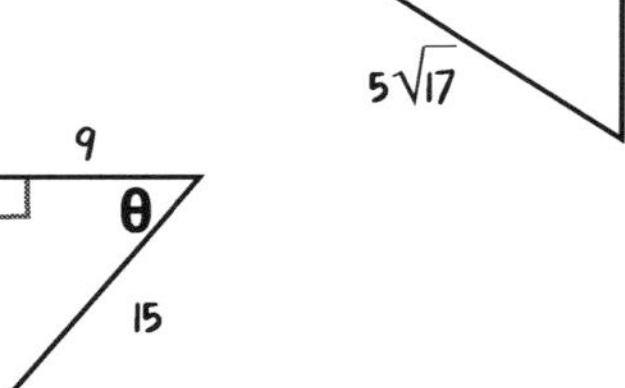

253. $\cot\theta$

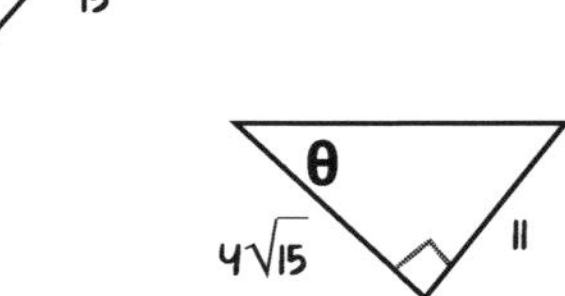

254. $\cos\theta$

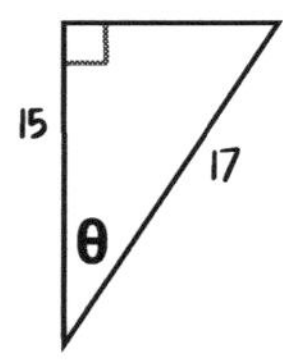

255. $\sec\theta$

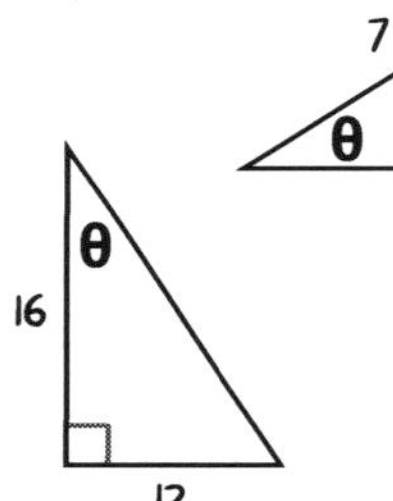

256. $\tan\theta$

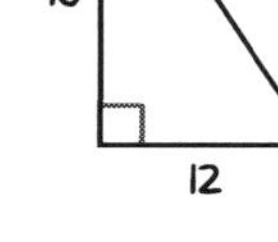

257. $\sec\theta$

258. $\csc\theta$

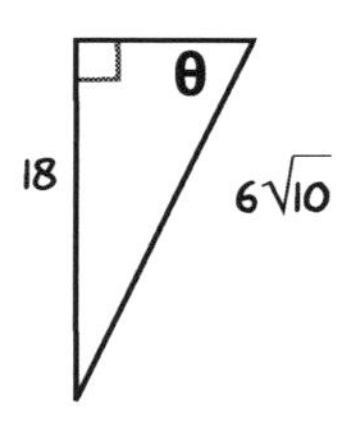

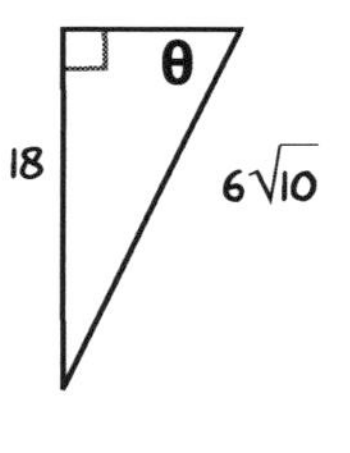

259. $\cot\theta$

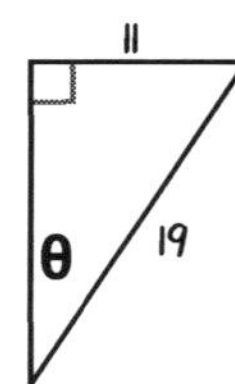

260. $\tan\theta$

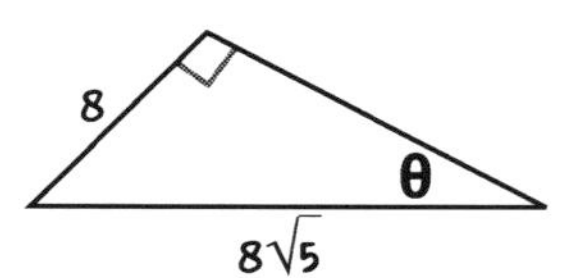

Section 2.1 Quiz

261. $\tan\theta$

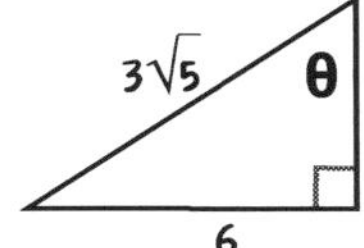

262. $\tan\theta$

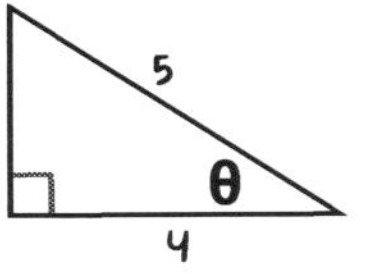

263. $\cos\theta$

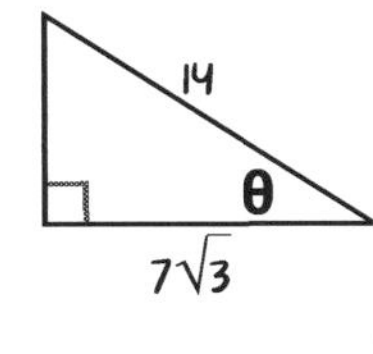

264. $\sin\theta$

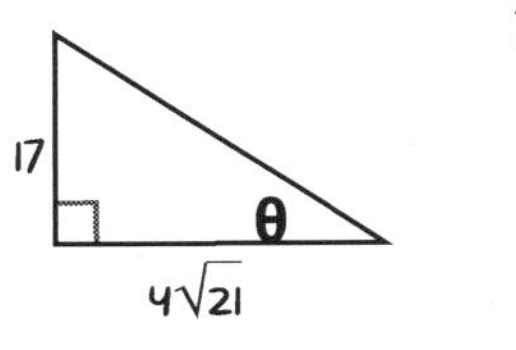

265. $\cos\theta$

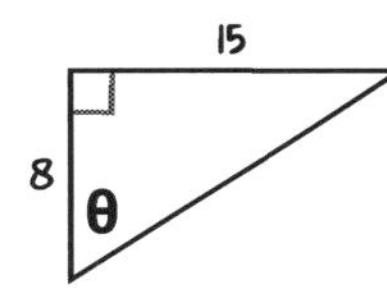

266. $\sin\theta$

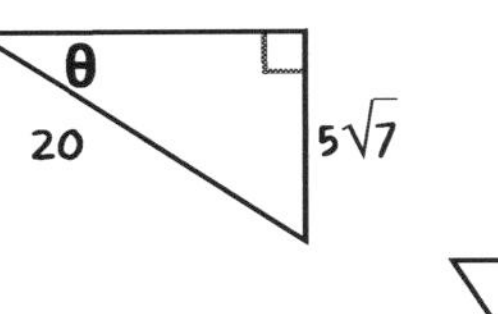

267. $\csc\theta$

268. $\sin\theta$

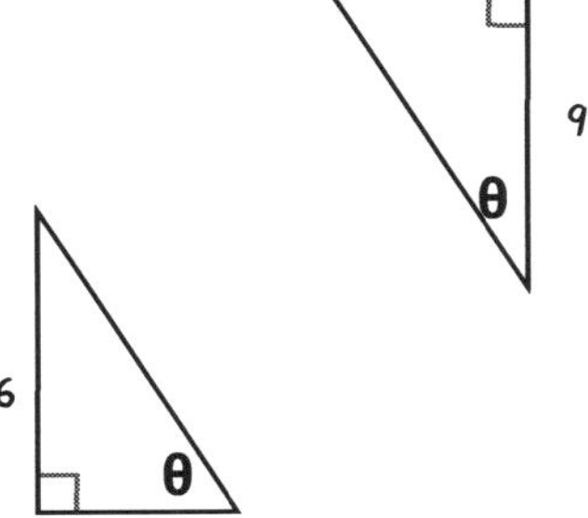

269. $\tan\theta$

270. $\sin\theta$

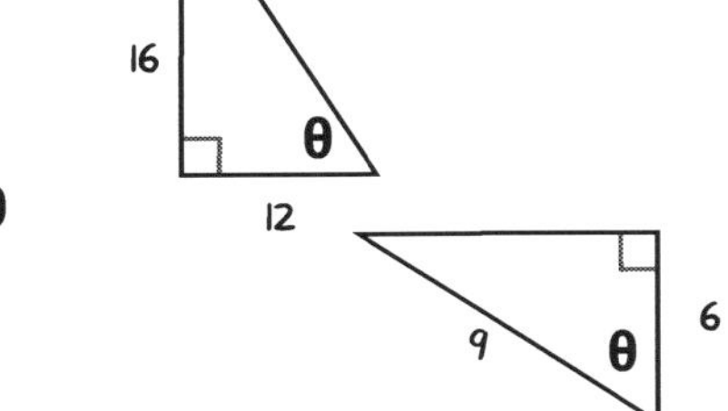

271. $\sec\theta$

272. $\cot\theta$

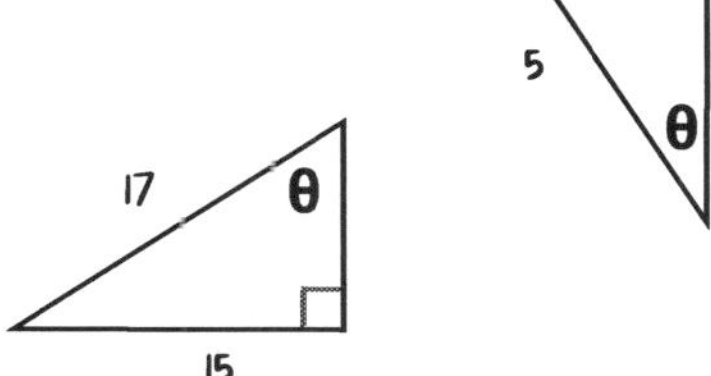

273. $\sec\theta$

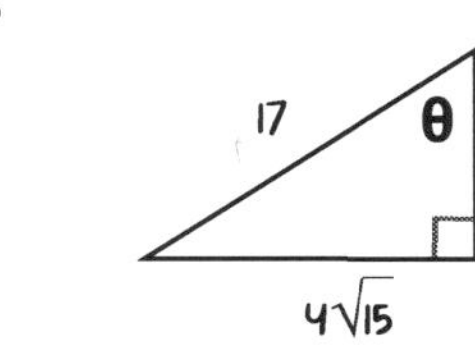

274. $\csc\theta$

275. $\cot\theta$

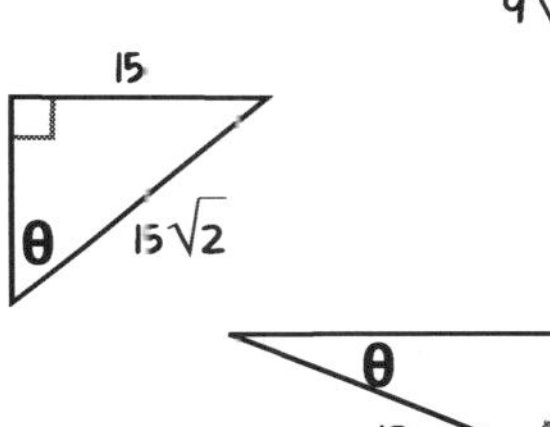

276. $\cos\theta$

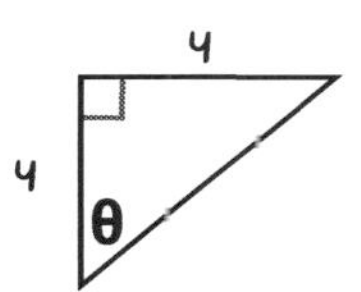

277. $\cot\theta$

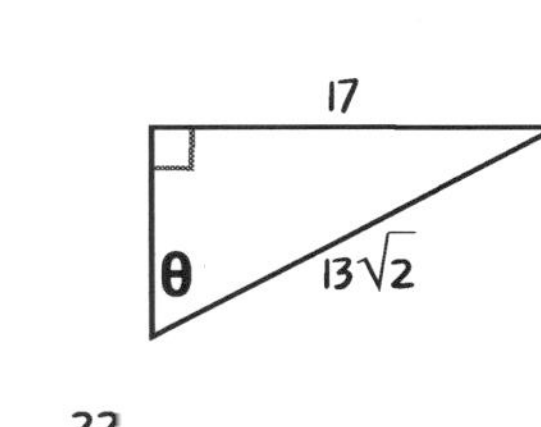

278. $\cot\theta$

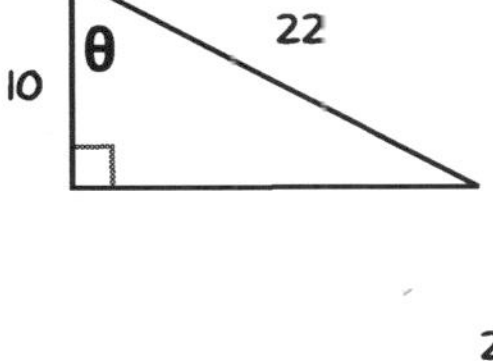

279. $\tan\theta$

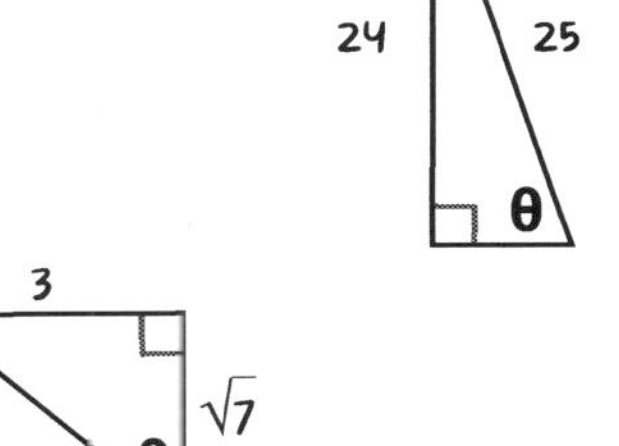

280. $\tan\theta$

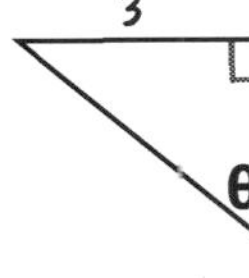

Section 2.1 Quiz

281. $\cos\theta$

282. $\cos\theta$

283. $\cos\theta$

284. $\csc\theta$

285. $\csc\theta$

286. $\tan\theta$

287. $\sin\theta$

288. $\cot\theta$

289. $\csc\theta$

290. $\cot\theta$

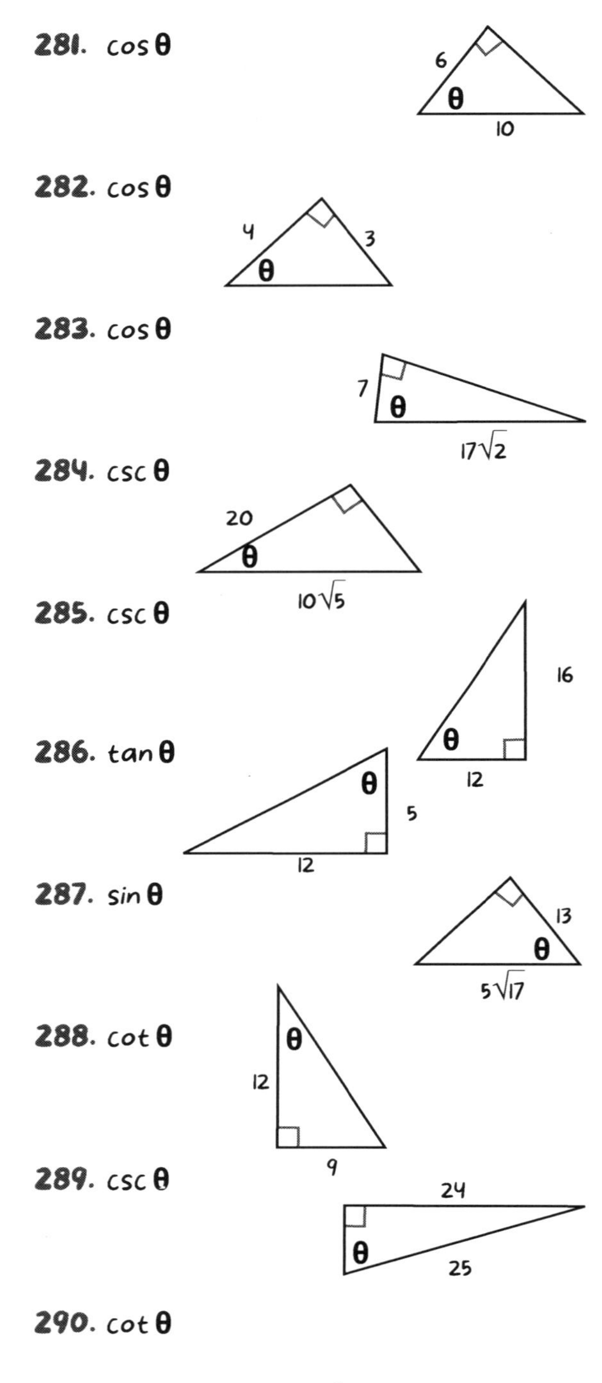

291. $\tan\theta$

292. $\csc\theta$

293. $\tan\theta$

294. $\cot\theta$

295. $\csc\theta$

296. $\tan\theta$

297. $\cot\theta$

298. $\sin\theta$

299. $\tan\theta$

300. $\csc\theta$

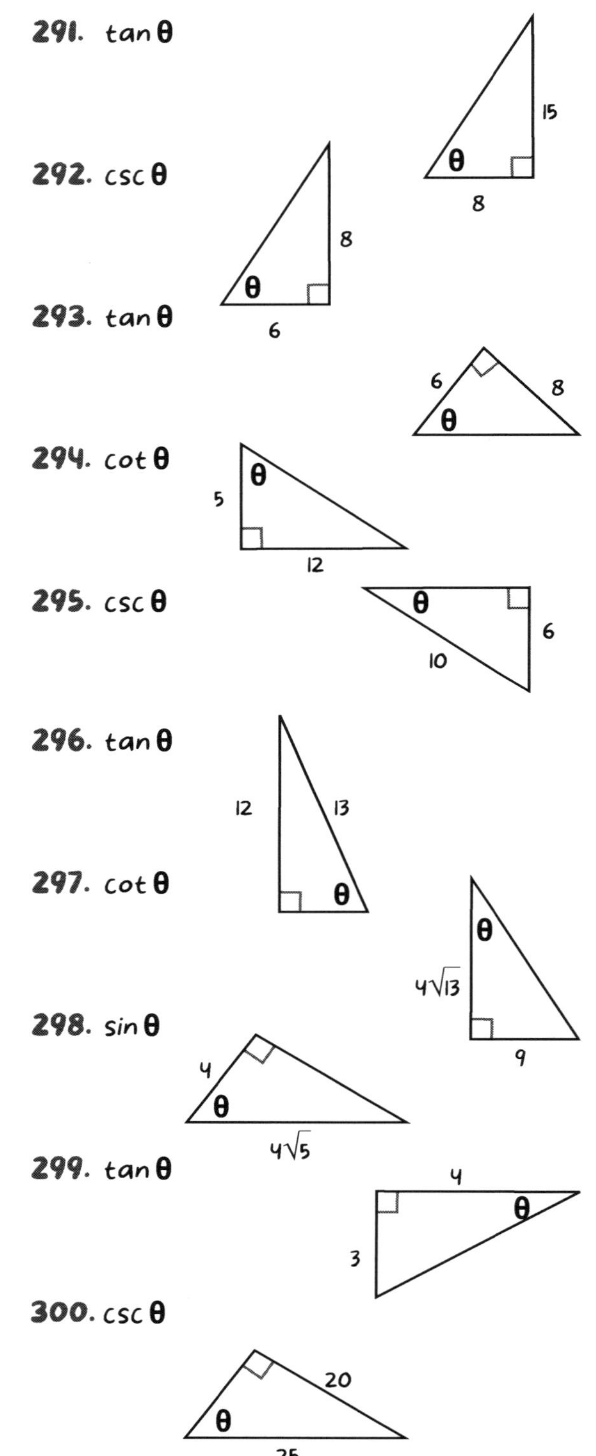

Section 2.2 Finding Missing Sides & Angles

Though it might seem like trigonometry is mostly confined to academic settings, you'd be surprised to discover its frequent applications in our daily lives. Trigonometry is used every day in aviation, navigation, construction sites, astronomy, and more.

Let's take a look at a few real-world examples while we **find** a missing side or a missing angle using sin, cos, or tan.

You will need to use the calculator for these problems. Most schools and math classes have students use the TI-84 calculator. If you do not have this specific calculator, do not worry! Simply look your calculator model online and make sure you know how to set the mode to radian **or** degree. Here is an image of the TI-84 calculator below.

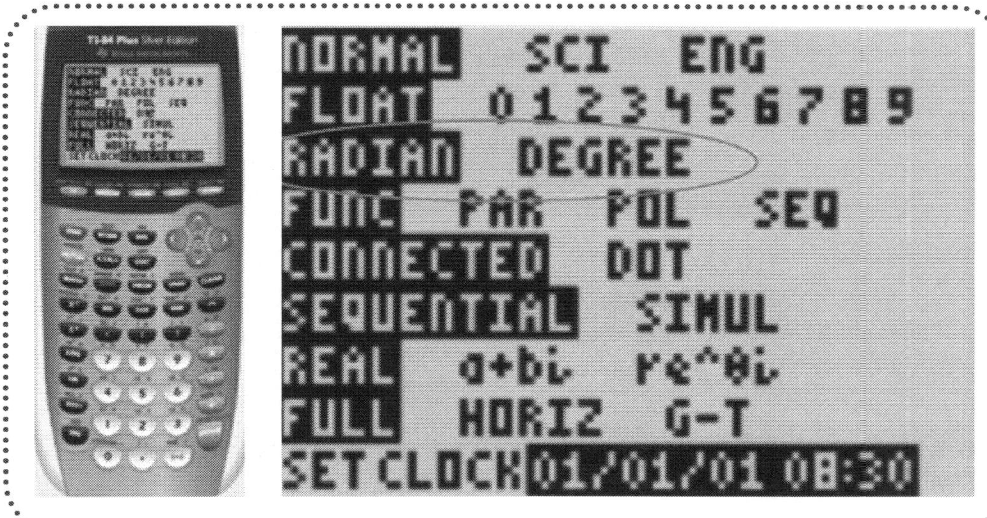

To toggle between Radian or Degree, you will need to click on the "2nd" button followed by the "Mode" button. Both of these buttons are found on the top left of the calculator. For these problems, you want to make sure you have the calculator set to **degrees.**

Real Life Example # 1

Carmen wants to measure the **height** of a tree. She walks exactly 100 feet from the **base** of the tree and looks up. The **angle** from the ground to the top of the tree is 33°. To the nearest foot, how tall is the tree?

We can use trigonometry to solve this problem. Notice that we can create a right-triangle.

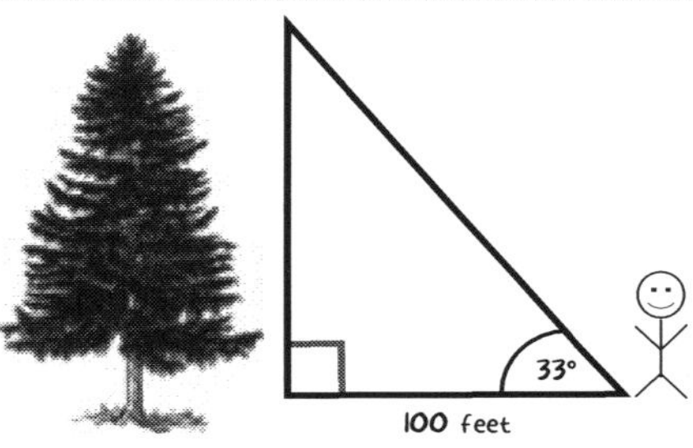

We know the angle from the ground to the top of the tree is **33°** which is labeled on the diagram above. We also know Carmen is **100** feet away, so that is labeled as well. The question asks us how tall is the tree.

Note that 100 feet is **adjacent** to 33° and we need to find "x" which is **opposite** to 33°. Let's add in that new information to our diagram.

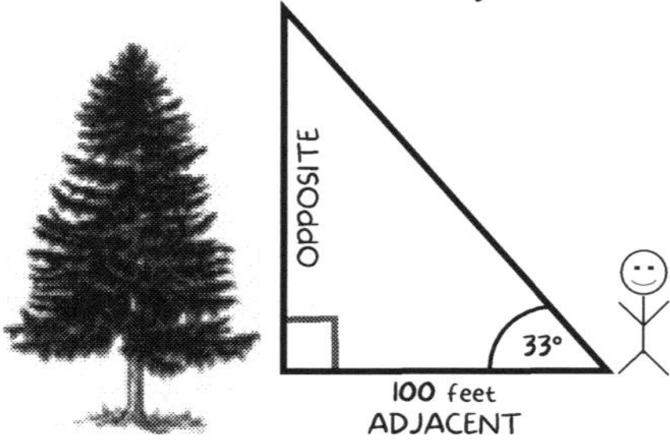

We have enough information to use trigonometry to solve this problem. We know the angel is 33°. We have the **adjacent** value and we need to find out the **opposite** value.

Which one of our trig function applies here? Remember the mnemonic device SOCAHTOA. **Here is a diagram reminder to refresh your memory.**

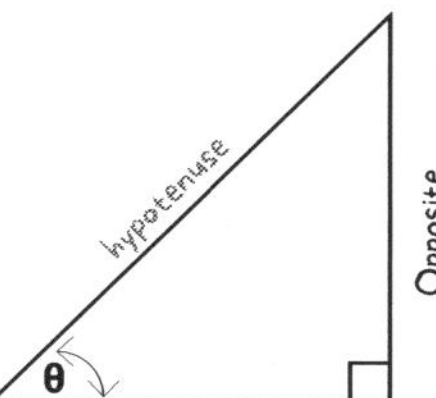

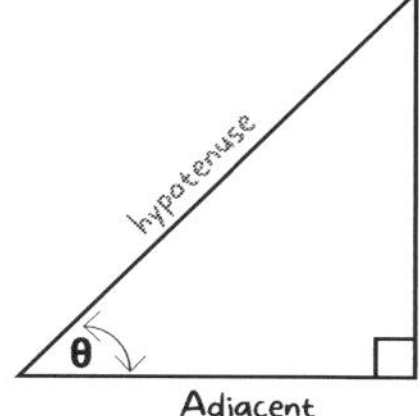

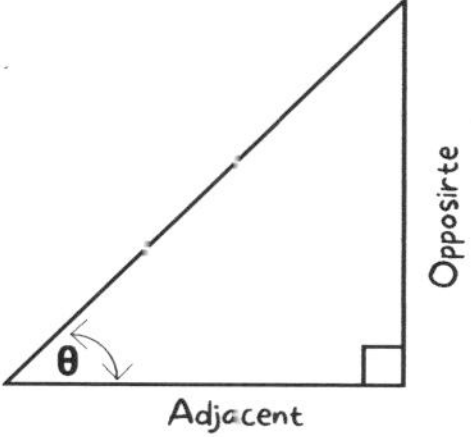

$\sin(\theta) = \dfrac{\text{opposite}}{\text{hypotenuse}}$ $\cos(\theta) = \dfrac{\text{adjacent}}{\text{hypotenuse}}$ $\tan(\theta) = \dfrac{\text{opposite}}{\text{adjacent}}$

SOH **CAH** **TOA**

We need to use $\tan\theta = \dfrac{\text{opposite}}{\text{adjacent}}$. Plug in the known values.

$\tan 33^\circ = \dfrac{x}{100}$.

$(100)(\tan 33^\circ) = x$ **You need to use a calculator for all these problems.**

$64.94 = x$

The problem states to round up to the nearest foot, so the answer is **65 feet tall.**

Always make sure your calculator is set up correct. For the example above, if we accidentally had our calculator set to the radian mode, we would get the value of tan(33) as -75.31 which is **wrong**.

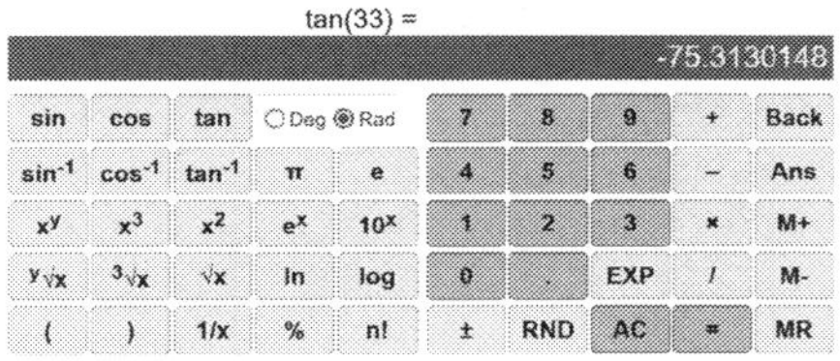

tan(33) = -75.3130148

We need to make sure our calculator is set to degrees.

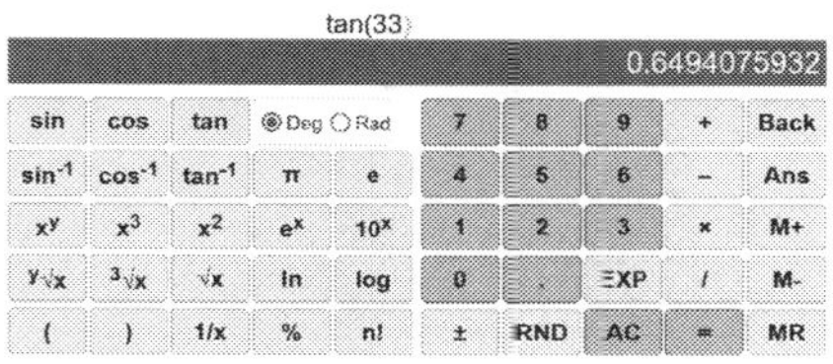

tan(33) 0.6494075932

This set up is correct

Real Life Example # 2

Joseph is standing **31 metres** away from the base of a skyscraper. He looks up to the top of the building at a **78° angle.** How **tall** is the skyscraper? Round to the nearest meter.

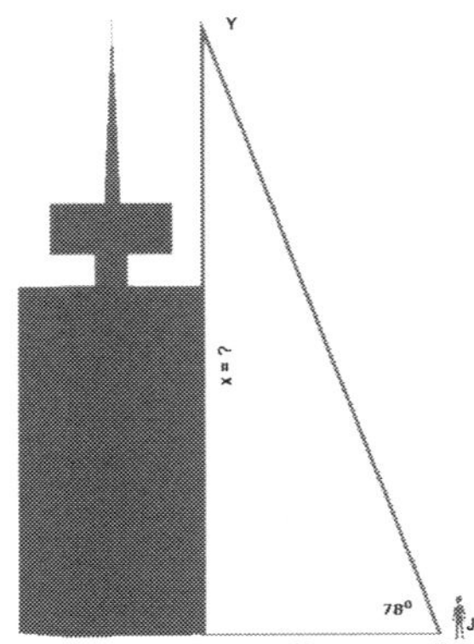

We need to use $\tan\theta = \frac{\text{opposite}}{\text{adjacent}}$. Plug in the known values.

$$\tan 78° = \frac{x}{31}$$

$$4.7046 = \frac{x}{31}$$

$$145.8426 = x$$

So $x = 145.8426$ meters.

The problem states to round up to the nearest meter, so the answer is **146 meters tall.**

Real Life Example # 3

In the diagram below, the cable makes a 38° angle with the seabed. The taut cable is 30 meters in length. We want to know how deep the water is from the the boat to the seabed.

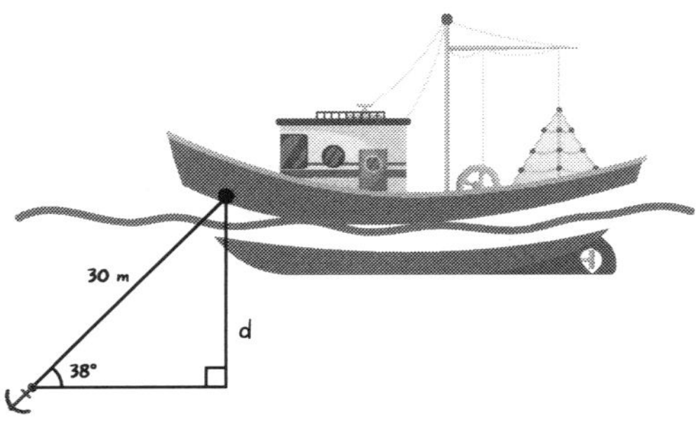

How can we solve this? We know the value of the **hypotenuse** and we know the cable makes a 38° angle. We are trying to solve for "d" which is **opposite** of the angle given.

Which one of our trig functions deal with hypotenuse and opposite?

$\sin\theta = \dfrac{\text{opposite}}{\text{hypotenuse}}$ Let's plug in our known values.

$\sin 38° = \dfrac{d}{30}$

$0.6156 = \dfrac{d}{30}$

$18.468 = d$

The depth is 18.47 meters. (rounded 2 decimal places)

Real Life Example # 4

The ladder leans against a wall as shown. The foot of the ladder is **6 feet** from the wall. The ladder reaches a **height** of **15 feet** on the wall. What is the **angle** that the ladder makes with the wall?

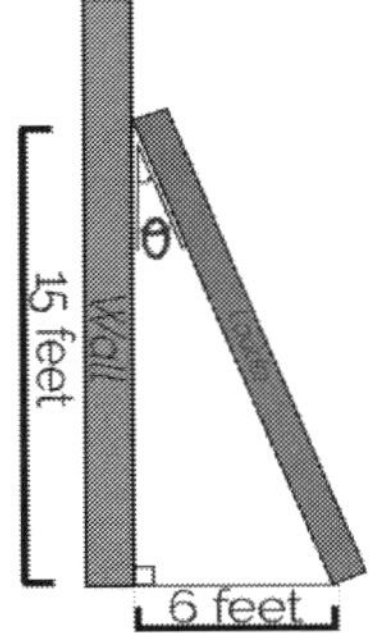

Notice in the last three examples, we were trying to find a missing **side**. In this problem, we are looking to solve for a **missing angle**.

How can we solve this? We know we are trying to solve for **θ** (the unknown angle).

Let's redraw the problem.

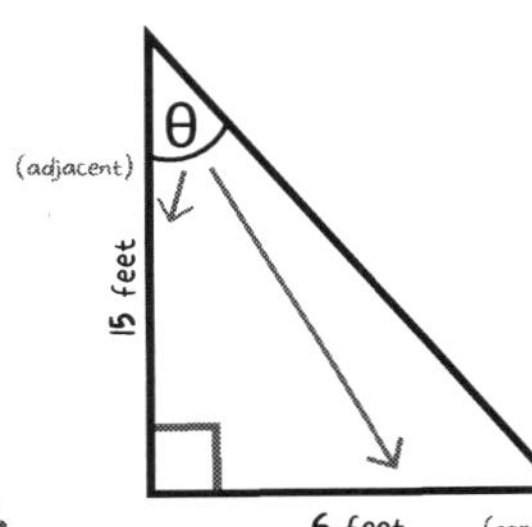

We know the **opposite** value is 6 and the **adjacent** value is 15 feet. Which one of our trig functions deal with opposite and adjacent?

We need to use $\tan\theta = \dfrac{\text{opposite}}{\text{adjacent}}$. Plug in the known values.

$\tan\theta = \dfrac{6}{15}$

In this step, we must follow an important rule when using the calculator.

When **SOLVING** for **angles,** we must use the **inverse function** on the calculator.

The **inverse sine function** is $\sin^{-1}$. This can also be called **arcsin.**

The **inverse cos function** is $\cos^{-1}$. This can also be called **arccos.**

The **inverse tan function** is $\tan^{-1}$. This can also be called **arctan.**

The inverse sin takes the **ratio** of the respective trig function and gives us an **angle.**

We have $\tan\theta = \frac{6}{15}$ $(6 \div 15 = 0.4$ so....)

$\tan\theta = 0.4$ (We need to take the inverse tan function or arctan)

$\theta = \tan^{-1}(0.4)$ (Plug that into your calculator)

$\theta = 21.8°$

arctan(0.4)

21.801409486

sin	cos	tan	Deg / Rad		7	8	9	+	Back
sin⁻¹	cos⁻¹	tan⁻¹	π	e	4	5	6	–	Ans
x^y	x^3	x^2	e^x	10^x	1	2	3	×	M+
$\sqrt[y]{x}$	$\sqrt[3]{x}$	$\sqrt{x}$	ln	log	0	.	EXP	/	M-
(	)	1/x	%	n!	±	RND	AC	=	MR

The angle between the ladder and the wall is 21.8°.

Real Life Example # 5

The distance from a boat to a lighthouse is **100 feet** and the lighthouse is **140 feet tall.** What is the angle of depression from the top of the Lighthouse to the boat?

We are provided with a word problem. Let's go ahead and solve this by drawing a diagram to assist us.

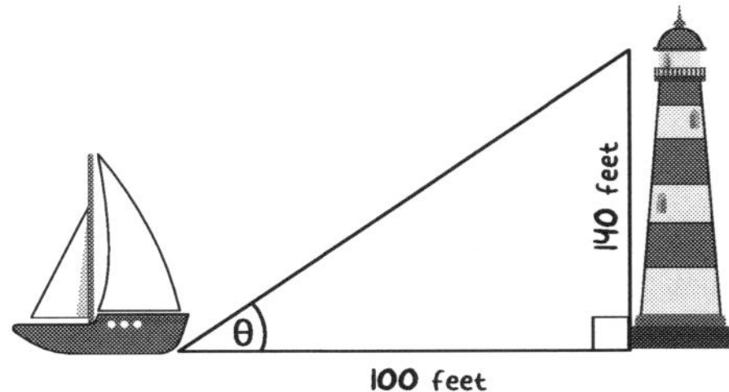

Your diagram should look like this. The angle of depression is the angle of elevation from the boat to the top of the light house.

How can we solve this? We know we are trying to solve for **θ** (the unknown angle).

We know the **opposite** value is 140 and the **adjacent** value is 100 feet.

Which one of our trig functions deal with opposite and adjacent?

We need to use $\tan \theta = \frac{\text{opposite}}{\text{adjacent}}$. Plug in the known values.

$\tan \theta = \frac{140}{100}$

$\tan \theta = 1.4$ (We need to take the inverse tan function or arctan)

$\theta = \tan^{-1}(1.4)$ (Plug that into your calculator)

$\theta = 54.46°$ → Round that to the nearest tenth and we get $\theta = 54.5°$. (Degrees are usually rounded to the nearest tenth unless the problem states otherwise).

Our answer is 54.5°.

You are now ready to tackle practice problems to find the missing side **or** missing angles.

Section 2.2 Quiz

Directions: Find the measure of each side indicated. Round your answer to the nearest tenth. Be sure to include the units in your answer.

1.

B
X
8 km
38°
A
C

2.

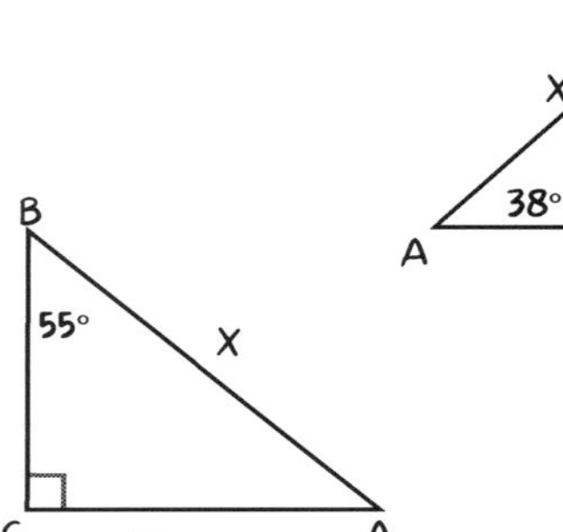

3.

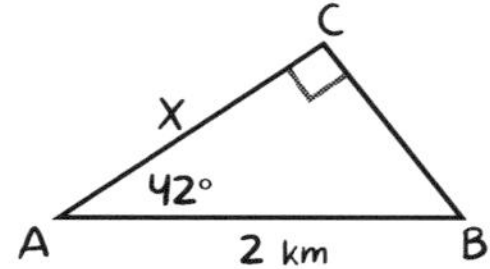

4.

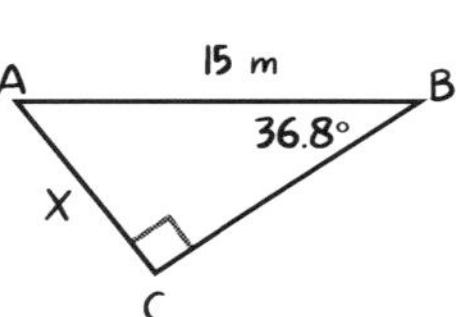

5.

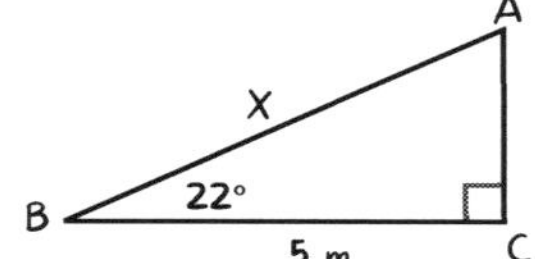

6.

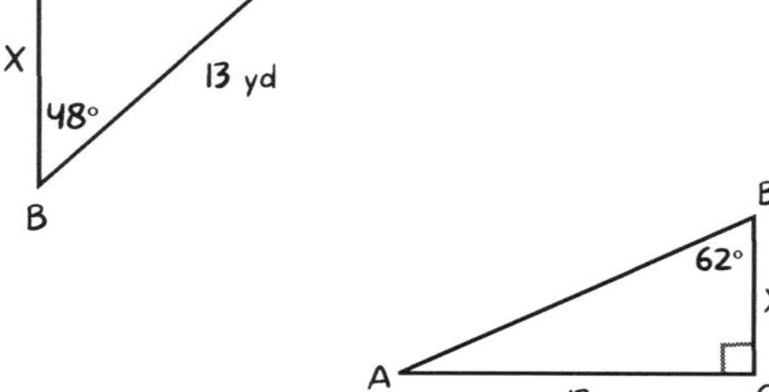

7.

8.

B
X
C
22.7°
15 km
A

9.

A
12 km
C
33°
X
B

10.

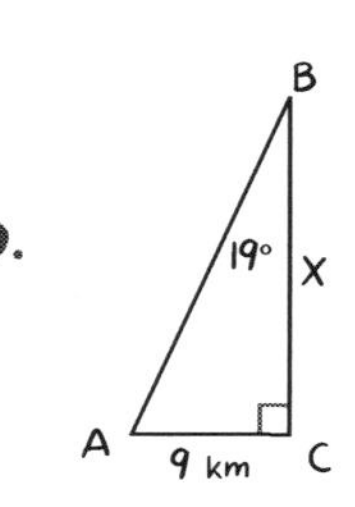

11.

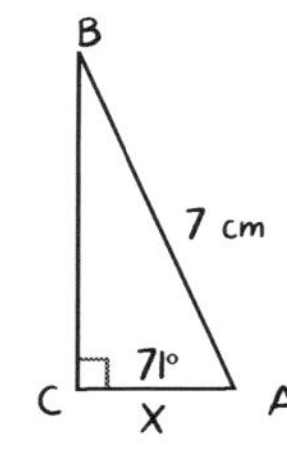

12.

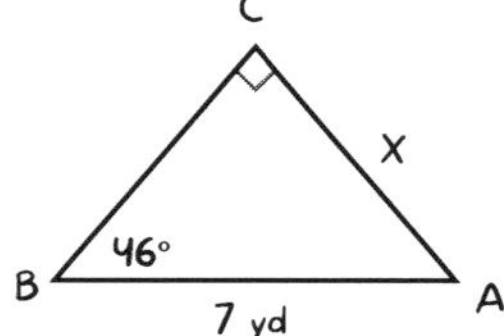

13.

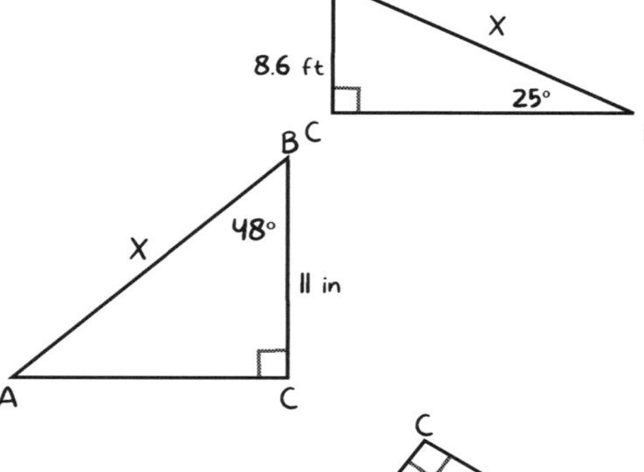

14.

15.

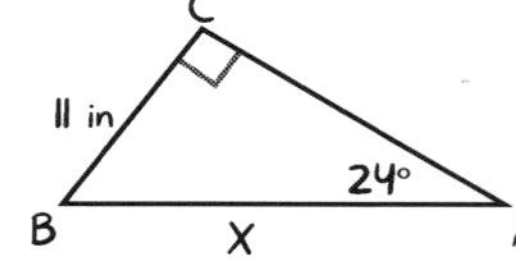

16.

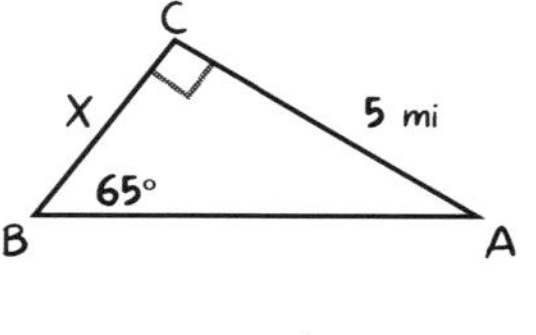

Section 2.2 Quiz

17. A, B, C; 16 yd; 17°; X

18.

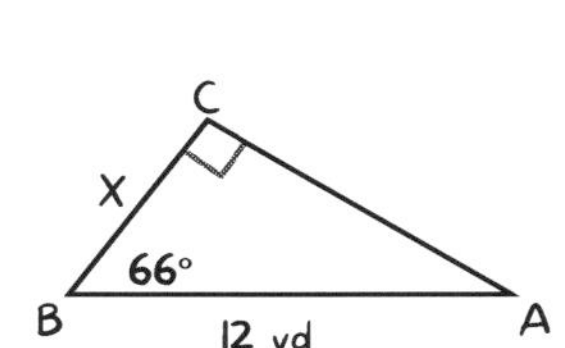

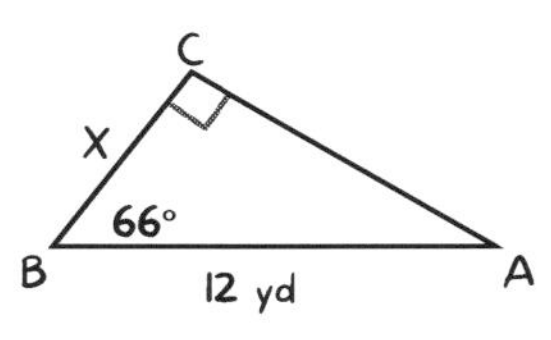

19. C, X, 26°, A, 6 m, B

20.

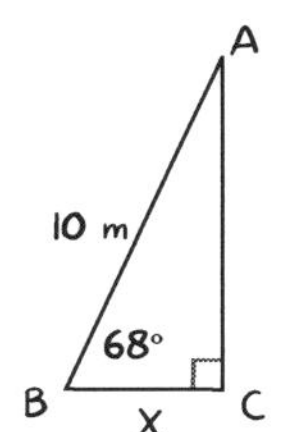

21. C, X, 65°, B, 15 ft, A

22.

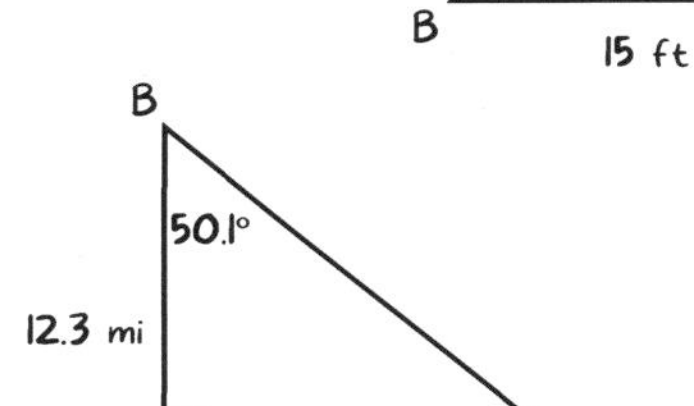

23. C, X, 66°, B, 11 cm, A

24.

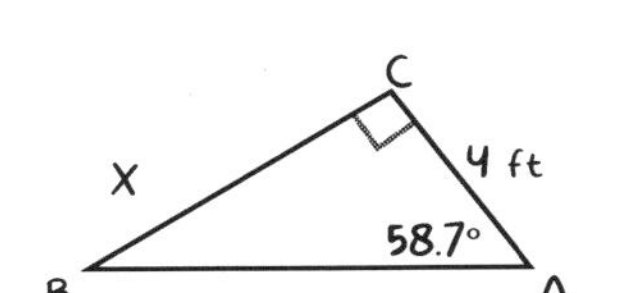

25.

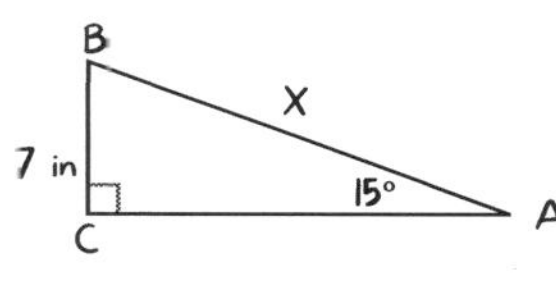

26.

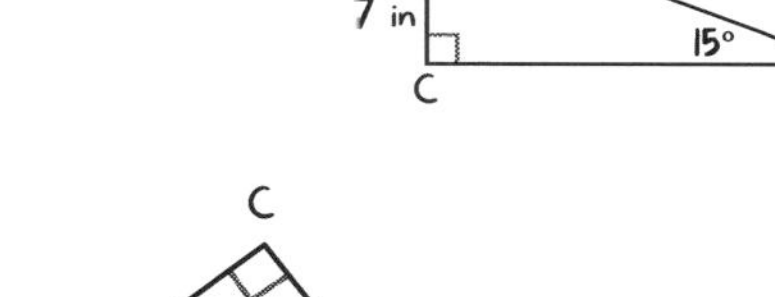

27.

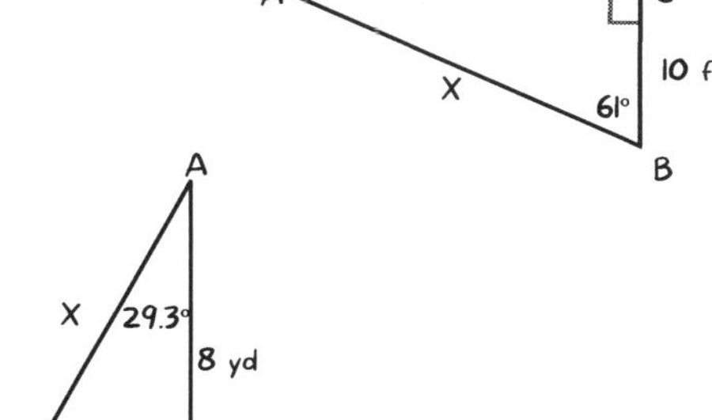

28. A, X, 29.3°, 8 yd, B, C

29.

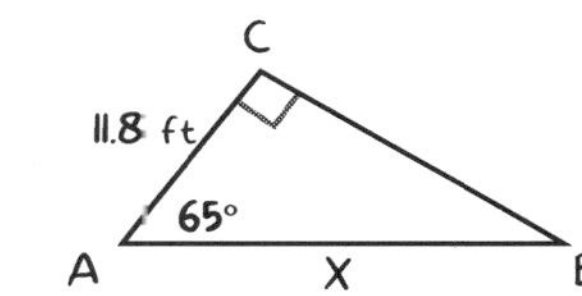

30.

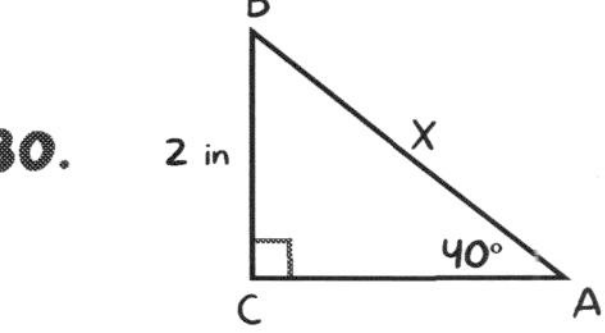

31.

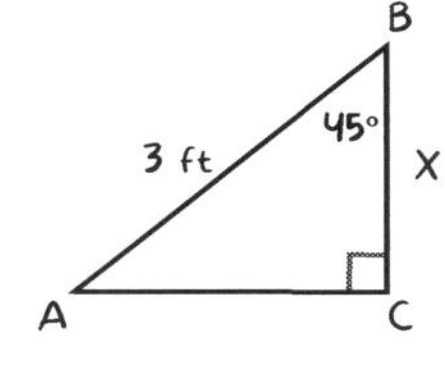

32.

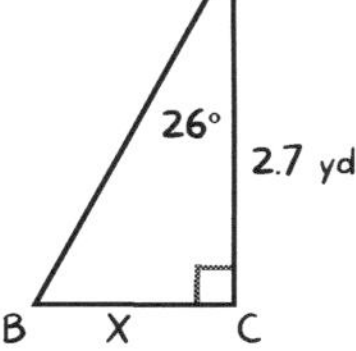

Section 2.2 Quiz

33.

34.

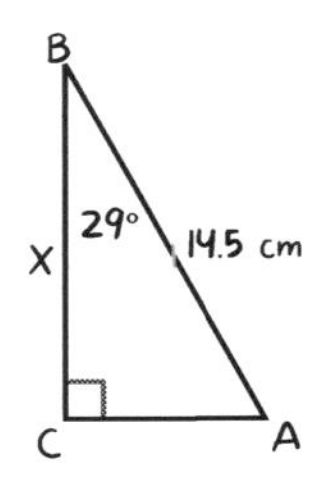

35.

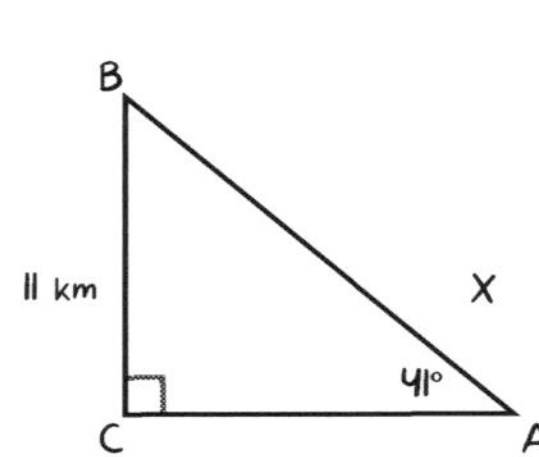

36.

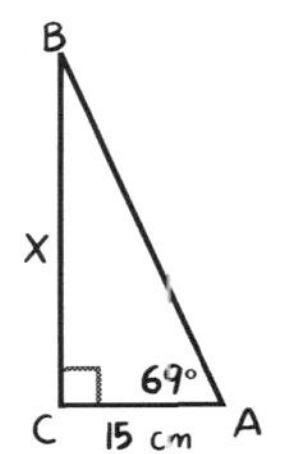
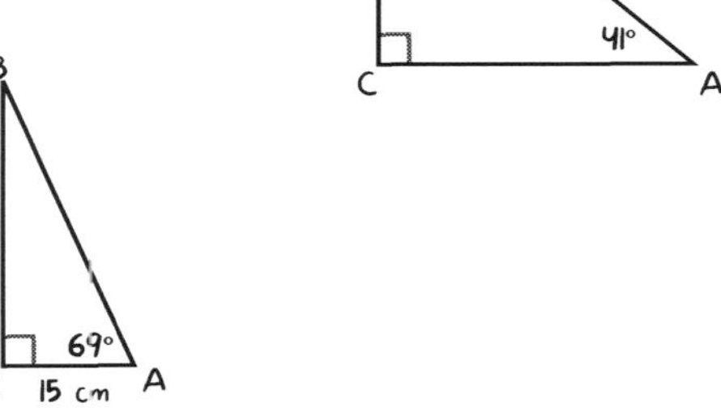

37.

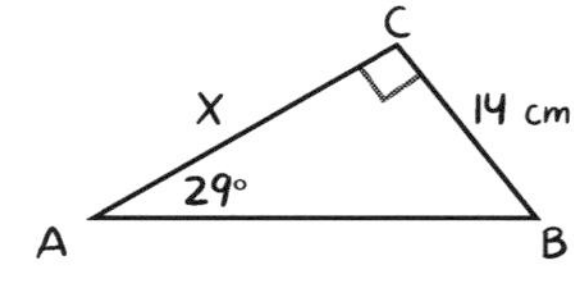

38.

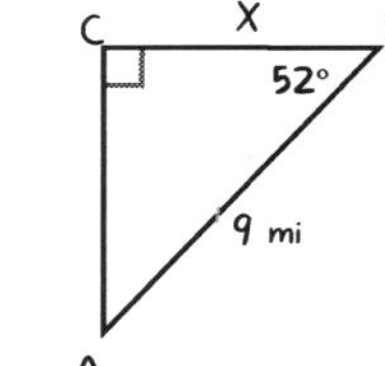
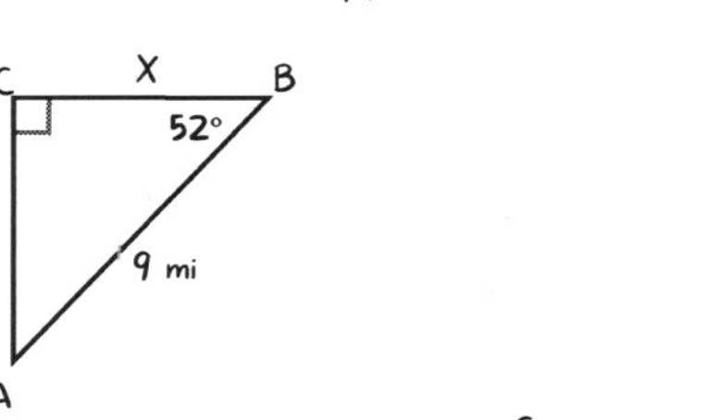

39.

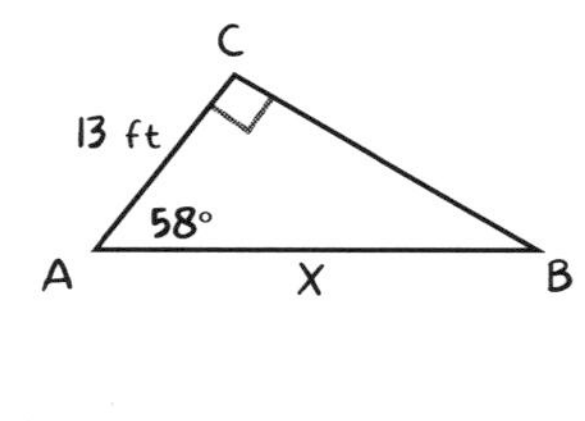

40.

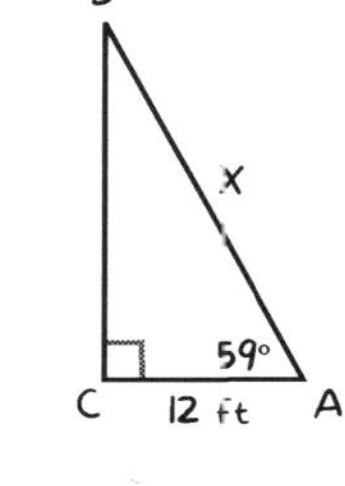

41.

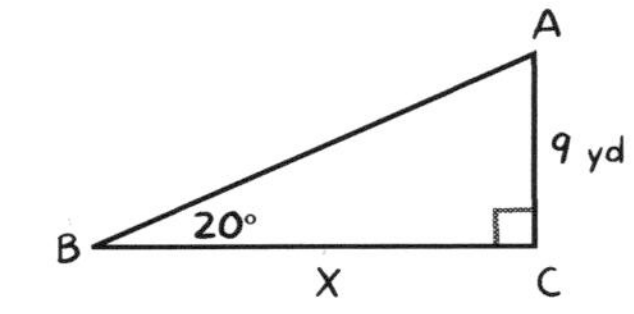

42.

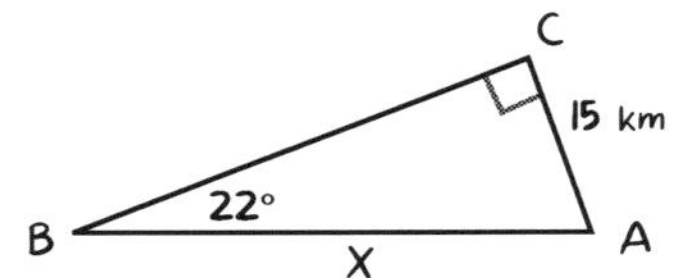

43.

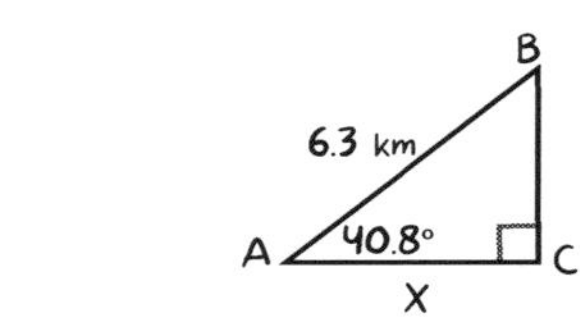

44.

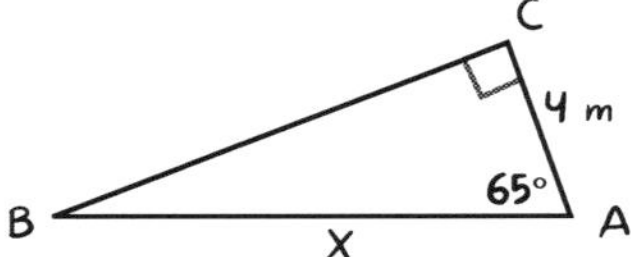

45.

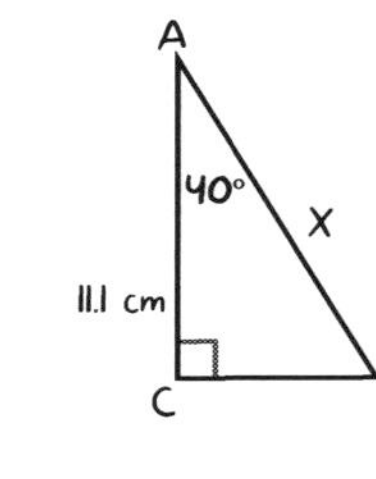

46.

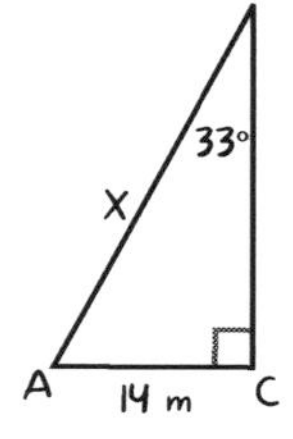

47.

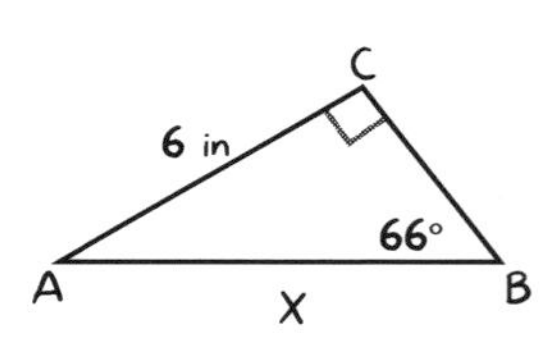

48.

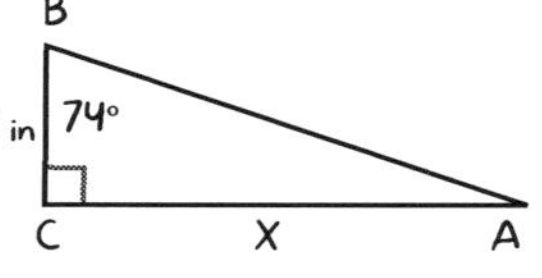

Section 2.2 Quiz

49.

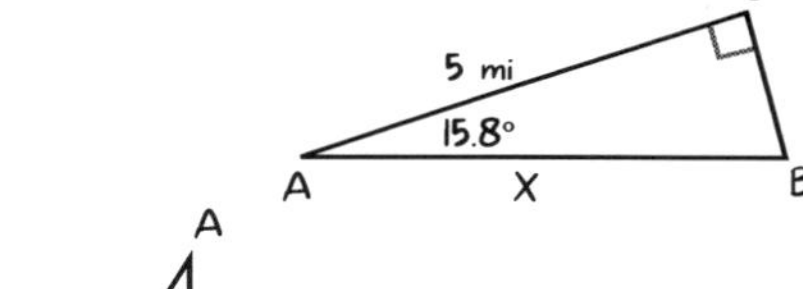

50.

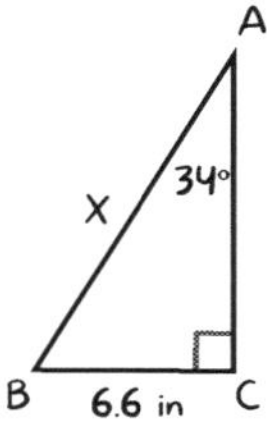

51.

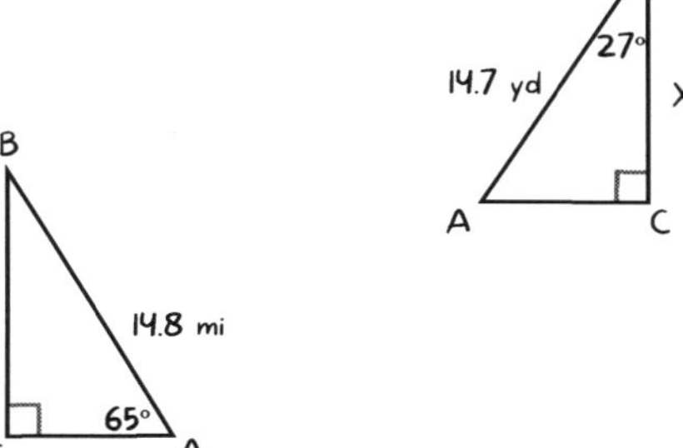

52.

53.

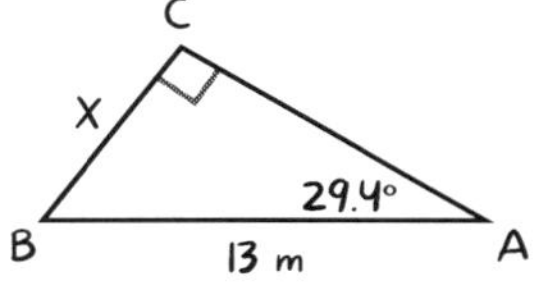

54.

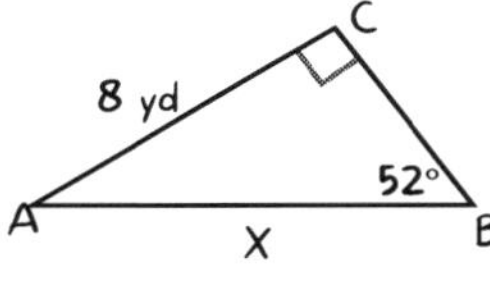

55.

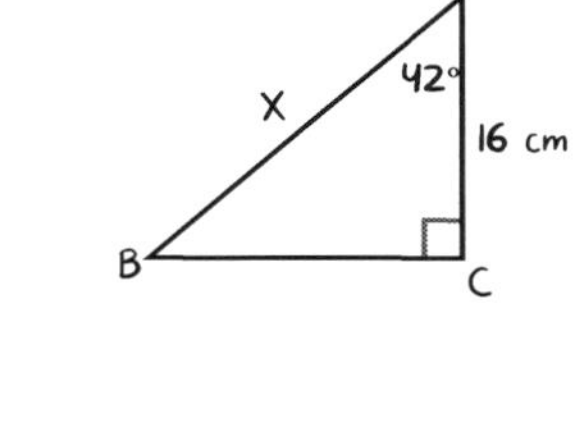

56.

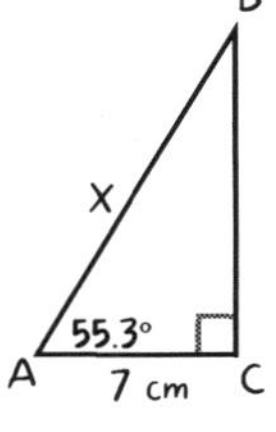

57.

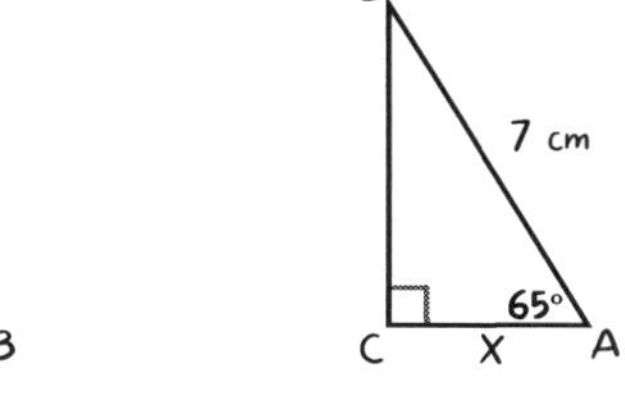

58.

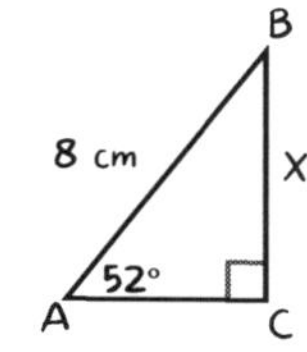

59.

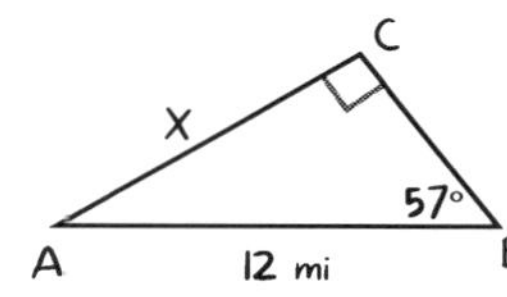

60.

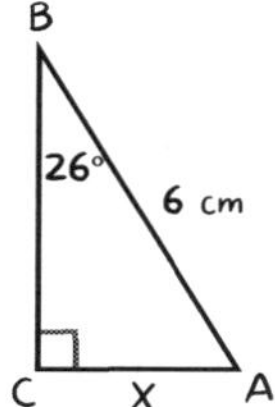

61.

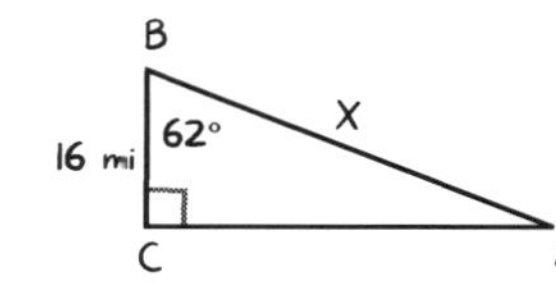

62.

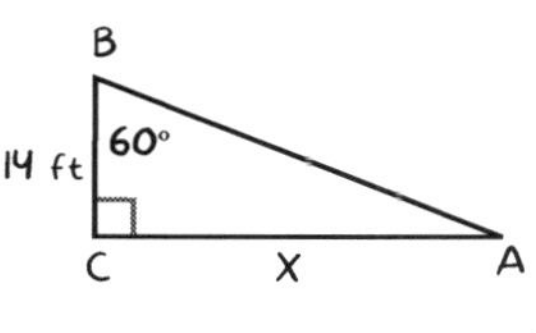

63.

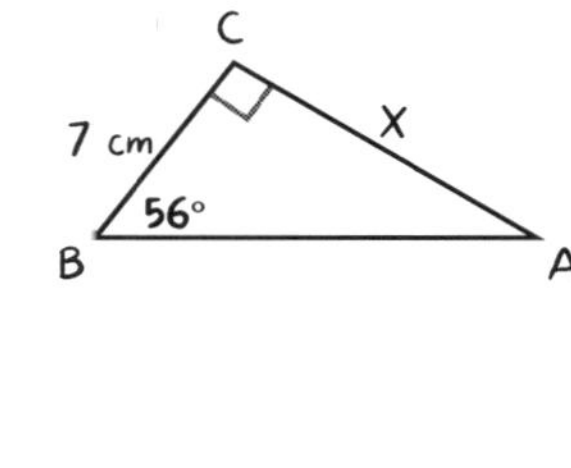

64.

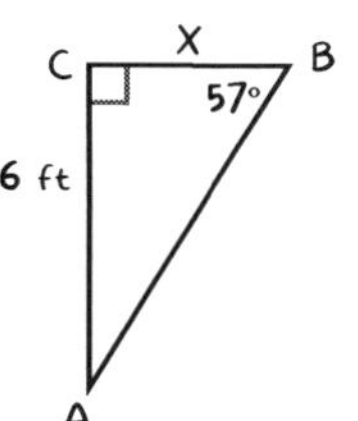

Section 2.2 Quiz

65.

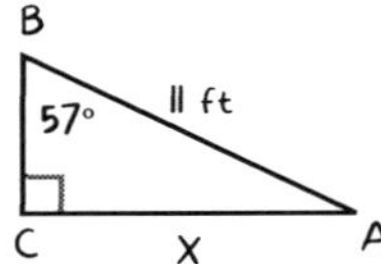

66.

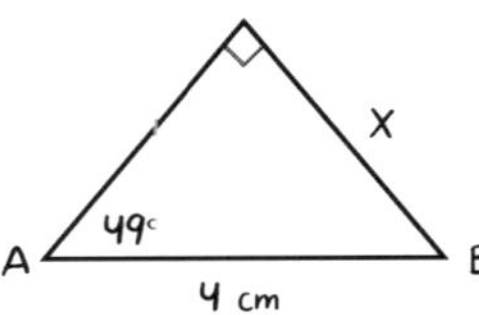

67.

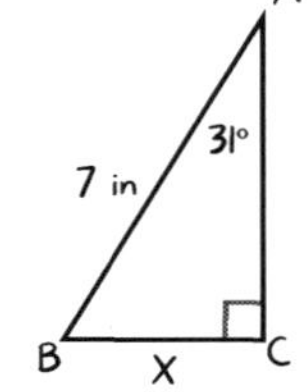

68.

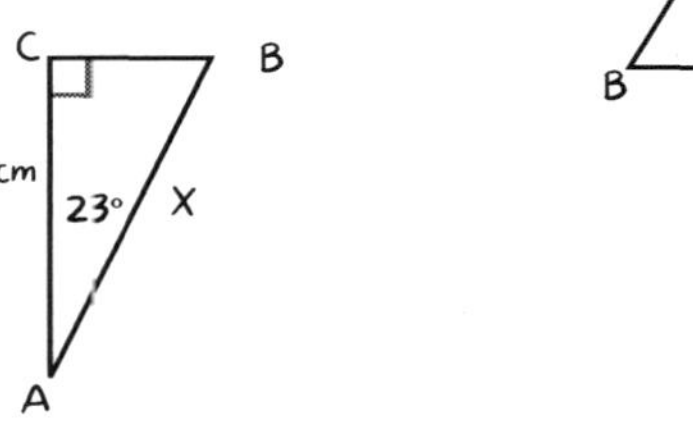

69.

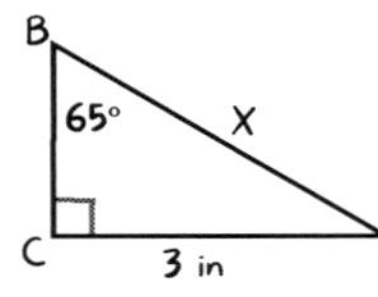

70.

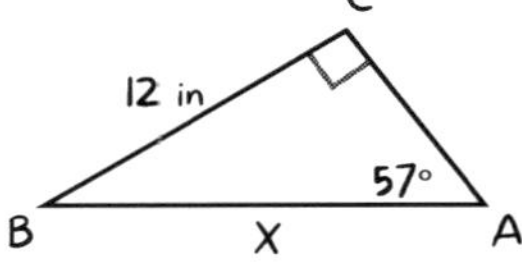

71.

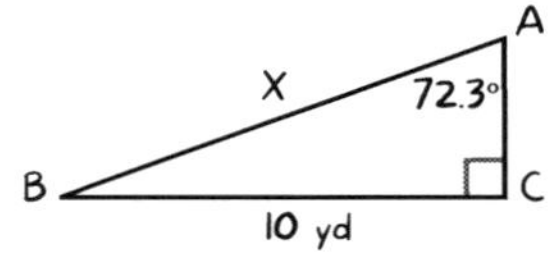

72.

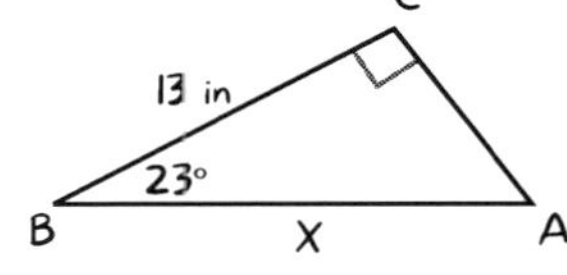

73.

B
11 in
X
C
63°
A

74.

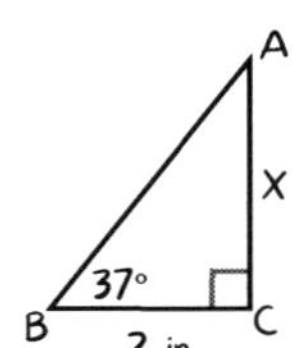

75.

B
29°
7 mi
C
X
A

76.

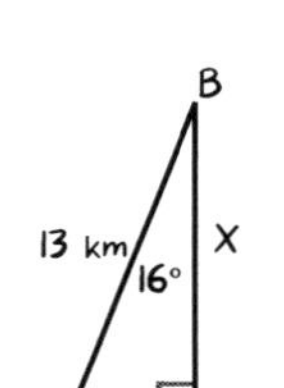

77.

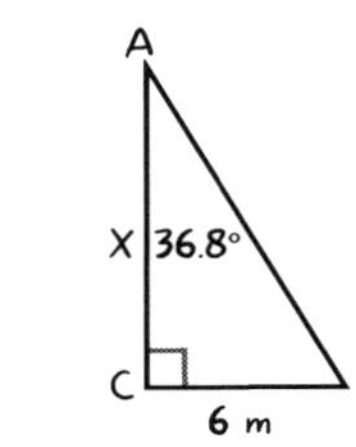

78.

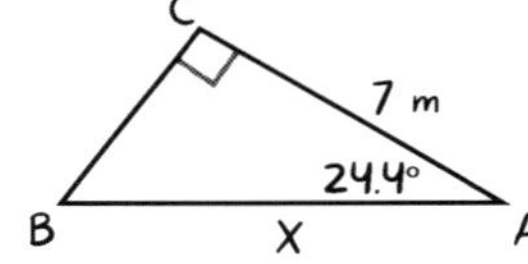

79.

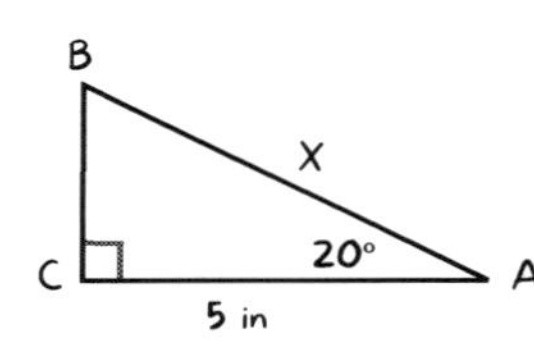

80.

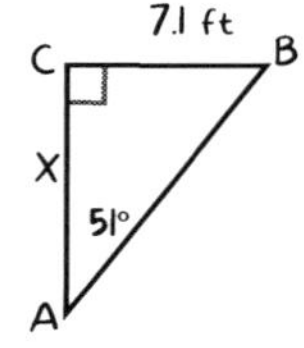

Section 2.2 Quiz

81.

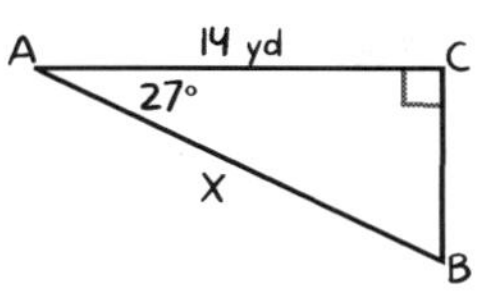

82.

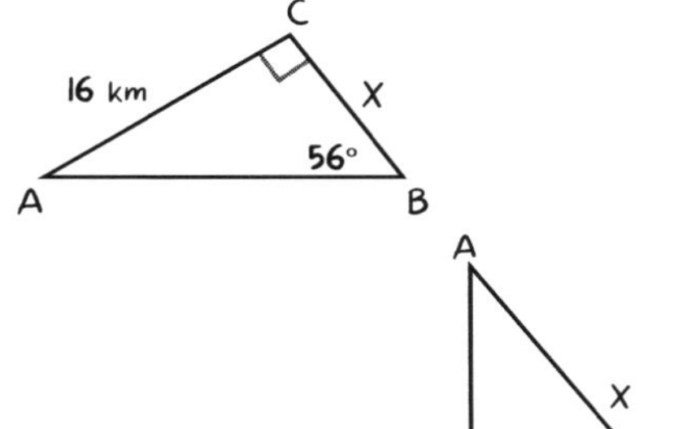

83.

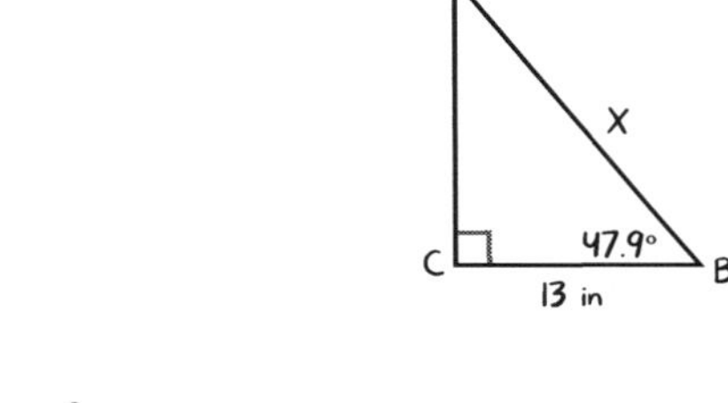

84.

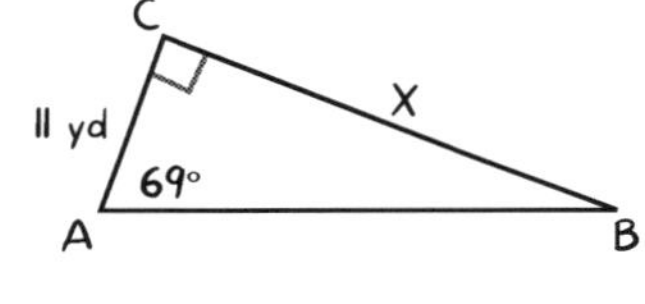

85.

B
4.3 in
X
A
55°
C

86.

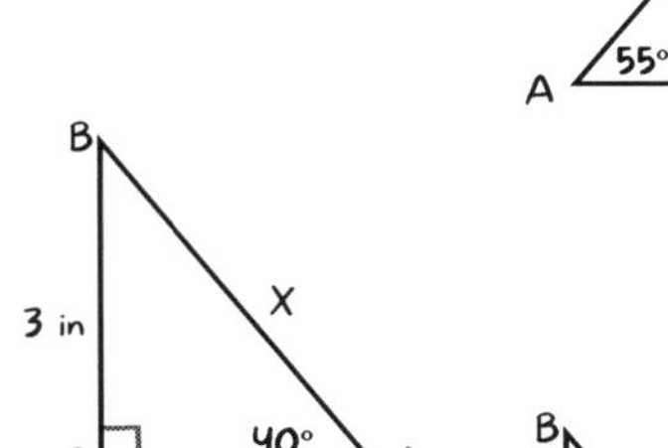

87.

B
X
C
42°
A
13 m

88.

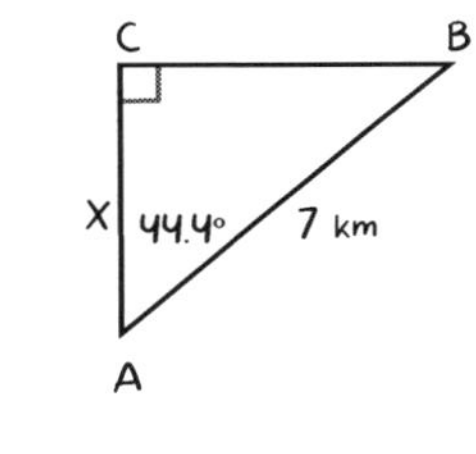

89.

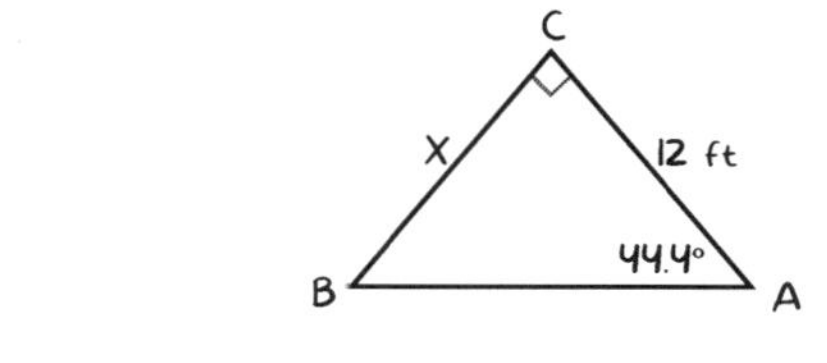

90.

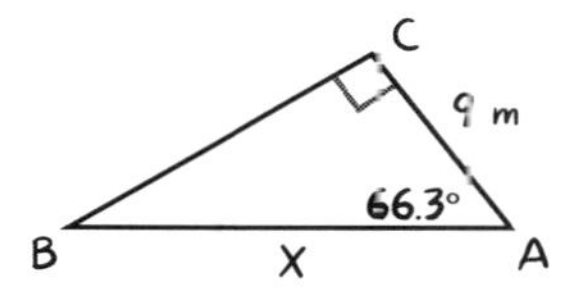

91.

92.

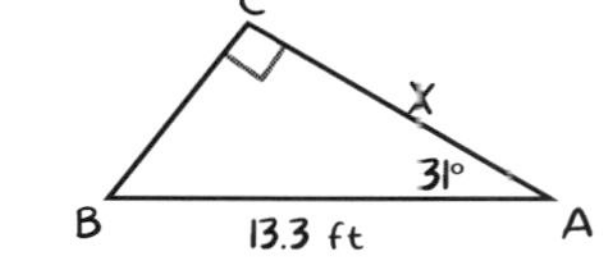

93.

A
7 ft
57°
X
B
C

94.

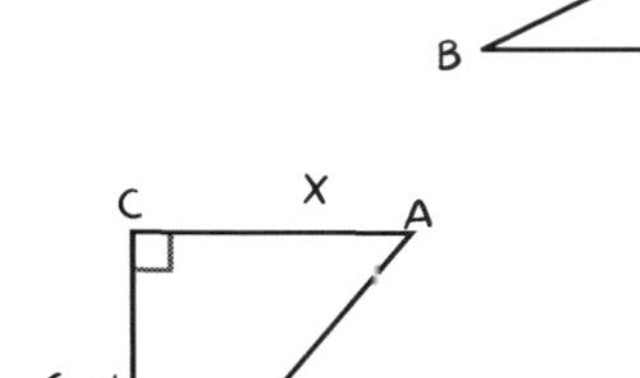

95.

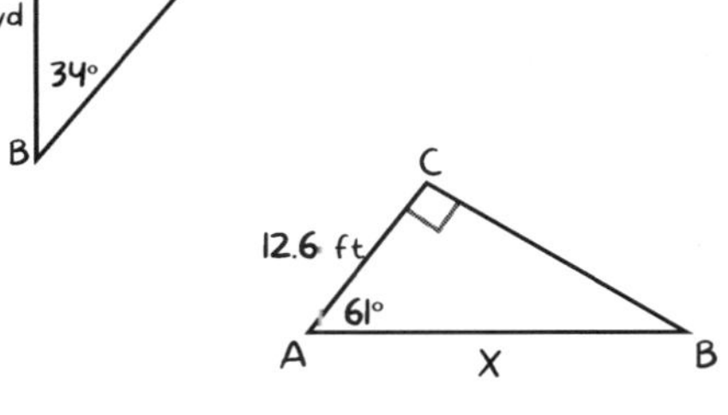

96.

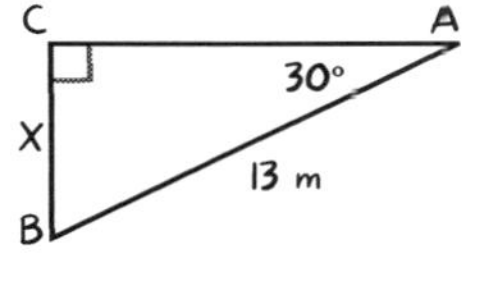

Section 2.2 Quiz

97.

99.

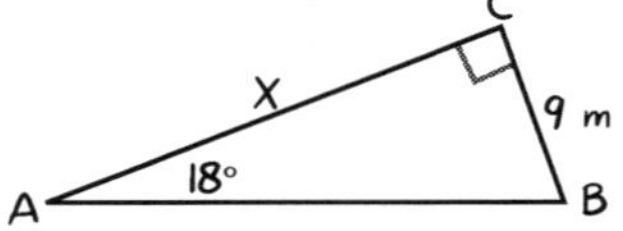

98.

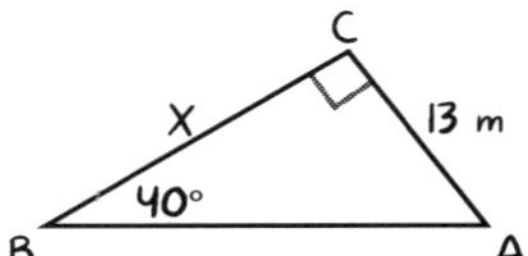

100.

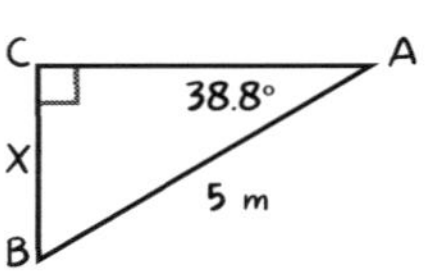

Directions: Find the measure of each **angle** indicated. Round your answer to the nearest tenth. Be sure to include the degree sign in your answer.

1.

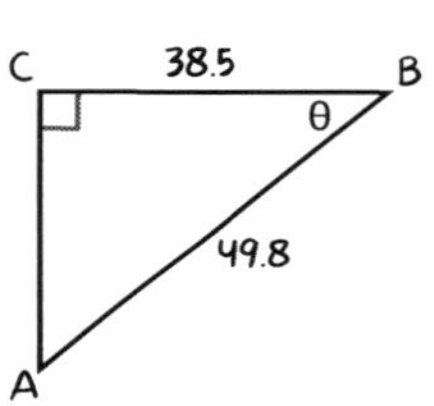

5.

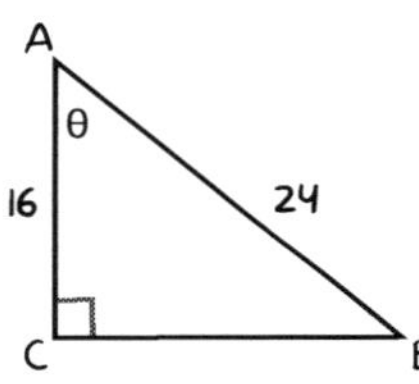

2.

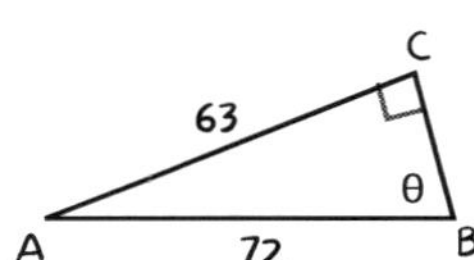

6.

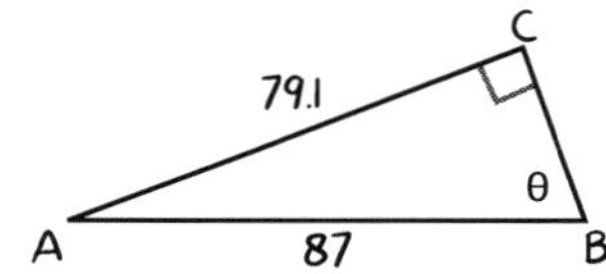

3.

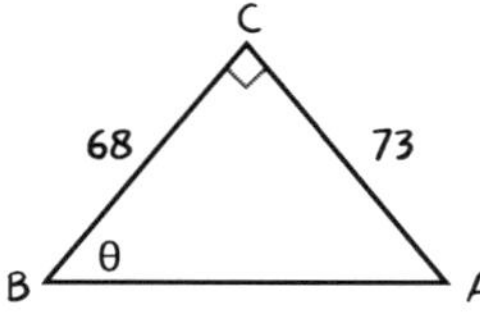

7.

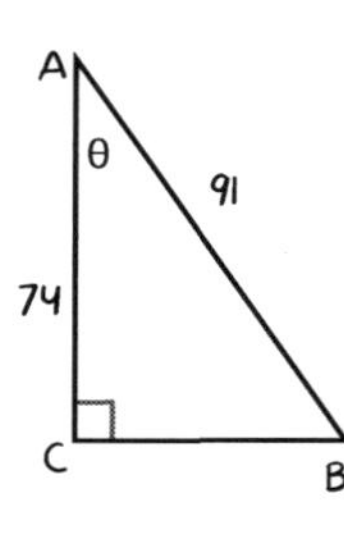

4.

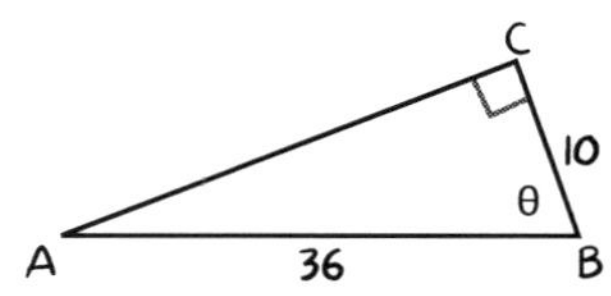

8.

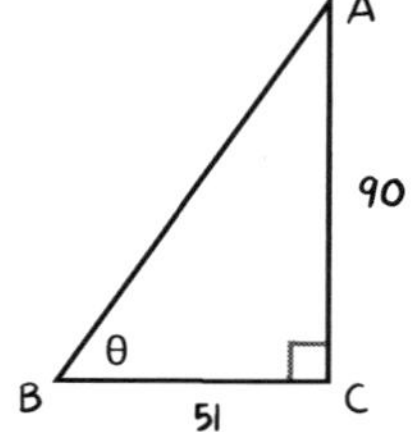

Section 2.2 Quiz

9.

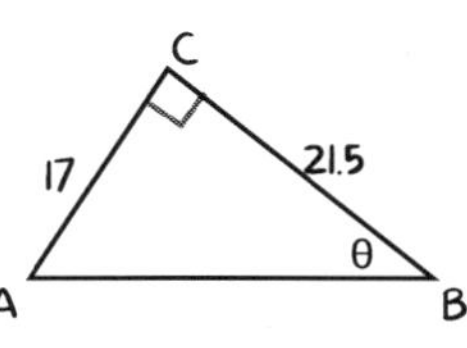

10.

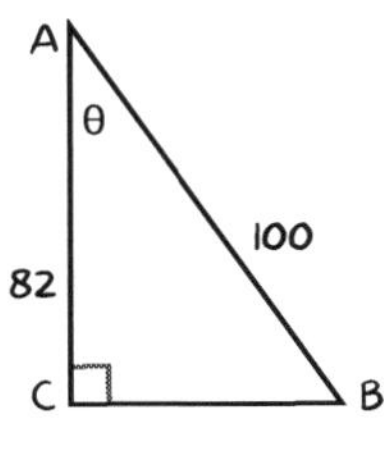

11.

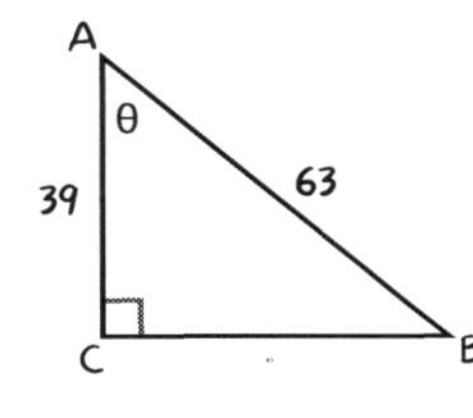

12.

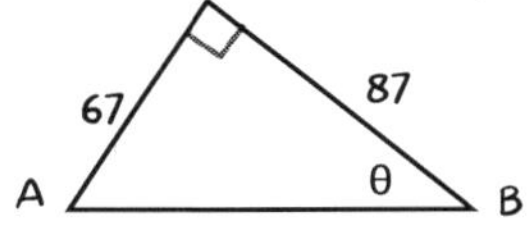

13.

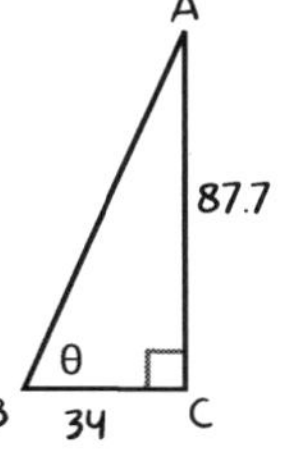

14.

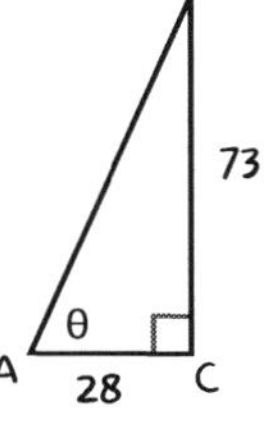

15.

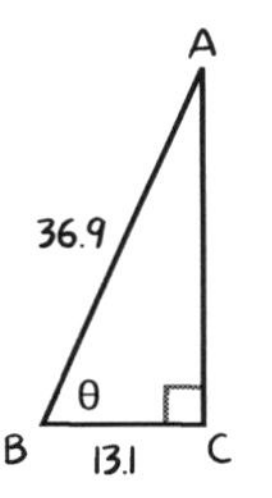

16.

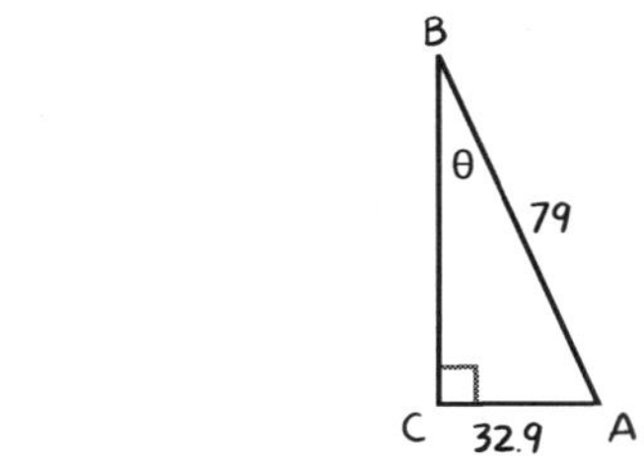

17.

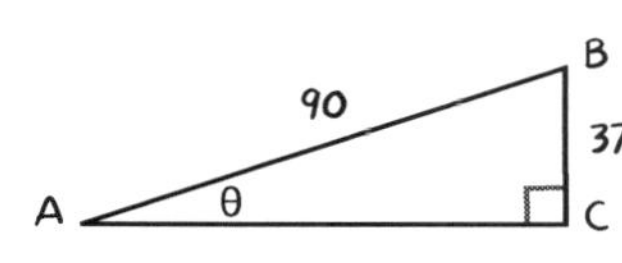

18.

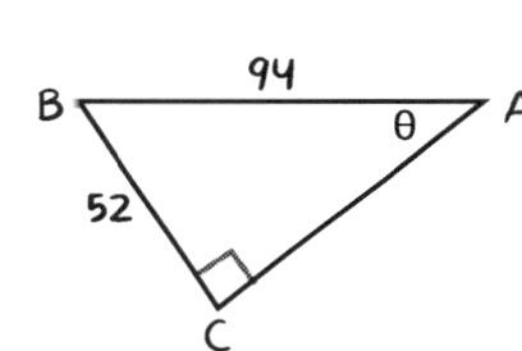

19.

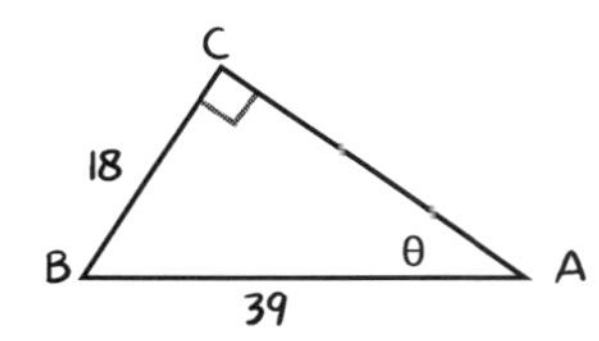

20.

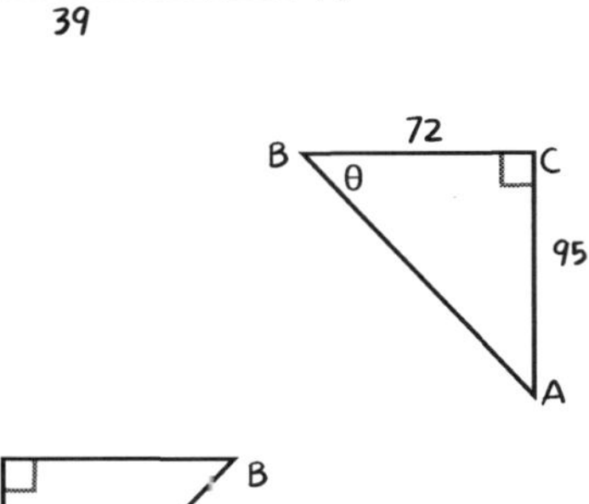

21.

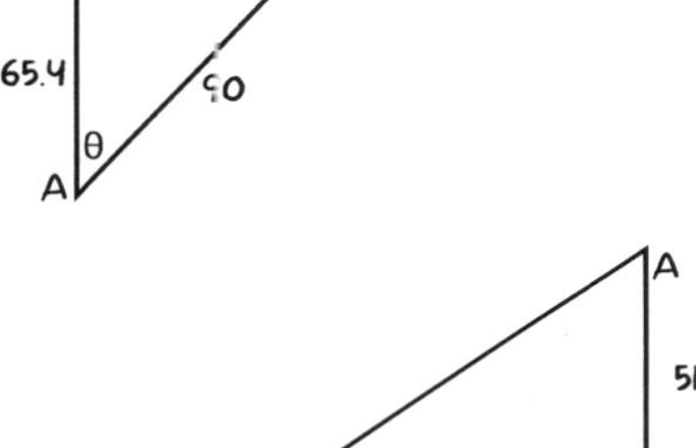

22.

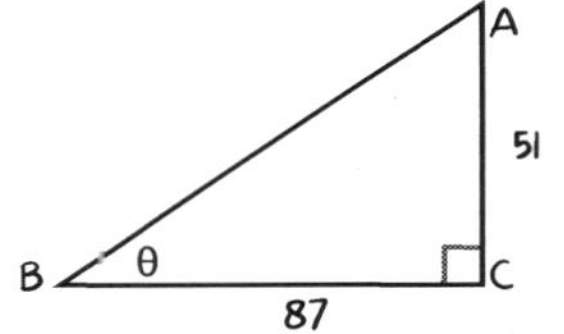

Section 2.2 Quiz

23.

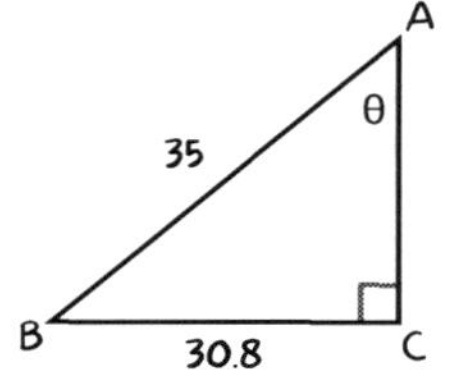

24.

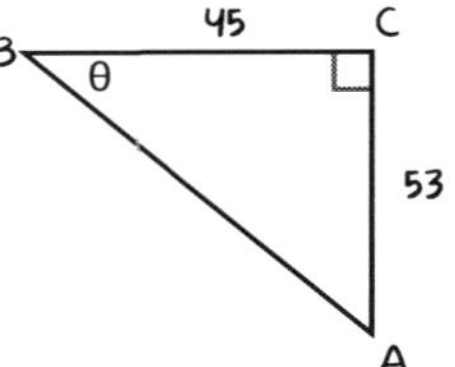

25.

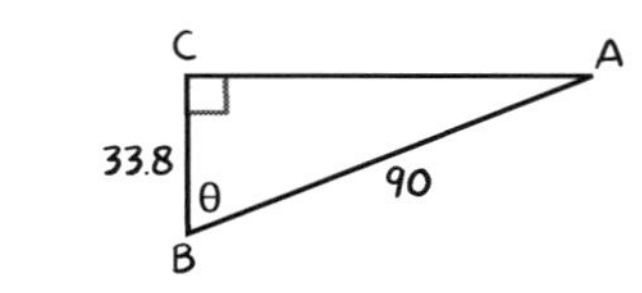

26.

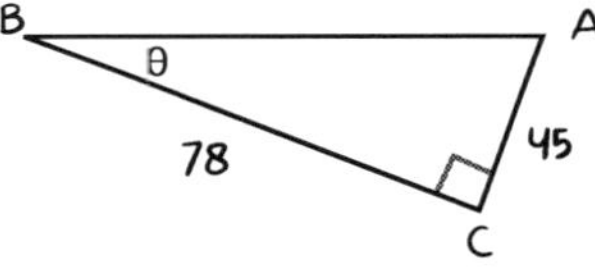

27.

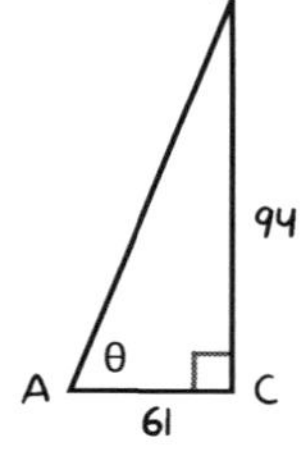

28.

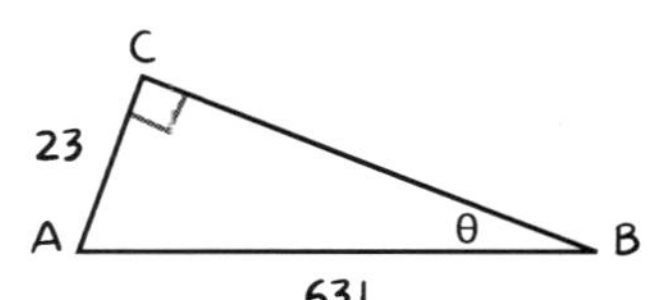

29.

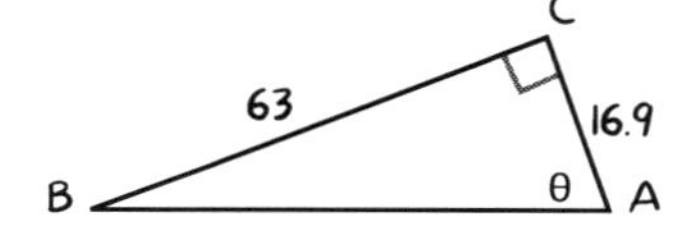

30.

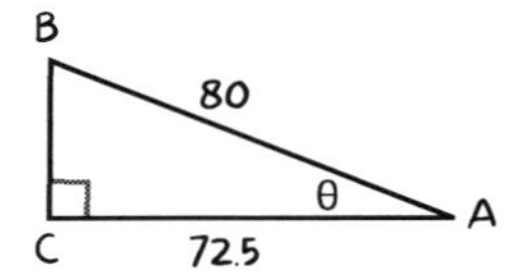

31.

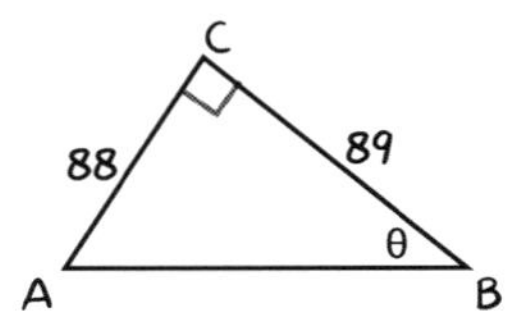

32.

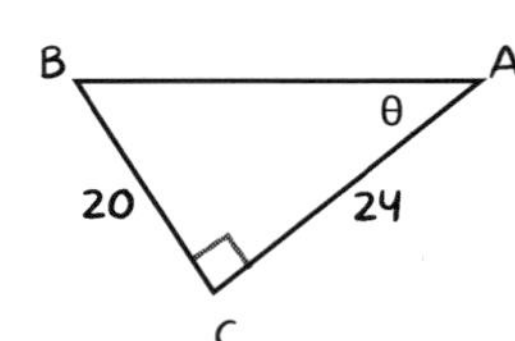

33.

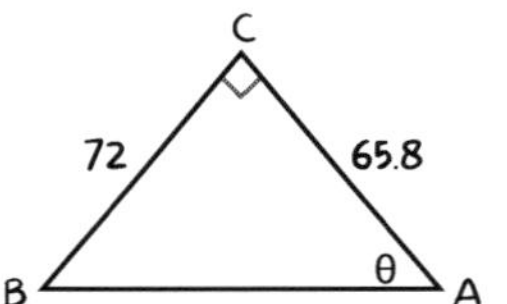

34.

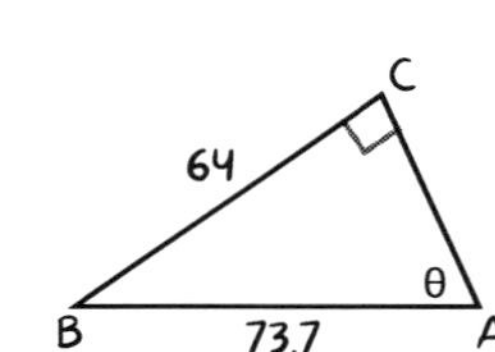

35.

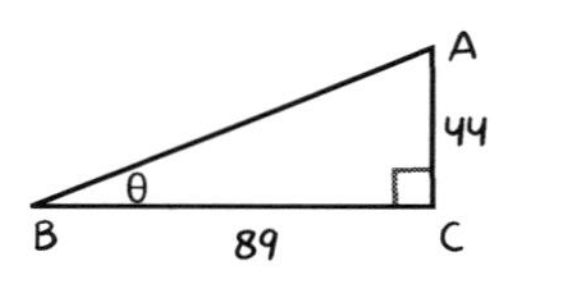

36.

Section 2.2 Quiz

37.

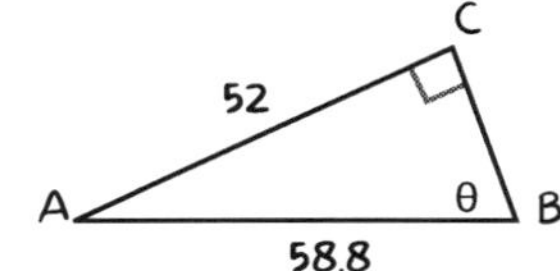

38.

39.

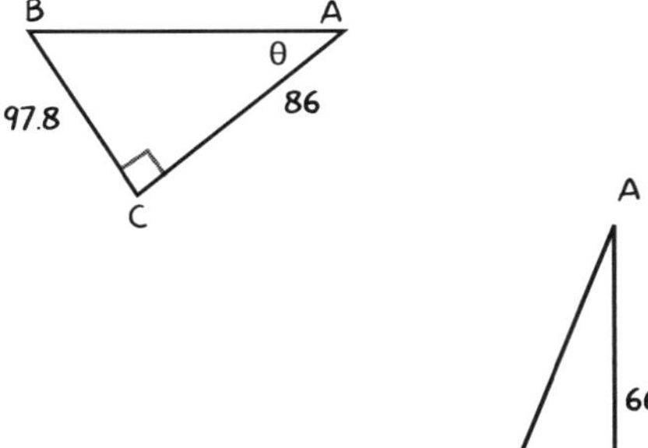

40.

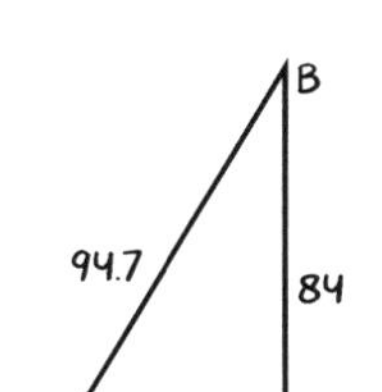

41.

42.

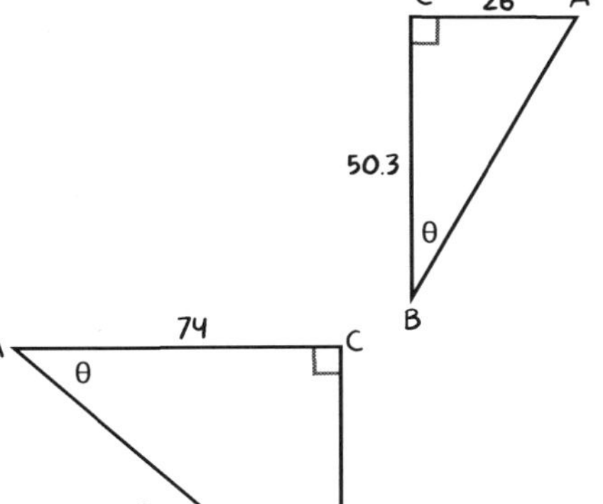

43.

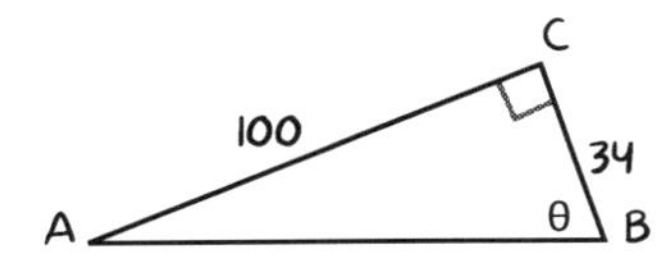

44.

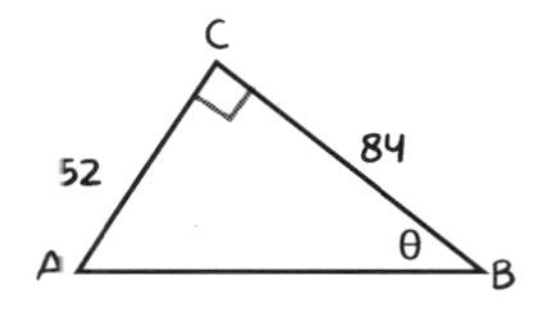

45.

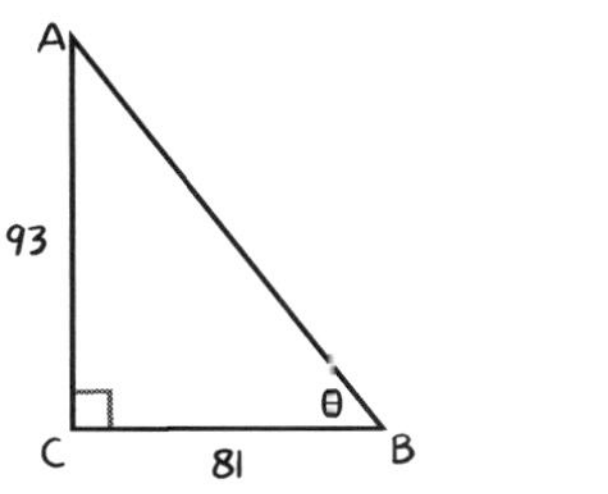

46.

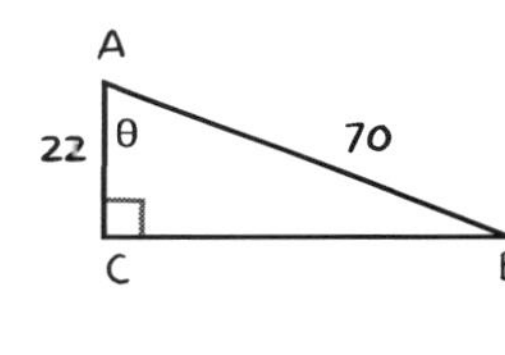

47.

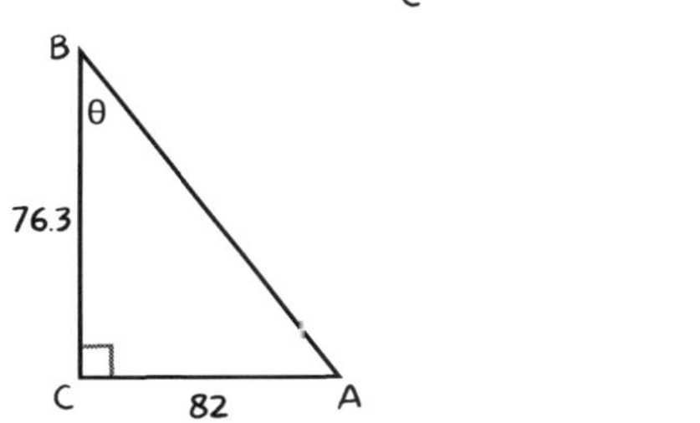

48.

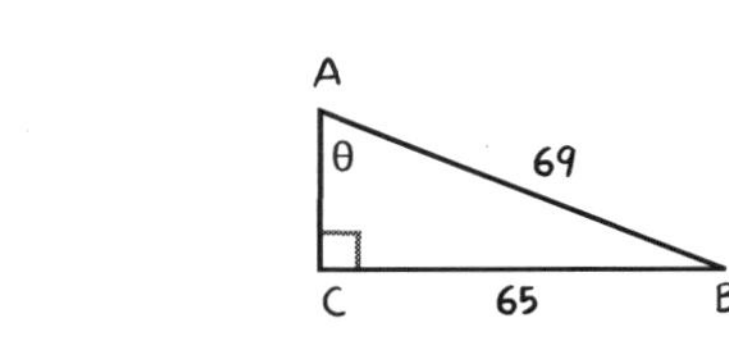

49.

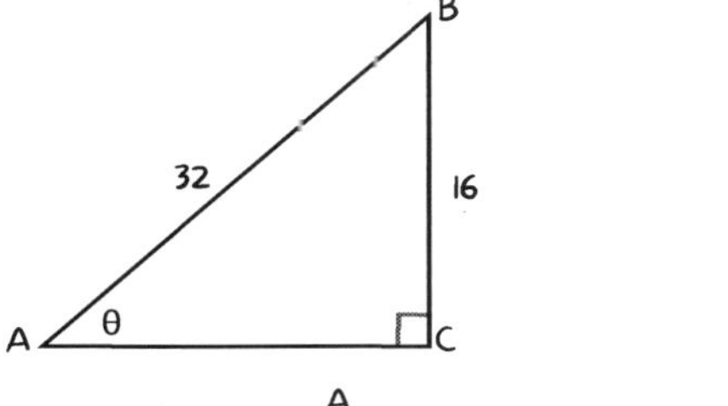

50.

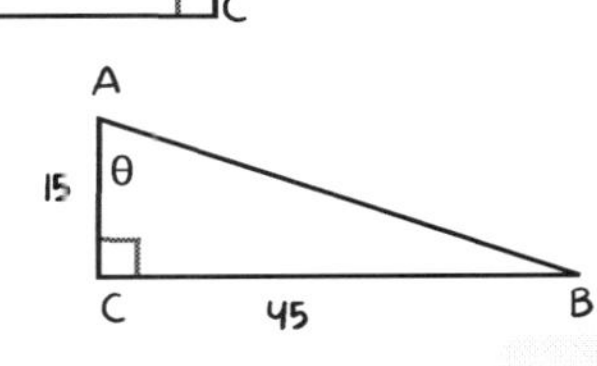

Section 2.2 Quiz

51.

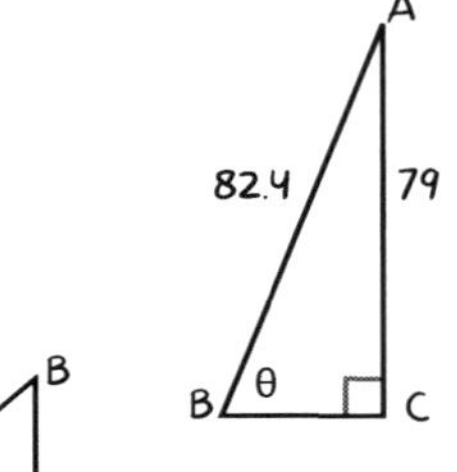

52.

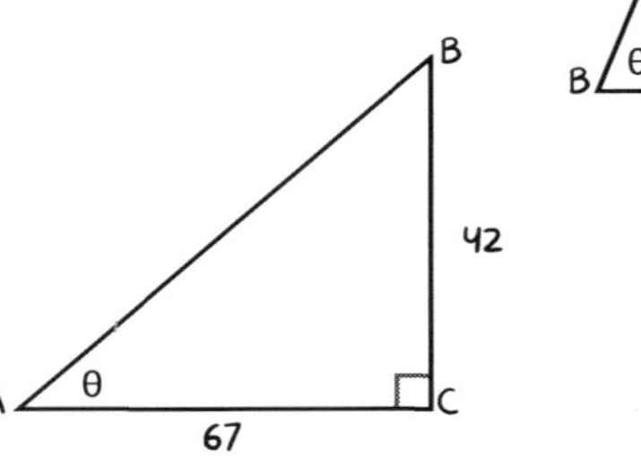

53.

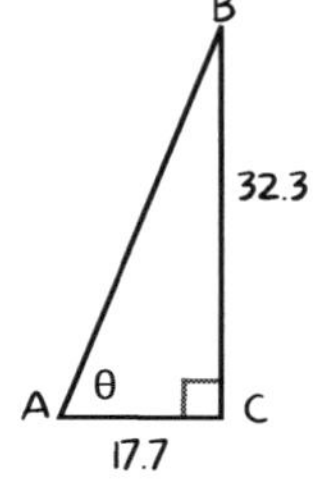

54.

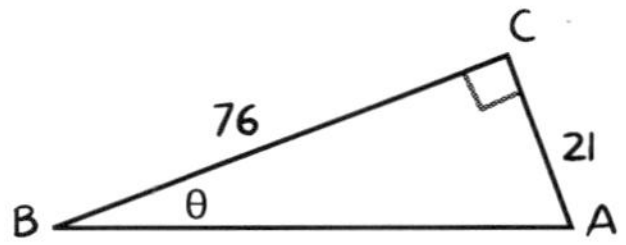

55.

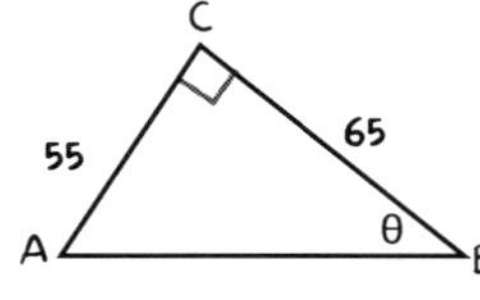

56.

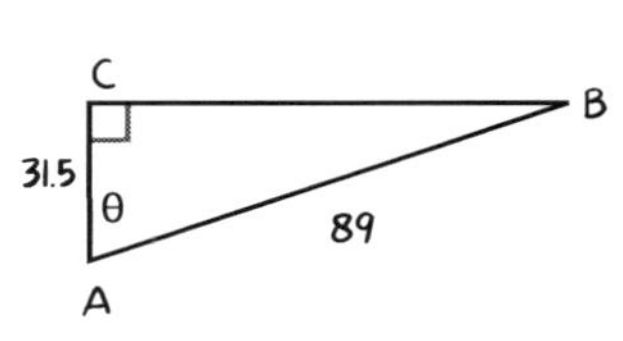

57.

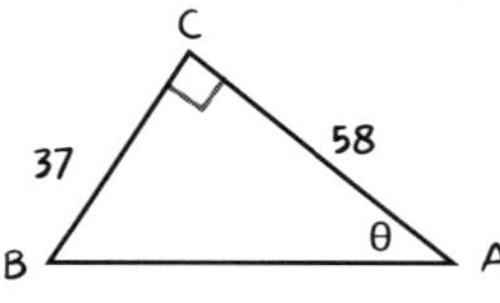

58.

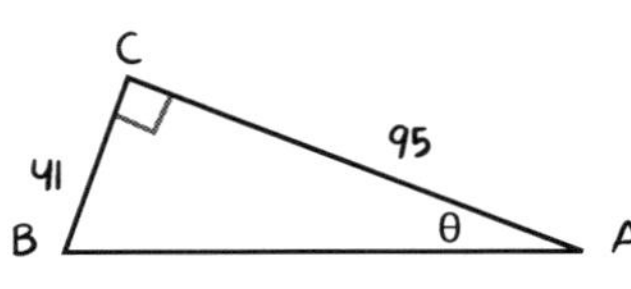

59.

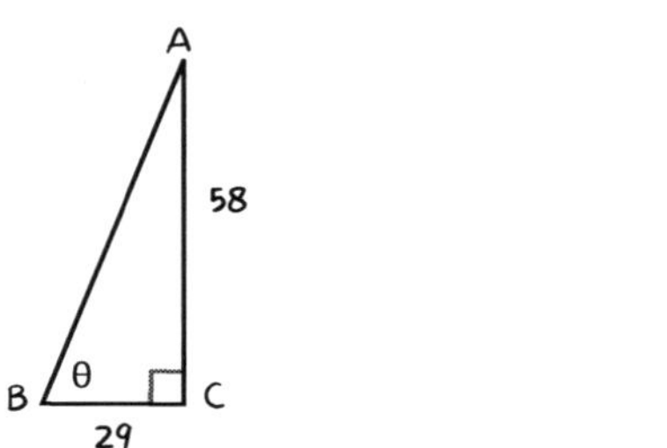

60.

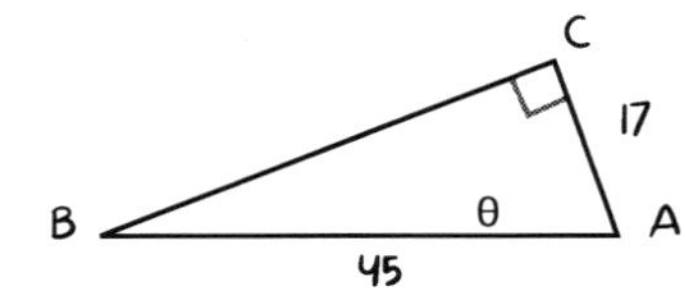

61.

62.

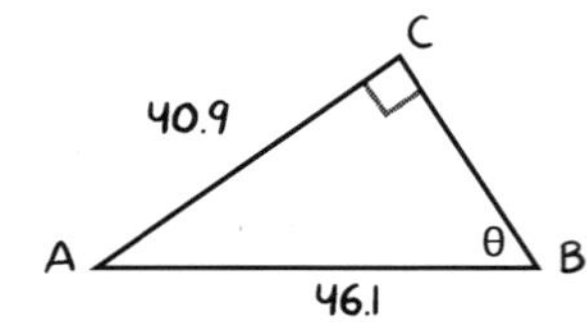

63.

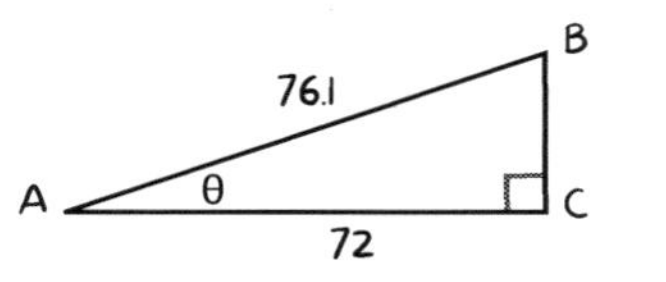

64.

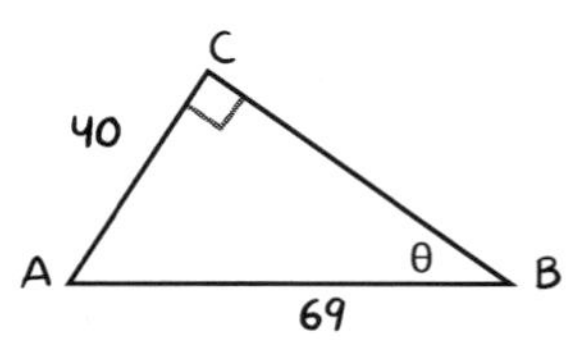

Section 2.2 Quiz

65.

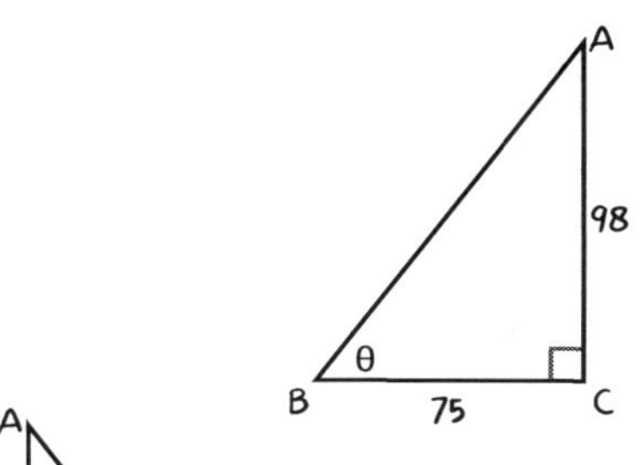

66.

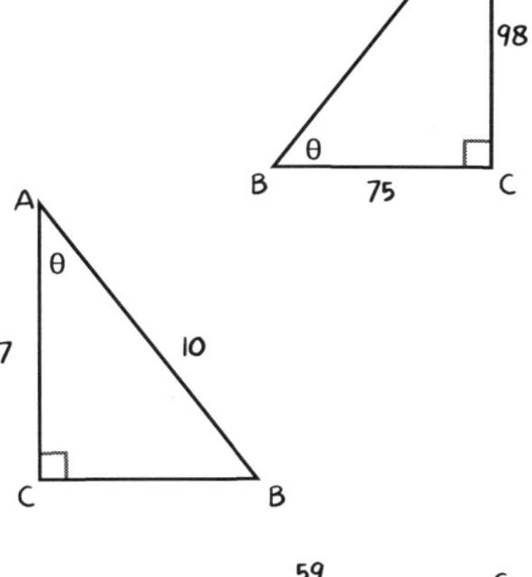

67.

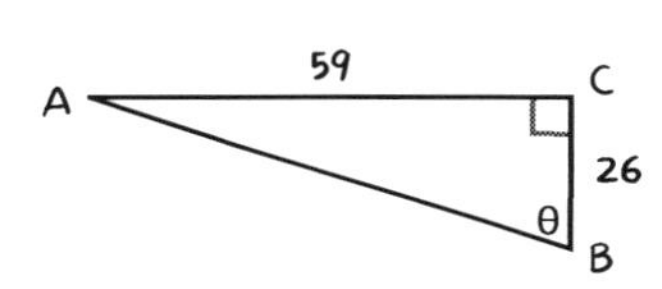

68.

69.

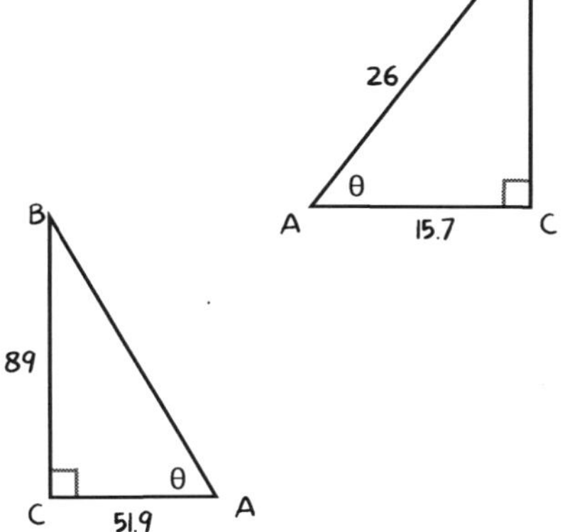

70.

71.

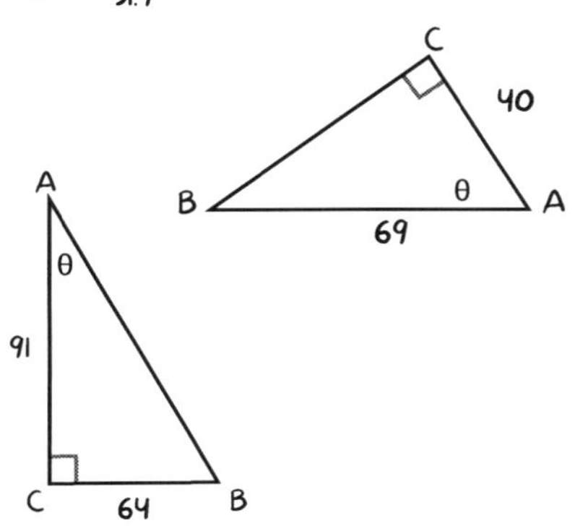

72.

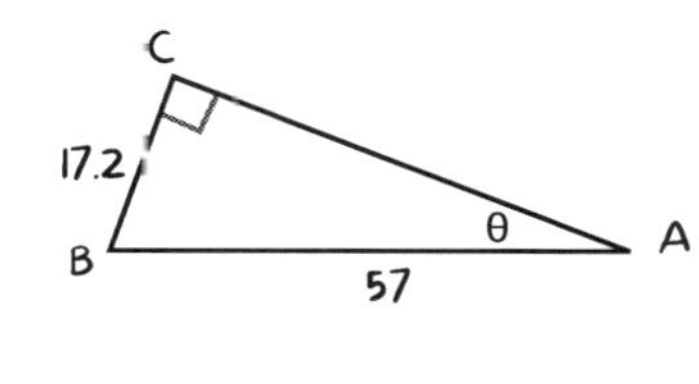

73.

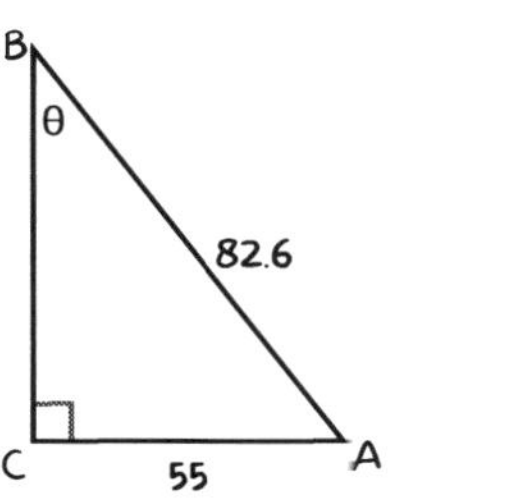

74.

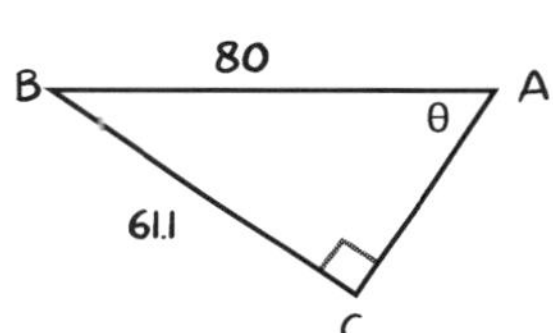

75.

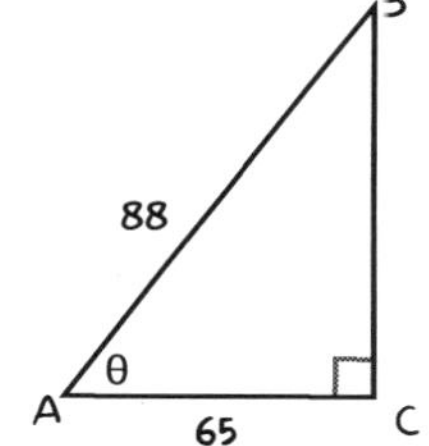

76.

77.

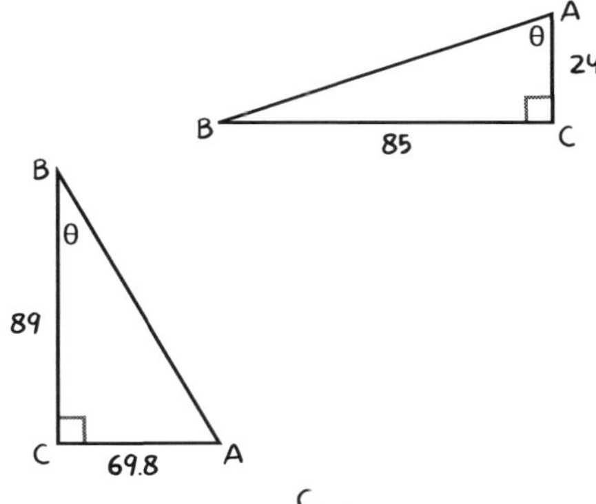

78.

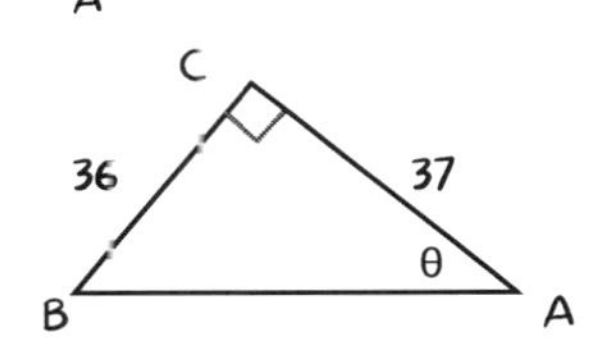

79.

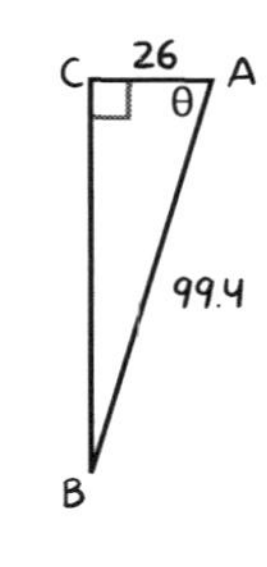

80.

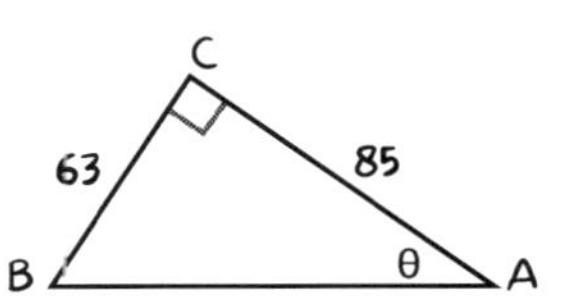

81.

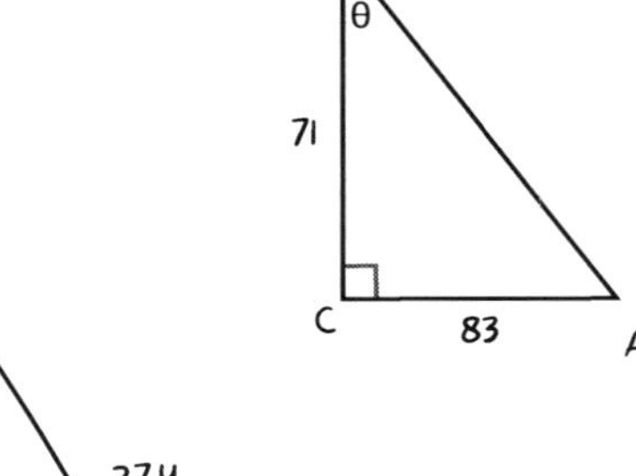

82.

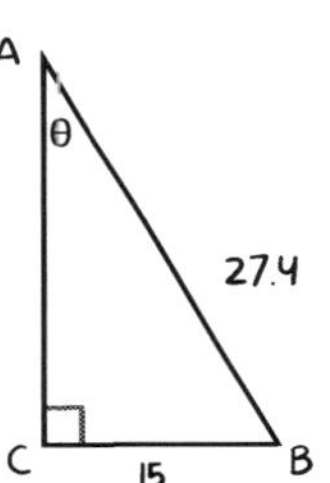

83.

84.

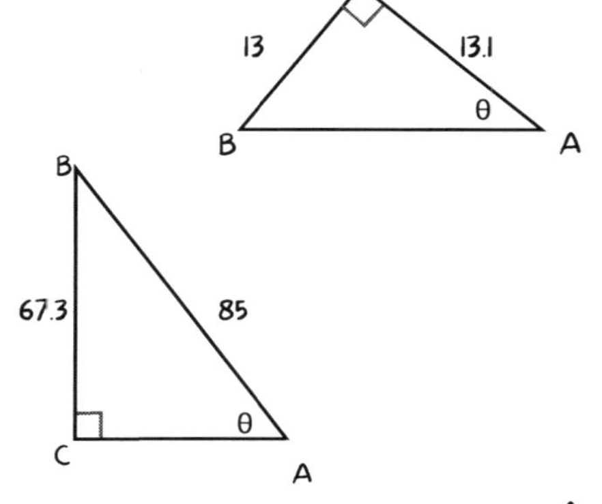

85.

C A θ 36.1 92 B

86.

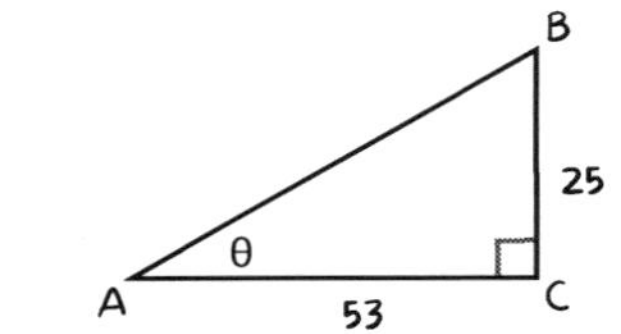

87.

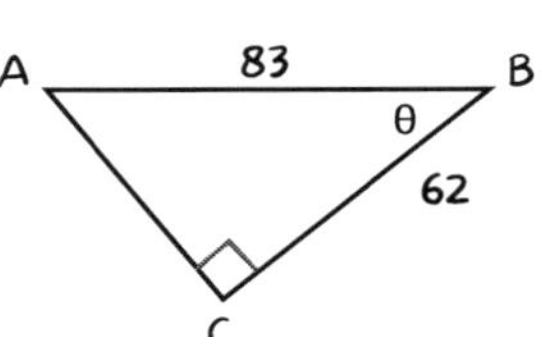

88.

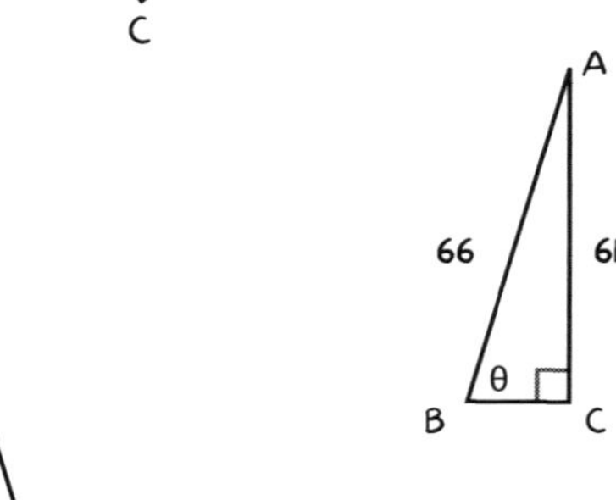

89.

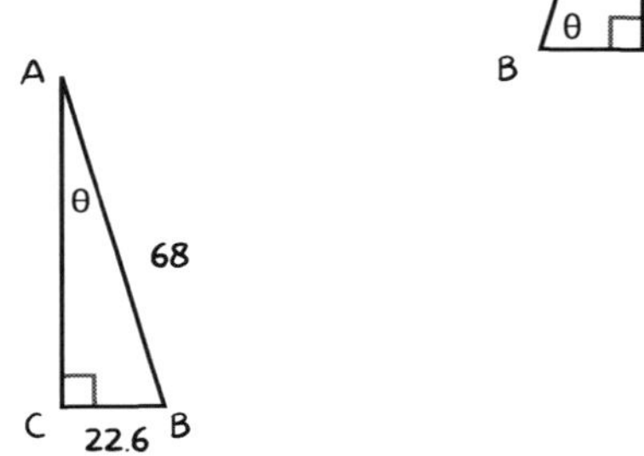

90.

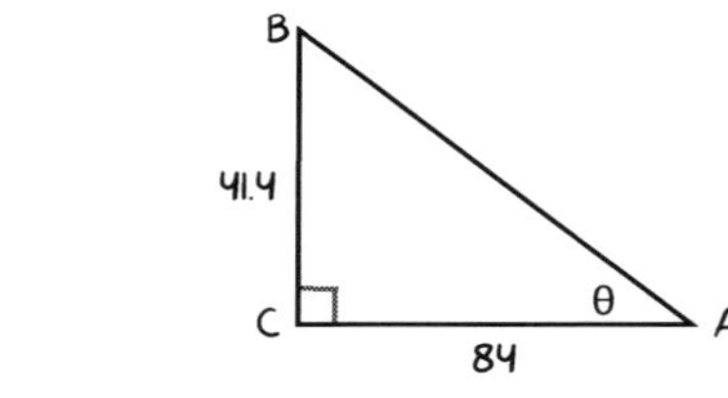

91.

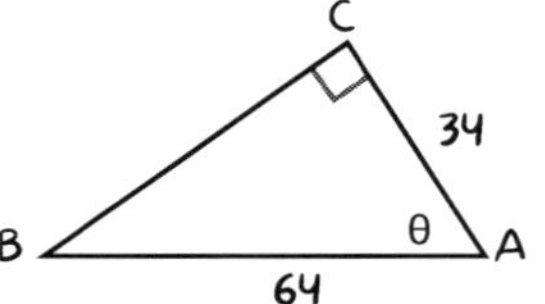

92.

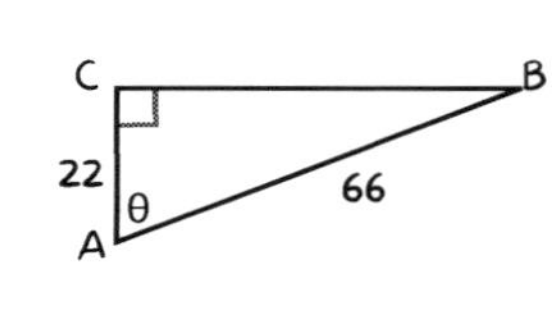

Section 2.2 Quiz

93.

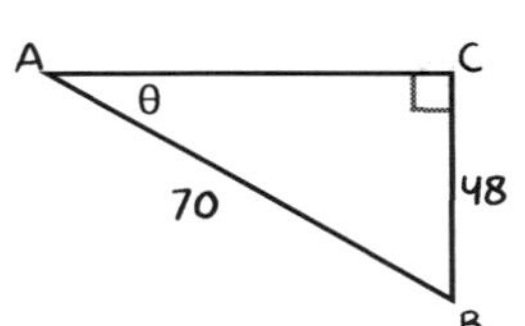

94.

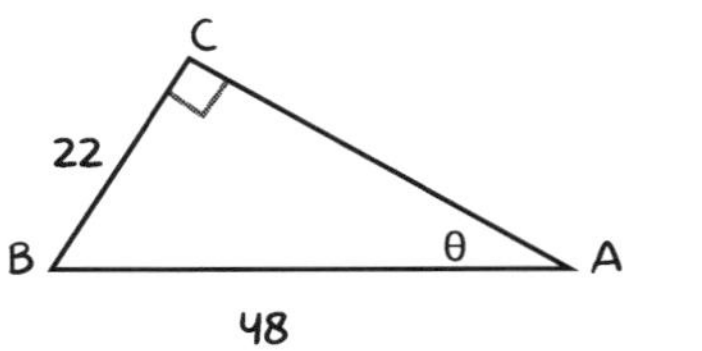

95.

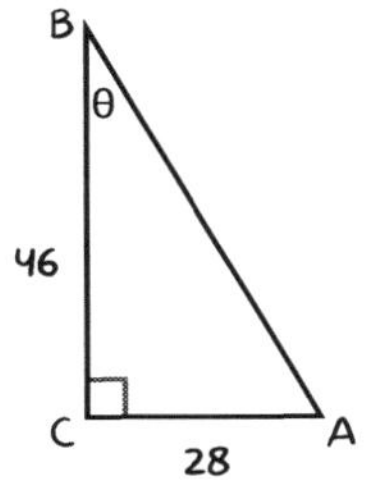

96.

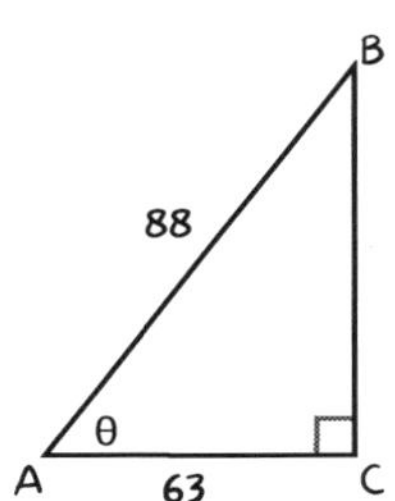

97.

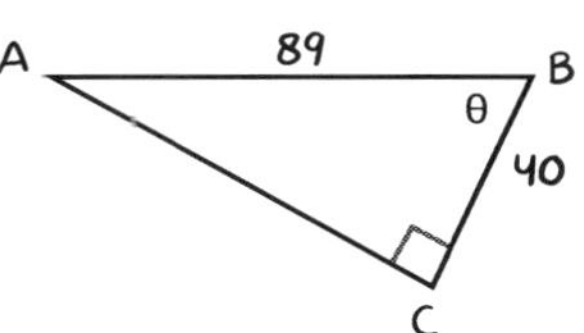

98.

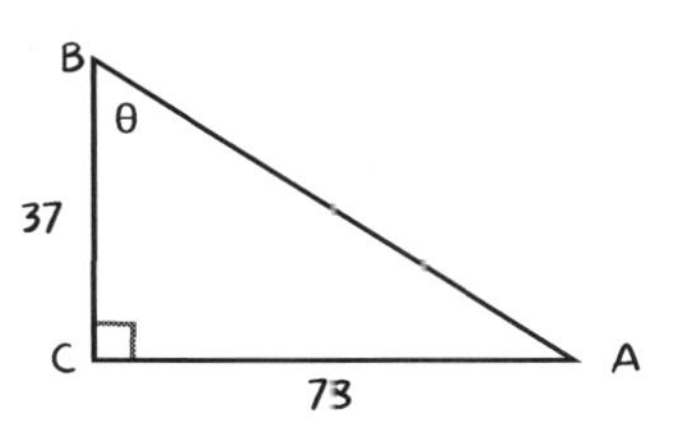

99.

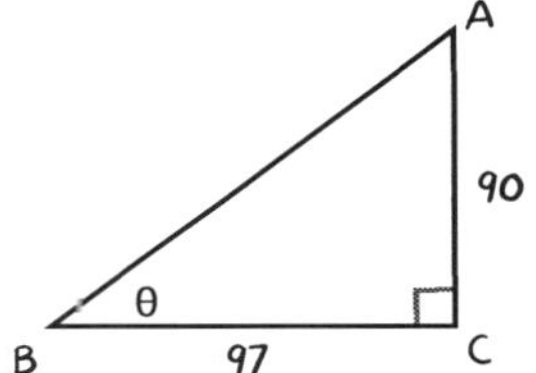

100.

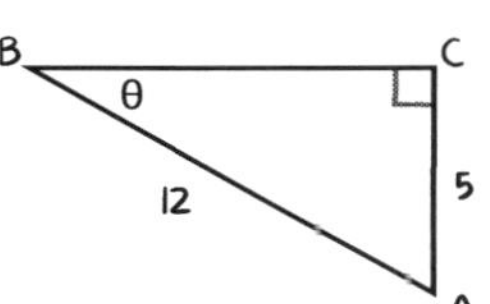

Section 3.1: 30-60-90 & 45-45-90 Right Triangle

In Chapter 2, you used a calculator to determine the values of sin, cos, and tan. In Chapter 3, we will learn about **two** special right triangles that are so common that it is useful to know the side ratios without doing the Pythagorean Theorem each time. We will **not** be using a calculator to solve any problem in Chapter 3.

The first special right triangle we will cover is the **30-60-90** triangle that has the angles 30°, 60°, and 90°. A 30-60-90 right triangle has the side ratios x, $x\sqrt{3}$, $2x$.

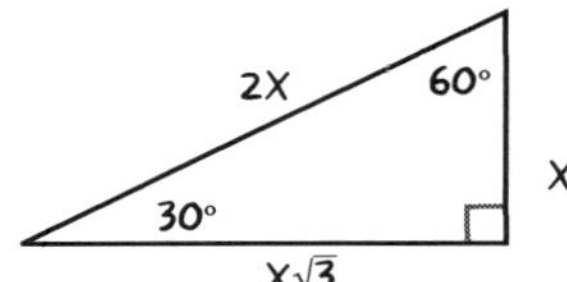

The side opposite of 30° is always the shortest side (x).

The side opposite of 60° is the longer leg ($x\sqrt{3}$).

The hypotenuse is always $2x$.

Knowing this ratio, we can find the value of 2 missing sides if we are provided with just **one** side value. Let's take a look at a few examples.

Example 1:

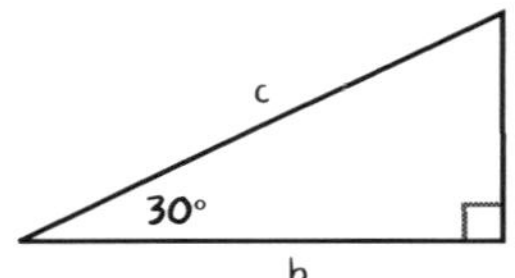

This is a 30-60-90 triangle. We know the value of the shorter leg (x) is 5.

b is $x\sqrt{3}$, but we know x is 5 so b is $5\sqrt{3}$.

c is the hypotenuse and is always $2x$. We know x is 5, so $2x$ is 10.

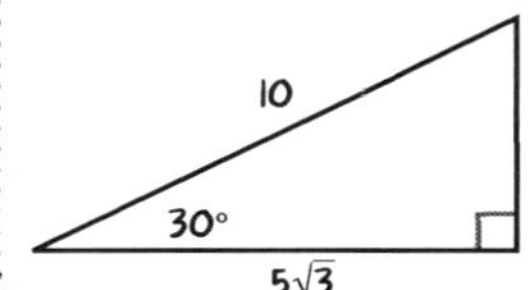

b = $5\sqrt{3}$ and c = 10

Example 2:

Find the length of the hypotenuse in the figure below.

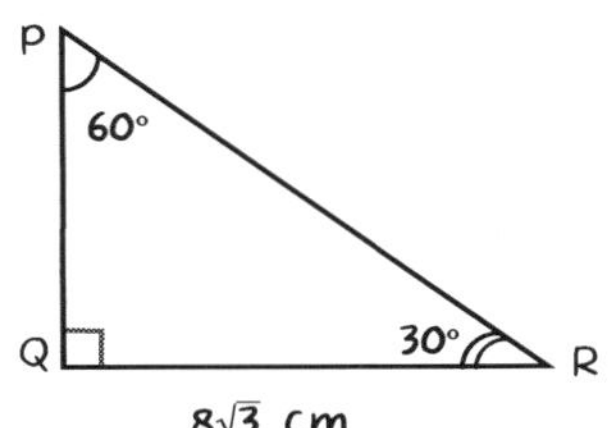

This is a 30-60-90 triangle. We are given the value of the longer leg which has the ratio $x\sqrt{3}$. We need to find the hypotenuse. We know the ratio of the hypotenuse is $2x$, and we should quickly realize $x = 8$. Therefore, $(8 \times 2 = 16)$. **The hypotenuse is 16 cm.**

Example 3:

Find the length of the hypotenuse in the figure below.

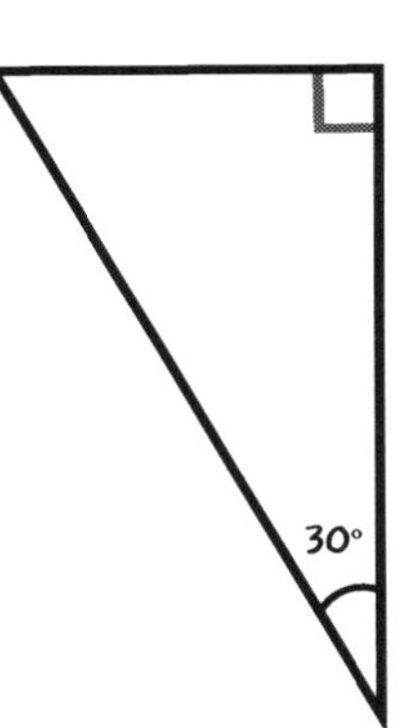

This is a 30-60-90 triangle. Opposite of 30°, we know the ratio is x. Opposite of 60° is $x\sqrt{3}$.

We can see that 18 is equal to $x\sqrt{3}$. If we want to figure out what x is, what can we do? We can divide by $\sqrt{3}$.

So $x = \frac{18}{\sqrt{3}}$, which is the shortest leg measure.

However, we must remember that we cannot have a square root in our denominator. We must rationalize this denominator.

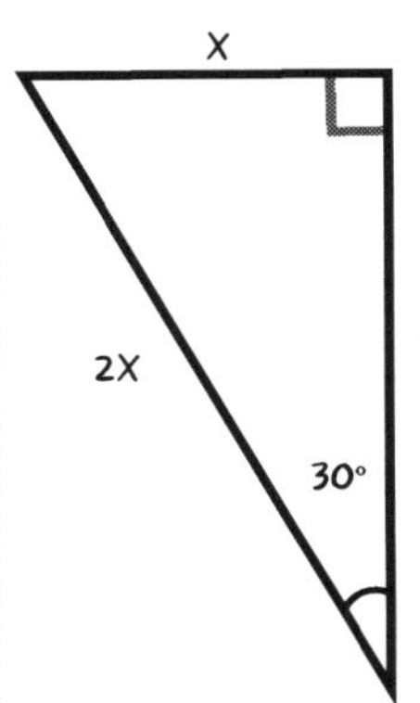

$$\frac{18}{\sqrt{3}} \times \frac{\sqrt{3}}{\sqrt{3}} = \frac{18\sqrt{3}}{3} = 6\sqrt{3}$$

$$\text{So } x = 6\sqrt{3}$$

We can easily find the hypotenuse now which is $2x$. $2(6\sqrt{3}) = 12\sqrt{3}$.

The hypotenuse of the figure above is $12\sqrt{3}$.

Example 4:

What is the value of x and y?

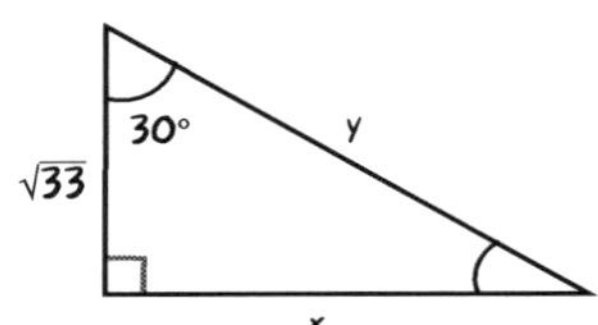

This is a **30-60-90** triangle. We are given the side of the longer leg $\sqrt{33}$, which has a ratio of $x\sqrt{3}$. Let's first figure out the value of the variable x, which has a ratio of x. We can divide $\sqrt{33}$ by by $\sqrt{3}$ to get what x is.

$$\frac{\sqrt{33}}{\sqrt{3}} = \frac{\sqrt{33}}{\sqrt{3}} \times \frac{\sqrt{3}}{\sqrt{3}} = \frac{\sqrt{99}}{3} = \frac{\sqrt{9}\sqrt{11}}{3} = \frac{3\sqrt{11}}{3} = \sqrt{11}$$

We rationalized the denominator, and then simplified to get $x = \sqrt{11}$.

To solve for y (the hypotenuse), we simply need to multiply by the value of x by **2**.

$(2)(\sqrt{11}) = 2\sqrt{11} \leftarrow$ We cannot simplify any further.
The value of $x = \sqrt{11}$.

The value of $y = 2\sqrt{11}$.

Example 5:

What is the value of x and y?

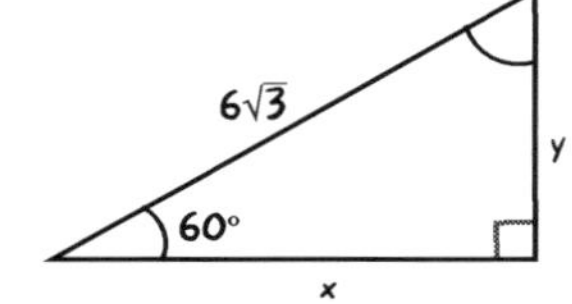

This is a **30-60-90** triangle. We are given the hypotenuse which is represented by the ratio $2x$.

Let's first solve for the value of x, which has a ratio of x. We need to divide the value of hypotenuse by **2**.

$\frac{6\sqrt{3}}{2} = 3\sqrt{3}$. This is our value of x.

Let's now solve for the value of y, which has a ratio of $x\sqrt{3}$. All we need to do is take our value of x and multiply by $\sqrt{3}$.

$3\sqrt{3} \times \sqrt{3} = 3\sqrt{9} = 3(3) = 9$

The value of $x = 3\sqrt{3}$. **The value of** $y = 9$.

Recap: You must memorize the 30-60-90 triangle ratio.

1. Short side (opposite the 30 degree angle) = x
2. Hypotenuse (opposite the 90 degree angle) = $2x$
3. Long side (opposite the 60 degree angle) = $x\sqrt{3}$

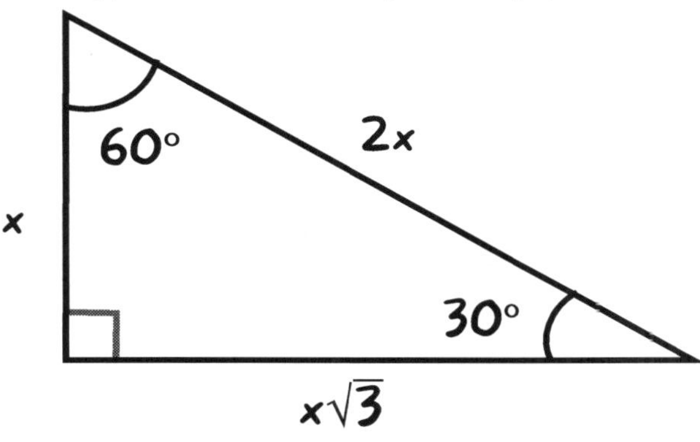

The second special right triangle we will cover is the 45-45-90 triangle that has the angles 45°, 45°, and 90°. A 45-45-90 right triangle has the side ratios x, x, $x\sqrt{2}$.

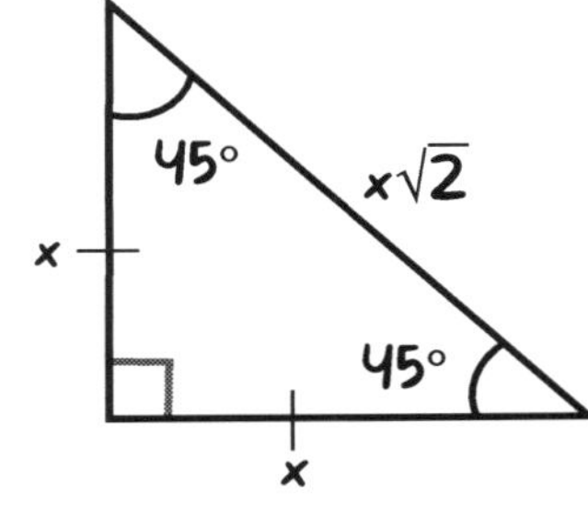

The hypotenuse always has the ratio of $x\sqrt{2}$ and the legs are x.

Let's take a look at a few examples.

Example 1:

What is the value of x and y?

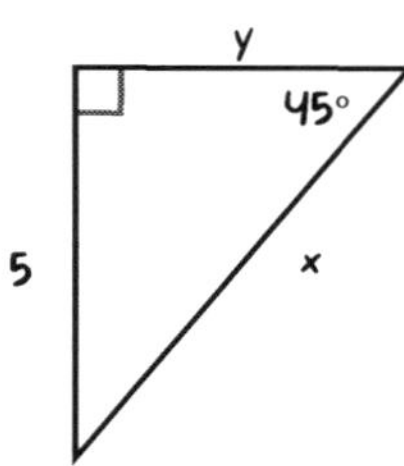

This triangle is a 45-45-90 right triangle. Given that one leg measures 5 units, the other leg, denoted as 'y', will also measure 5 units.

Now we need to determine the value of x, in this case our hypotenuse. We just learned that the hypotenuse has a ratio of $x\sqrt{2}$, in a 45-45-90 right triangle. We know $x = 5$, so the hypotenuse is $5\sqrt{2}$.

The value of $y = 5$.

The value of $x = 5\sqrt{2}$.

Example 2:

What is the value of u and v?

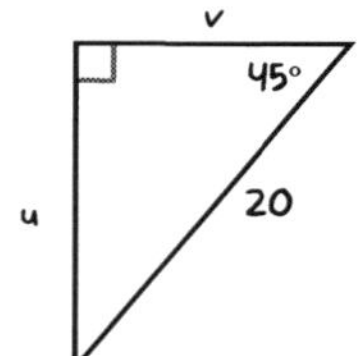

In a 45-45-90 right triangle, the legs are congruent, and the hypotenuse is $\sqrt{2}$ times longer than one of the legs.

Since the hypotenuse is 20, in order to solve for the length of a leg, we will divide by $\sqrt{2}$.

$\frac{20}{\sqrt{2}} = \frac{20}{\sqrt{2}} \times \frac{\sqrt{2}}{\sqrt{2}} = \frac{20\sqrt{2}}{2} = 10\sqrt{2} \leftarrow$ We rationalized the denominator and simplified.

The value of $u = 10\sqrt{2}$.

The value of $v = 10\sqrt{2}$.

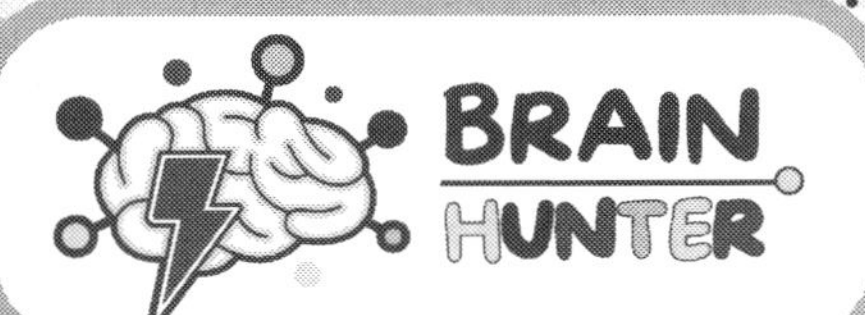

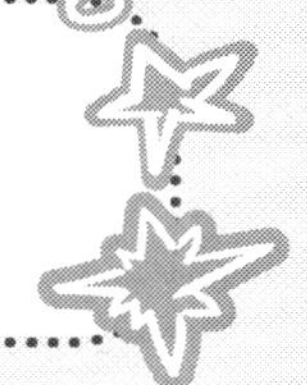

Example 3:

What is the value of x and y?

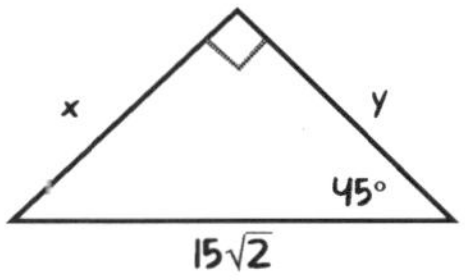

In a 45-45-90 right triangle, the legs are congruent, and the hypotenuse is $\sqrt{2}$ times longer than one of the legs.

Since the hypotenuse is $15\sqrt{2}$, in order to solve for the length of a leg, we will divide by $\sqrt{2}$.

$\frac{15\sqrt{2}}{\sqrt{2}} = 15$. So the value of each leg is 15.

The value of $x = 15$.

The value of $y = 15$.

Recap: You must memorize the 30-60-90 triangle ratio.

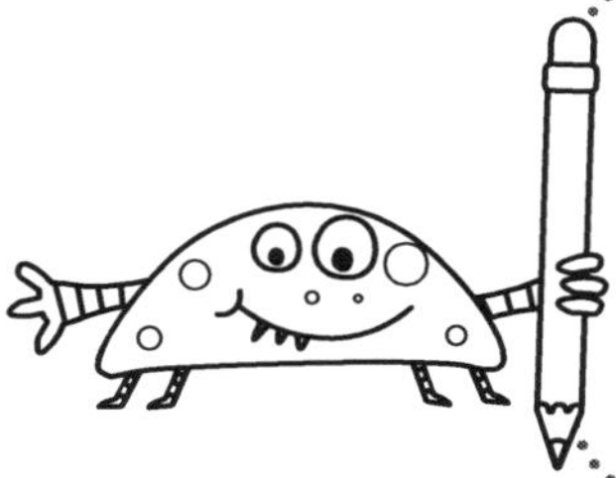

The hypotenuse always has the ratio of $x\sqrt{2}$ and the legs are x.

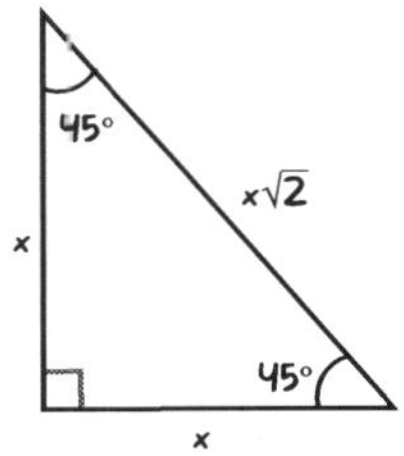

You should **memorize** this information. Most classes and exams require you to remember these two special right triangles. Here is an overview one last time before we move on to practice questions.

30-60-90 right triangle	45-45-90 right triangle
The side opposite of 30° is always the shortest side (x). The side opposite of 60° is the longer leg ($x\sqrt{3}$). The hypotenuse is always $2x$. 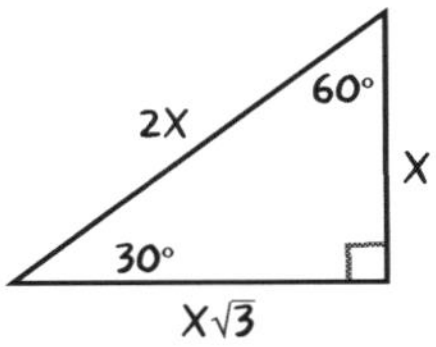 	A 45-45-90 right triangle has the side ratios x, x, $x\sqrt{2}$. The hypotenuse always has the ratio of $x\sqrt{2}$ and the legs are x. 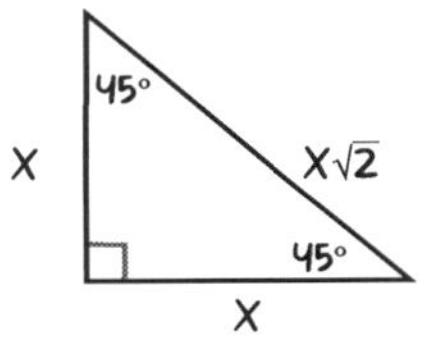

Section 3.1 Quiz

Directions: The following problems are a 30-60-90 right triangle or a 45-45-90 right triangle. Solve for the variables asked. Do **not** use a calculator. Make sure your answers are in the simplest form.

1.

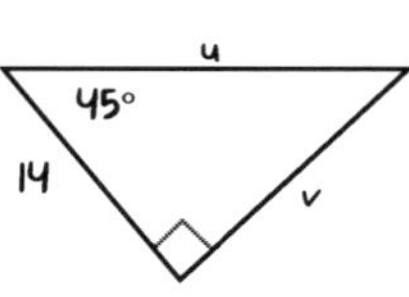

2.

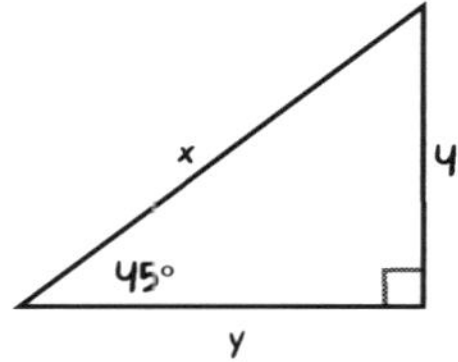

3.

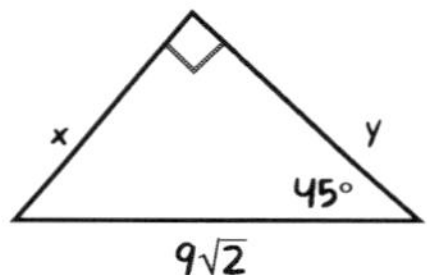

4.

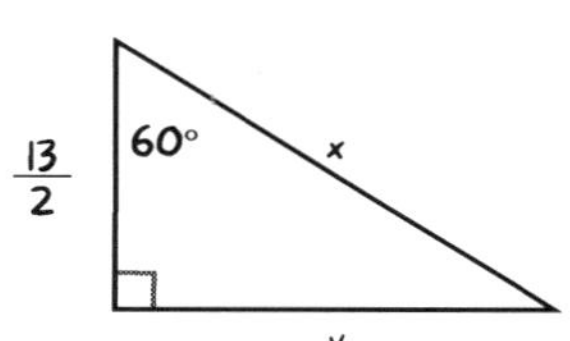

5.

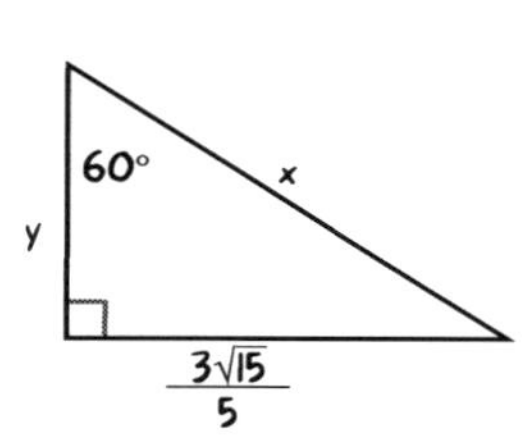

6.

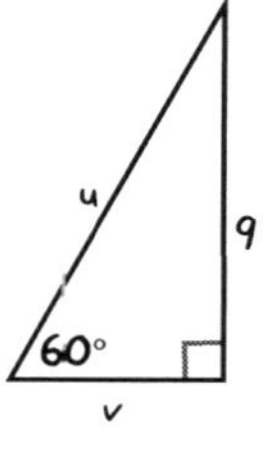

7.

$3\sqrt{6}$
60°
n
m

8.

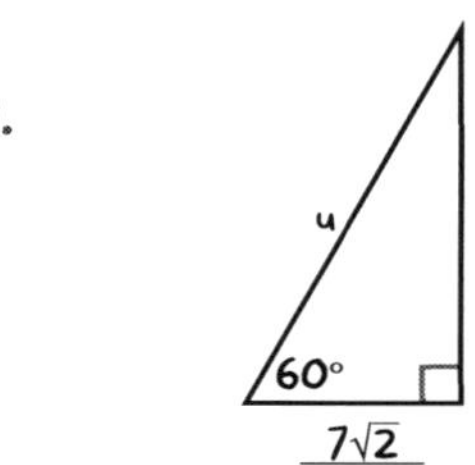

9.

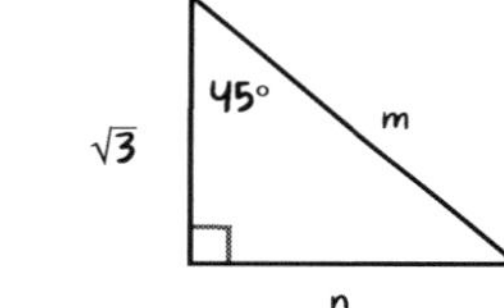

10.

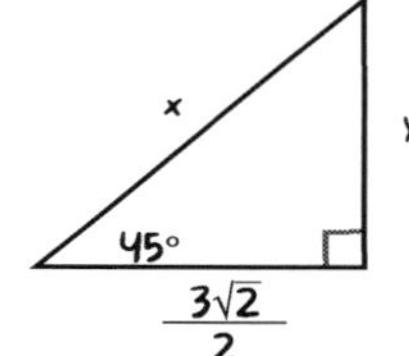

11.

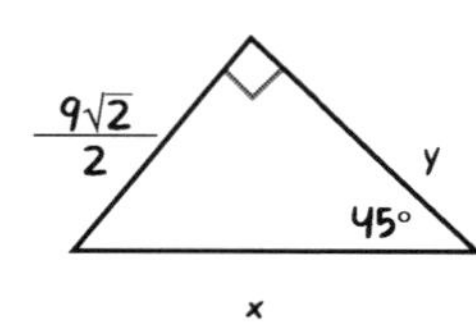

12.

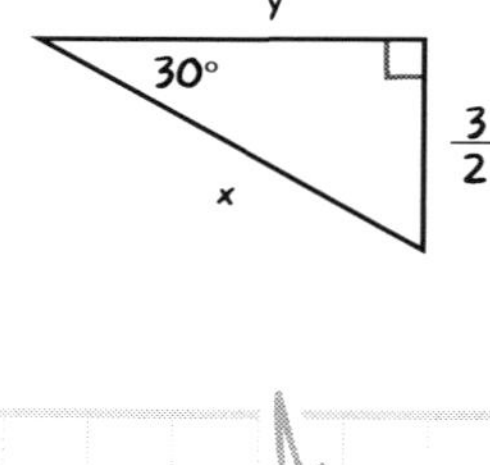

Section 3.1 Quiz

13.

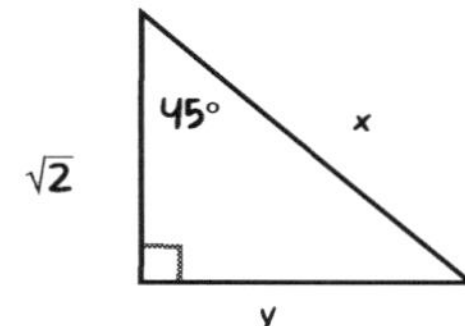

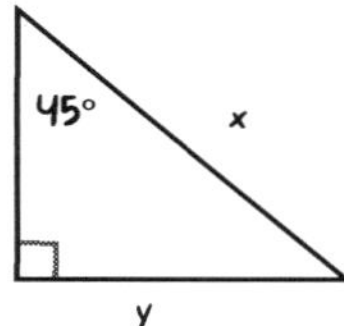

14.

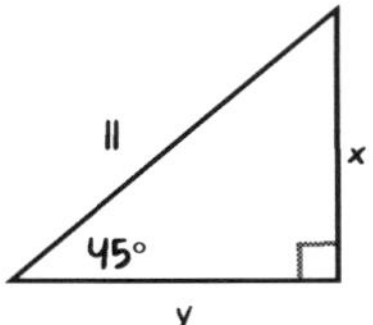

15.

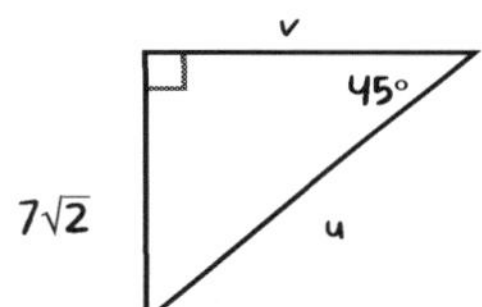

16.

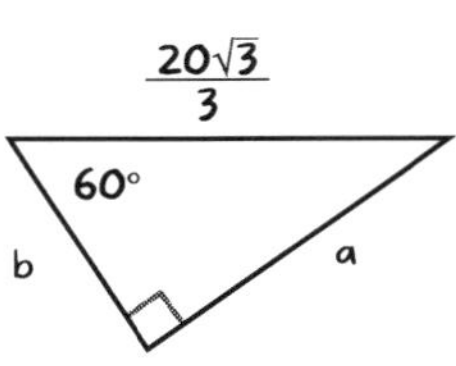

17.

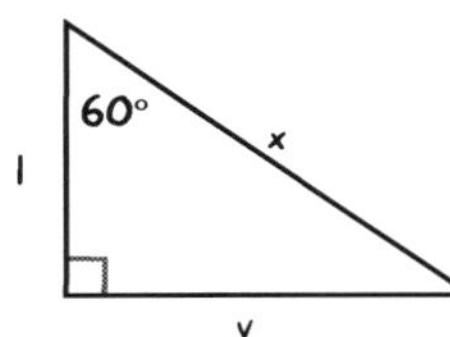

18.

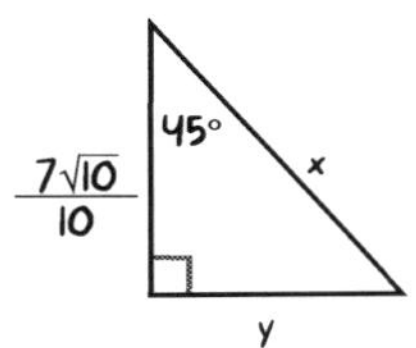

19.

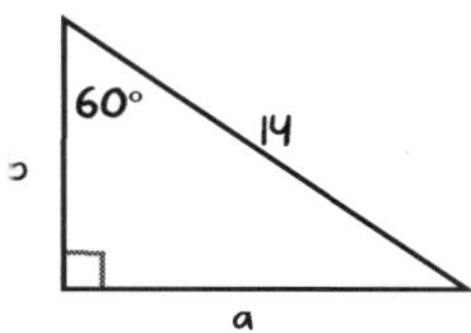

20.

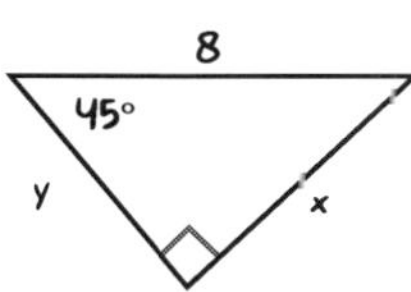

21.

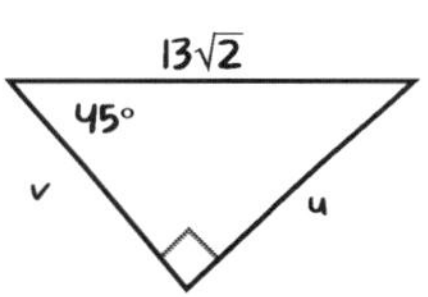

22.

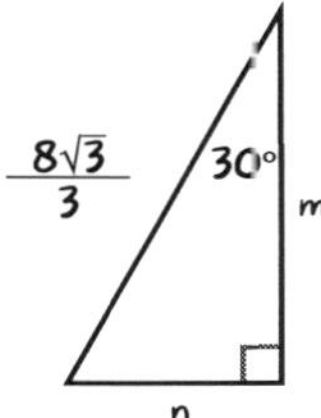

23.

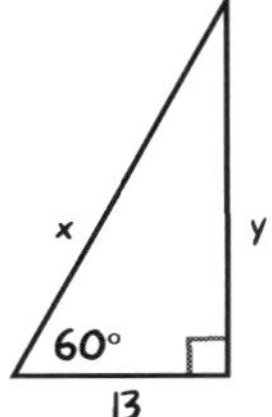

24.

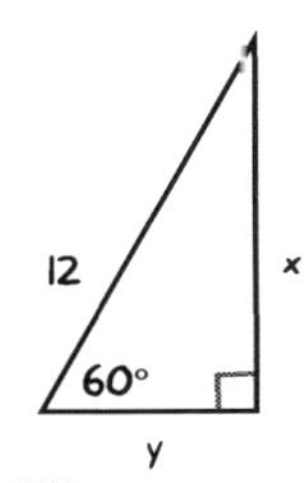

Section 3.1 Quiz

25.

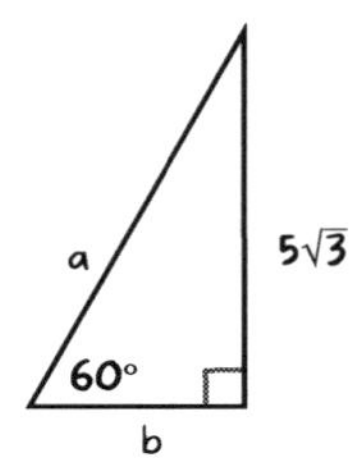

26.

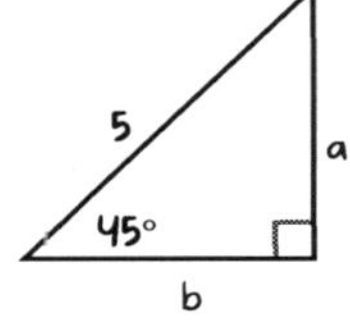

27.

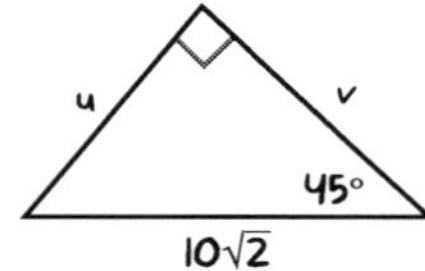

28.

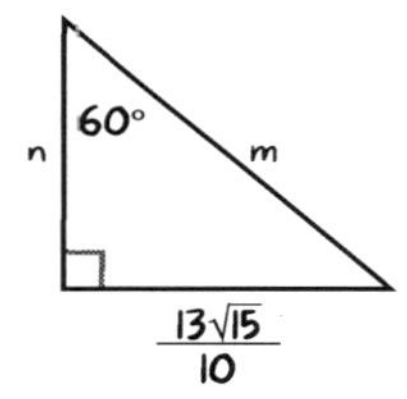

29.

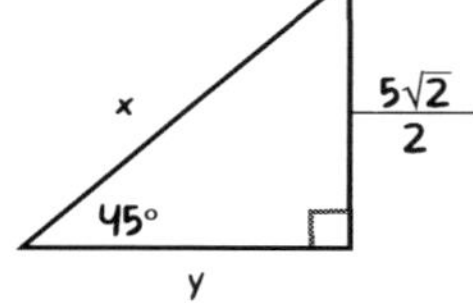

30.

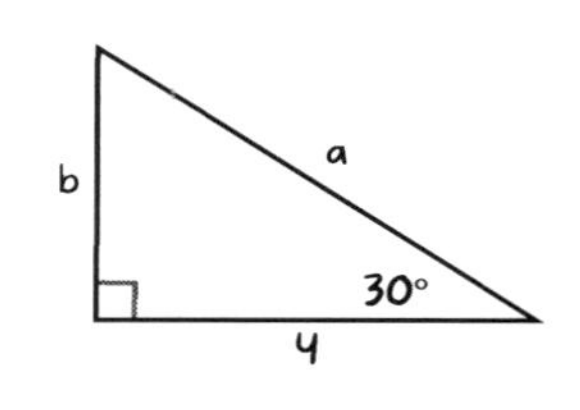

31.

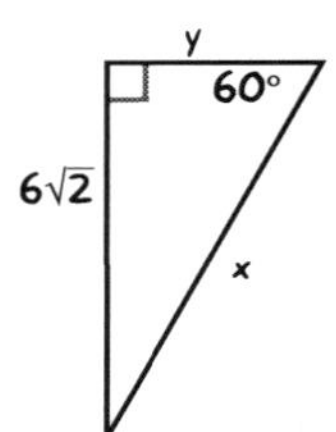

32.

33.

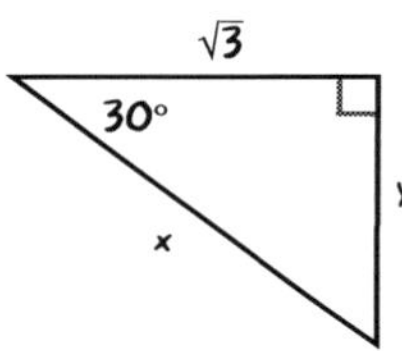

34.

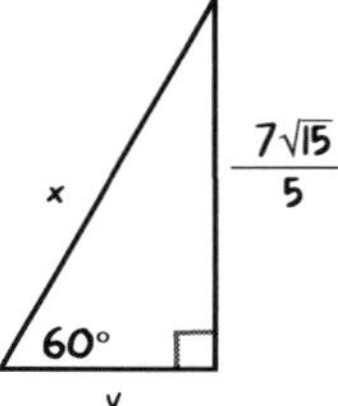

35.

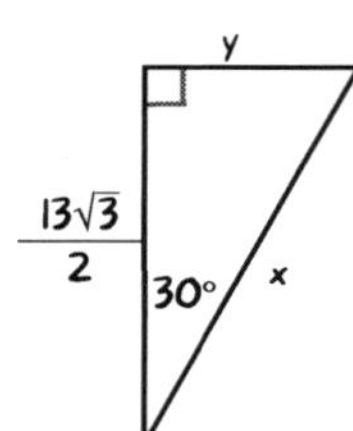

36.

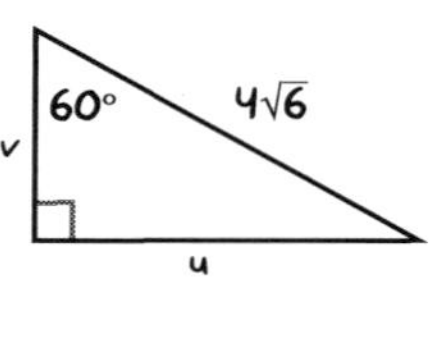

Section 3.1 Quiz

37.

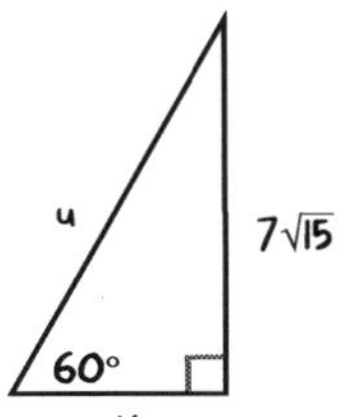

38.

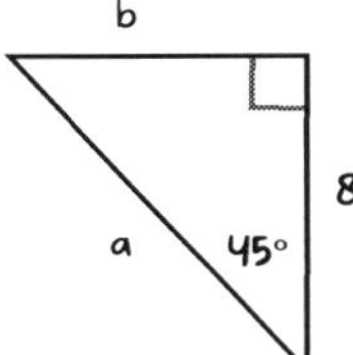

39.

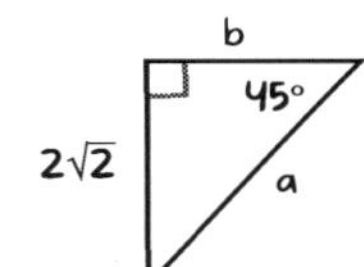

40.

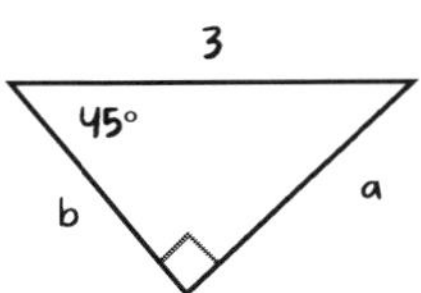

41.

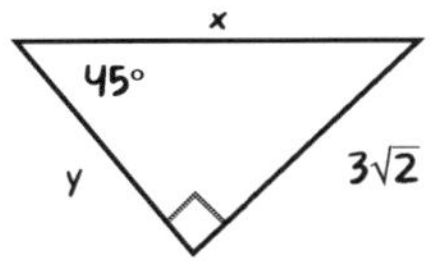

x
45°
y
$3\sqrt{2}$

42.

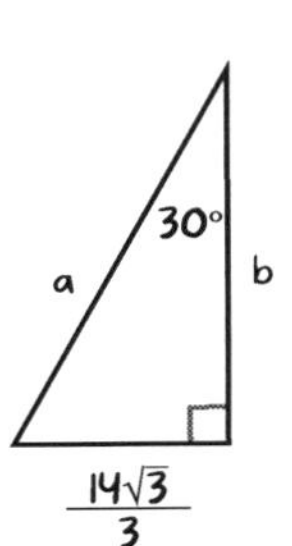

43.

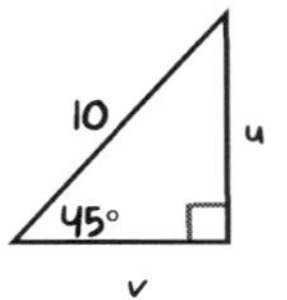

44.

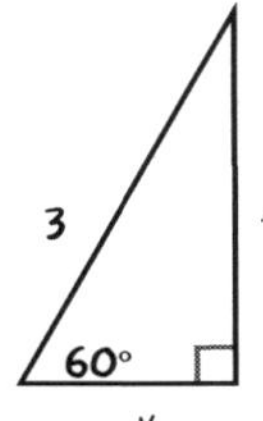

45.

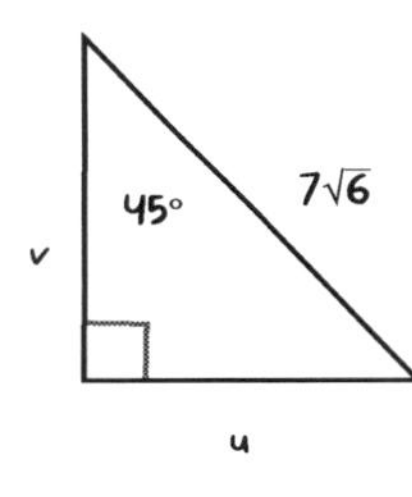

46.

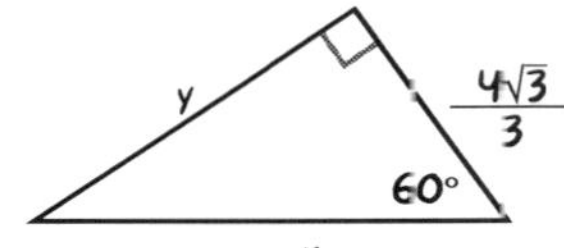

47.

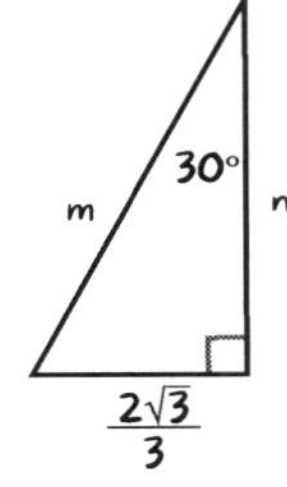

48.

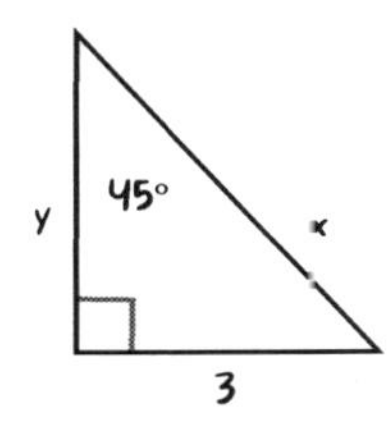

49.

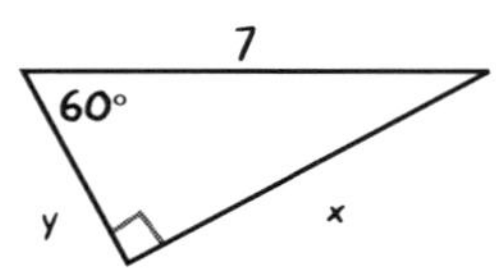

50.

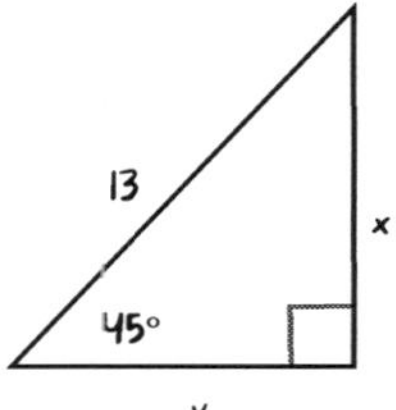

51.

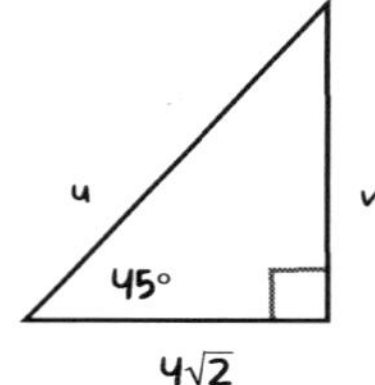

52.

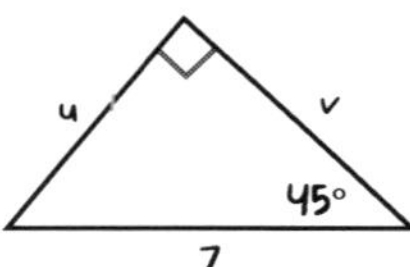

53.

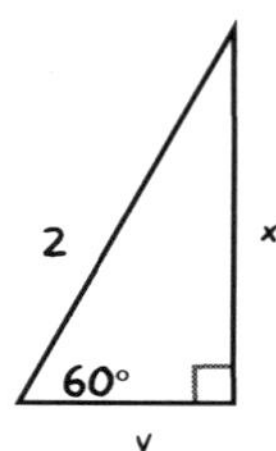

54.

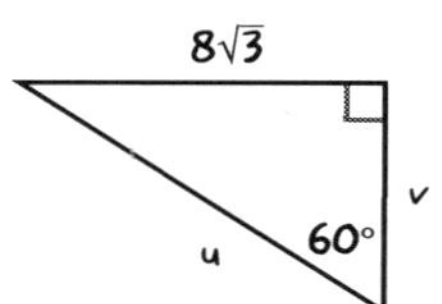

55.

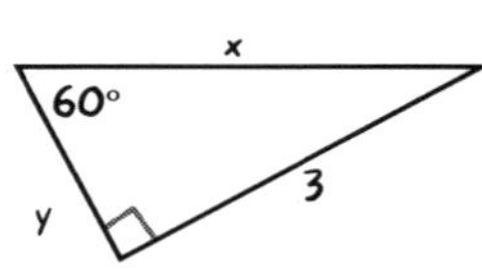

56.

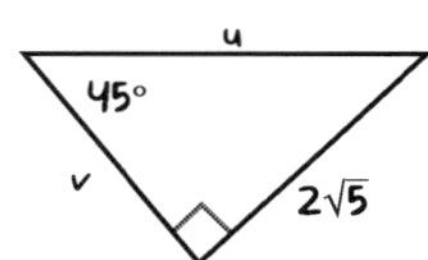

57.

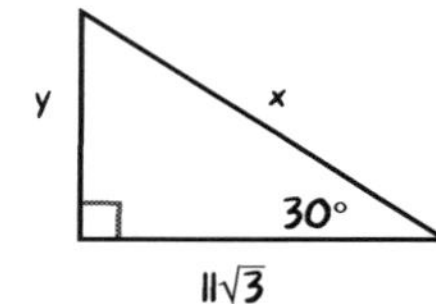

58.

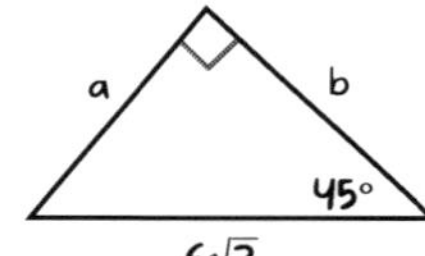

59.

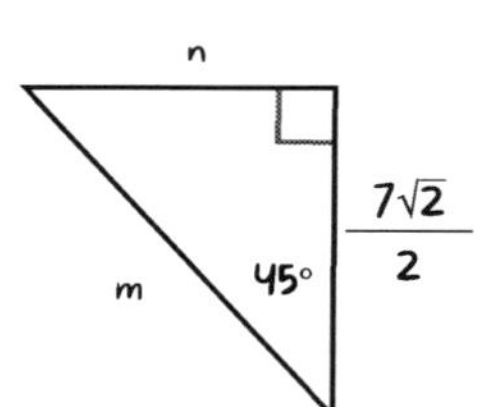

60.

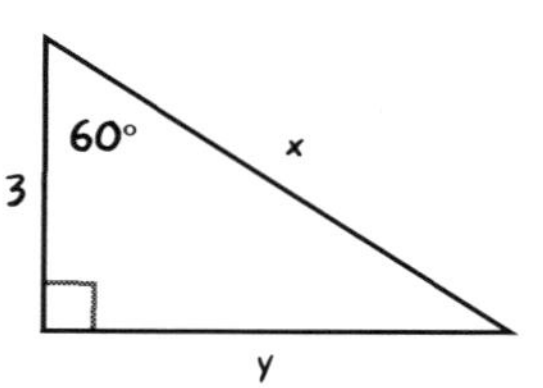

Section 3.1 Quiz

61.

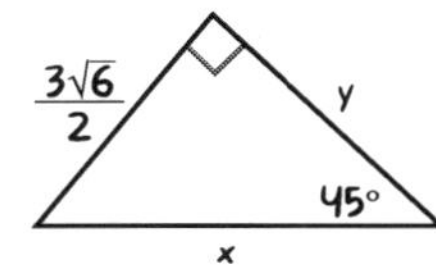

62.

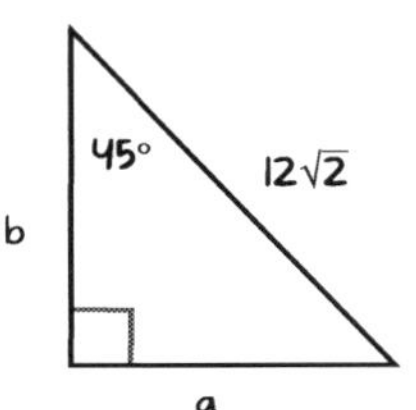

63.

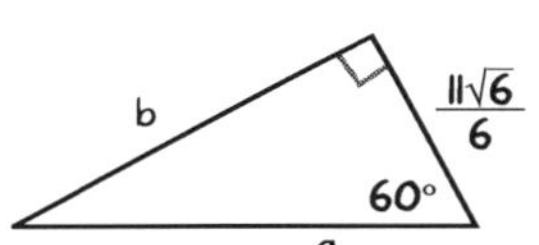

64.

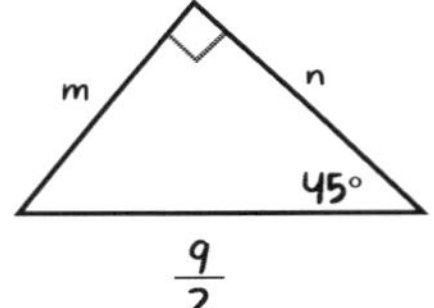

65.

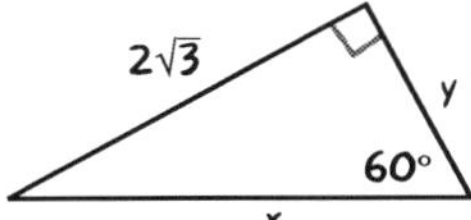

66.

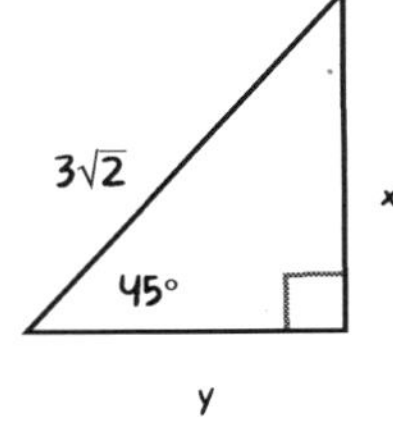

67.

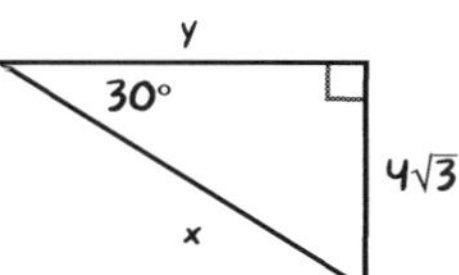

68.

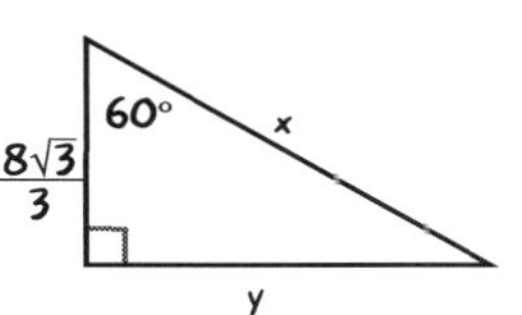

69.

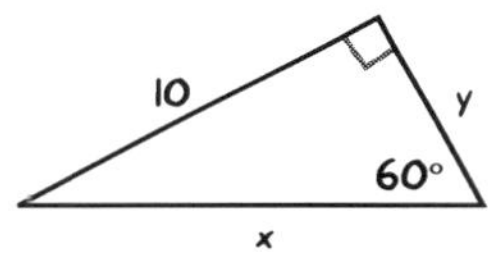

70.

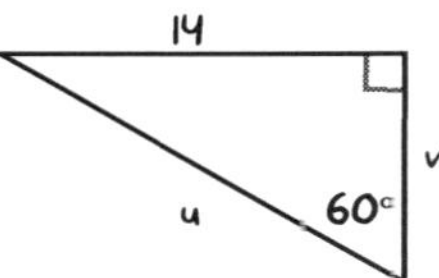

71.

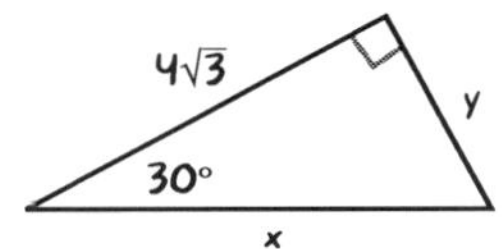

72.

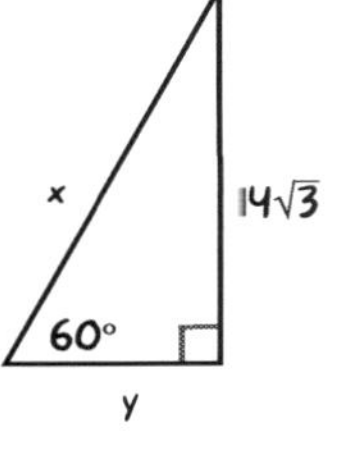

Section 3.1 Quiz

73.

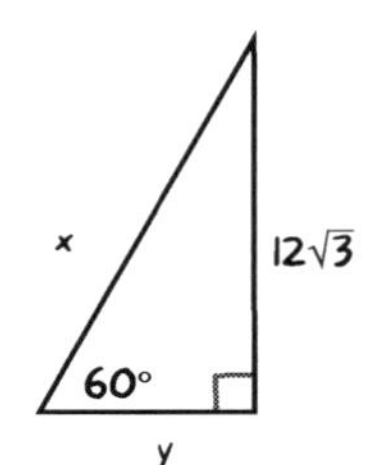

74.

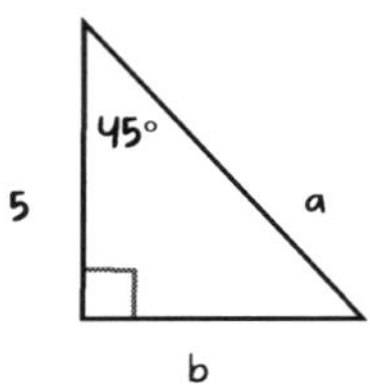

75.

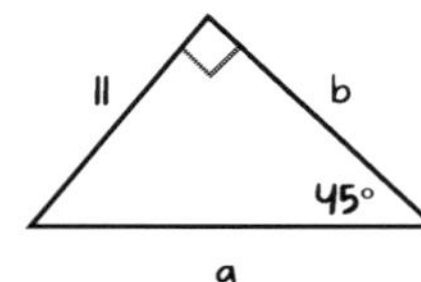

76.

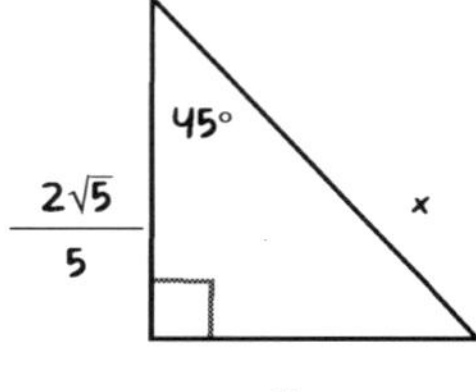

77.

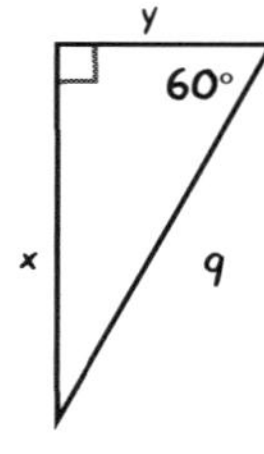

78.

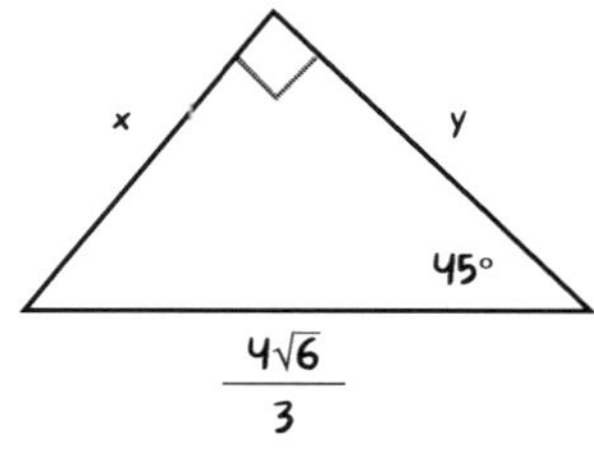

79.

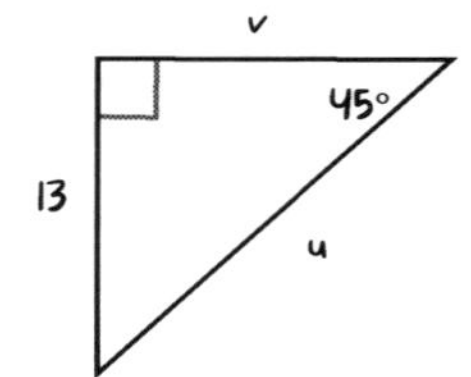

80.

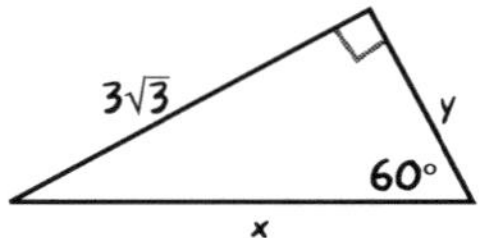

81.

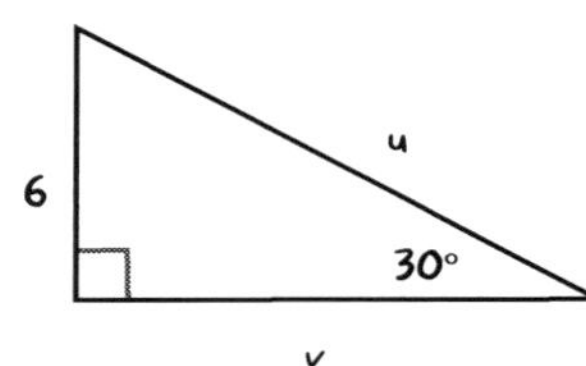

82.

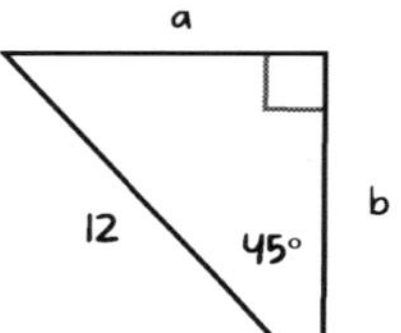

83.

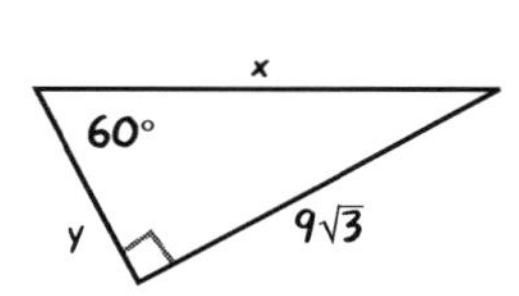

84.

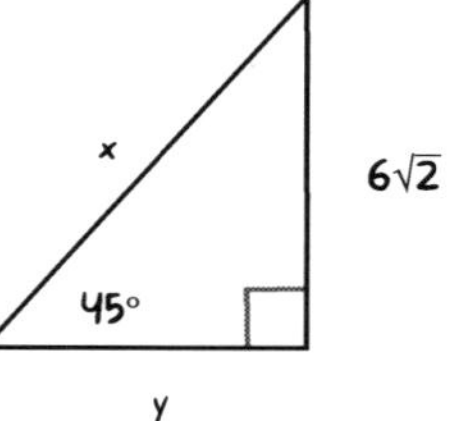

Section 3.1 Quiz

85.

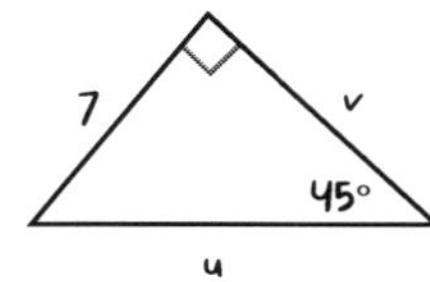

86.

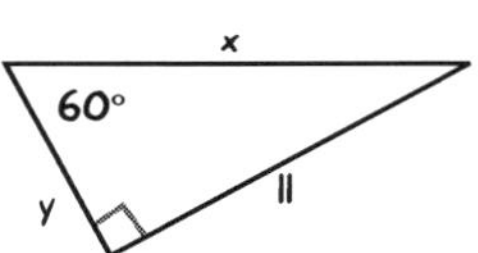

87.

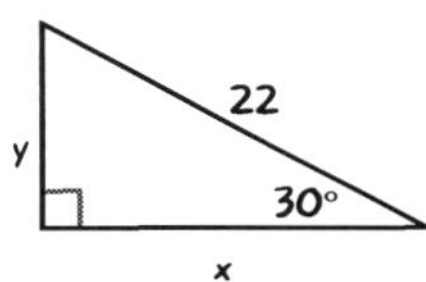

88.

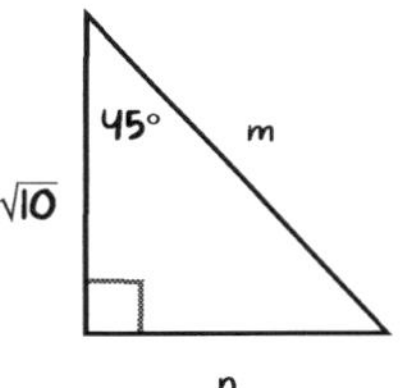

89.

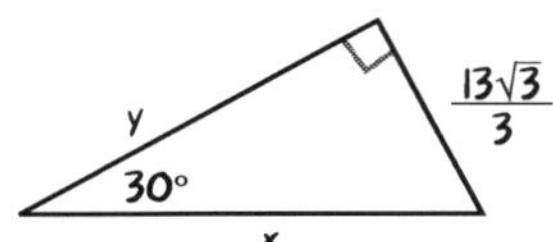

90.

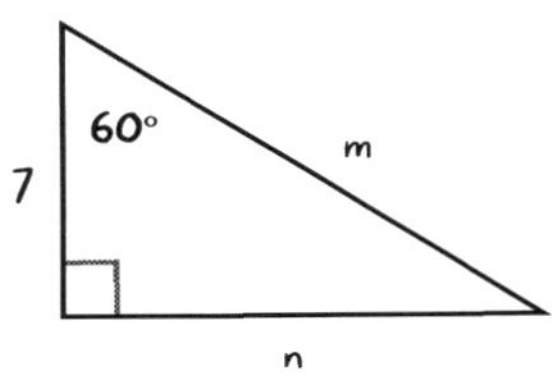

91.

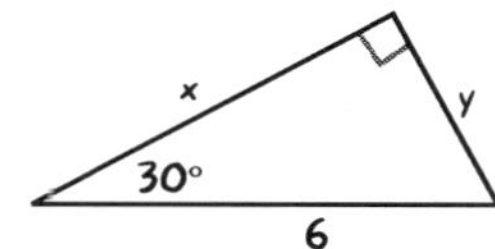

92.

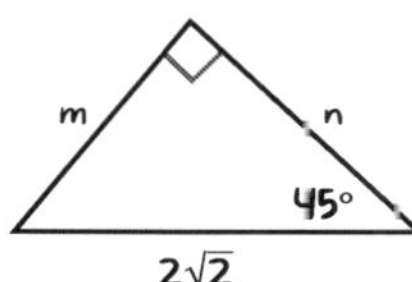

93.

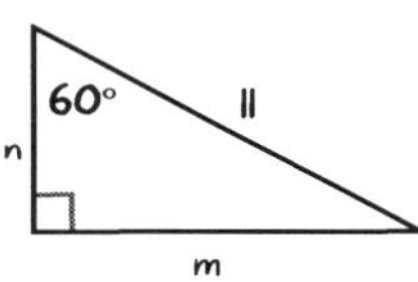

94.

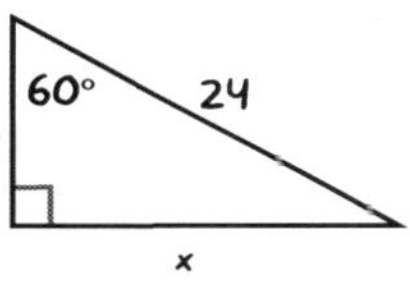

95.

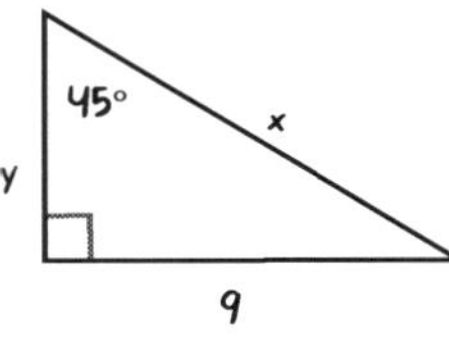

96.

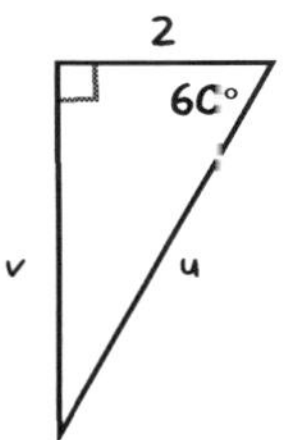

97.

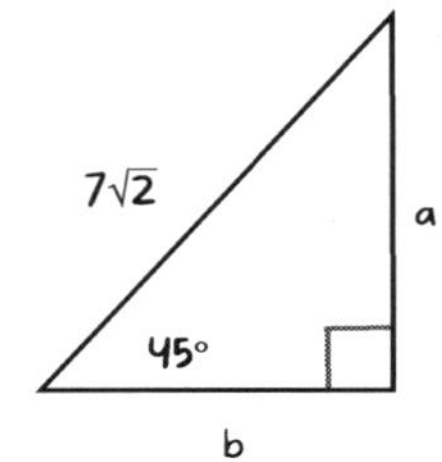

98.

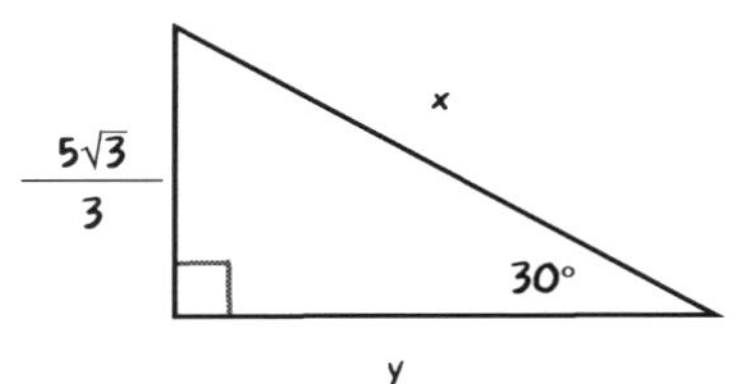

99.

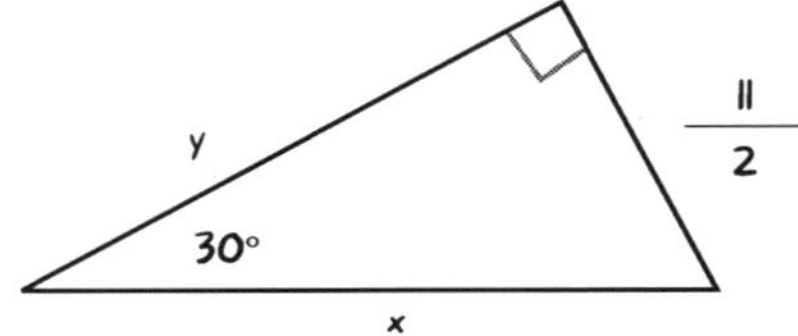

100.

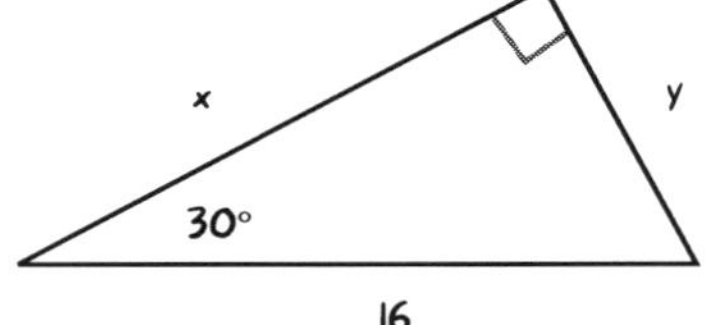

Section 3.2: 30-60-90 & 45-45-90 Right Triangle (Advanced Problems)

In Section 3.1 we learned about the two special right triangles and their ratios. In this section, we will take a look at problems that are slightly more advanced.

Example 1:

What is the value of x in the diagram below?

We need to figure out the value of x. We can see in this diagram we have **two** right triangles, one of them being the 30-60-90 triangle and the other a 45-45-90 triangle.

In order to figure out the value of x, we need to figure out the value of the hypotenuse on the 45-45-90 triangle.

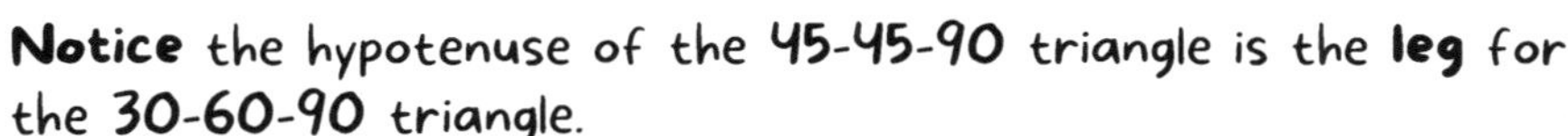

Notice the hypotenuse of the 45-45-90 triangle is the **leg** for the 30-60-90 triangle.

Let's recall our ratios for a 30-60-90 triangle.

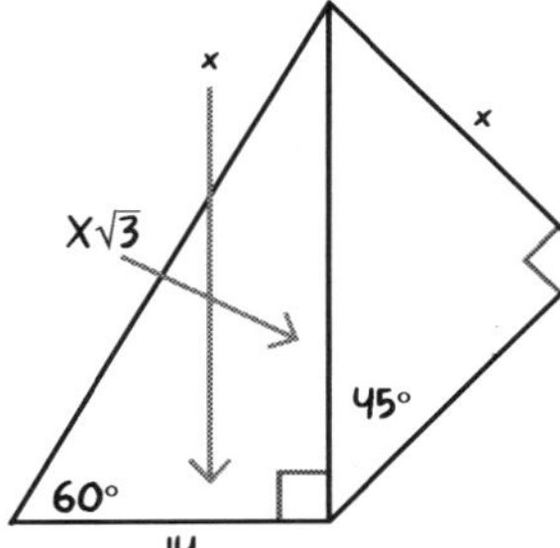

14 is the value of "x" in the 30-60-90 right triangle.

We can easily determine the other leg value, as we know the ratio is $x\sqrt{3}$. The value is $14\sqrt{3}$.

Now let's re-draw just the 45-45-90 triangle.

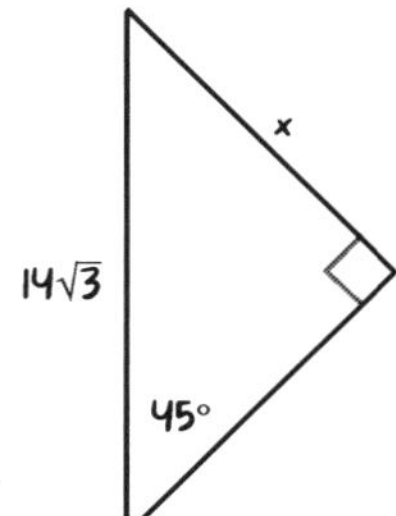

Now we can use our ratios that we know for this 45-45-90 triangle.

We know a 45-45-90 right triangle has the side ratios x, x, $x\sqrt{2}$.

$14\sqrt{3}$ represents the ratio $x\sqrt{2}$. How can we identify what x is? Simply divide by $\sqrt{2}$.

$$\frac{14\sqrt{3}}{\sqrt{2}} = \frac{14\sqrt{3}}{\sqrt{2}} \times \frac{\sqrt{2}}{\sqrt{2}} = \frac{14\sqrt{6}}{2} = 7\sqrt{6}$$

Our answer to this problem is $7\sqrt{6}$.

Example 2:

What is the value of x in the diagram below?

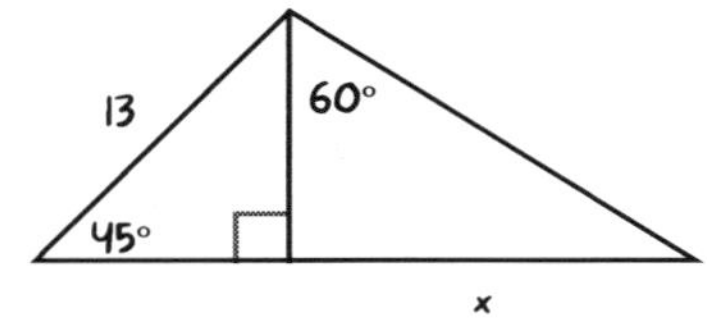

We need to figure out the value of x. We can see in this diagram we have **two** right triangles, one of them being the 45-45-90 triangle and the other a 30-60-90 triangle.

We need to first tackle the 45-45-90 right triangle because we were provided with the hypotenuse value. We know a 45-45-90 right triangle has the side ratios $x, x, x\sqrt{2}$.

If 13 represents $x\sqrt{2}$, how do we find x (the legs)? Divide by $\sqrt{2}$!

$$\frac{13}{\sqrt{2}} = \frac{13}{\sqrt{2}} \times \frac{\sqrt{2}}{\sqrt{2}} = \frac{13\sqrt{2}}{2}$$

Let's re-draw just the 30-60-90 right triangle with our new known value for one of the sides.

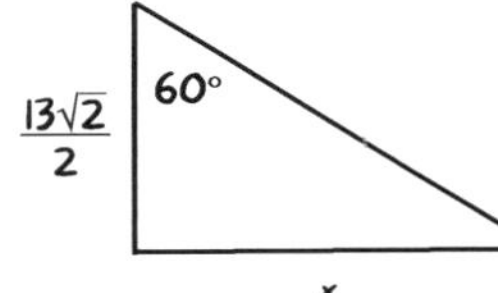

Let's also label this with our known ratios.

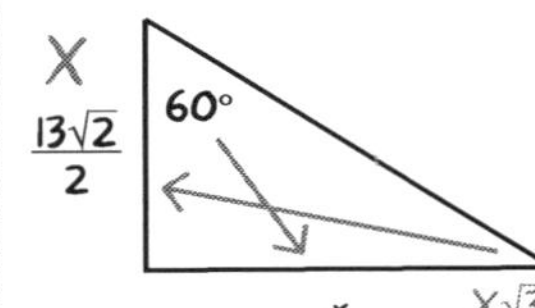

It's very important to label because as you can see the variable x in the original problem can confuse us.

$\frac{13\sqrt{2}}{2}$ is the value of x **and** the side we are trying to solve for is represented by the ratio $x\sqrt{3}$. So, we need to multiply $\frac{13\sqrt{2}}{2}$ by $\sqrt{3}$ to get the answer to this problem.

$$\frac{13\sqrt{2}}{2} \times \sqrt{3} = \frac{13\sqrt{6}}{2}$$

Our answer to this problem is $\frac{13\sqrt{6}}{2}$.

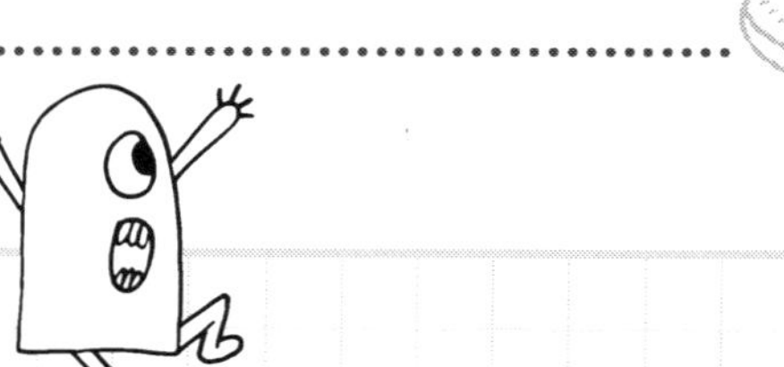

Example 3:

What is the value of y in the diagram below?

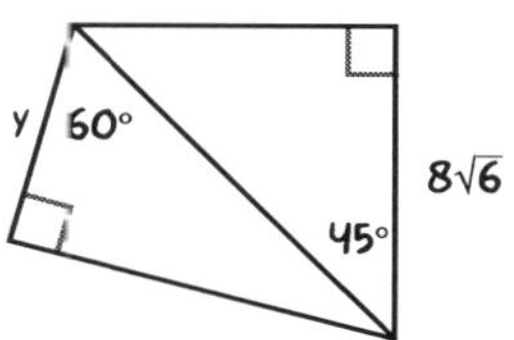

We need to figure out the value of x. We can see in this diagram we have **two** right triangles, one of them being the 45-45-90 triangle and the other a 30-60-90 triangle.

We need to first tackle the 45-45-90 right triangle because we were provided with the leg value. We know a 45-45-90 right triangle has the side ratios x, x, $x\sqrt{2}$.

We know the leg value $8\sqrt{6}$ represents the side ratio x. We can determine the hypotenuse by multiplying $8\sqrt{6}$ by $\sqrt{2}$.

$$8\sqrt{6} \times \sqrt{2} = 8\sqrt{12} = 8\sqrt{4}\sqrt{3} = (8)(2)\sqrt{3} = 16\sqrt{3}$$

The hypotenuse is $16\sqrt{3}$.

Let's re-draw the 30-60-90 right triangle with the new information we know.

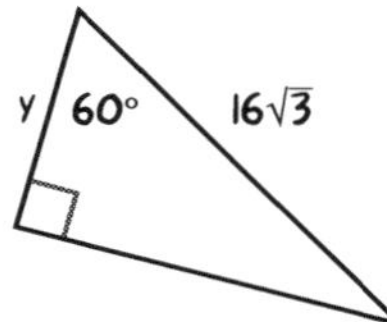

A 30-60-90 right triangle has the side ratios x, $x\sqrt{3}$, $2x$.

Let's also label this with our known ratios.

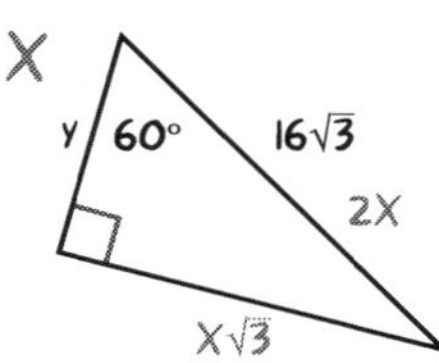

We need to figure out what the variable y is. We can see y represents the ratio x, and we know the hypotenuse, $16\sqrt{3}$, which represents the ratio $2x$.

What do we need to do? Simply divide $16\sqrt{3}$ by 2.

$$\frac{16\sqrt{3}}{2} = 8\sqrt{3}$$

Our answer to this problem is $8\sqrt{3}$.

Let's practice!

Section 3.2 Quiz

Directions: Find the missing side length. Do **not** use a calculator. Make sure your answers are in the simplest form.

1.

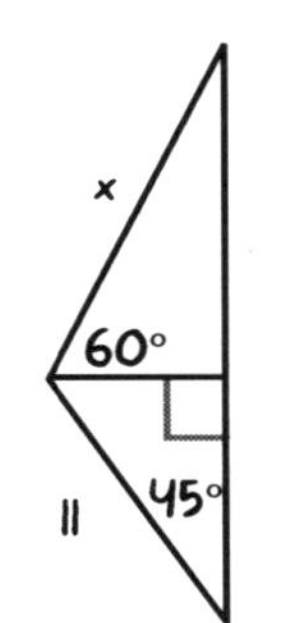

2.

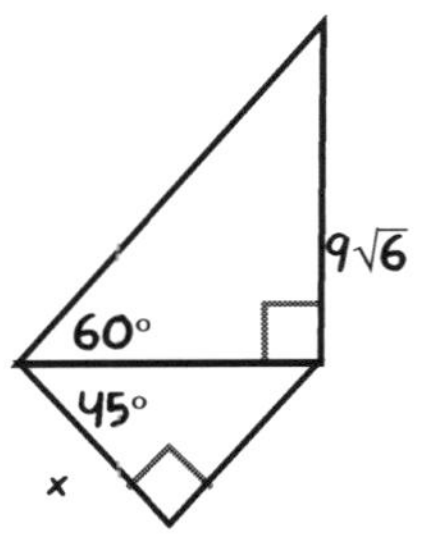

3.

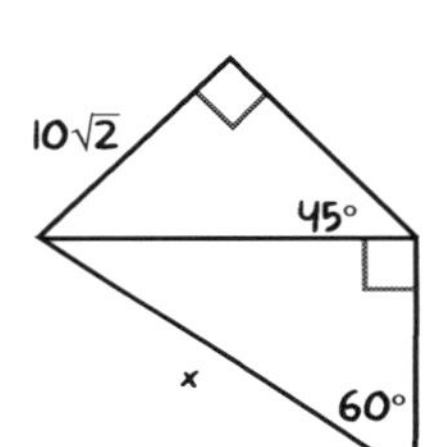

4.

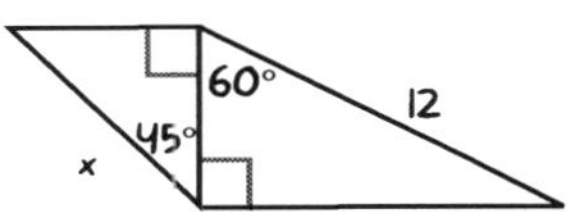

5.

6.

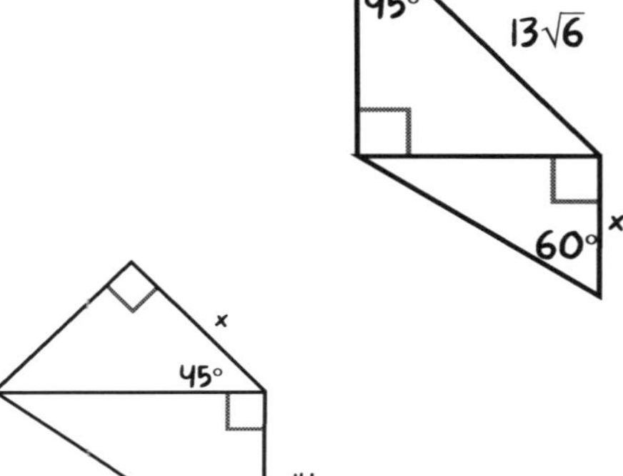

7.

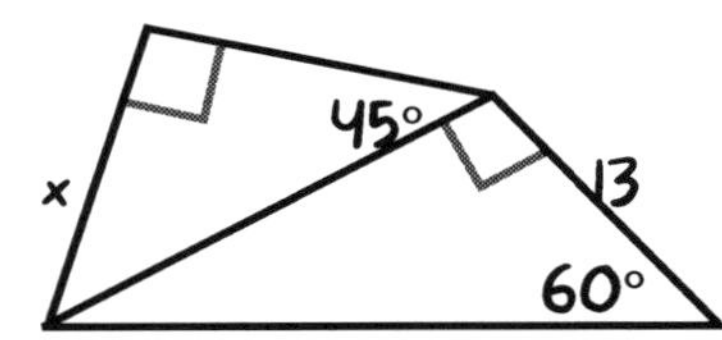

8.

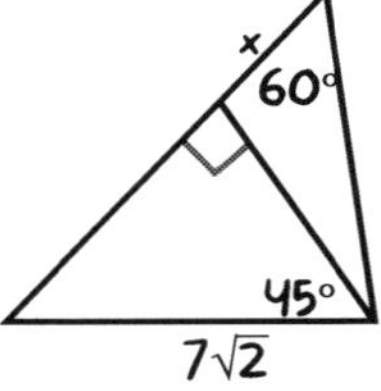

9.

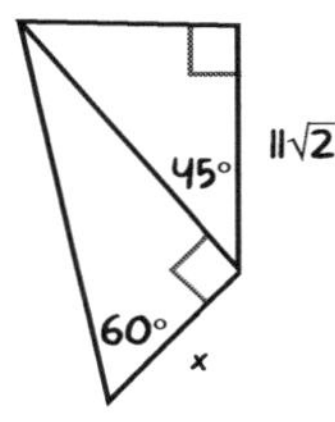

10.

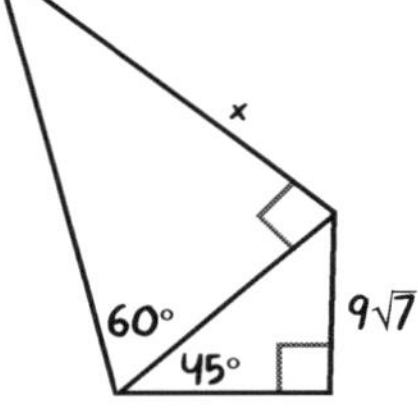

11.

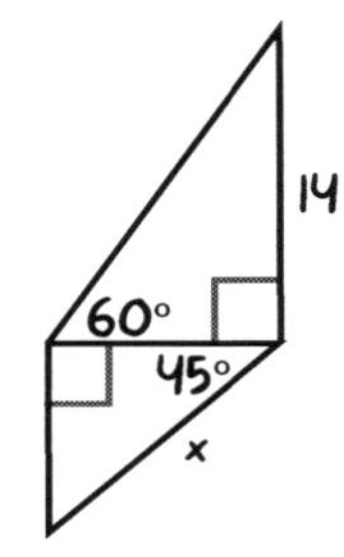

12.

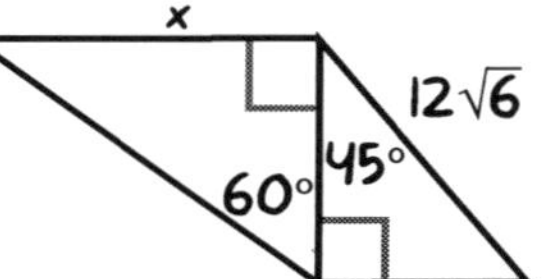

Section 3.2 Quiz

13.

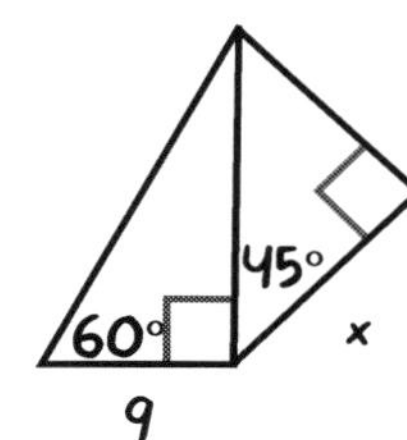

14.

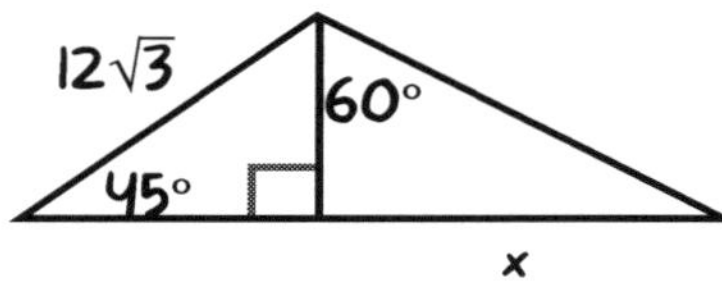

15.

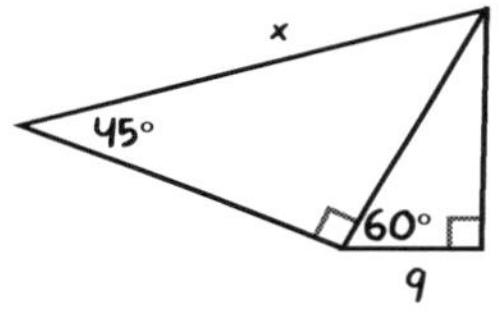

16.

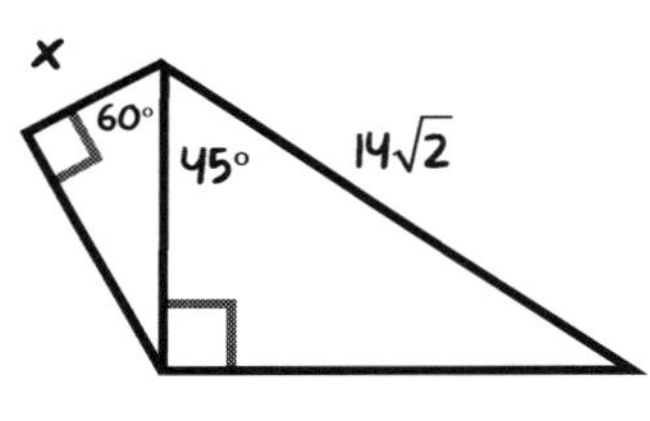

17.

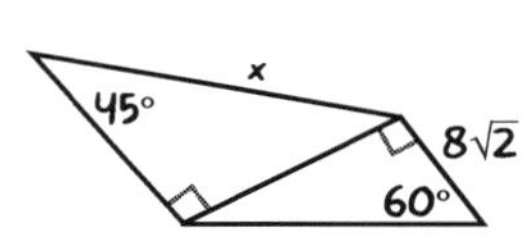

18.

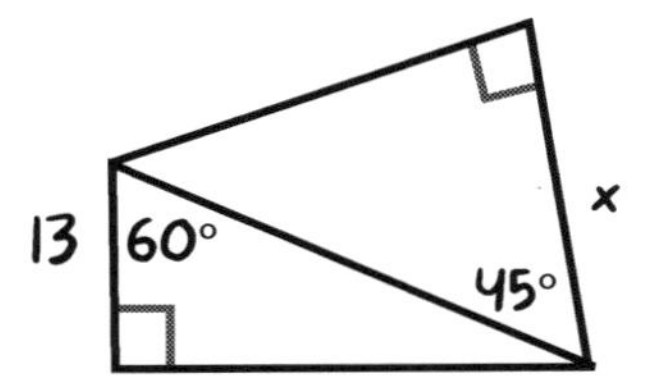

19.

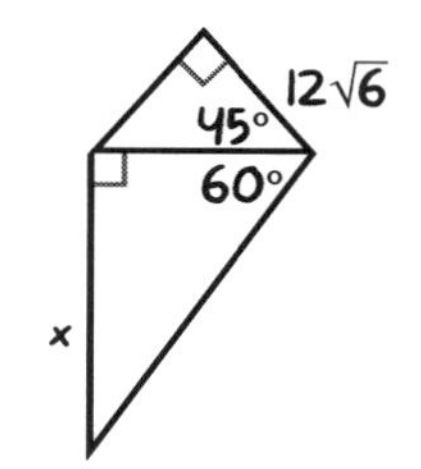

20.

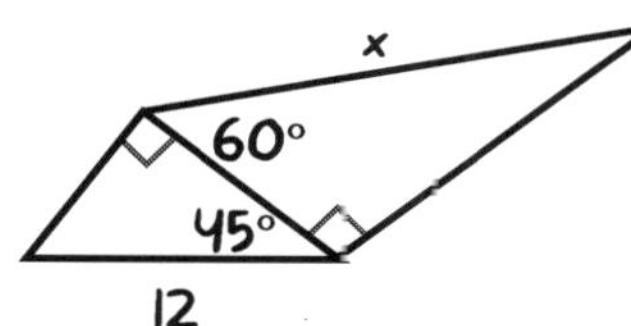

21.

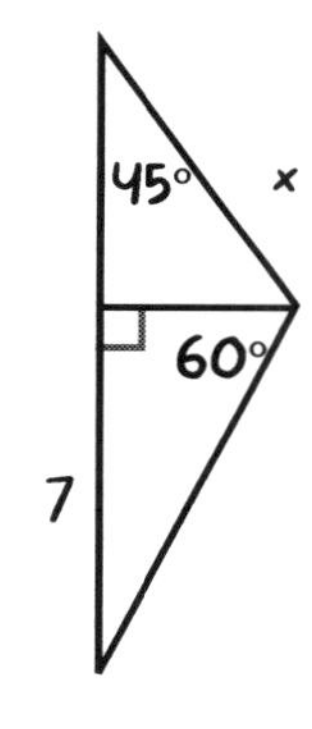

22.

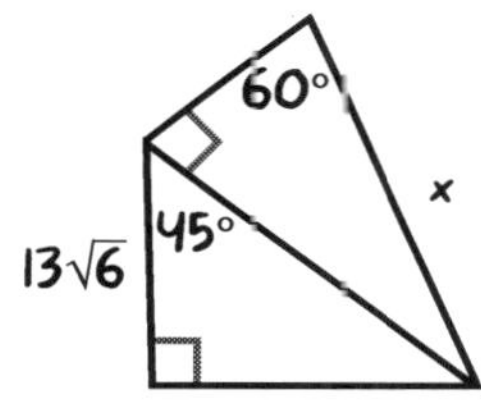

23.

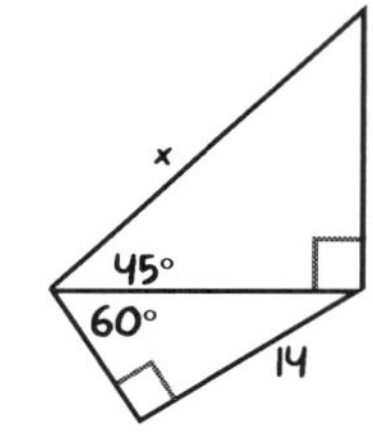

24.

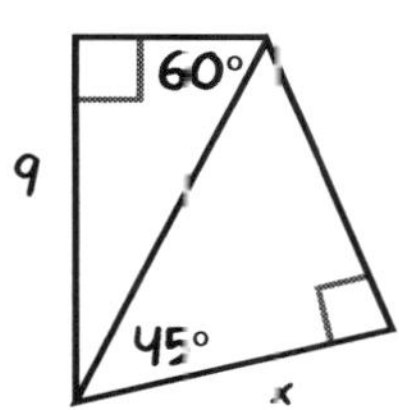

25.

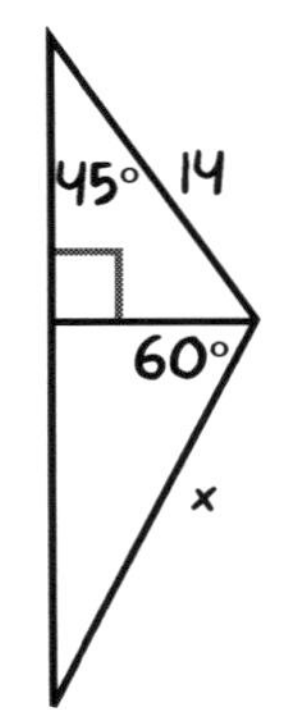

26.

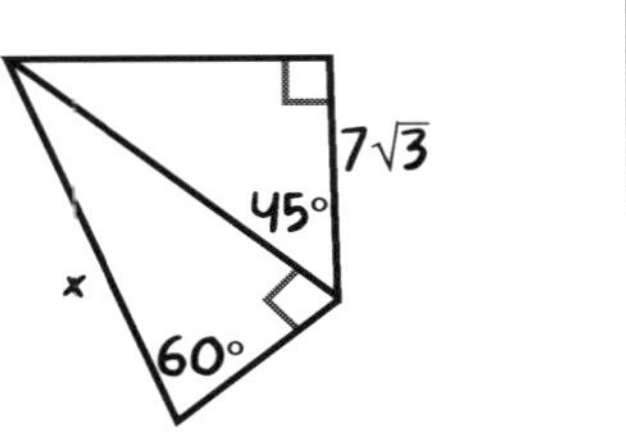

27.

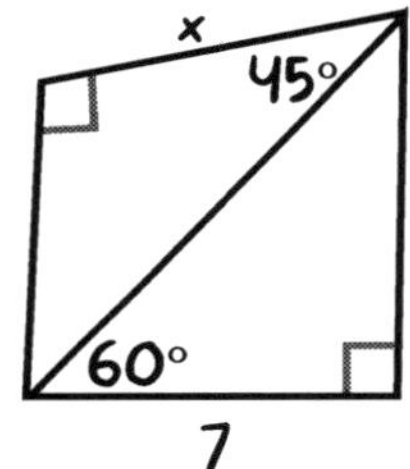

28.

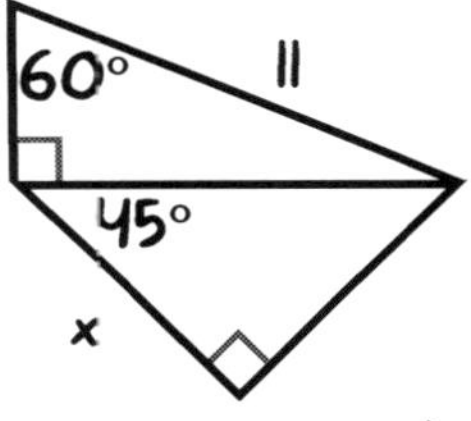

29.

30.

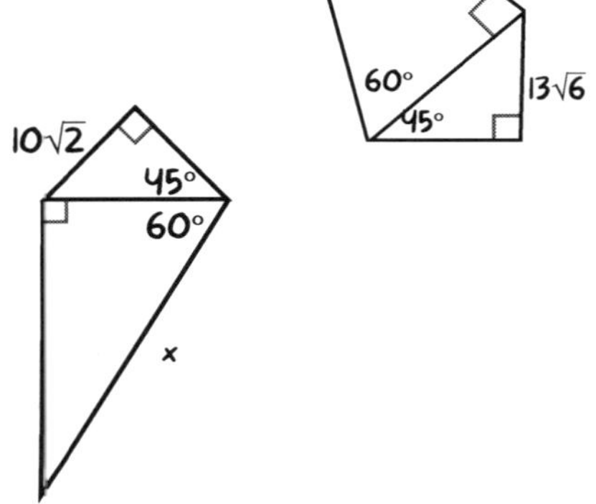

31.

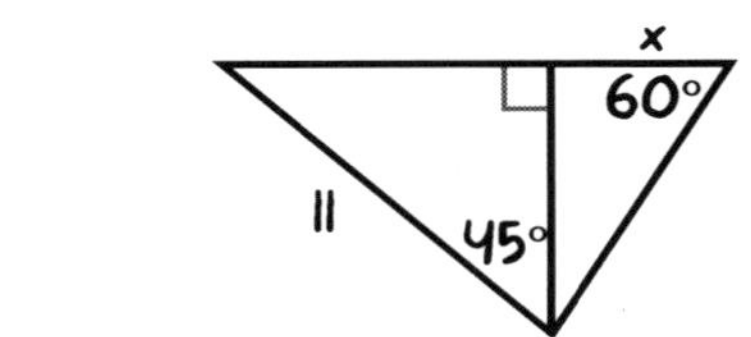

32.

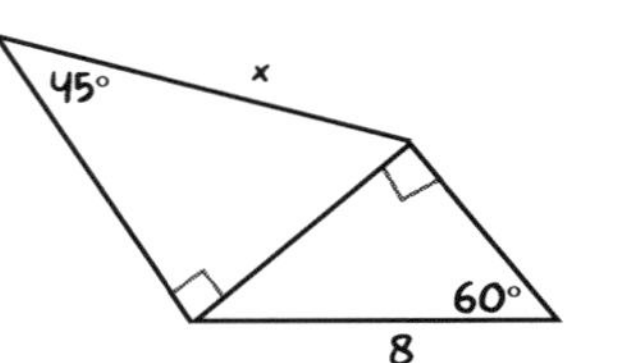

33.

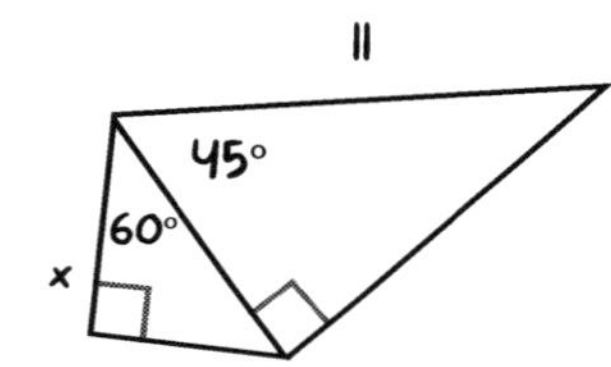

34.

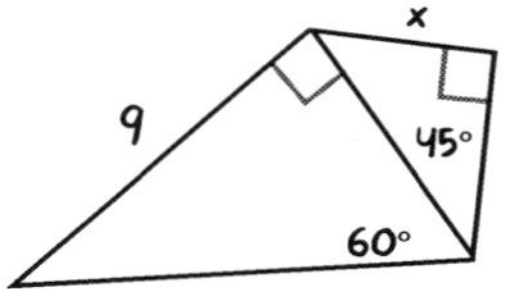

35.

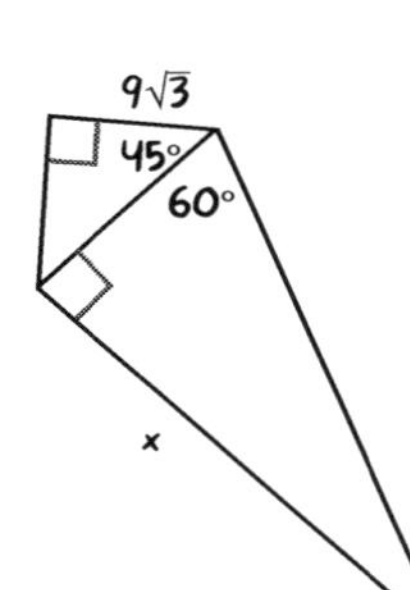

36.

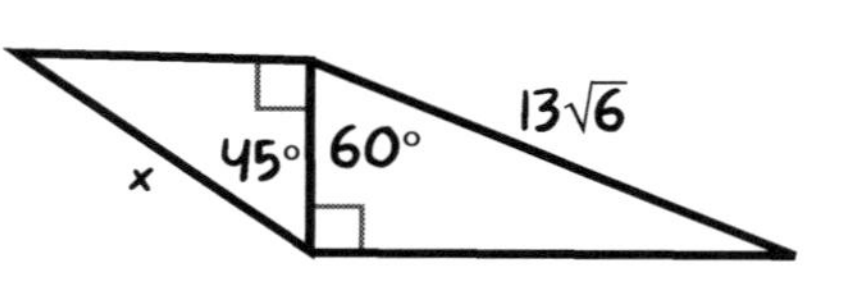

Section 3.2 Quiz

37.

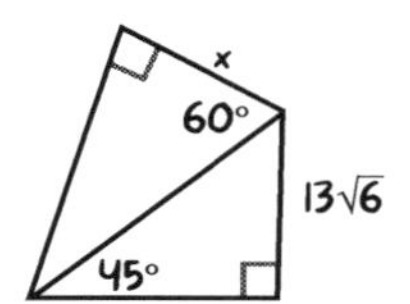

38.

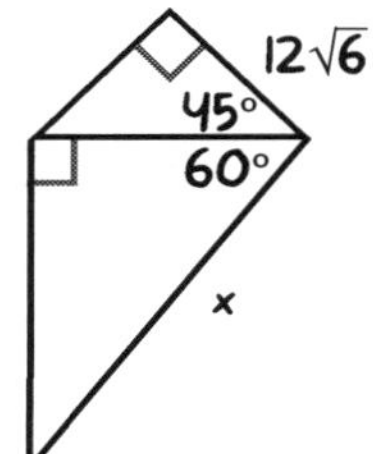

39.

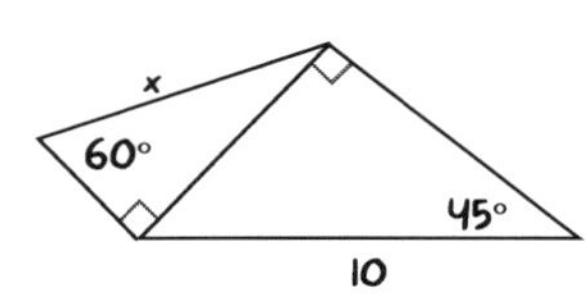

40.

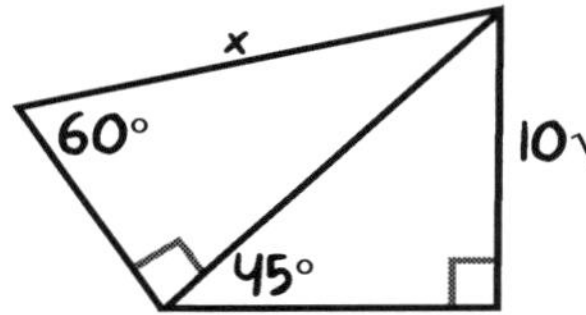

41.

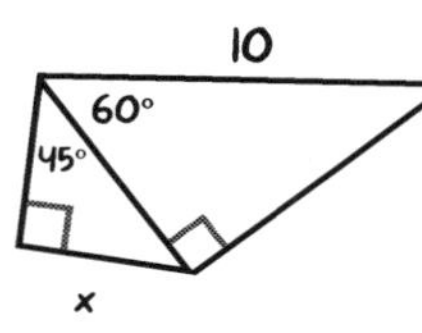

42.

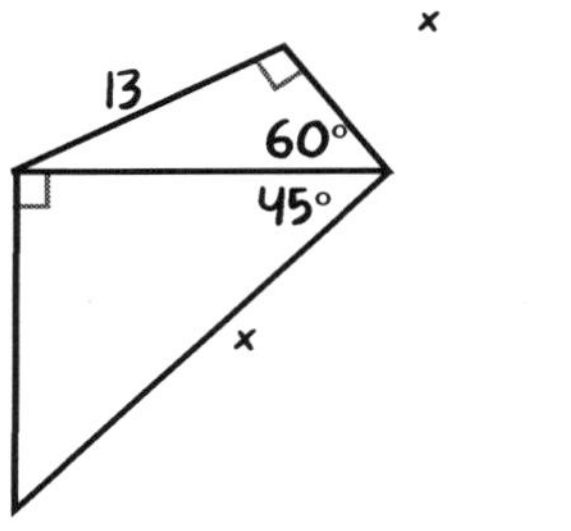

43.

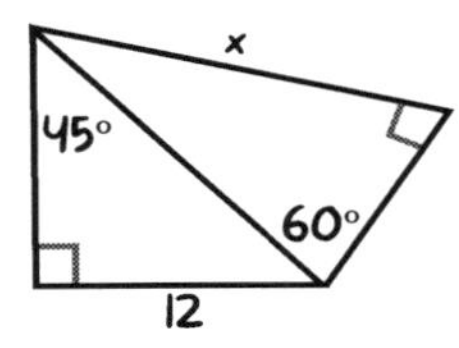

44.

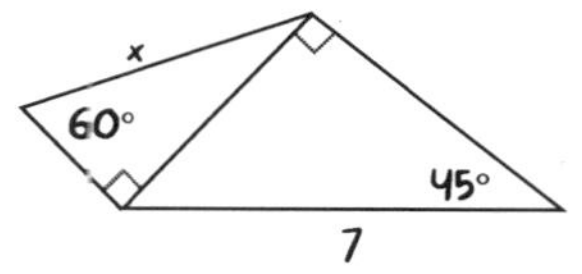

45.

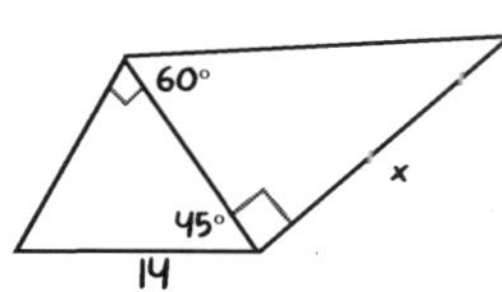

46.

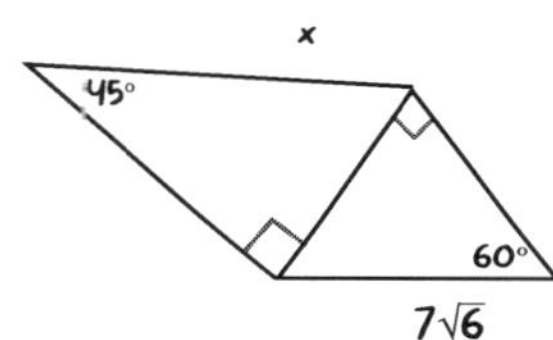

47.

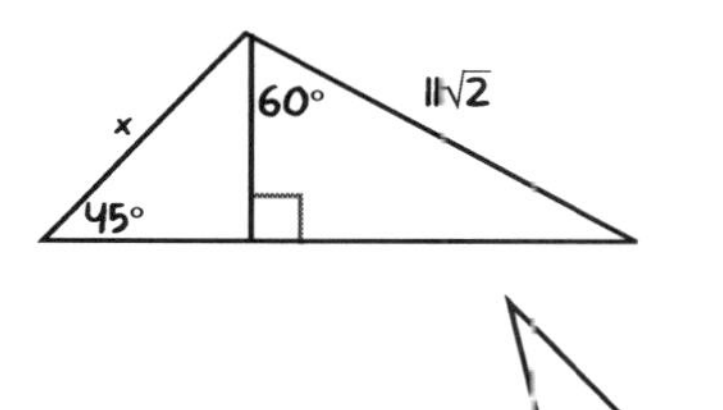

48.

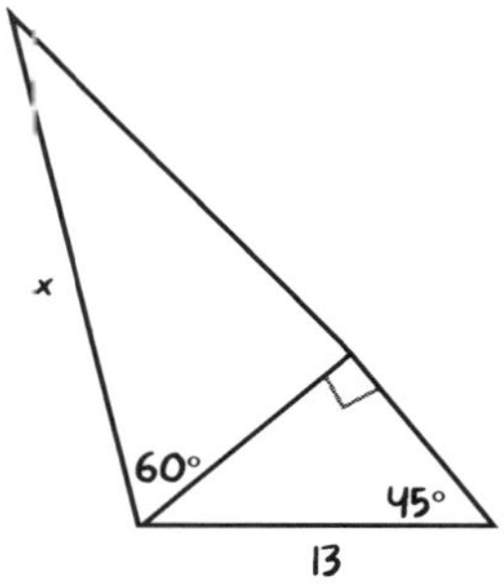

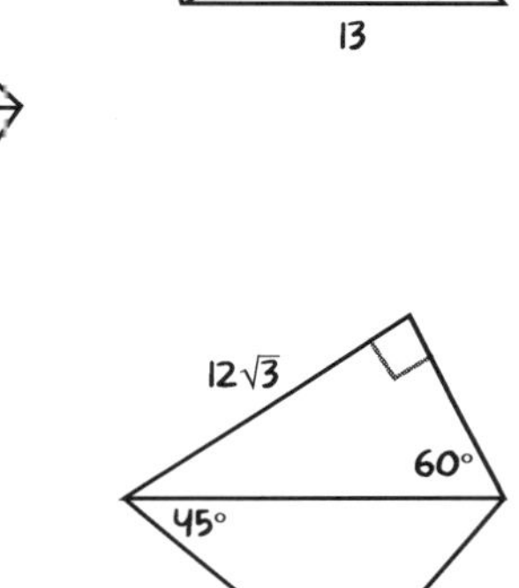

49.

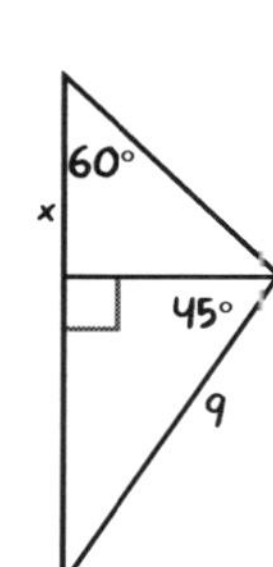

50.

$12\sqrt{3}$, 60°, 45°, x

In Chapter 3, we learned about the 45-45-90 right triangle.

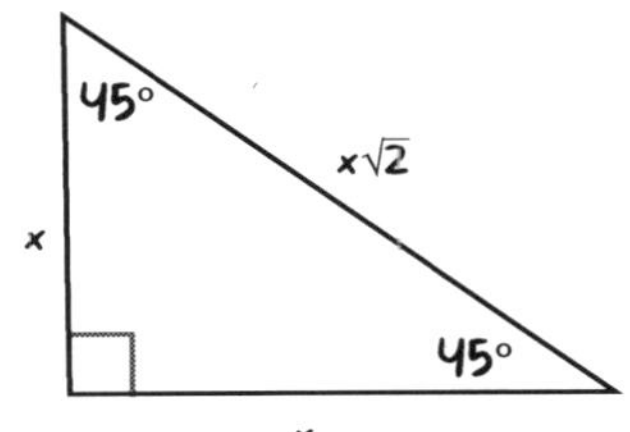

This can also be written as →

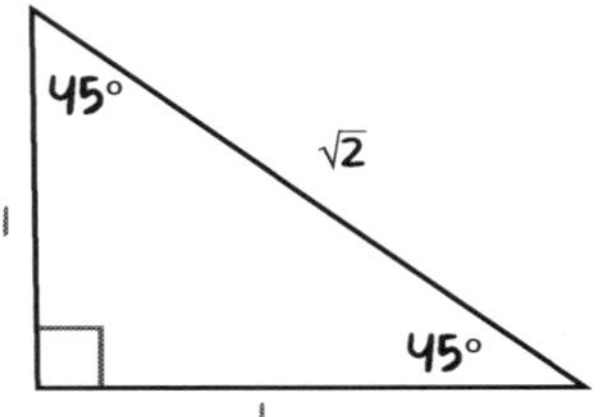

In this chapter, we will derive the values of sine, cosine, and tangent for 0°, 30°, 45°, 60° and 90°.

Let's start with finding the sine, cosine, and tangent values for 45° by using this diagram.

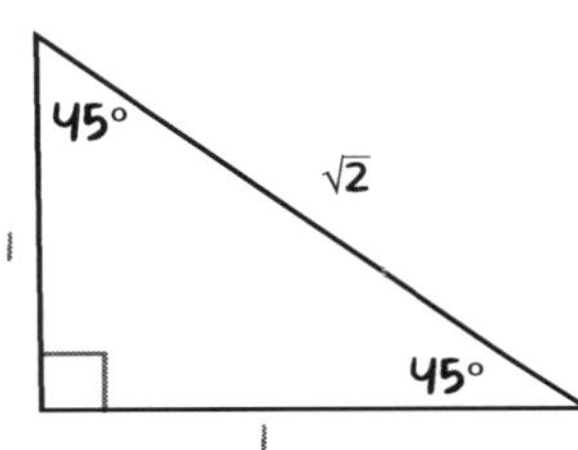

Recall that $\sin = \dfrac{\text{opposite}}{\text{hypotenuse}}$, so $\sin(45°) = \dfrac{1}{\sqrt{2}}$

Recall that $\cos = \dfrac{\text{adjacent}}{\text{hypotenuse}}$, so $\cos(45°) = \dfrac{1}{\sqrt{2}}$

Recall that $\tan(\theta) = \dfrac{\sin(\theta)}{\cos(\theta)} = \dfrac{\text{opposite}}{\text{adjacent}}$, $\tan(45°) = \dfrac{1}{1} = 1$

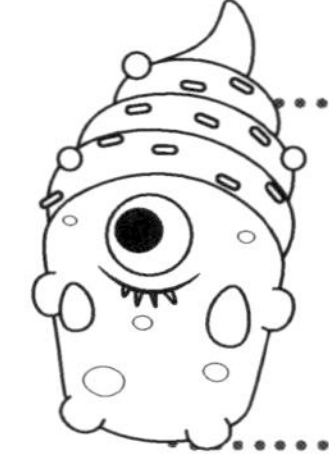

Awesome!

Let's find the values of sine, cosine, and tangent for 30° and 60° using what we learned about the 30-60-90 right triangle.

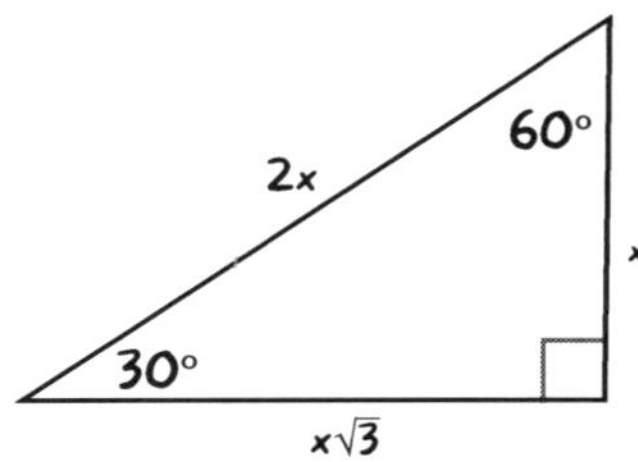

This can also be written as →

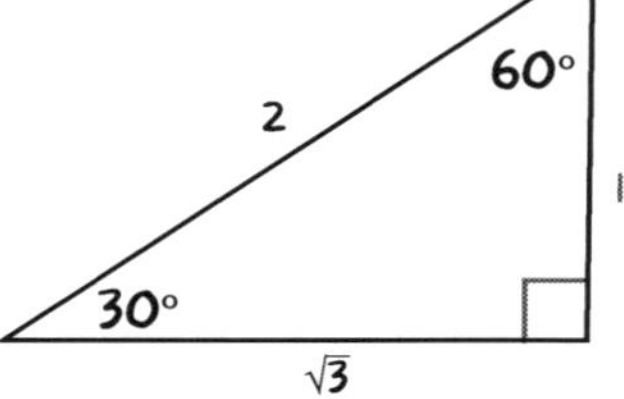

Let's find sine, cosine, and tangent values for 60° and 90° by using this diagram.

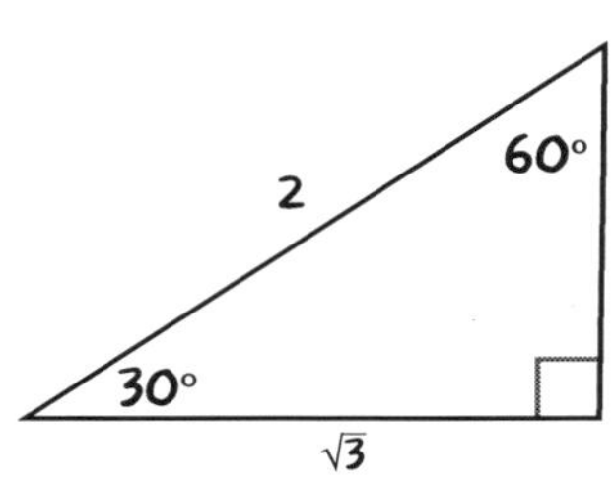

Recall that $\sin = \frac{\text{opposite}}{\text{hypotenuse}}$, so $\sin(60°) = \frac{\sqrt{3}}{2}$

Recall that $\cos = \frac{\text{adjacent}}{\text{hypotenuse}}$, so $\cos(60°) = \frac{1}{2}$

Recall that $\tan(\theta) = \frac{\sin(\theta)}{\cos(\theta)} = \frac{\text{opposite}}{\text{adjacent}}$, $\tan(60°) = \frac{\sqrt{3}}{1} = \sqrt{3}$

Recall that $\sin = \frac{\text{opposite}}{\text{hypotenuse}}$, so $\sin(30°) = \frac{1}{2}$

Recall that $\cos = \frac{\text{adjacent}}{\text{hypotenuse}}$, so $\cos(30°) = \frac{\sqrt{3}}{2}$

Recall that $\tan(\theta) = \frac{\sin(\theta)}{\cos(\theta)} = \frac{\text{opposite}}{\text{adjacent}}$, $\tan(30°) = \frac{1}{\sqrt{3}} = \frac{1}{\sqrt{3}} \times \frac{\sqrt{3}}{\sqrt{3}} = \frac{\sqrt{3}}{3}$

We just derived the following values.

	30°	45°	60°
sin	$\frac{1}{2}$	$\frac{1}{\sqrt{2}}$	$\frac{\sqrt{3}}{2}$
cos	$\frac{\sqrt{3}}{2}$	$\frac{1}{\sqrt{2}}$	$\frac{1}{2}$
tan	$\frac{1}{\sqrt{3}}$	1	$\sqrt{3}$

Most teachers will **require** you to **memorize** these values. The good news is this table is easy to memorize or derive the values if you forget.

Watch this video to understand the trig function values for 0 and 90 degrees.
https://tinyurl.com/3e4abax9

In the table below, you will see **0°** and **90°** added for sin, cos, and tan. You are expected to memorize all the values in this chart.

θ	0°	30°	45°	60°	90°
sin θ	0	$\frac{1}{2}$	$\frac{\sqrt{2}}{2}$	$\frac{\sqrt{3}}{2}$	1
cos θ	1	$\frac{\sqrt{3}}{2}$	$\frac{\sqrt{2}}{2}$	$\frac{1}{2}$	0
tan θ	0	$\frac{\sqrt{3}}{3}$	1	$\sqrt{3}$	undefined

You are also **required** to know the cosecant, secant, and cotangent trig functions for the angles above. However, this is **easy** to remember. All you need to remember is:

$$\csc\theta = \frac{1}{\sin\theta}$$

$$\sec\theta = \frac{1}{\cos\theta}$$

$$\cot\theta = \frac{1}{\tan\theta}$$

Let's take a look at a few practice examples to make sure we understand how to find the values for cosecant, secant, and cotangent trig functions.

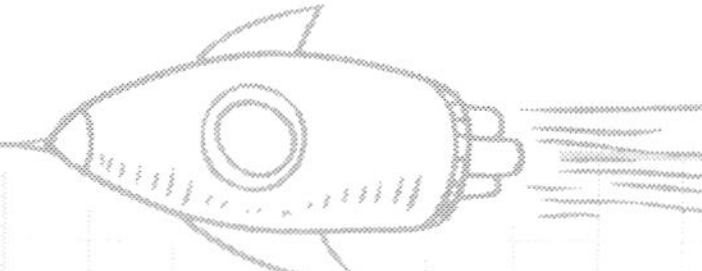

Question 1:

What is cot 60°?

First, let's remember $\cot\theta = \frac{1}{\tan\theta}$, so $\cot 60° = \frac{1}{\tan 60°}$

What is tan 60°? For now, refer back to our table. We know tan 60° s $\sqrt{3}$. So our answer is $\frac{1}{\sqrt{3}}$. **However,** we cannot leave the answer like this. We **must** rationalize the denominator.

$\frac{1}{\sqrt{3}} \times \frac{\sqrt{3}}{\sqrt{3}} = \frac{\sqrt{3}}{3}$ ← That is our answer.

So $\cot 60° = \frac{\sqrt{3}}{3}$.

Question 2:

What is csc 30°?

First, let's remember $\csc\theta = \frac{1}{\sin\theta}$, so $\csc 30° = \frac{1}{\sin 30°}$

What is sin 30°? For now, refer back to our table. We know sin 30° is $\frac{1}{2}$. So our answer is $\frac{1}{\frac{1}{2}}$. We can re-write that as $1 \times \frac{2}{1} = 2$.

So csc 30° = 2.

Let's switch it up. What if the angle provided was in radians?

Question 3:

What is $\cos(\frac{\pi}{3})$?

We must first convert the radians into degrees. If you do not remember how to convert radians to degrees, refer back to Chapter 1, section 1.3.

To convert radians to degrees, multiply by $\frac{180°}{\pi}$

$$\frac{\pi}{3} \times \frac{180°}{\pi} = \frac{180°}{3} = 60°$$

Now that we converted radians to degrees, we can answer the question.

What is $\cos 60°$?

Referring back to our table, the answer is $\frac{1}{2}$.

Question 4:

What is $\cot 0°$?

First, let's remember $\cot \theta = \frac{1}{\tan \theta}$, so $\cot 0° = \frac{1}{\tan 0°}$

What is $\tan 0°$? For now, refer back to our table. We know $\tan 0°$ is 0. If we plug that back into $\frac{1}{0}$ we see the answer is **undefined.** Remember, dividing by 0 results in an **undefined** value.

Let's take a look at this chart again. As stated earlier, you will most likely be required to know all of these values by memory.

θ	0°	30°	45°	60°	90°
sin θ	0	$\frac{1}{2}$	$\frac{\sqrt{2}}{2}$	$\frac{\sqrt{3}}{2}$	1
cos θ	1	$\frac{\sqrt{3}}{2}$	$\frac{\sqrt{2}}{2}$	$\frac{1}{2}$	0
tan θ	0	$\frac{\sqrt{3}}{3}$	1	$\sqrt{3}$	undefined

Thankfully, there's a method to help you easily remember this chart.

Step 1: Draw the following table on a piece of paper.

θ	0°	30°	45°	60°	90°
sin θ					
cos θ					

Step 2: On the first blank row labeled "**Sin**", write the numbers 0 through 4 in sequential order: 0, 1, 2, 3, and 4. On the "**Cos**" row, write these numbers in the opposite order: 4, 3, 2, 1, and 0.

θ	0°	30°	45°	60°	90°
sin θ	0	1	2	3	4
cos θ	4	3	2	1	0

Step 3: Square root each of the numbers.

θ	0°	30°	45°	60°	90°
sin θ	$\sqrt{0}$	$\sqrt{1}$	$\sqrt{2}$	$\sqrt{3}$	$\sqrt{4}$
cos θ	$\sqrt{4}$	$\sqrt{3}$	$\sqrt{2}$	$\sqrt{1}$	$\sqrt{0}$

Step 4: Divide the numbers by 2.

θ	0°	30°	45°	60°	90°
sin θ	$\frac{\sqrt{0}}{2}$	$\frac{\sqrt{1}}{2}$	$\frac{\sqrt{2}}{2}$	$\frac{\sqrt{3}}{2}$	$\frac{\sqrt{4}}{2}$
cos θ	$\frac{\sqrt{4}}{2}$	$\frac{\sqrt{3}}{2}$	$\frac{\sqrt{2}}{2}$	$\frac{\sqrt{1}}{2}$	$\frac{\sqrt{0}}{2}$

Step 5: Simplify where possible.

θ	0°	30°	45°	60°	90°
sin θ	0	$\frac{1}{2}$	$\frac{\sqrt{2}}{2}$	$\frac{\sqrt{3}}{2}$	1
cos θ	1	$\frac{\sqrt{3}}{2}$	$\frac{\sqrt{2}}{2}$	$\frac{1}{2}$	0

Those are the values for sin and cos!

How do you remember the values for tan? Remember $\tan(x)$ is just $\frac{\sin(x)}{\cos(x)}$ so you can easily fill in the values for tan.

$$\tan(0°) = \frac{0}{1} = 0$$

$$\tan(30°) = \frac{1}{2} \div \frac{\sqrt{3}}{2} = \frac{1}{2} \times \frac{2}{\sqrt{3}} = \frac{2}{2\sqrt{3}} = \frac{2}{2\sqrt{3}} \times \frac{2\sqrt{3}}{2\sqrt{3}} = \frac{4\sqrt{3}}{(4)(3)} = \frac{4\sqrt{3}}{12} = \frac{\sqrt{3}}{3}$$

$$\tan(45°) = \frac{\sqrt{2}}{2} \div \frac{\sqrt{2}}{2} = \frac{\sqrt{2}}{2} \times \frac{2}{\sqrt{2}} = \frac{2\sqrt{2}}{2\sqrt{2}} = 1$$

$$\tan(60°) = \frac{\sqrt{3}}{2} \div \frac{1}{2} = \frac{\sqrt{3}}{2} \times \frac{2}{1} = \frac{2\sqrt{3}}{2} = \sqrt{3}$$

$$\tan(90°) = \frac{1}{0} = \text{Undefined}$$

Let's add those values to the chart by adding another row for tan.

θ	0°	30°	45°	60°	90°
sin θ	0	$\frac{1}{2}$	$\frac{\sqrt{2}}{2}$	$\frac{\sqrt{3}}{2}$	1
cos θ	1	$\frac{\sqrt{3}}{2}$	$\frac{\sqrt{2}}{2}$	$\frac{1}{2}$	0
tan θ	0	$\frac{\sqrt{3}}{3}$	1	$\sqrt{3}$	undefined

Once you practice this method several times on a piece of paper, you will be an expert in no time!

Now that you know these values and also remember how to convert angles in radians to degrees, it's time to practice. Work through these problems carefully. It's easy to make careless mistakes.

Angle θ				
Degrees	**Radians**	**sin θ**	**cos θ**	**tan θ**
0	0	0	1	0
30	$\frac{\pi}{6}$	$\frac{1}{2}$	$\frac{\sqrt{3}}{2}$	$\frac{1}{\sqrt{3}}$
45	$\frac{\pi}{4}$	$\frac{1}{\sqrt{2}}$	$\frac{1}{\sqrt{2}}$	1
60	$\frac{\pi}{3}$	$\frac{\sqrt{3}}{2}$	$\frac{1}{2}$	$\sqrt{3}$
90	$\frac{\pi}{2}$	1	0	undefined

Chapter 4 Quiz

Directions: Find the value of each trig function. Do **not** use your calculator.

1. $\cos 30°$
2. $\tan 90°$
3. $\tan \frac{\pi}{4}$
4. $\tan 0$
5. $\sin \frac{\pi}{6}$
6. $\sec \frac{\pi}{6}$
7. $\tan 30°$
8. $\tan \frac{\pi}{2}$
9. $\sec \mathbf{0}$
10. $\cot 60°$
11. $\sin 60°$
12. $\cos \frac{\pi}{6}$
13. $\csc 0$
14. $\sec 60°$
15. $\sec 30°$
16. $\cot 0°$
17. $\sec \frac{\pi}{2}$
18. $\tan 60°$
19. $\csc \frac{\pi}{6}$
20. $\sec 45°$

Chapter 4 Quiz

21. sin 90°

22. cos 0°

23. cos 45°

24. cos $\frac{\pi}{2}$

25. cos $\frac{\pi}{6}$

26. cot 45°

27. cos 0°

28. sin 90°

29. csc 30°

30. tan 45°

31. sec 45°

32. sec 90°

33. csc 90°

34. sec 60°

35. cos 30°

36. tan 0°

37. tan 60°

38. tan 30°

39. cos 90°

40. cot 45°

Chapter 4 Quiz

41. $\cos 60^\circ$

42. $\csc 0^\circ$

43. $\cos 45^\circ$

44. $\sin 30^\circ$

45. $\csc 45^\circ$

46. $\cot 0^\circ$

47. $\csc 60^\circ$

48. $\sin 45^\circ$

49. $\sec 30^\circ$

50. $\sin 0^\circ$

51. $\cot 90^\circ$

52. $\cot 30^\circ$

53. $\cot 60^\circ$

54. $\sin 60^\circ$

55. $\sec 0^\circ$

56. $\tan 90^\circ$

57. $\sec \frac{\pi}{3}$

58. $\tan \frac{\pi}{2}$

59. $\sec \frac{\pi}{6}$

60. $\cot \frac{\pi}{4}$

61. $\cot \frac{\pi}{6}$

Chapter 4 Quiz

62. $\sin \frac{\pi}{2}$

63. $\tan \frac{\pi}{3}$

64. $\sin \frac{\pi}{6}$

65. $\cos \frac{\pi}{6}$

66. $\csc \frac{\pi}{2}$

67. $\sin \frac{\pi}{4}$

68. $\csc \frac{\pi}{6}$

69. $\sin \frac{\pi}{3}$

70. $\cos \frac{\pi}{4}$

71. $\cot \frac{\pi}{3}$

72. $\cos \frac{\pi}{2}$

73. $\cot \frac{\pi}{2}$

74. $\sec \frac{\pi}{4}$

75. $\csc \frac{\pi}{4}$

76. $\tan \frac{\pi}{6}$

77. $\csc \frac{\pi}{3}$

78. $\tan \frac{\pi}{4}$

79. $\sec \frac{\pi}{2}$

80. $\cos \frac{\pi}{3}$

Section 5.1: Reference Angle

In the previous chapter, you learned the trig function values for **sin, cos, tan, csc, sec,** and **cot** for 0°, 30°, 45°, 60° and 90°.

In Chapter 5, we will learn how to **evaluate** a trig function at an angle **between** 90° and 360°. In order to solve these types of problems, we must be able to determine the **reference angle.** Reference angles make it possible to evaluate trigonometric functions for angles outside the first quadrant.

A reference angle is the acute angle (less than or equal to 90°) that an angle θ makes with the x-axis when it is projected onto one of the coordinate axes. It provides a simplified way to determine the trigonometric values for any angle, regardless of its location in the coordinate system.

* The reference angle is always positive and lies between 0° and 90°.

Determining Reference Angles: To find the reference angle for a given angle θ in **degrees**, we can use these following rules.

Quadrant I ($0° < \theta < 90°$): The angle itself is its reference angle.

Quadrant II ($90° < \theta < 180°$): The reference angle is 180° minus the given angle.

Quadrant III ($180° < \theta < 270°$): The reference angle is the given angle minus 180°.

Quadrant IV ($270° < \theta < 360°$): The reference angle is 360° minus the given angle.

Quadrant II	**Quadrant I**
Reference angle = 180 - Given angle	Reference angle = Given angle
Quadrant III	**Quadrant IV**
Reference angle = Given angle - 180	Reference angle = 360 - Given angle

Here's another diagram to visualize.

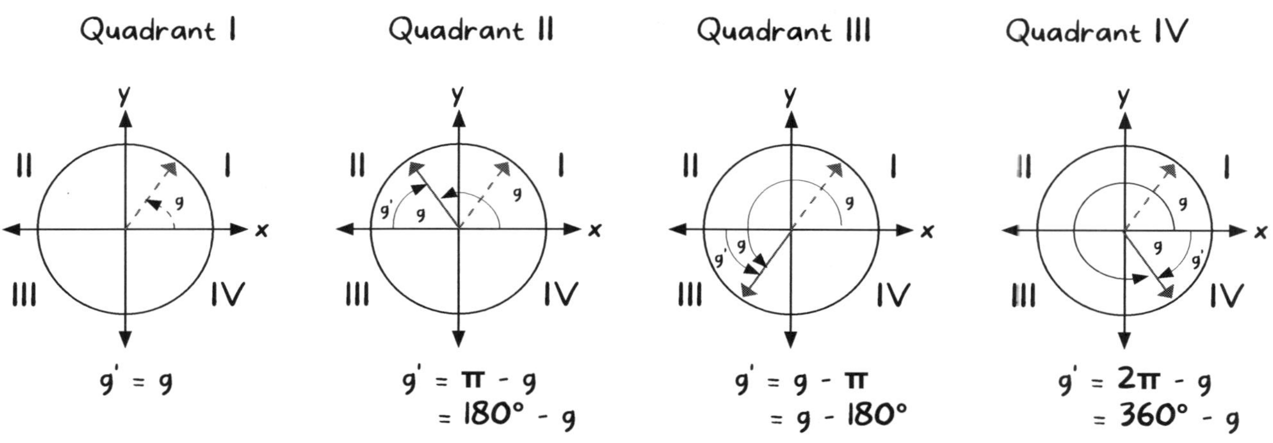

Take a look at this diagram below that has an angle of 135°. We know 135° belongs in Quadrant II and we can use the rule 180° - 135° to get the reference angle which is 45°.

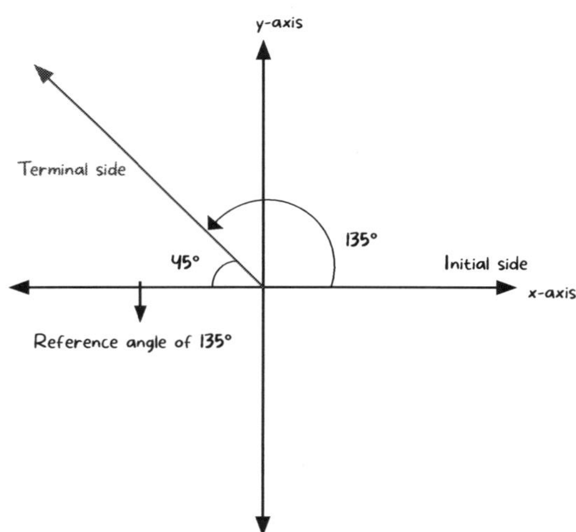

Just to cover our terminology, let's define **initial side** and **terminal side** as noted on the diagram above. In trigonometry, when discussing angles in their standard position, two key terms come into play: the initial side and the terminal side.

The initial side of an angle in standard position is the starting position of the angle. When an angle is in standard position, its vertex is located at the origin of the coordinate plane, and the initial side lies along the positive x-axis. This side remains **fixed** and does **not** move. It serves as the **starting** point from which the rotation of the angle begins.

The terminal side is where the angle ends after rotating from the initial side. The position of the terminal side depends on the magnitude and direction of the angle:

* Positive angles rotate counterclockwise from the initial side.
* Negative angles rotate clockwise from the initial side.

How do we find a reference angle for a negative degree?

We need to follow two steps.

Step 1: **Make the Angle Positive**

For a negative angle, add 360° repeatedly until you get a positive angle between 0° and 360°. Example: For -450°, add 360°. You'll get -90°. Add 360° again, and you get 270°.

Step 2: **Find the Reference Angle**

The same exact rules apply that you learned above. Take your positive angle (we call this the **coterminal angle**).

If the positive angle is in Quadrant I (0° to 90°): It's already the reference angle.
If in Quadrant II (90° to 180°): Subtract the angle from 180°.
If in Quadrant III (180° to 270°): Subtract 180° from the angle.
If in Quadrant IV (270° to 360°): Subtract the angle from 360°.

In this case, 270° falls in Quadrant III. 270° - 180° = 90°.

The reference angle for -450° is 90°.

How do we find a reference angle for an angle exceeding 360 degrees?

If an angle is more than 360°, it means it has spun past a full circle. To get its reference angle, bring it between 0° and 360° by **subtracting** 360°. For example, for an angle of 400°, take away 360° to get 40°.

Then follow the rules as usual based on the quadrant. In this case, 40° is in Quadrant I, meaning it is already the reference angle.

What is the reference angle of 950°? First, we need to subtract 950° - 360° = 590°. This is still more than 360°, so subtract that number again by 360°.

590° - 360° = 230°. We know that 230° falls in Quadrant III, so we need to apply the rule **subtract the given angle by 180°.**

230° - 180° = 50°. The reference angle is 50°.

Take a look at these guided practice problems before you solve the quest ons on your own.

Example 1:

What is the reference angle of 485°?

485° - 360° = 125°.

125° falls in Quadrant II, which states we need to follow the rule **"180° minus the given angle"**. 180° - 125° = 55°.

55° is our reference angle.

Example 2:

What is the reference angle of -100°?

-100° + 360°= 260°.

260° falls in Quadrant III, so we need to apply the rule **subtract the given angle by 180°.**

260° - 180° = 80°.

80° is our reference angle.

Example 3:

What is the reference angle of 355°?

355° falls in Quadrant IV. The rule is **360 minus the given angle.**

360° - 355° = 5°

5° is our reference angle.

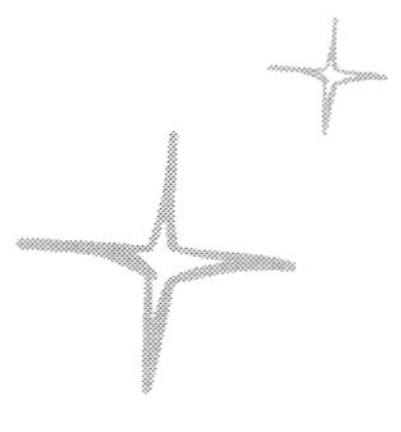

Section 5.1 Quiz

Directions: Find the reference angle. Show your work on a separate piece of paper.

1. 560°
2. 700°
3. 245°
4. 710°
5. 195°
6. -510°
7. -120°
8. 520°
9. -610°
10. 535°
11. 480°
12. -620°
13. 685°
14. -100°
15. 640°
16. 160°
17. 565°
18. -575°
19. -650°
20. 500°
21. 620°
22. 130°
23. -265°
24. 430°
25. -605°
26. 385°
27. -165°
28. 485°
29. -530°
30. -680°
31. 655°
32. 525°
33. -420°
34. -110°
35. 570°
36. -425°
37. -440°
38. -225°
39. 330°
40. 110°
41. 475°
42. 355°
43. 315°
44. -470°
45. -275°
46. 530°
47. 100°
48. -550°
49. 650°
50. 600°
51. 150°
52. -560°
53. 125°
54. 610°
55. 660°
56. -580°
57. 135°
58. -350°
59. -245°
60. -460°
61. -590°
62. 345°
63. -370°
64. -485°

Section 5.1 Quiz

65. -355°
66. 405°
67. 555°
68. 705°
69. -435°
70. -455°
71. -700°
72. -600°
73. 545°
74. -130°
75. -400°
76. -695°
77. 390°
78. 305°
79. 120°
80. -290°
81. 170°
82. 590°
83. -570°
84. 310°
85. 350°
86. 395°
87. 580°
88. -405°
89. -585°
90. -160°
91. 190°
92. -410°
93. -330°
94. 410°
95. 510°
96. 595°
97. -635°
98. 440°
99. -340°
100. -660°
101. -260°
102. 320°
103. 130°
104. -430°
105. 315°
106. -700°
107. -210°
108. 230°
109. -225°
110. -300°
111. 470°
112. -370°
113. -495°
114. 600°
115. 550°
116. -400°
117. 110°
118. 350°
119. -470°
120. -440°
121. 285°
122. 330°
123. -530°
124. -115°
125. -510°
126. -555°
127. -525°
128. -105°
129. 115°
130. 485°
131. -620°
132. 410°

Section 5.1 Quiz

133. -585°
134. 250°
135. 220°
136. -135°
137. -640°
138. -185°
139. 155°
140. -350°
141. -190°
142. 570°
143. 310°
144. 240°
145. -140°
146. 595°
147. 715°
148. 590°
149. 390°
150. 565°
151. -490°
152. -705°
153. -590°
154. 480°
155. 205°
156. 160°
157. -250°
158. 420°
159. 685°
160. -595°
161. 440°
162. -645°
163. 705°
164. -100°
165. -110°
166. 425°
167. -420°
168. 700°
169. -325°
170. -280°
171. -680°
172. 560°
173. 300°
174. -600°
175. -120°
176. -255°
177. 430°
178. 455°
179. -380°
180. -345°
181. -455°
182. 395°
183. 545°
184. -625°
185. -385°
186. -230°
187. 120°
188. 170°
189. -170°
190. -545°
191. -375°
192. 660°
193. 150°
194. -160°
195. 520°
196. -355°
197. -570°
198. 510°
199. 240°
200. -245°

Section 5.2: Solving Trig Functions for Quadrants II, III, and IV

In Chapter 4, we covered the values of trigonometric functions for particular angles. By now, these values should be familiar to you. For your convenience, we've provided a reference chart below.

θ	0°	30°	45°	60°	90°
sin θ	0	$\frac{1}{2}$	$\frac{\sqrt{2}}{2}$	$\frac{\sqrt{3}}{2}$	1
cos θ	1	$\frac{\sqrt{3}}{2}$	$\frac{\sqrt{2}}{2}$	$\frac{1}{2}$	0
tan θ	0	$\frac{\sqrt{3}}{3}$	1	$\sqrt{3}$	undefined

$$\csc\theta = \frac{1}{\sin\theta}$$

$$\sec\theta = \frac{1}{\cos\theta}$$

$$\cot\theta = \frac{1}{\tan\theta}$$

Earlier in this chapter, we also discussed how to determine a reference angle. With this foundation, we're now equipped to **compute** trigonometric functions for angles in any of the four quadrants.

We need to follow **three steps** when evaluating a trig function.

Step 1: Determine the reference angle.

Step 2: Use the Reference Angle to find the trig function value.

Step 3: Assign the Correct Sign (Positive or Negative) Based on the Quadrant.

*We did **not** cover the signs on a quadrant. Let's do that now!

All trig functions (sin, cos, and tan) are positive in **Quadrant I.**

Only **Sine** is positive in **Quadrant II.**
Only **Tangent** is positive in **Quadrant III.**
Only **Cosine** is positive in **Quadrant IV.**

We can use the acronym **"All Students Take Calculus"** to remember the signs of the trig functions in each quadrant:

All: All trig functions are positive in Quadrant I.
Students: Only Sine is positive in Quadrant II.
Take: Only Tangent is positive in Quadrant III.
Calculus: Only Cosine is positive in Quadrant IV.

How about cosecant, secant, and cotangent?

They have the **same signs** as sin, cos, and tan respectively. Here's a chart to put it all together.

Quadrant	sin θ	cos θ	tan θ	sec θ	csc θ	cot θ
I	+	+	+	+	+	+
II	+	-	-	-	+	-
III	-	-	+	-	-	+
IV	-	+	-	+	-	-

Try not to get frustrated! This table is easy to remember

* if you know the acronym **"All Students Take Calculus"**
* cosecant (csc) is the reciprocal of sine (sin), so they share the same sign.
* secant (sec) is the reciprocal of cosine (cos), so they also share the same sign.
* cotangent (cot) is the reciprocal of tangent (tan), so they have the same sign too.

Let's work on a few practice problems together.

Question 1:

What is sec 600°?

Let's follow the three steps.

Step 1: Determine the reference angle.
Step 2: Use the Reference Angle to find the trig function value.
Step 3: Assign the Correct Sign (Positive or Negative) Based on the Quadrant.

What is our reference angle? Since this angle is greater than 360°, we need to keep subtracting it until we have an angle between 0° and 360°.

$$600° - 360° = 240°$$

240° falls in Quadrant III, and we need to use the rule **Given Angle minus 180°.**
*If you need a refresher, revisit section 5.1.

$$240° - 180° = 60°$$

So, 60° is our reference angle.

Let's move on to **Step 2**.

Instead of sec 600°, we can now ask ourself what is sec 60°?

Remember $\sec\theta = \frac{1}{\cos\theta}$, so $\sec 60° = \frac{1}{\cos 60°}$. Do you remember what cos 60° is?
You should have that memorized. If not, the table is at the beginning of this section.

cos 60° is $\frac{1}{2}$

So we have cos 60° $= \frac{1}{\cos 60°} = \frac{1}{\frac{1}{2}} = 1 \div \frac{1}{2} = 1 \times \frac{2}{1} = \frac{2}{1} = 2.$

Let's move on to **Step 3** to assign the correct sign (positive or negative).

Recall 240° falls in Quadrant III. So I can check my table for $\sec\theta$, Quadrant III.
There is a **negative sign** there.

So the answer is -2.

Here is a great overview video for a general trigonometry refresher if you prefer videos! https://t.ly/TPHV4

Question 2:

What is tan 135°?

Let's follow the three steps.

Step 1: Determine the reference angle.
Step 2: Use the Reference Angle to find the trig function value.
Step 3: Assign the Correct Sign (Positive or Negative) Based on the Quadrant.

What is our reference angle?

135° falls in Quadrant II, and we need to use the rule **180 minus the given angle.**

$$180° - 135° = 45°$$

So, 45° is our reference angle.

Let's move on to **Step 2**.

Instead of tan 135°, we can now ask ourself what is tan 45°?

Do you remember what tan 45° is? You should have that memorized. If not, the table is at the beginning of this section.

tan 45° is 1.

Let's move on to **Step 3** to assign the correct sign (positive or negative).

Recall 135° falls in Quadrant II. So I can check my table for tan θ, Quadrant II. There is a **negative sign** there.

So the answer is -1.

Question 3:

What is csc -630°?

Let's follow the three steps.

Step 1: Determine the reference angle.
Step 2: Use the Reference Angle to find the trig function value.
Step 3: Assign the Correct Sign (Positive or Negative) Based on the Quadrant.

What is our reference angle?

Since -630° is negative, we need to keep adding 360° to it until we get a value between 0° and 360°.

$-630° + 360° = -270°$

$-270° + 360° = 90°$, that already falls in Quadrant I meaning 90° is also our reference angle.

Let's move on to **Step 2**.

Instead of csc -630°, we can now ask ourself what is csc 90°?

Remember $\csc \theta = \frac{1}{\sin \theta}$, so $\csc 90° = \frac{1}{\sin 90°}$. Do you remember what sin 90° is?

You should have that memorized. If not, the table is at the beginning of this section.

sin 90° is 1.

Let's move on to **Step 3** to assign the correct sign (positive or negative).

90° falls in Quadrant I. All trig functions are positive in Quadrant I.

So the answer is 1.

Question 4:

What is cot 990°?

Let's follow the three steps.

Step 1: Determine the reference angle.
Step 2: Use the Reference Angle to find the trig function value.
Step 3: Assign the Correct Sign (Positive or Negative) Based on the Quadrant.

What is our reference angle? Since this angle is greater than 360°, we need to keep subtracting it until we have an angle between 0° and 360°.

$990° - 360° = 630°$

$630° - 360° = 270°$

270° falls in Quadrant III, and we need to use the rule **Given Angle minus 180°.**

So, 90° is our reference angle.

Let's move on to **Step 2**.

Instead of cot 990°, we can now ask ourself what is cot 90°?

Remember $\cot\theta = \dfrac{1}{\tan\theta}$, so $\cot 90° = \dfrac{1}{\tan 90°}$. Do you remember what tan 90° is?
You should have that memorized. If not, the table is at the beginning of this section.

tan 90° is **undefined** or $\dfrac{1}{0}$.

So we have $\cot 90° = \dfrac{1}{\tan 90°} = \dfrac{1}{\frac{1}{0}} = 1 \div \dfrac{1}{0} = 1 \times \dfrac{0}{1} = \dfrac{0}{1} = 0$.

Our answer is 0°.

You are ready to rock and roll!

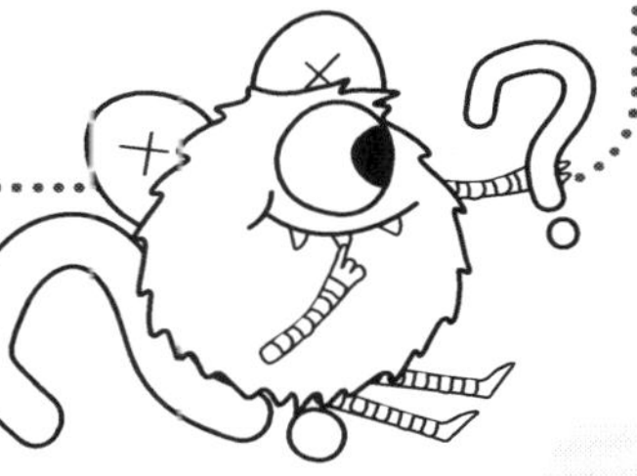

Section 5.2 Quiz

Directions: Find the value of each of these trigonometric functions. You do **not** need a calculator for any of these problems. Work on a piece of paper. Double check your work. Students make careless mistakes with these problems.

1. tan 855°
2. cot -60°
3. sin -60°
4. csc 120°
5. cos -300°
6. sec -585°
7. tan 60°
8. sin 450°
9. cos 495°
10. csc -810°
11. csc 420°
12. cos -900°
13. csc -630°
14. sin -30°
15. sin -945°
16. cos 780°
17. sin -660°
18. csc 1020°
19. cot 840°
20. cot -765°
21. cos 750°
22. csc -450°
23. cot 690°
24. sec -225°
25. cot 315°
26. sec -510°
27. sec 30°
28. tan 600°
29. cot 45°
30. sec 300°
31. sin 690°
32. cot 630°
33. cot -510°
34. csc 765°
35. sec 660°
36. sec -60°
37. sin -1020°
38. cot -675°
39. sec 420°
40. sec 1035°
41. cos -225°
42. csc -360°
43. sin 210°
44. cot 420°
45. sec -360°
46. sin 315°
47. sin -840°
48. cot 765°
49. cos 480°
50. cos -330°
51. sin 945°
52. sin -90°
53. sec 120°
54. csc -390°
55. cot 990°
56. cot 600°
57. sec 600°
58. tan -135°
59. csc 900°
60. csc 1035°

Section 5.2 Quiz

61. csc -780°
62. cos -630°
63. tan 150°
64. csc 690°
65. sec 675°
66. sin -330°
67. sec -690°
68. tan 990°
69. cot 180°
70. cos 960°
71. cot -315°
72. tan -210°
73. csc -750°
74. cos -690°
75. cot 945°
76. tan 960°
77. sec -300°
78. sec -930°
79. tan 630°
80. cos -495°
81. csc 780°
82. sec -150°
83. cos 870°
84. csc 330°
85. tan 225°
86. tan 0°
87. csc 90°
88. cos -765°
89. csc 240°
90. cot 510°
91. cos 855°
92. sec -315°
93. csc -720°
94. csc -150°
95. cot -1050°
96. sec 810°
97. tan -945°
98. cot -120°
99. sec -900°
100. cos -855°
101. tan -450°
102. cot -1035°
103. cos -1020°
104. cot -960°
105. tan 690°
106. cos -930°
107. tan -1050°
108. csc -990°
109. sin 675°
110. tan 30°
111. tan -1020°
112. tan 300°
113. cot 810°
114. tan 45°
115. sin -690°
116. cot -990°
117. tan 780°
118. tan -1035°
119. tan -300°
120. cot 765°

Section 5.2 Quiz

121. sin 570°
122. cos -300°
123. sin -780°
124. cot 150°
125. cos -180°
126. sin -120°
127. cot 1020°
128. cot -660°
129. cos 210°
130. cot 495°
131. tan -990°
132. cot 930°
133. sin -765°
134. sec 0°
135. tan 990°
136. cot 870°
137. sec -210°
138. sin 315°
139. tan -120°
140. sec -180°
141. csc 600°
142. sec -270°
143. cot -315°
144. tan 600°
145. tan 1035°
146. tan -480°
147. sin -510°
148. sec -600°
149. sin 0°
150. cot 855°
151. cos 675°
152. cot -45°
153. cot -150°
154. sin -585°
155. sec 420°
156. sec 840°
157. tan 90°
158. tan -180°
159. csc -750°
160. csc 585°
161. tan -690°
162. csc -540°
163. tan -210°
164. sec 600°
165. sec 675°
166. sin 45°
167. csc -765°
168. csc 945°
169. sec -930°
170. sin -405°
171. csc 570°
172. csc 135°
173. sin -900°
174. sin -30°
175. tan -900°
176. csc -405°
177. cos 0°
178. sec 315°
179. cot -1050°
180. csc -570°

Section 5.2 Quiz

181. $\sin 540^\circ$
182. $\sec -945^\circ$
183. $\sin 495^\circ$
184. $\sin 855^\circ$
185. $\csc -30^\circ$
186. $\cot 600^\circ$
187. $\cot 660^\circ$
188. $\sec 510^\circ$
189. $\csc 480^\circ$
190. $\cos -420^\circ$
191. $\tan 1050^\circ$
192. $\sin 225^\circ$
193. $\csc -600^\circ$
194. $\cos -270^\circ$
195. $\cot -405^\circ$
196. $\sec -405^\circ$
197. $\cot 120^\circ$
198. $\sin 405^\circ$
199. $\csc -945^\circ$
200. $\cot 930^\circ$
201. $\cos 30^\circ$
202. $\cos -315^\circ$
203. $\tan 420^\circ$
204. $\cot -1035^\circ$
205. $\csc 135^\circ$
206. $\tan -150^\circ$
207. $\cos 990^\circ$
208. $\cos 495^\circ$
209. $\sin -570^\circ$
210. $\cot -930^\circ$
211. $\csc -240^\circ$
212. $\cot -45^\circ$
213. $\cos -900^\circ$
214. $\cot -810^\circ$
215. $\csc 30^\circ$
216. $\sec 750^\circ$
217. $\sin 1035$
218. $\tan -60^\circ$
219. $\sec -720^\circ$
220. $\csc -960^\circ$
221. $\cot 600^\circ$
222. $\sin -330^\circ$
223. $\cos -540^\circ$
224. $\sin -420^\circ$
225. $\tan 945^\circ$
226. $\sin 225^\circ$
227. $\sin -720^\circ$
228. $\sin -1050^\circ$
229. $\cot 870^\circ$
230. $\sin 630^\circ$
231. $\cos 480^\circ$
232. $\cot -990^\circ$
233. $\csc -390^\circ$
234. $\csc 570^\circ$
235. $\csc 600^\circ$
236. $\cos 510^\circ$
237. $\cot -780^\circ$
238. $\cot -720^\circ$
239. $\cot -960^\circ$
240. $\cot -750^\circ$

Section 5.2 Quiz

241. csc -270°
242. sec -270°
243. sec -900°
244. cot 495°
245. csc 240°
246. tan 120°
247. csc -225°
248. cos -420°
249. sec 930°
250. sin 315°
251. cos 150°
252. csc -60°
253. sin -495°
254. sin 960°
255. sin 720°
256. tan -135°
257. sin 405°
258. cot -600°
259. csc -135°
260. tan 585°
261. cot -180°
262. csc -1050°
263. csc -540°
264. sec -90°
265. sec 960°
266. csc -720°
267. cot -315°
268. cot 210°
269. cot -390°
270. tan 180°
271. sin -810°
272. tan -1050°
273. sin -240°
274. sin 495°
275. sec -300°
276. sec 780°
277. sec 0°
278. csc 90°
279. cos -990°
280. tan 840°
281. sec 120°
282. cos 930°
283. sin 360°
284. csc 450°
285. tan -570°
286. csc -930°
287. tan 135°
288. csc 0°
289. sec 450°
290. sec 330°
291. cot -495°
292. tan -810°
293. sec 810°
294. csc 855°
295. tan 990°
296. csc -630°
297. tan -300°
298. csc 60°
299. csc -120°
300. sec -930°

Section 6.1: The Law of Sines

Law of Sines:
Imagine you have an **oblique** triangle (a triangle with no right triangle) with sides of lengths a, b, and c, and the angles opposite these sides are A, B, and C respectively.

The Law of Sines states that the **ratio** of a side length to the sine of its opposite angle is the same for all three sides of the triangle.

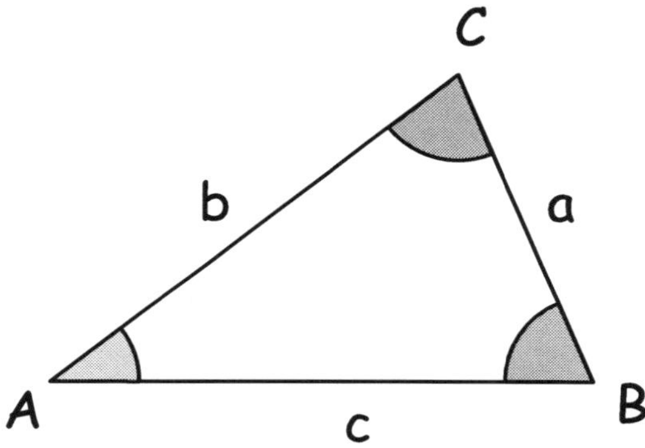

Mathematically:

$$\frac{a}{\sin(A)} = \frac{b}{\sin(B)} = \frac{c}{\sin(C)}$$

Why is this useful?
If you know the lengths of two sides of a triangle and the measure of one of the non-included angles, you can use the Law of Sines to find other angles or sides.

Let's take a look at a few practice examples to understand how to use the Law of Sines formula.

Example 1:

What is $m\angle C$?

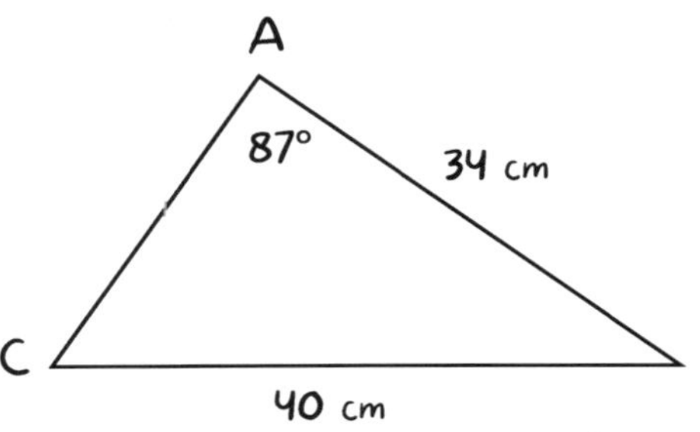

We need to find the angle measure of C. We can use the law of sines to solve this problem.

$\frac{40\text{ cm}}{\sin(87^\circ)} = \frac{34\text{ cm}}{\sin(C)}$ ← Cross multiply to get $40 \times \sin(\theta) = 34 \times \sin(87^\circ)$.

You will **need a calculator for these problems.**

$40 \times \sin(C) = 34 \times \sin(87^\circ)$

$40 \times \sin(C) = 34 \times 0.9986$

$40 \times \sin(C) = 33.9534$ ← Now divide both sides by 40

$\sin(C) = 0.8488$ ← How do we solve this? We must use **inverse sin** (arcsin) function on our calculator to get the angle.

arcsin(0.8488)

58.081389672

sin	cos	tan	Deg / Rad		7	8	9	+	Back
$\sin^{-1}$	$\cos^{-1}$	$\tan^{-1}$	π	e	4	5	6	–	Ans
x^y	x^3	x^2	e^x	10^x	1	2	3	×	M+
$\sqrt[y]{x}$	$\sqrt[3]{x}$	$\sqrt{x}$	ln	log	0	.	EXP	/	M-
(	)	1/x	%	n!	±	RND	AC	=	MR

$C = 58.1^\circ$ ← We usually always round to the nearest tenths for angles.

$m\angle C = 58.1^\circ$

Example 2:

What is AB?

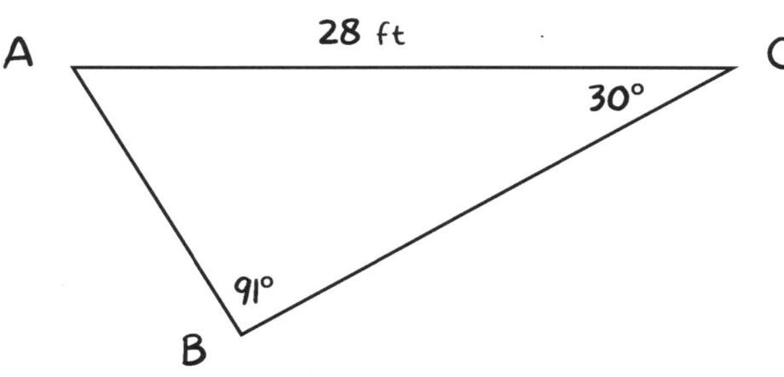

We need to find the length of AB. We can use the law of sines to solve this problem. **Remember**, you can use the Law of Sines if you are provided either

* Two angles and one side (AAS or ASA) OR
* Two sides and an angle opposite one of them (SSA)

$\frac{x \text{ ft}}{\sin(30°)} = \frac{28 \text{ ft}}{\sin(91°)}$ ⟵ Cross multiply to get $x(\sin(91°)) = 28(\sin(30°))$

Use your calculator to solve.

$x(\sin(91°)) = 28(\sin(30°))$

$x(0.9998) = 14$ ← Divide both sides by 0.9998

$x = 14.00$ ← We usually round to the nearest hundredths for distance. In this case, the answer is just 14. **Don't forget the units** (feet).

AB = 14 ft

The Law of Sines is not just a mathematical curiosity. It's an incredibly **useful** tool with a range of applications in both theoretical and practical scenarios. This law has many practical uses. For instance, in navigation and cartography, sailors and pilots use the Law of Sines to find distances and angles between points on a map. It's also used in architecture, engineering, and physics to solve various problems.

Section 6.1 Quiz

Directions: Solve these problems using the Law of Sines. You will need to use a calculator. Be sure to show your work on a separate piece of paper.

1. Find $m\angle B$

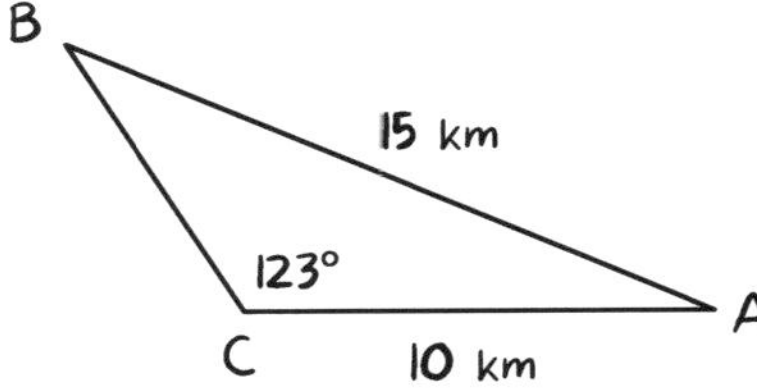

2. Find $m\angle B$

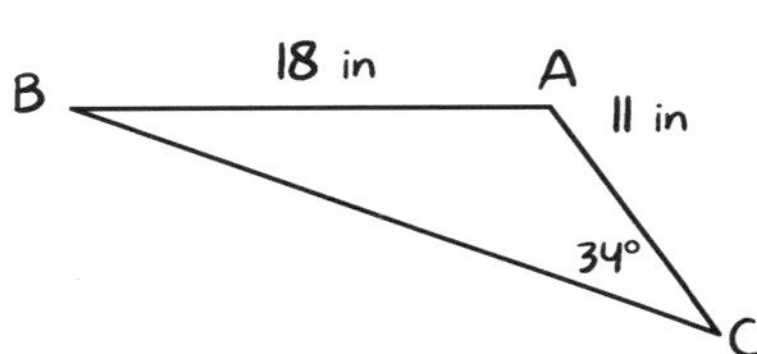

3. Find $m\angle C$

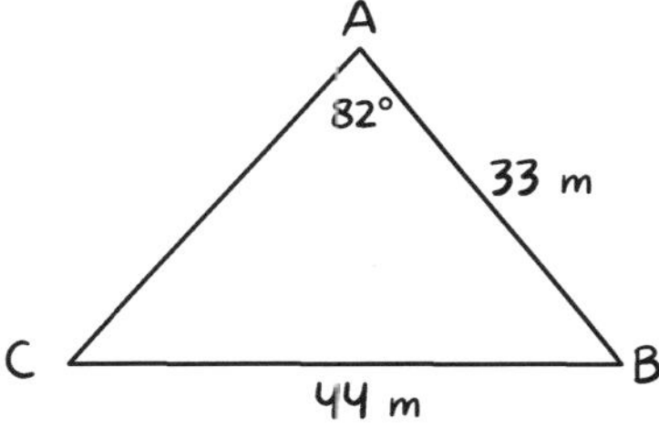

4. Find $m\angle C$

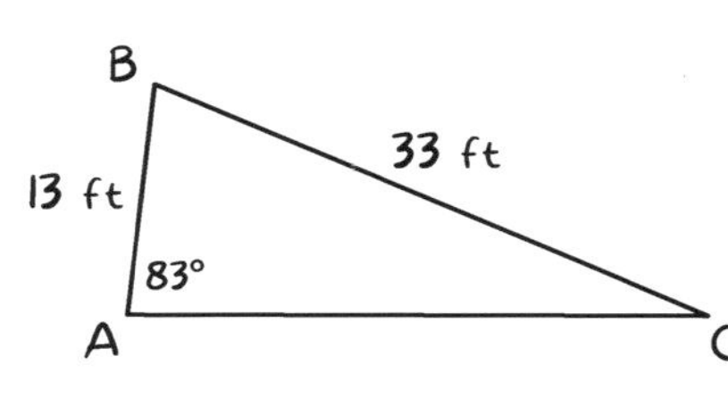

5. Find $m\angle B$

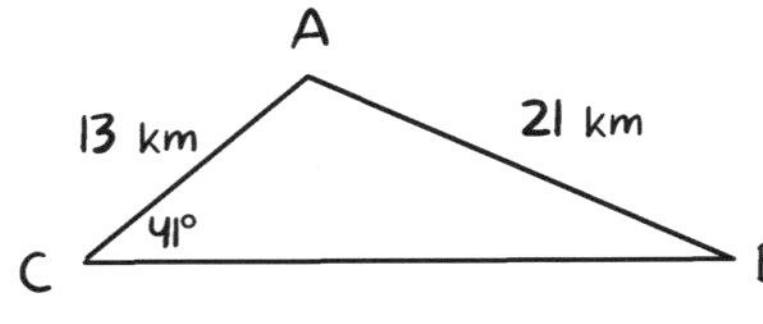

6. Find $m\angle A$

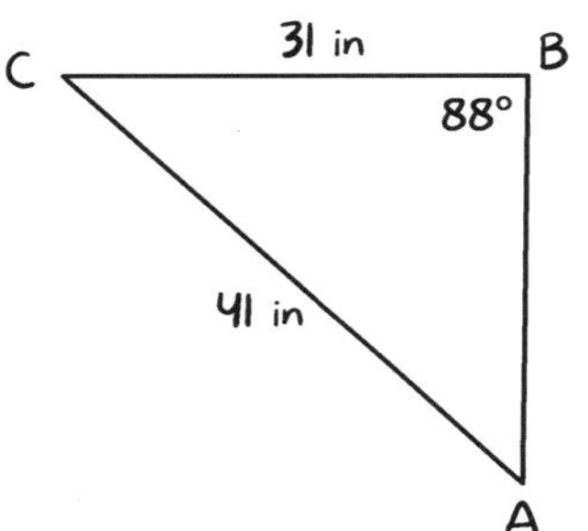

7. Find $m\angle B$

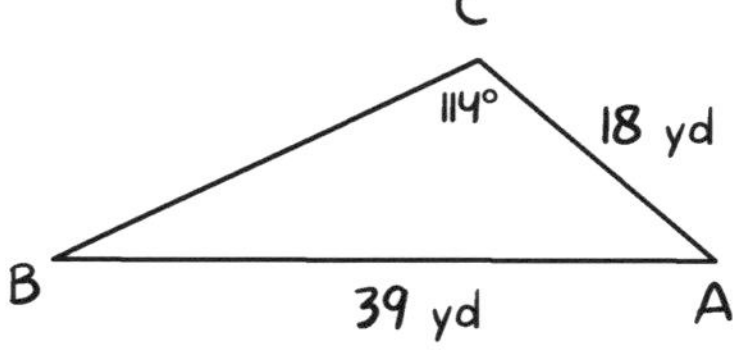

8. Find $m\angle C$

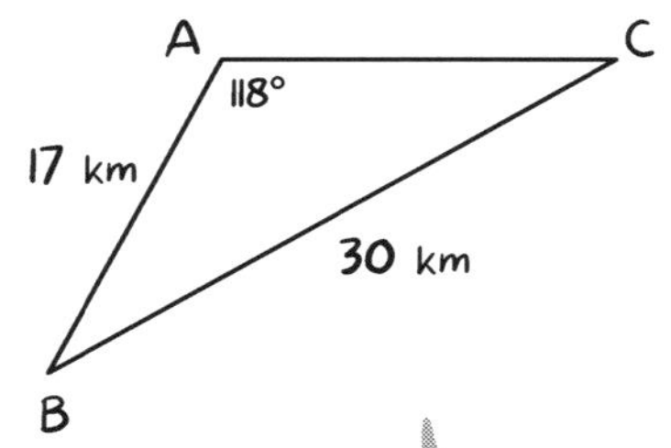

9. Find $m\angle C$

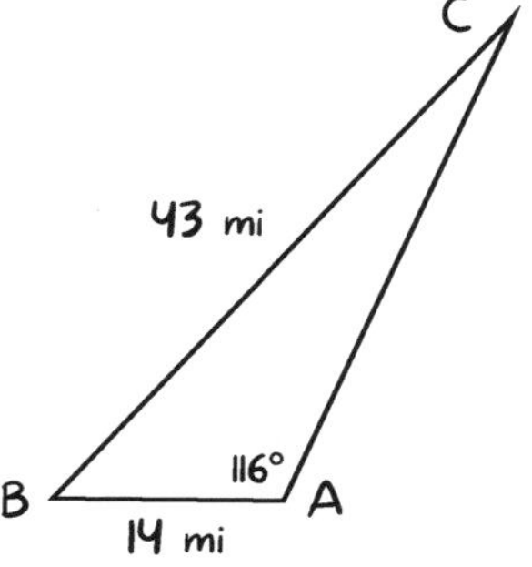

10. Find $m\angle C$

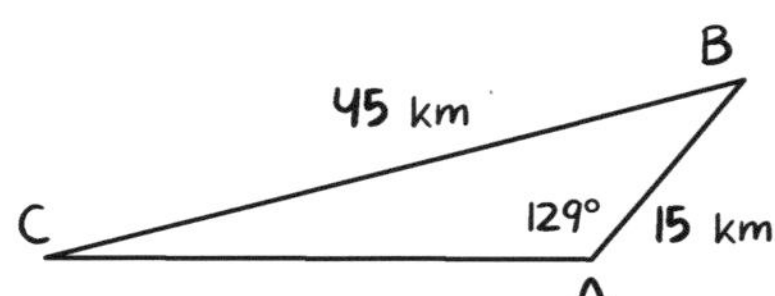

11. Find $m\angle B$

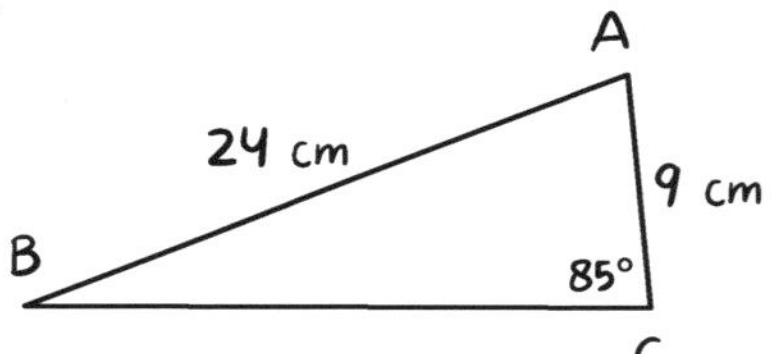

12. Find $m\angle C$

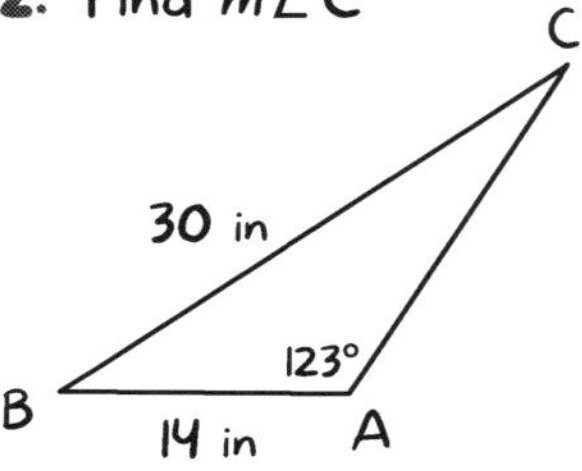

Section 6.1 Quiz

13. Find $m\angle B$

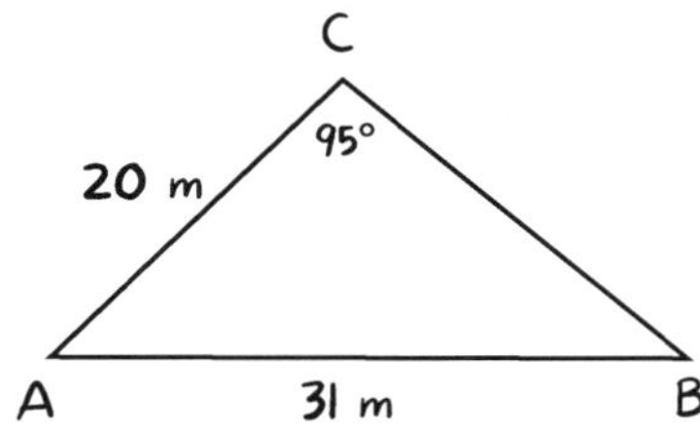

14. Find $m\angle B$

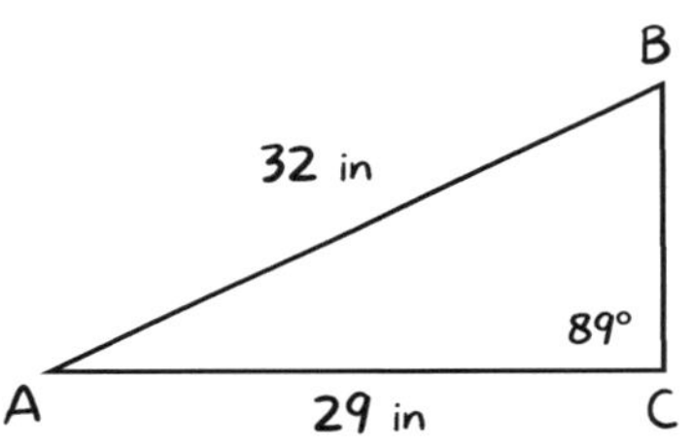

15. Find $m\angle C$

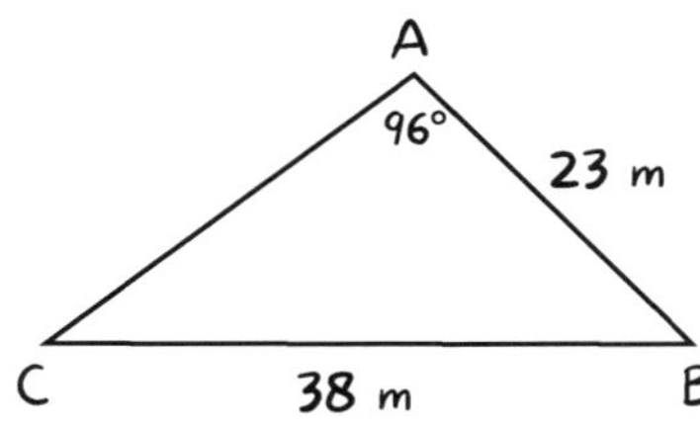

16. Find $m\angle A$

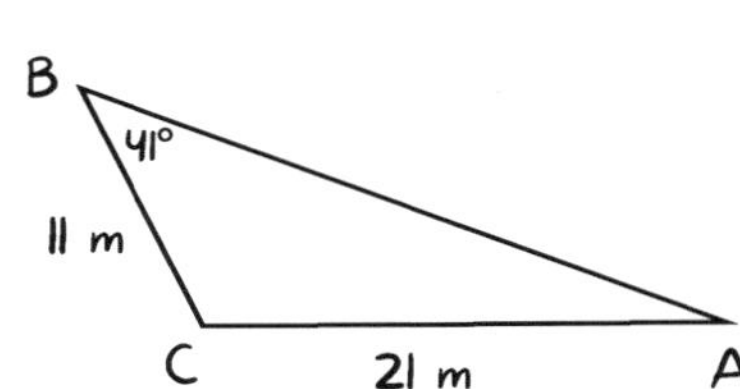

17. Find $m\angle B$

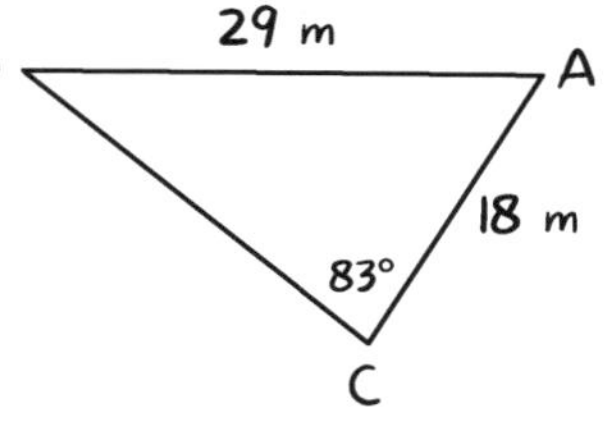

18. Find $m\angle B$

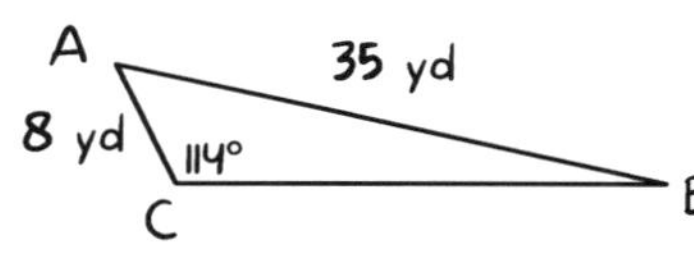

19. Find $m\angle C$

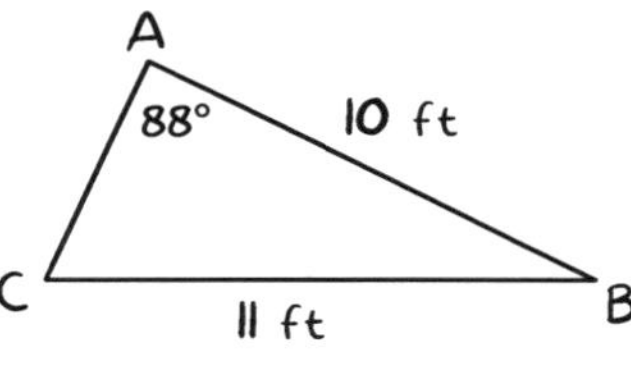

20. Find $m\angle B$

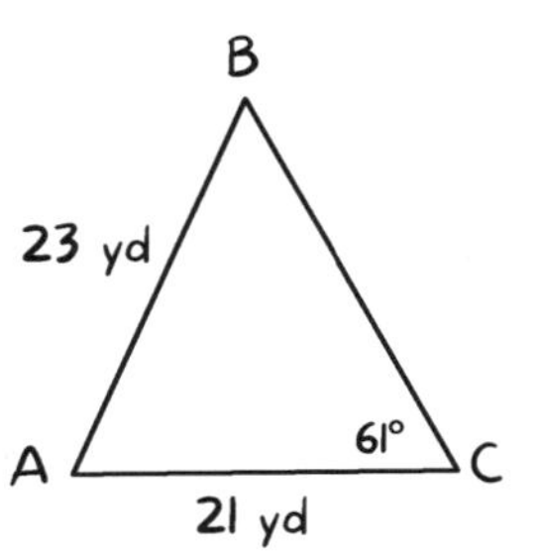

21. Find $m\angle B$

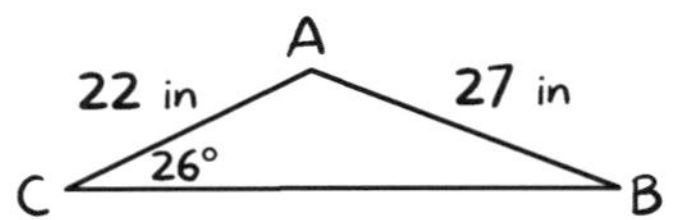

22. Find $m\angle C$

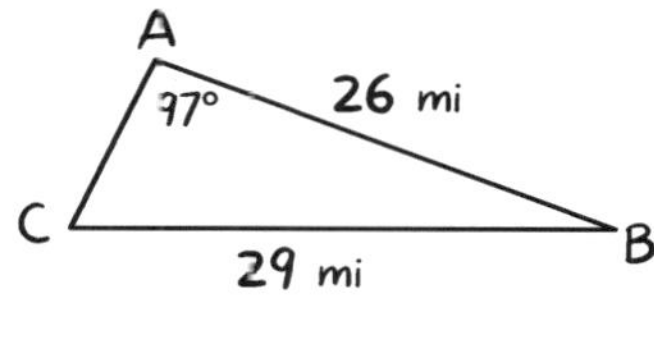

23. Find $m\angle C$

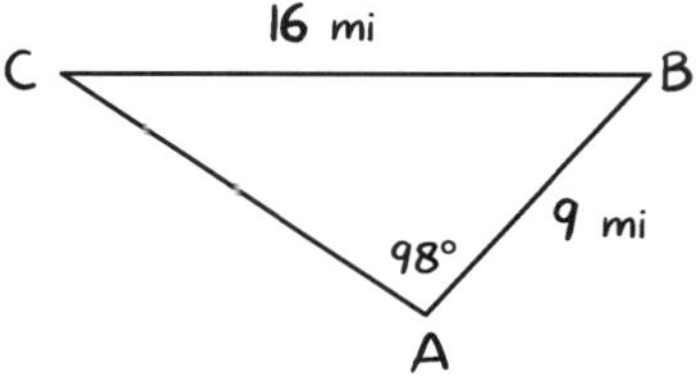

24. Find $m\angle C$

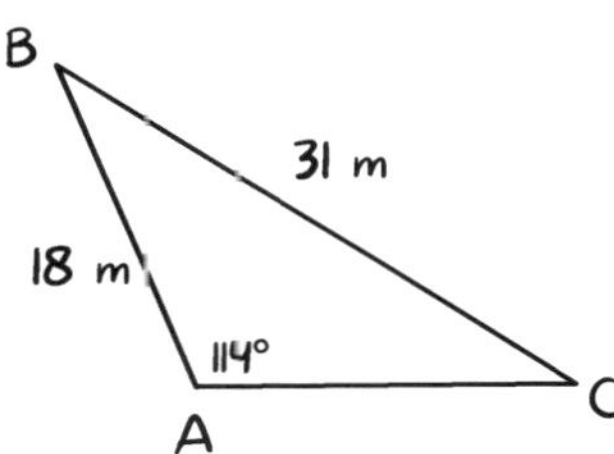

25. Find $m\angle C$

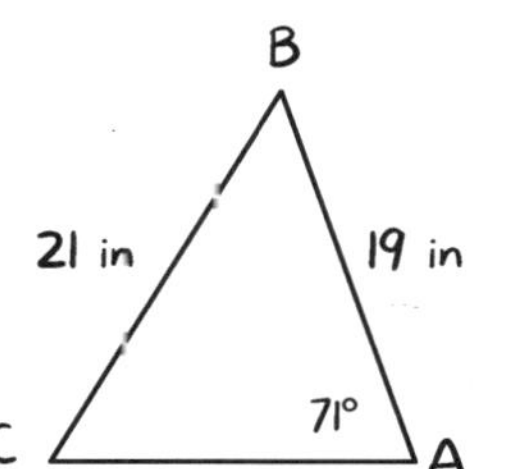

Section 6.1 Quiz

26. Find $m\angle A$

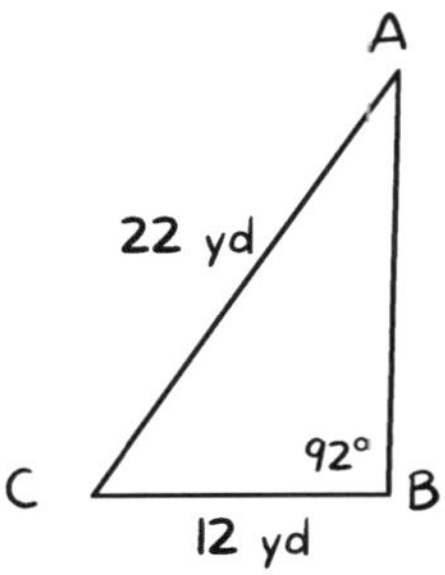

27. Find $m\angle C$

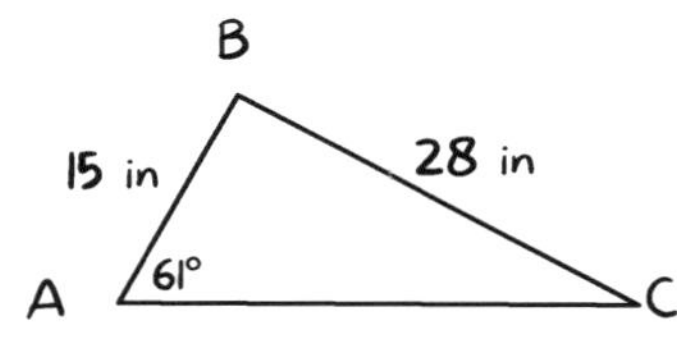

28. Find $m\angle A$

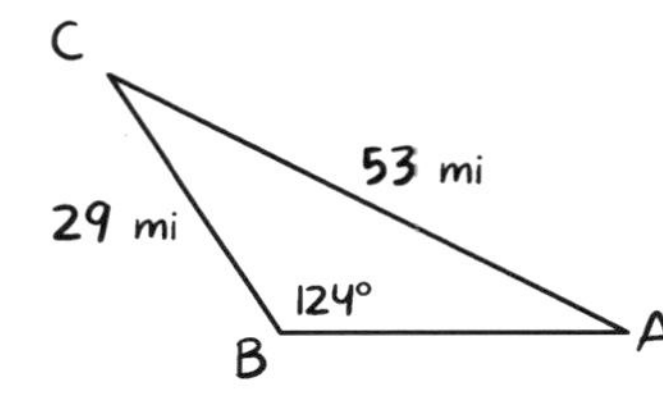

29. Find $m\angle A$

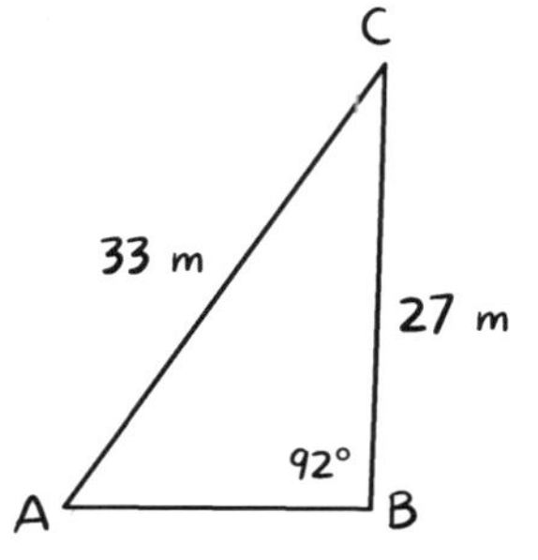

30. Find $m\angle C$

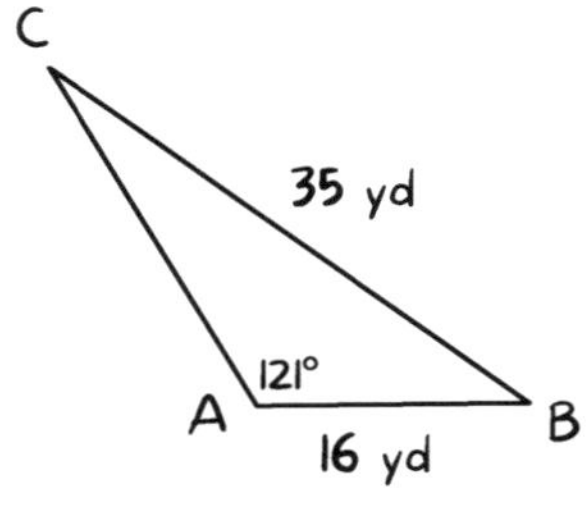

31. Find $m\angle C$

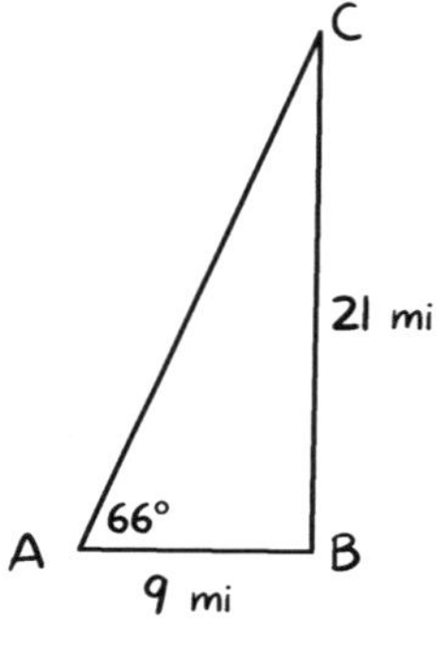

32. Find $m\angle B$

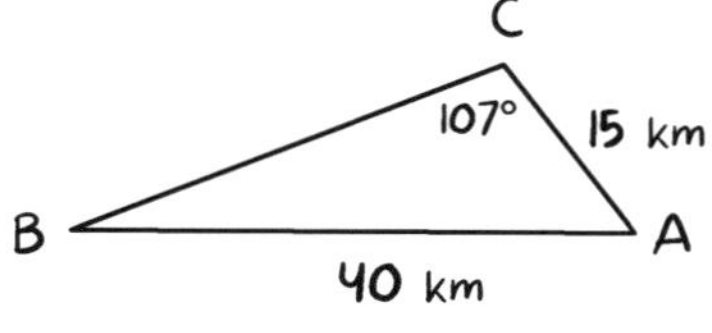

33. Find $m\angle A$

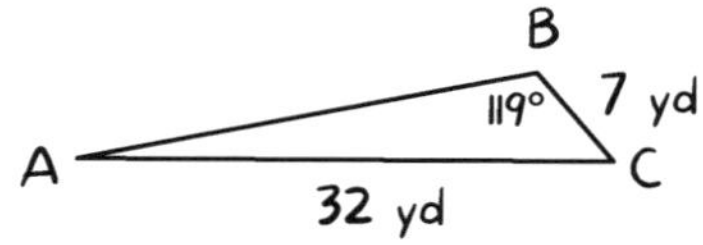

34. Find $m\angle C$

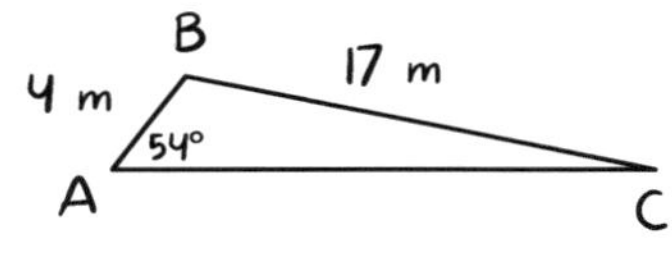

35. Find $m\angle C$

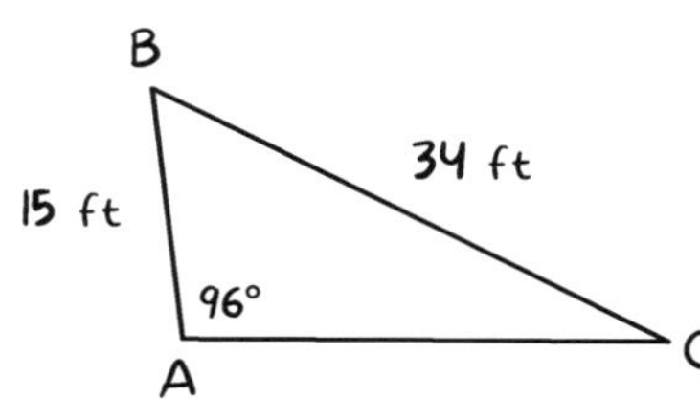

36. Find $m\angle B$

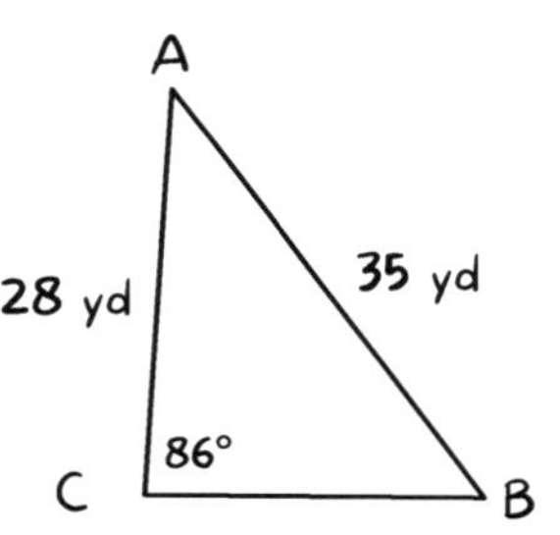

37. Find $m\angle A$

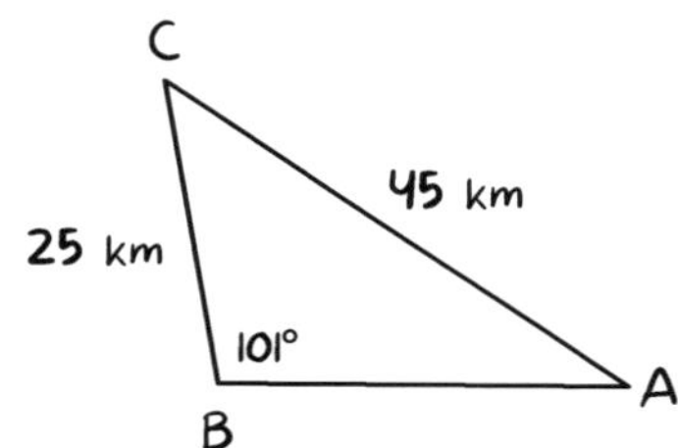

38. Find $m\angle A$

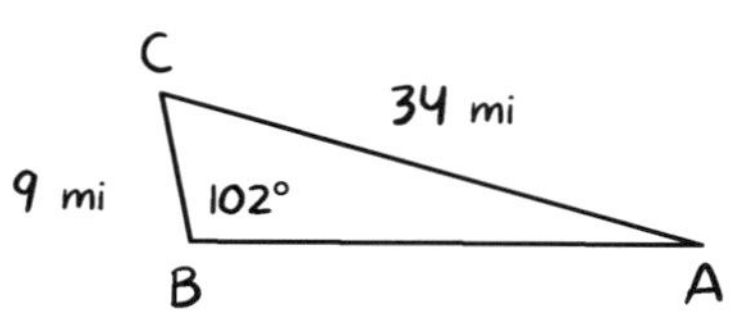

Section 6.1 Quiz

39. Find $m\angle C$

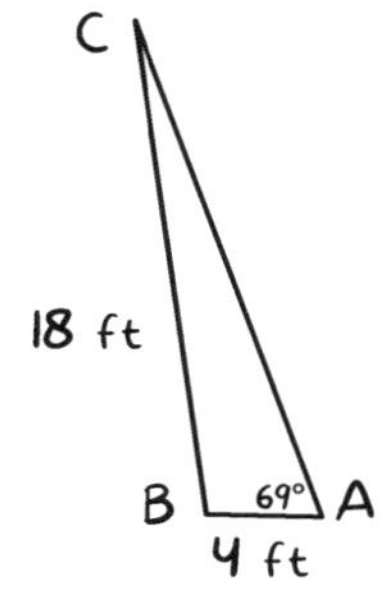

40. Find $m\angle B$

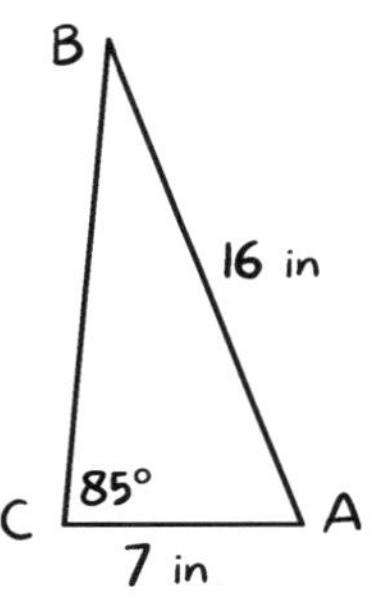

41. Find $m\angle C$

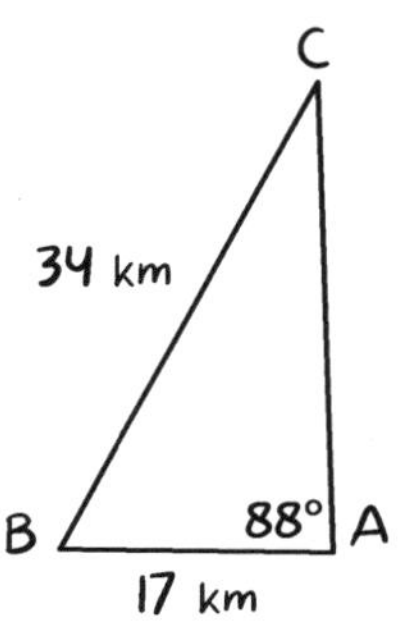

42. Find $m\angle B$

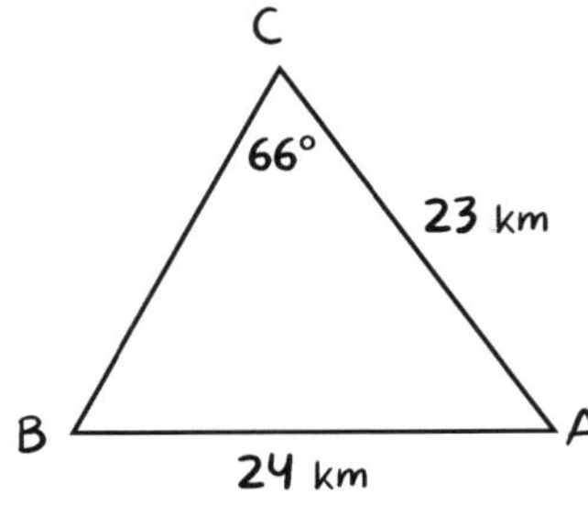

43. Find $m\angle C$

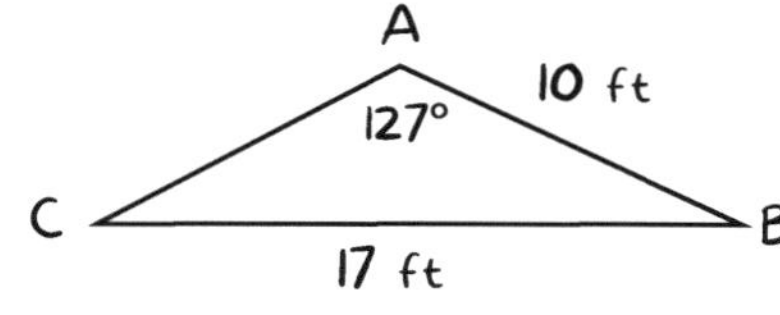

44. Find $m\angle C$

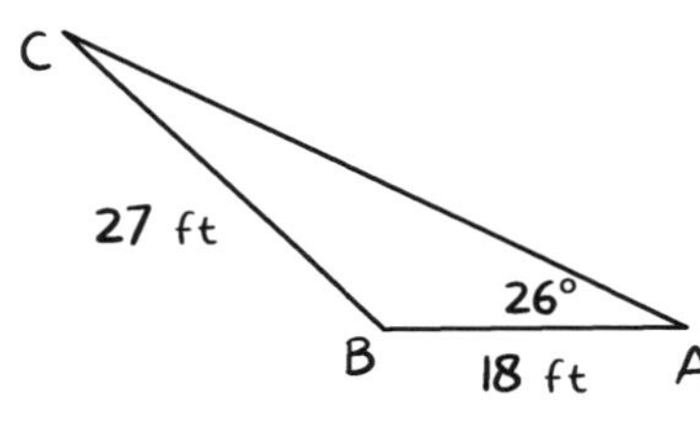

45. Find $m\angle A$

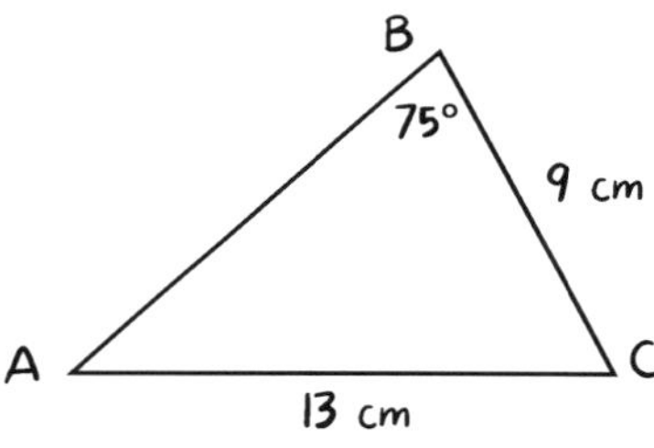

46. Find $m\angle C$

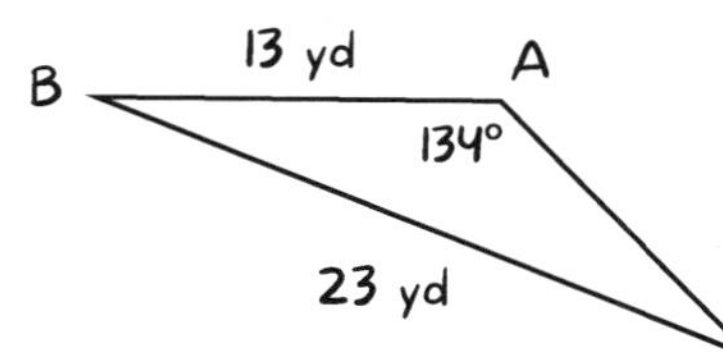

47. Find $m\angle C$

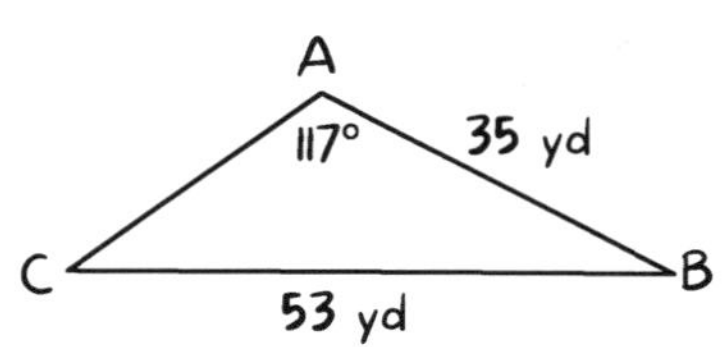

48. Find $m\angle B$

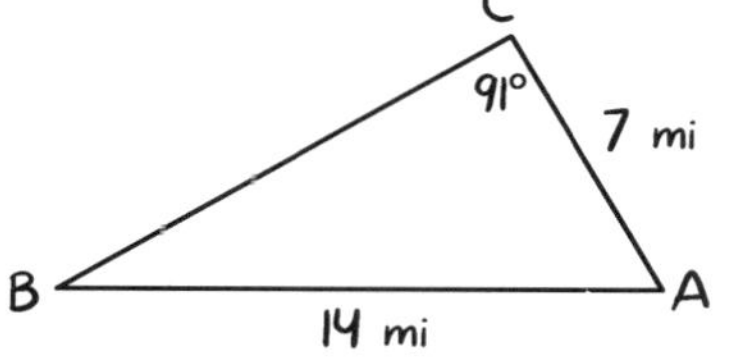

49. Find $m\angle A$

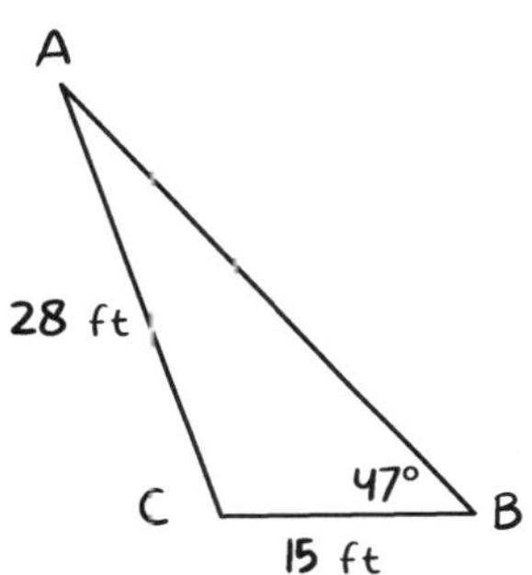

50. Find $m\angle B$

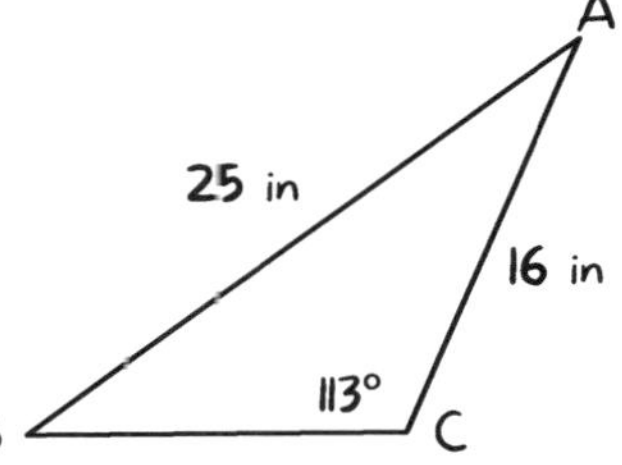

51. Find $m\angle A$

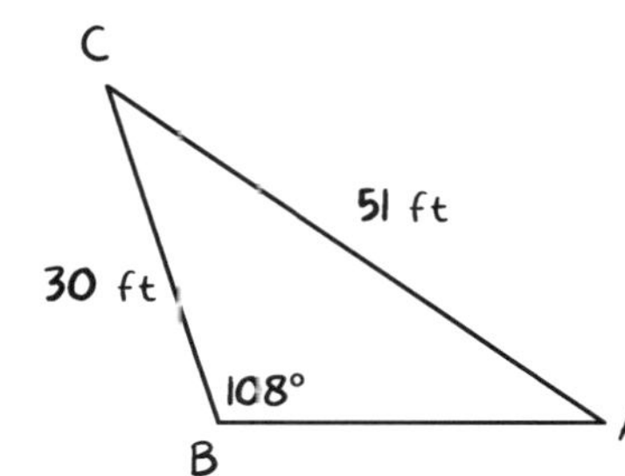

Section 6.1 Quiz

52. Find $m\angle A$

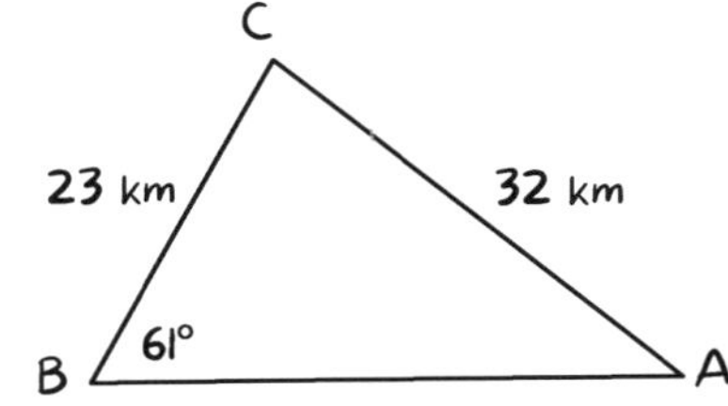

53. Find $m\angle B$

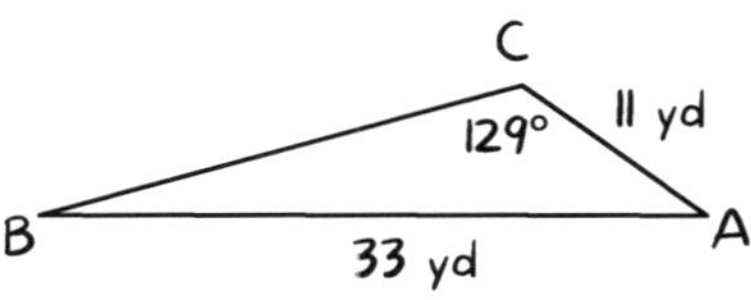

54. Find $m\angle C$

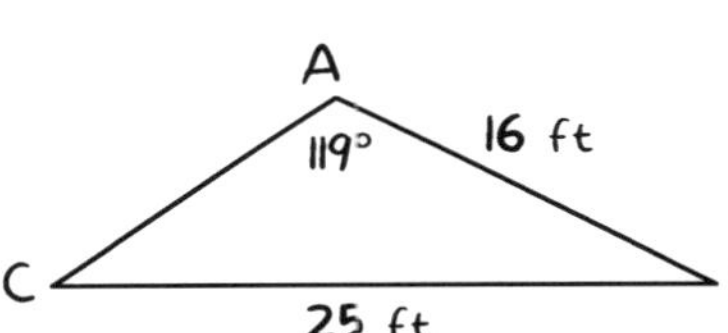

55. Find $m\angle A$

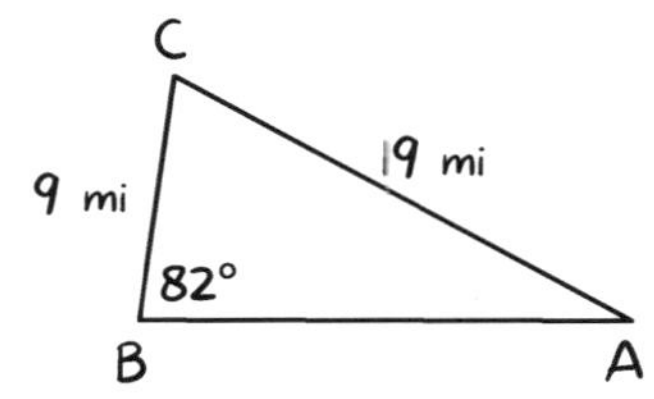

56. Find $m\angle B$

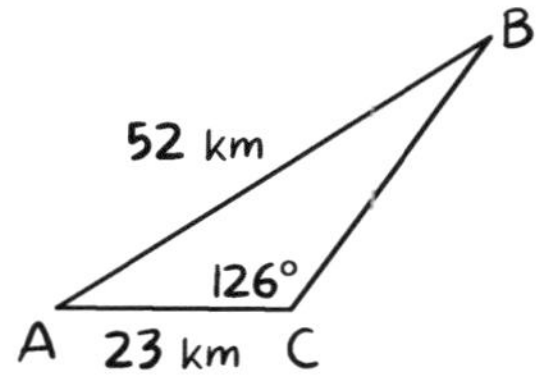

57. Find $m\angle C$

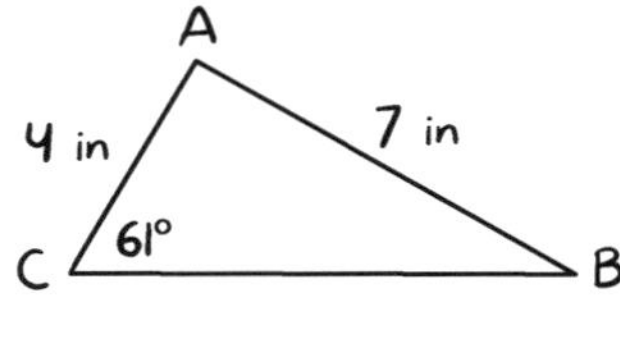

58. Find $m\angle B$

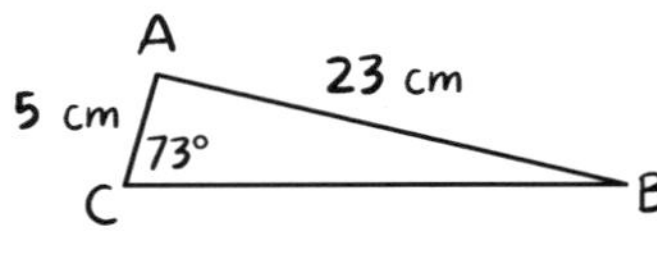

59. Find $m\angle C$

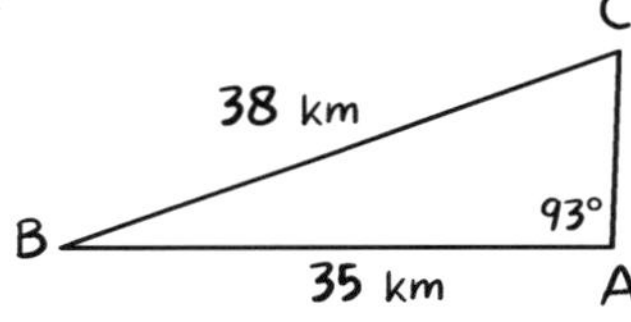

60. Find $m\angle A$

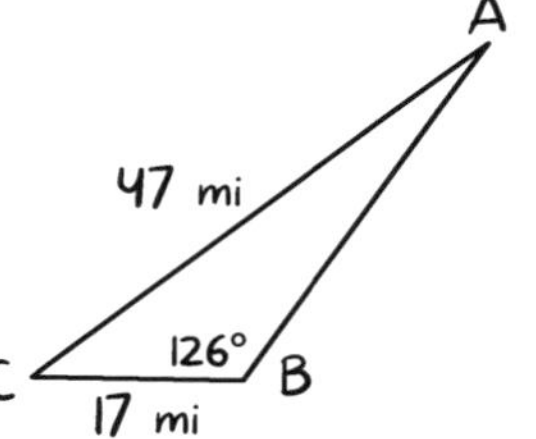

61. Find $m\angle A$

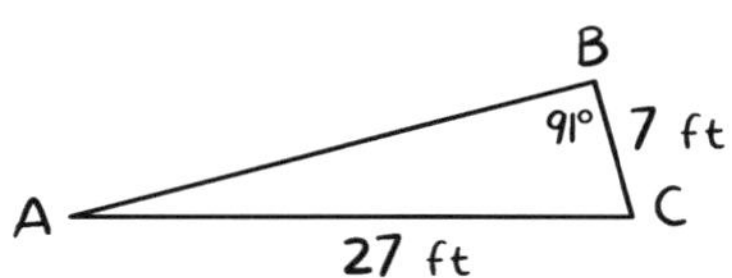

62. Find $m\angle A$

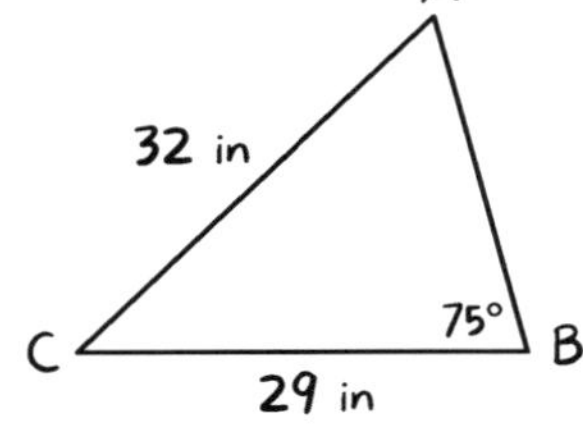

63. Find $m\angle B$

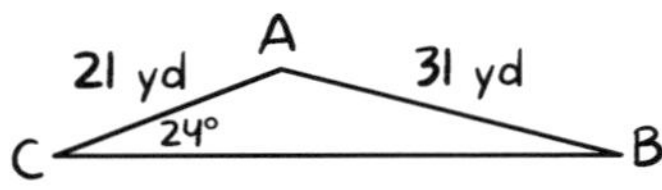

64. Find $m\angle A$

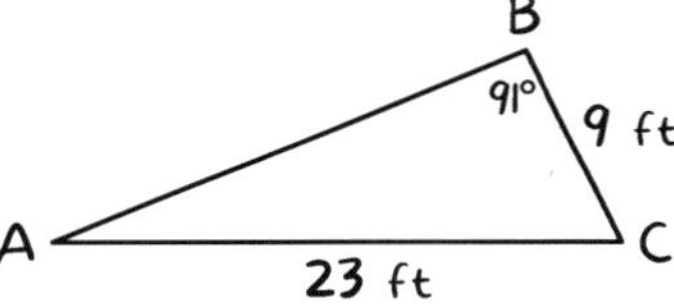

65. Find $m\angle C$

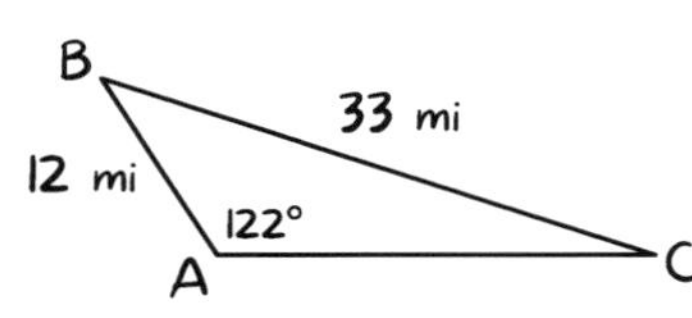

66. Find $m\angle B$

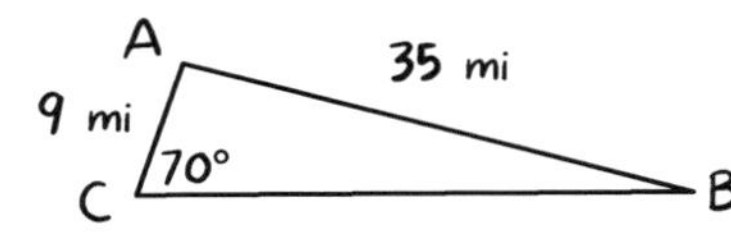

Section 6.1 Quiz

67. Find $m\angle A$

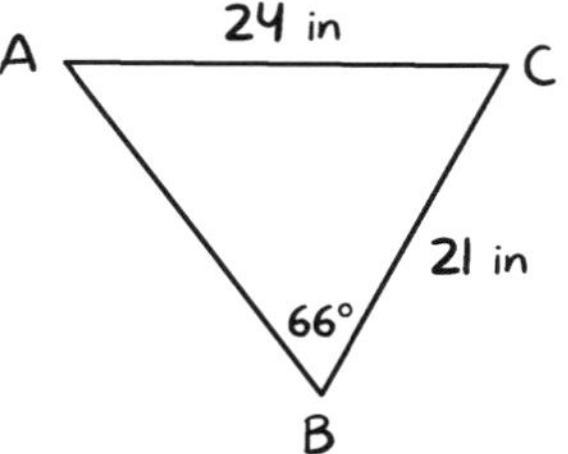

68. Find $m\angle B$

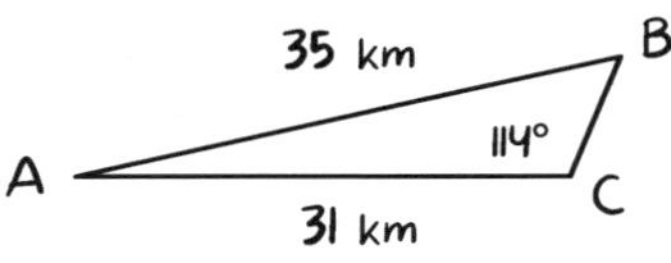

69. Find $m\angle C$

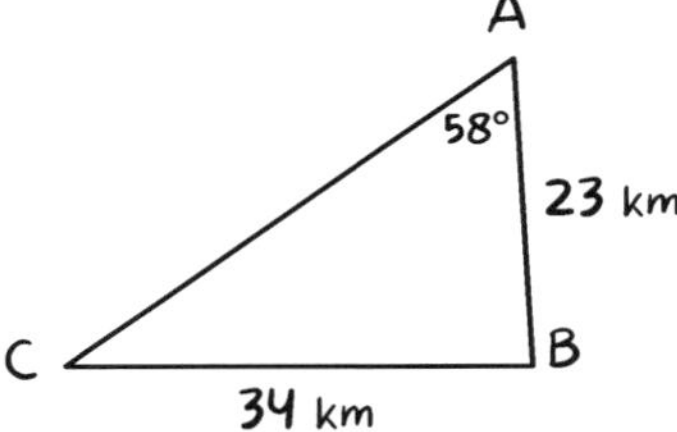

70. Find $m\angle B$

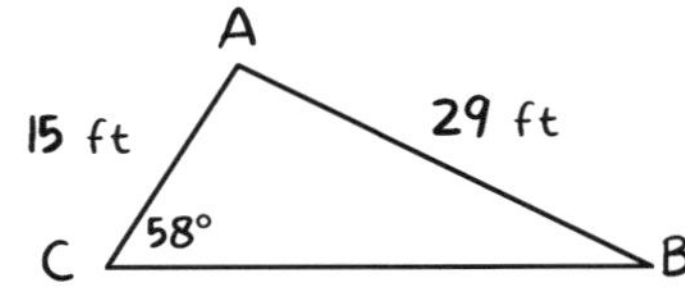

71. Find $m\angle B$

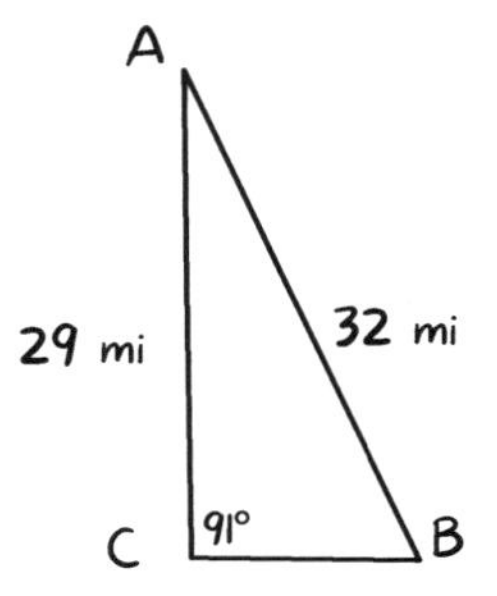

72. Find $m\angle A$

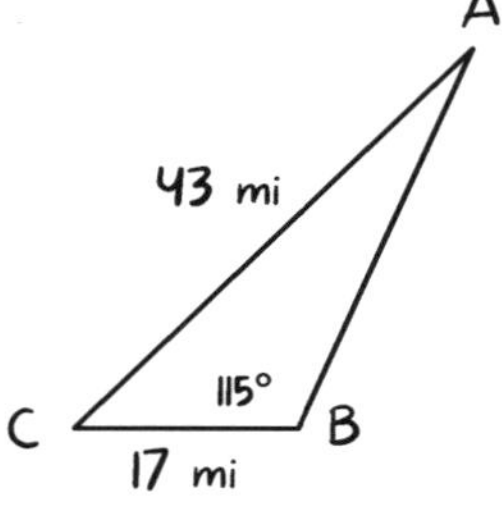

73. Find $m\angle B$

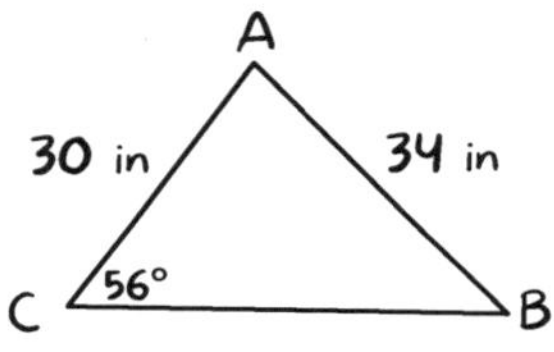

74. Find $m\angle C$

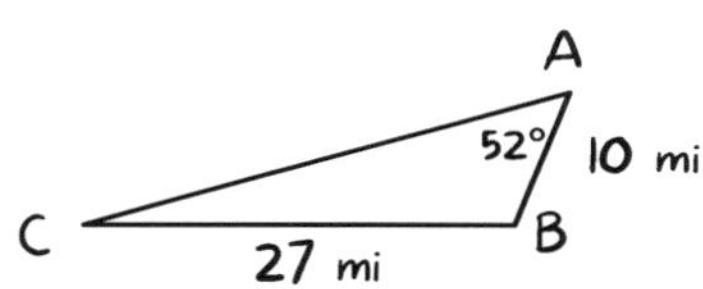

75. Find $m\angle C$

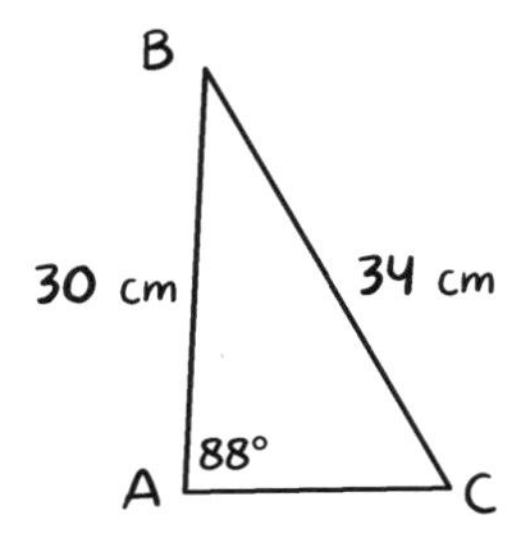

76. Find $m\angle B$

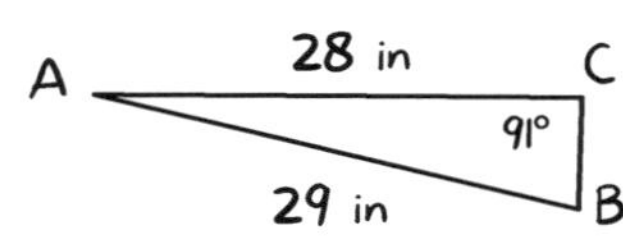

77. Find $m\angle C$

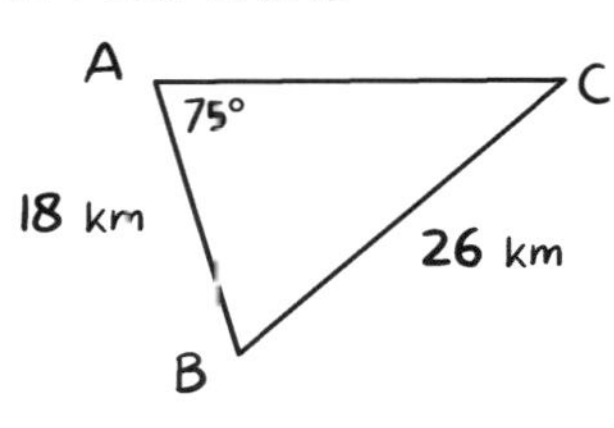

78. Find $m\angle A$

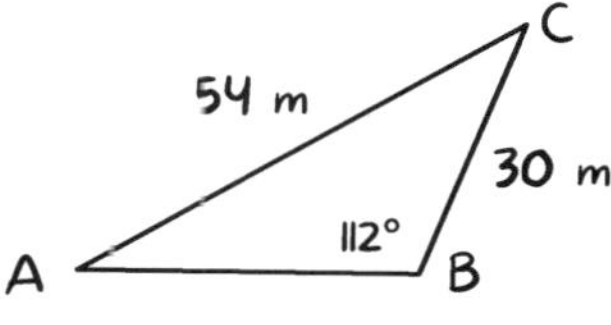

79. Find $m\angle C$

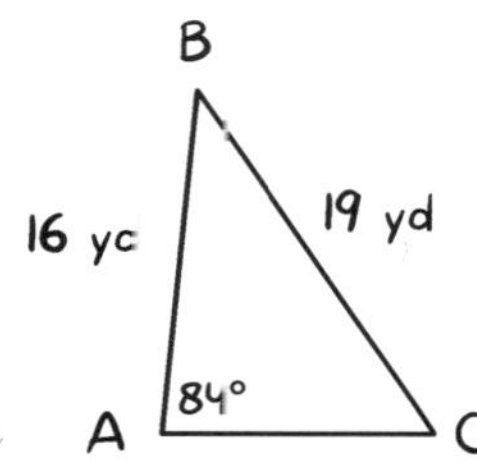

80. Find $m\angle B$

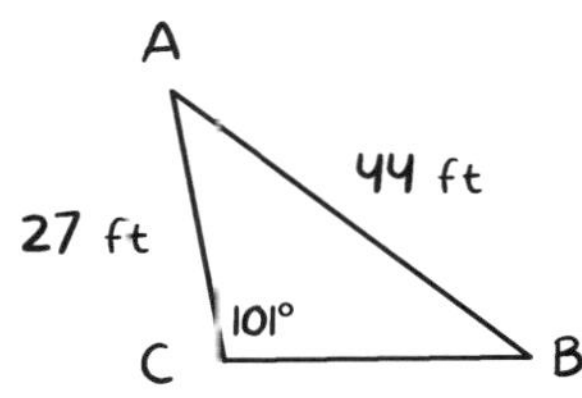

81. Find $m\angle A$

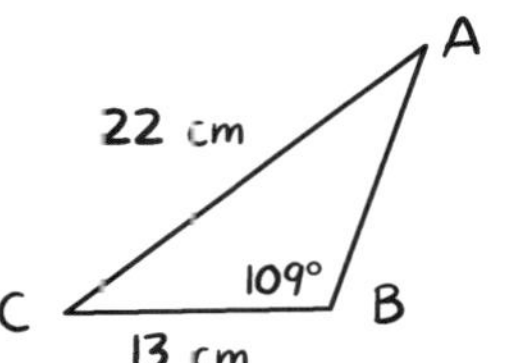

Section 6.1 Quiz

82. Find $m\angle B$

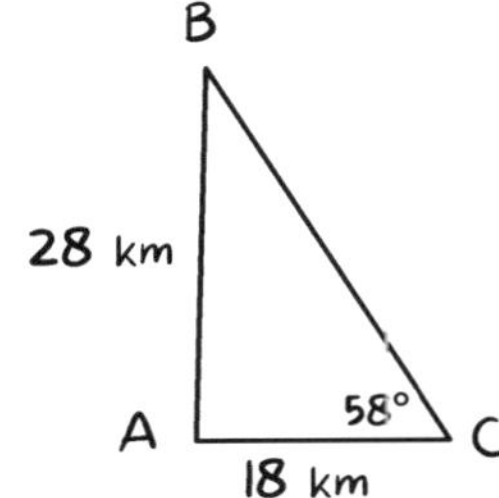

83. Find $m\angle C$

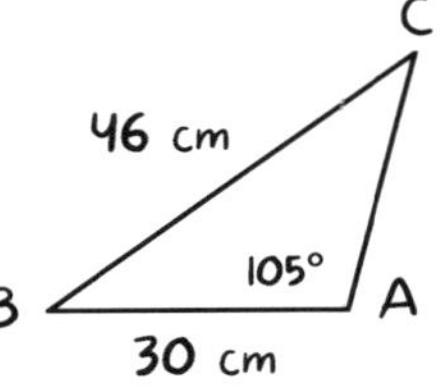

84. Find $m\angle C$

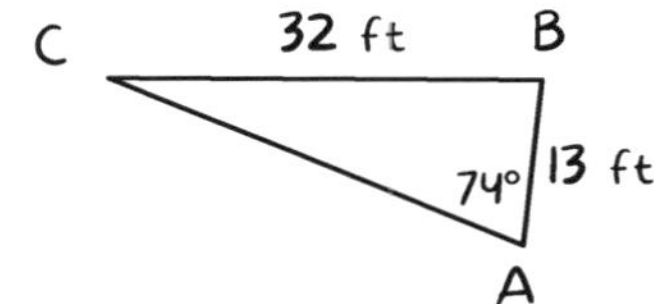

85. Find $m\angle A$

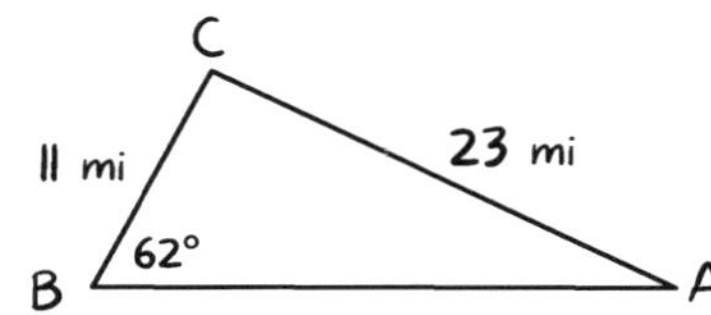

86. Find $m\angle A$

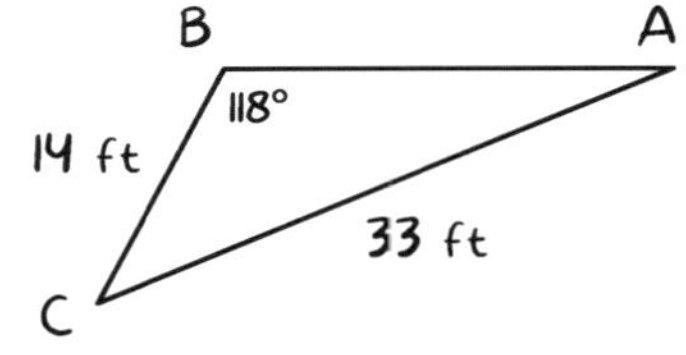

87. Find $m\angle A$

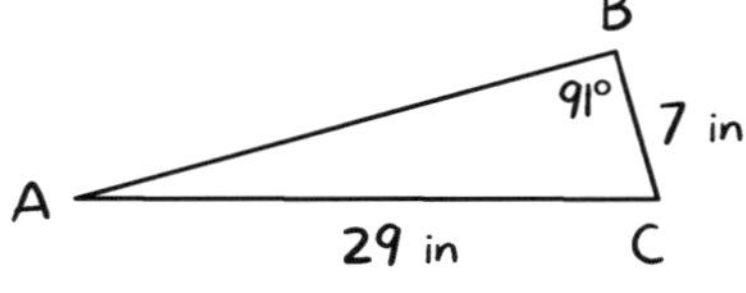

88. Find $m\angle B$

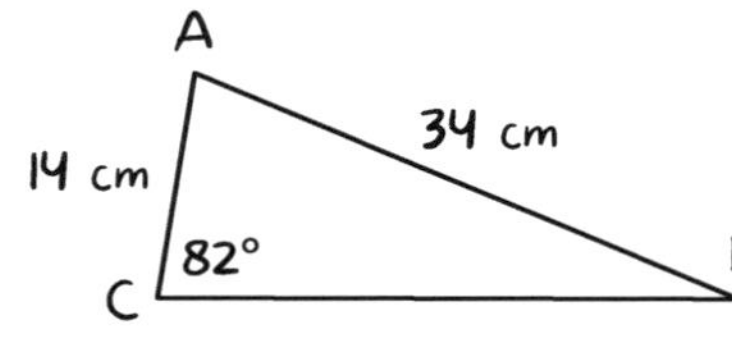

89. Find $m\angle B$

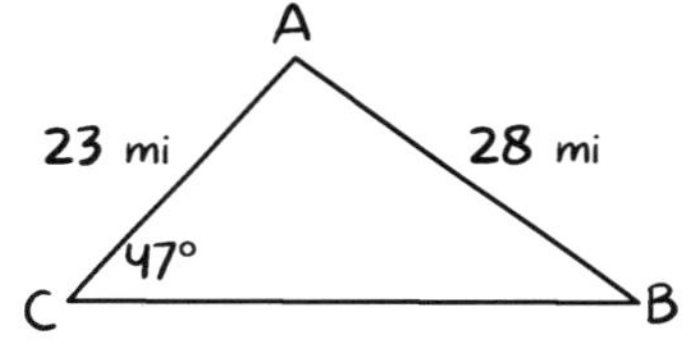

90. Find $m\angle C$

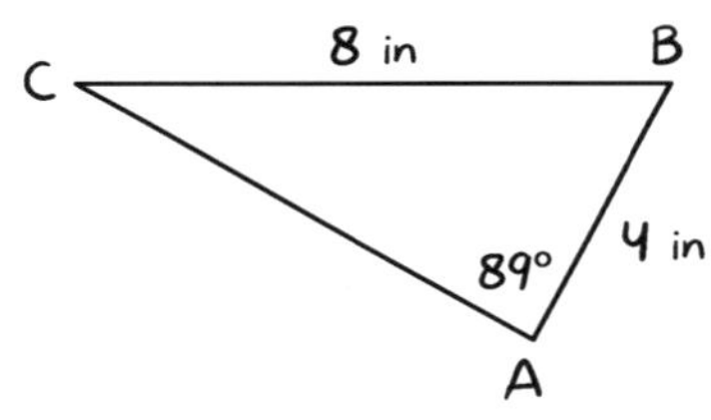

91. Find $m\angle C$

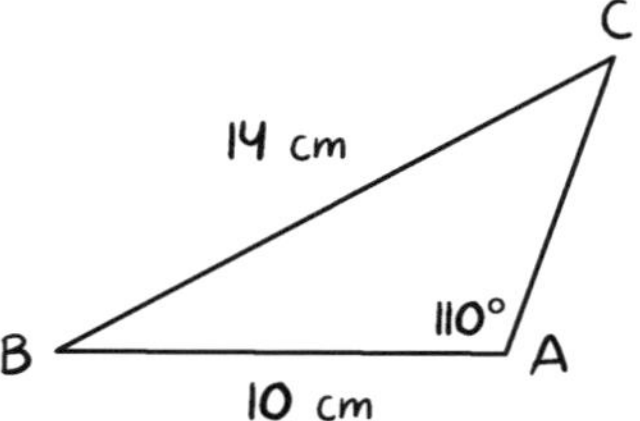

92. Find $m\angle B$

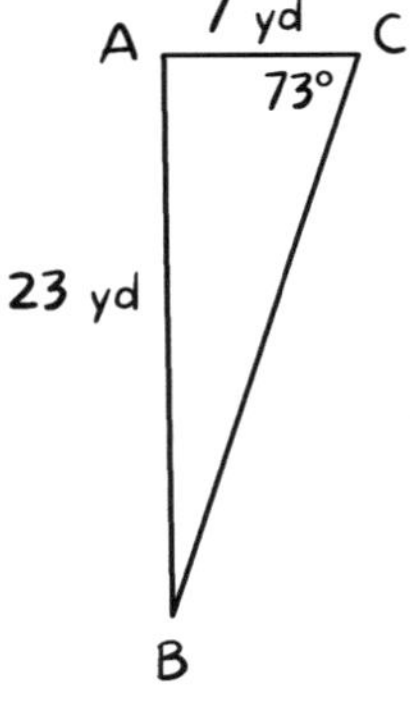

93. Find $m\angle C$

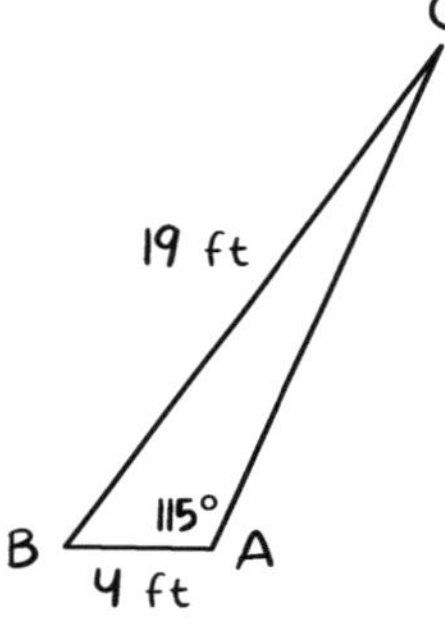

94. Find $m\angle A$

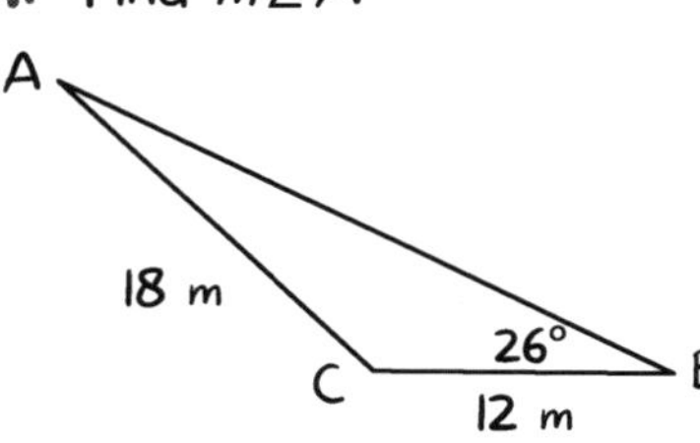

95. Find $m\angle A$

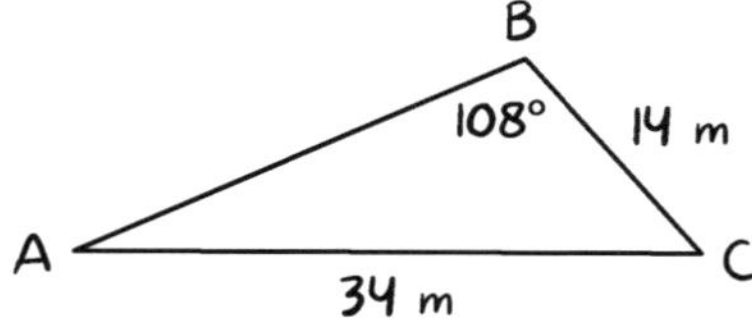

Section 6.1 Quiz

96. Find $m\angle A$

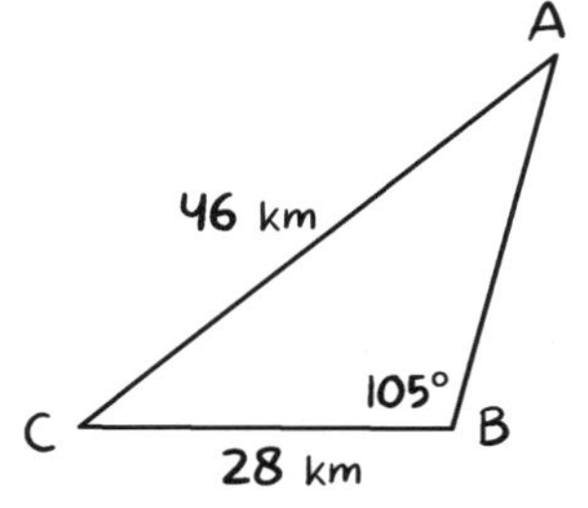

97. Find $m\angle A$

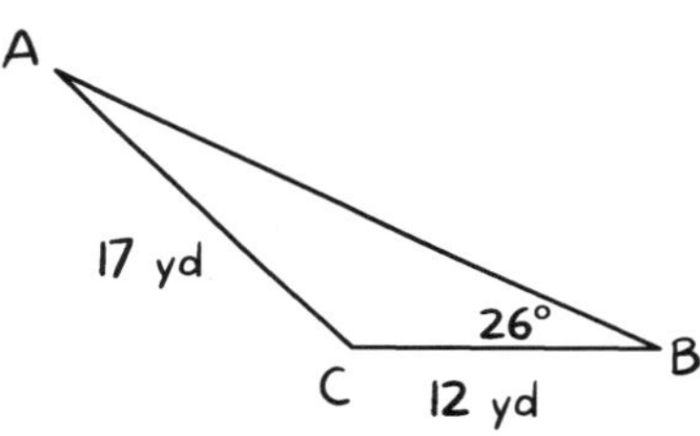

98. Find $m\angle B$

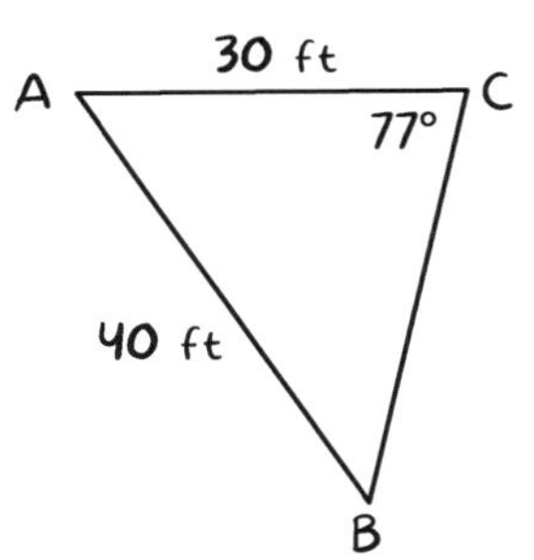

99. Find $m\angle A$

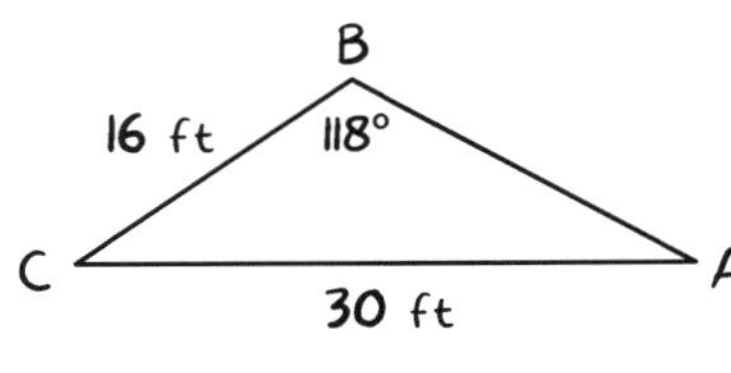

100. Find $m\angle A$

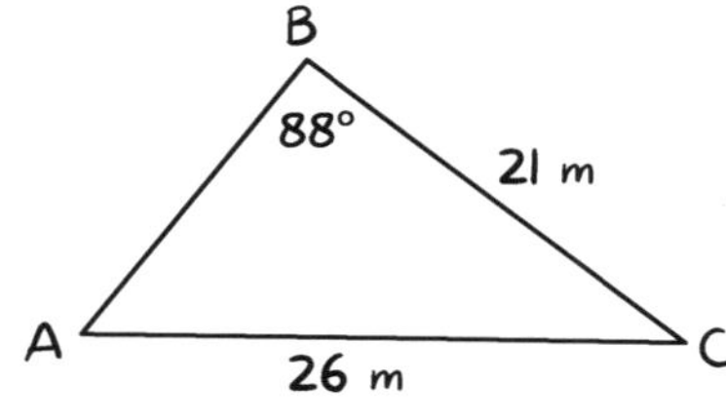

101. Find BC

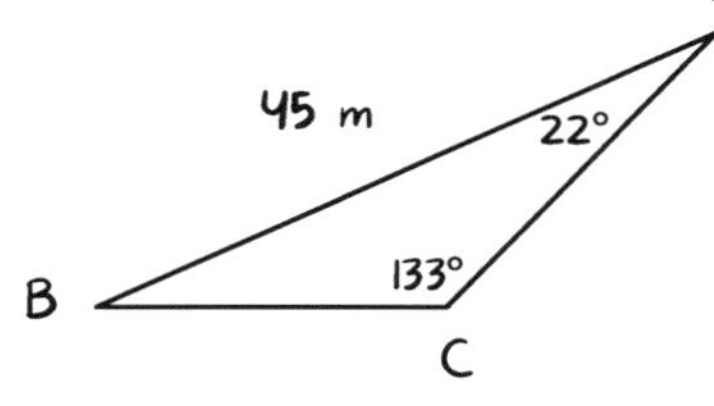

102. Find AC

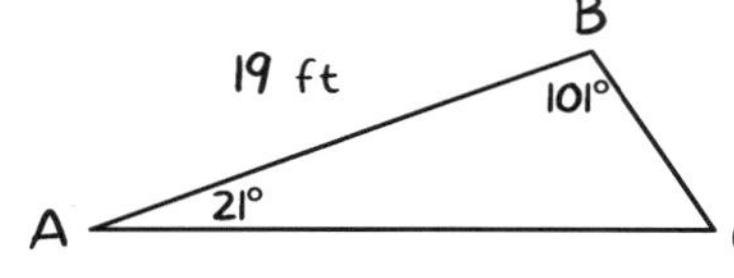

103. Find AC

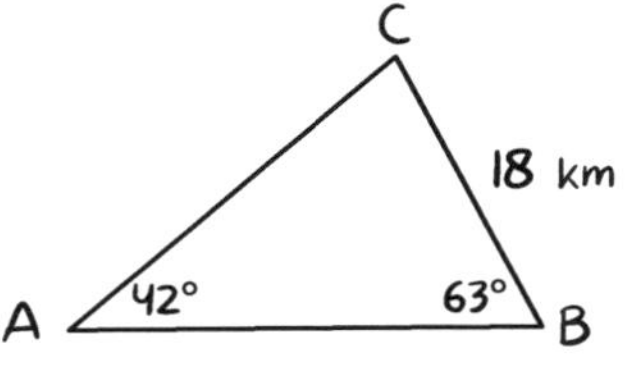

104. Find AB

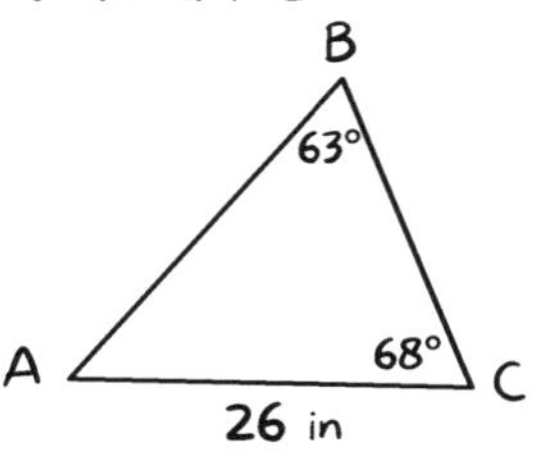

105. Find AB

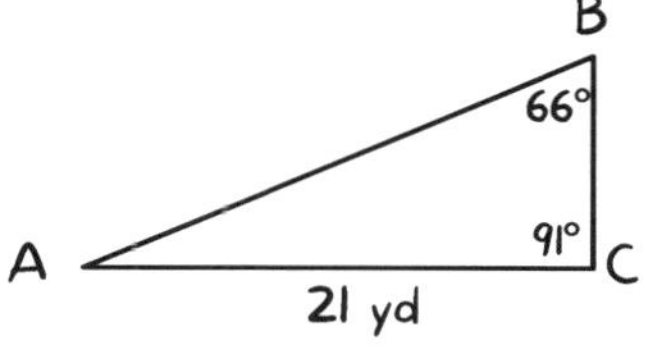

106. Find AC

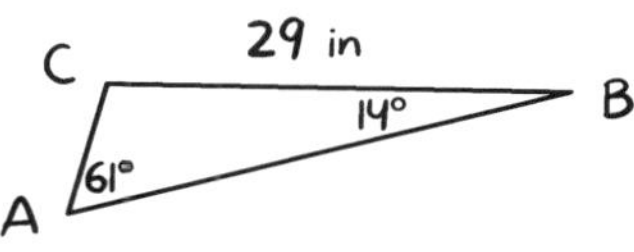

107. Find AC

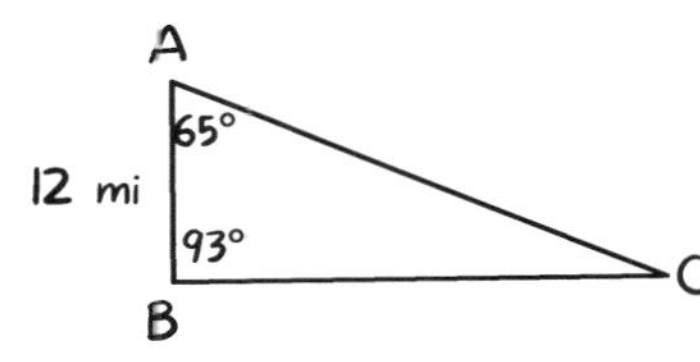

108. Find BC

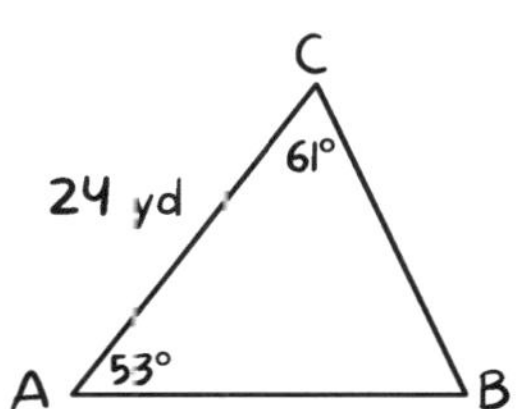

109. Find BC

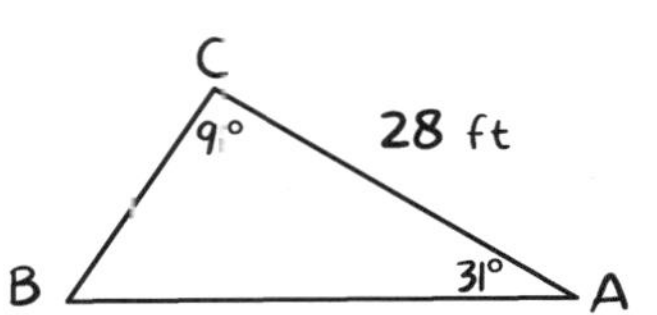

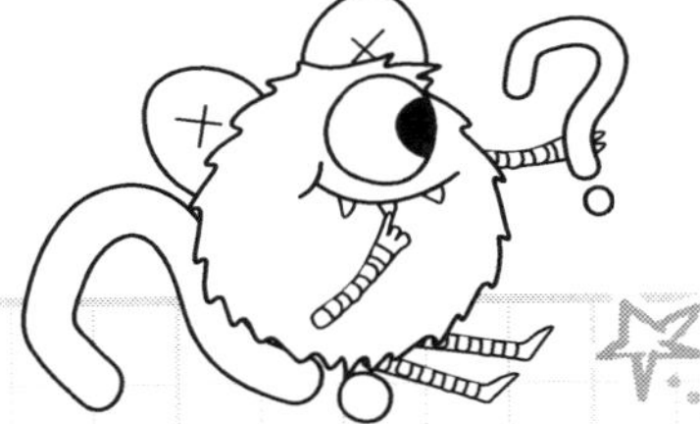

Section 6.1 Quiz

110. Find AC

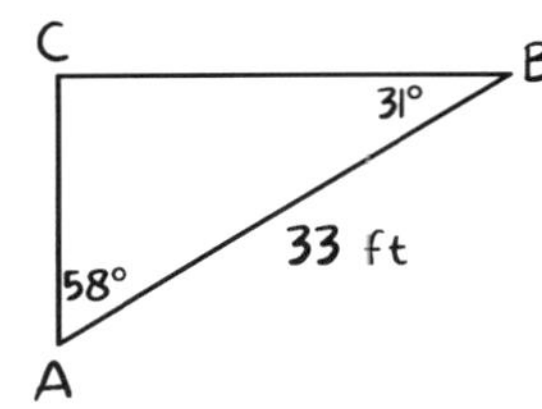

111. Find BC

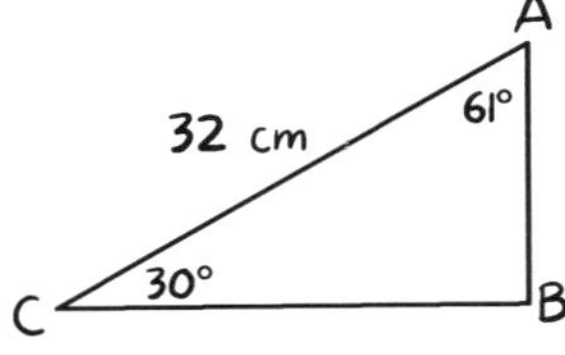

112. Find AC

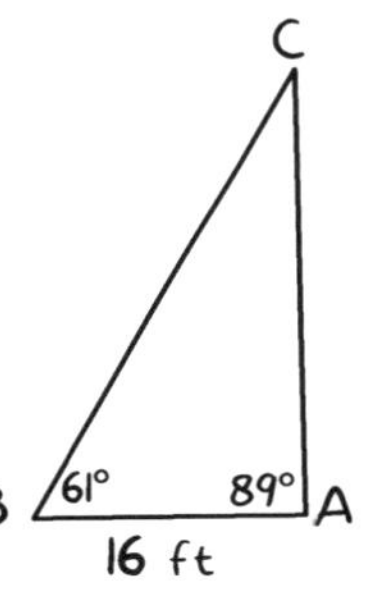

113. Find AC

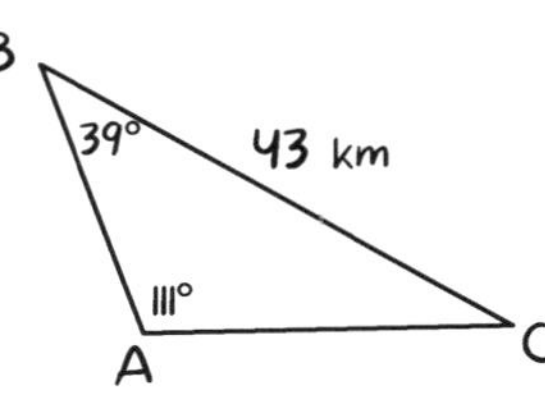

114. Find BC

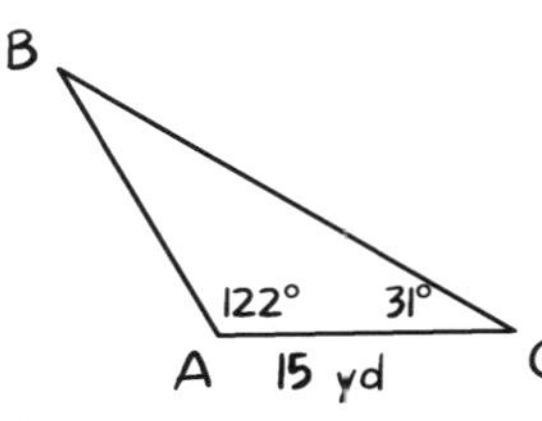

115. Find BC

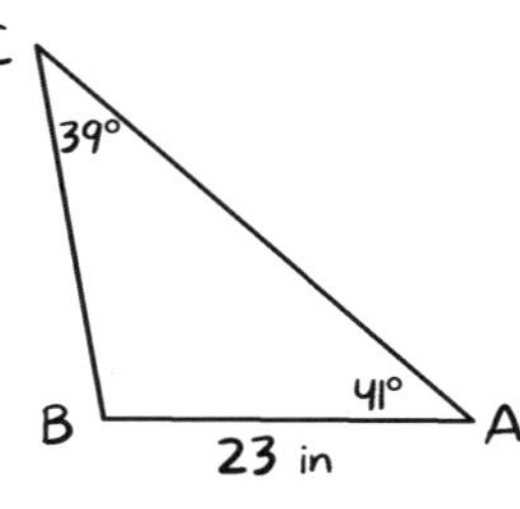

116. Find BC

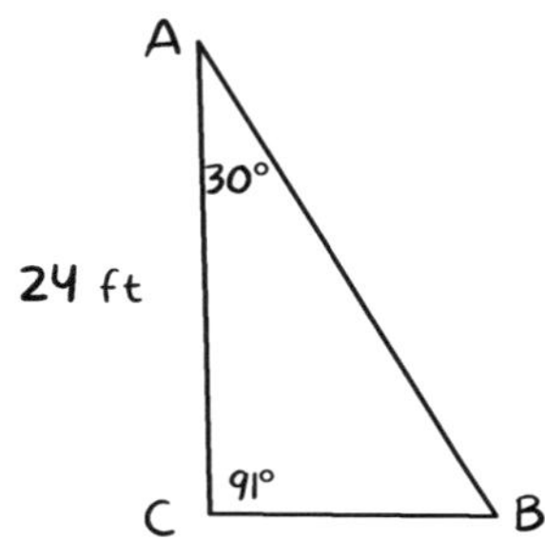

117. Find AB

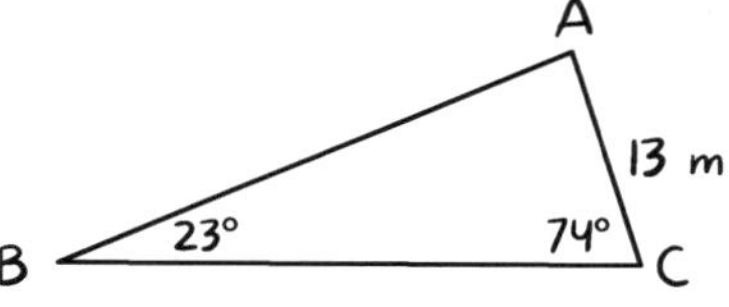

118. Find AC

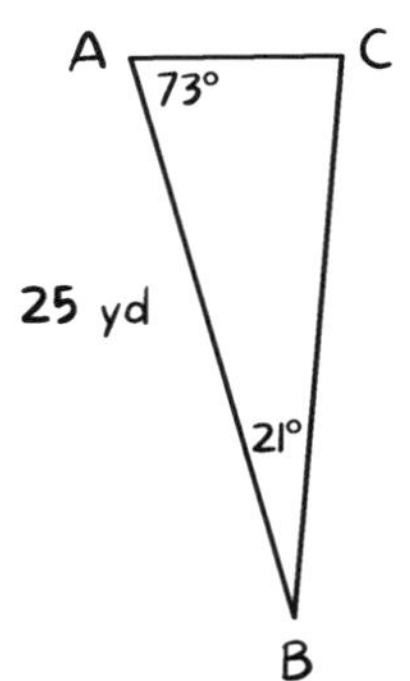

119. Find AB

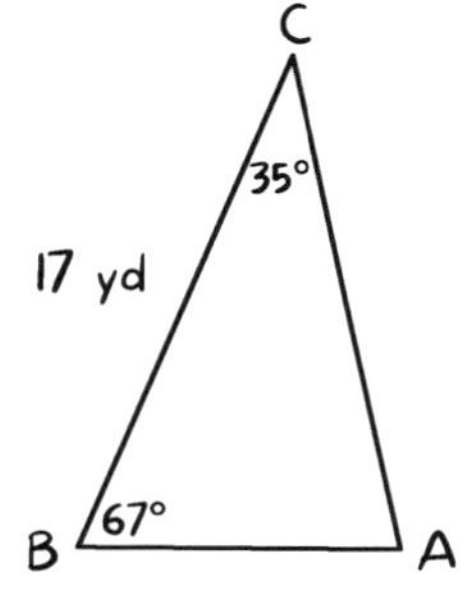

120. Find AB

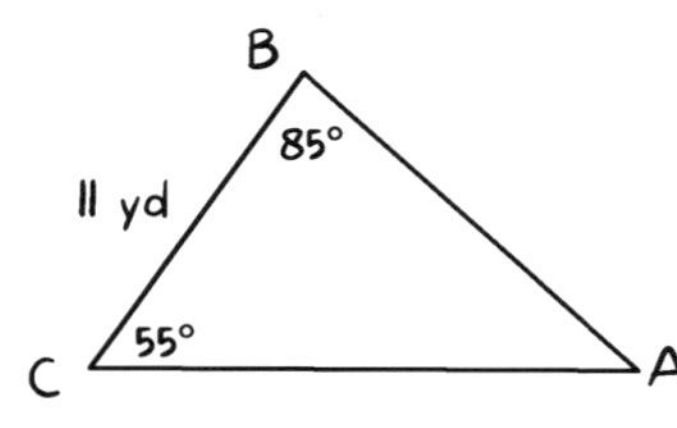

121. Find BC

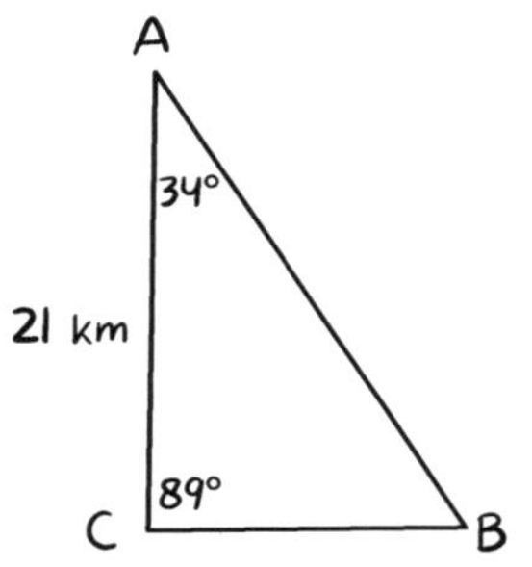

122. Find BC

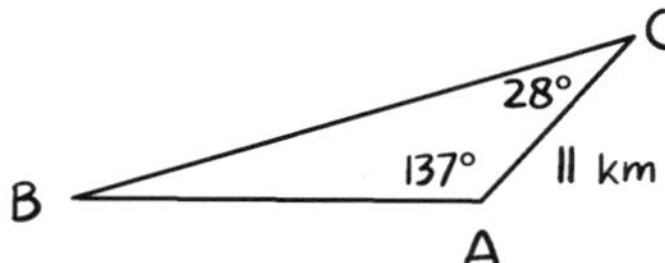

123. Find BC

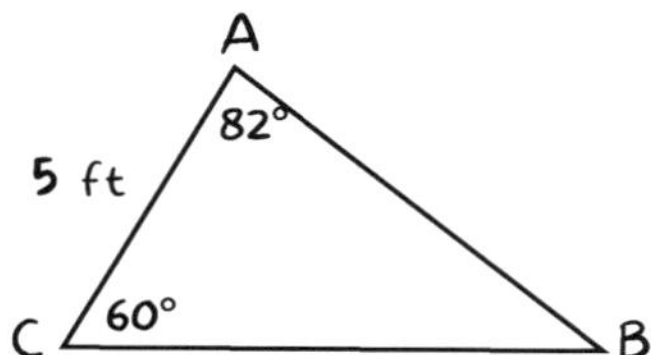

Section 6.1 Quiz

124. Find BC

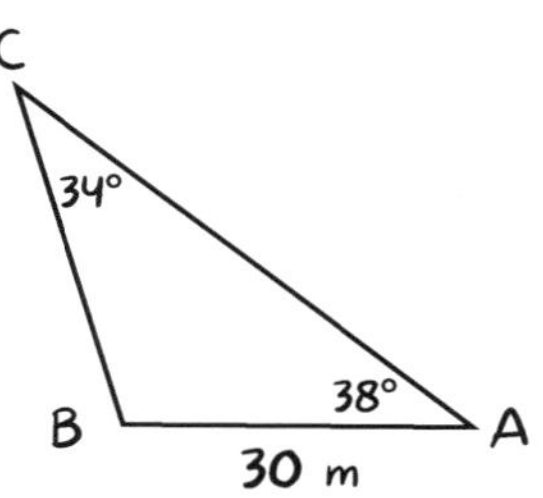

125. Find AC

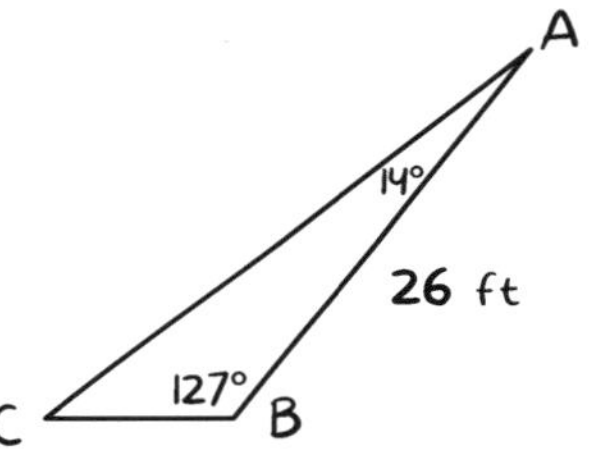

126. Find AC

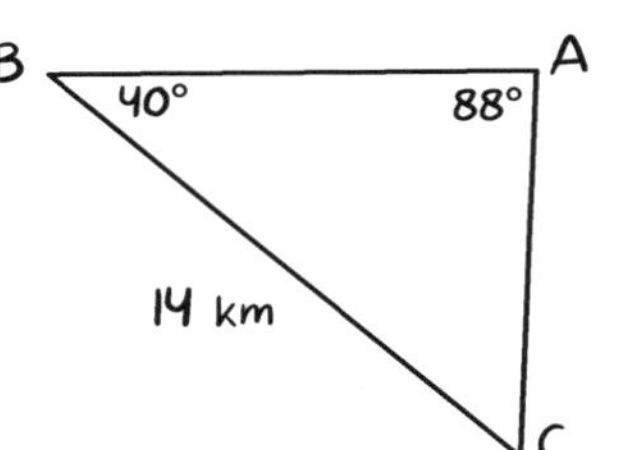

127. Find AC

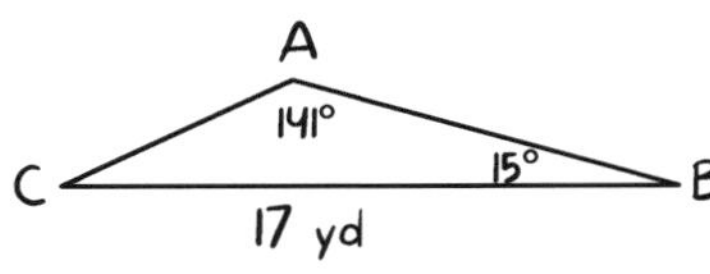

128. Find AC

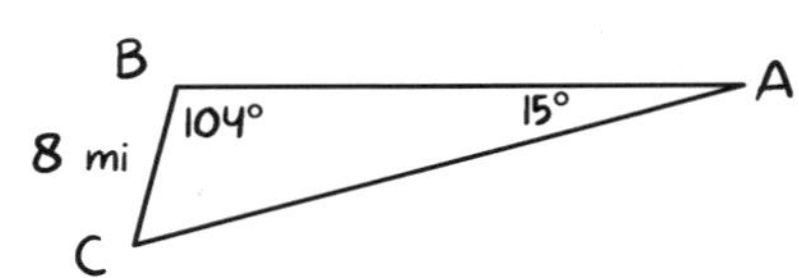

129. Find BC

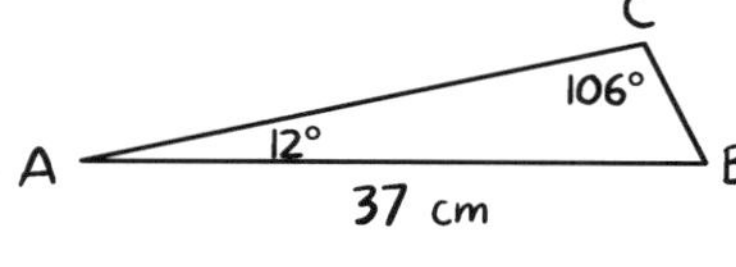

130. Find AB

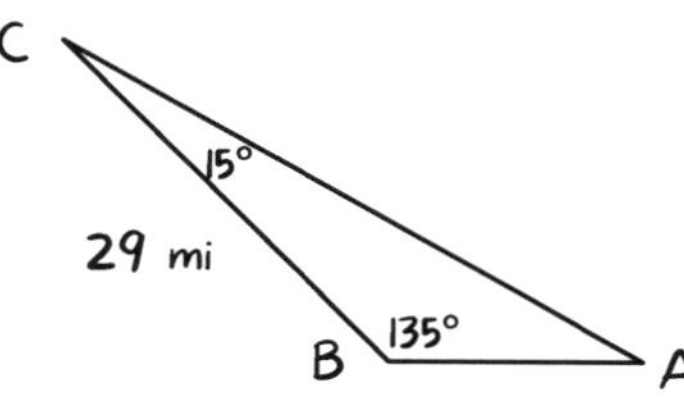

131. Find AC

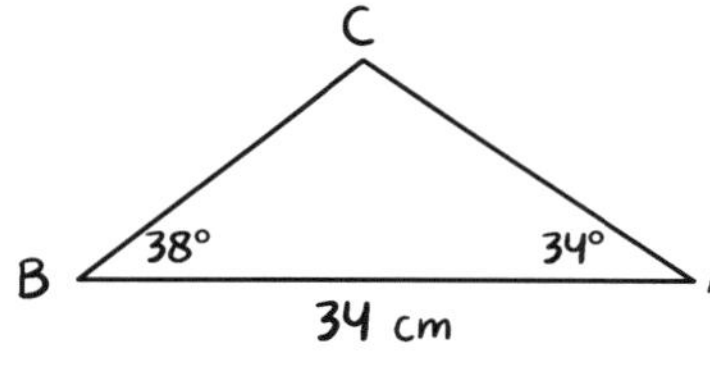

132. Find BC

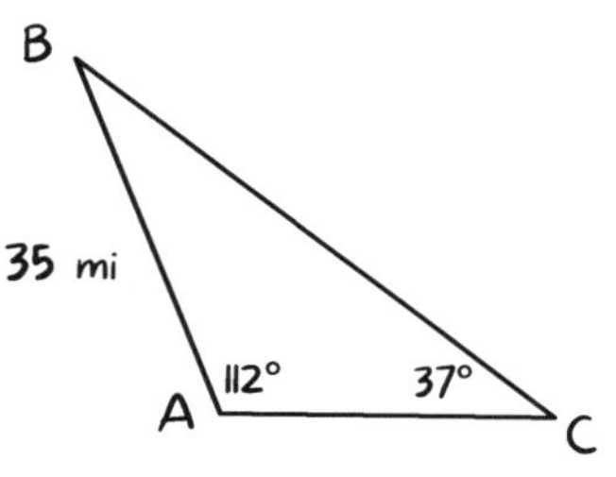

133. Find AB

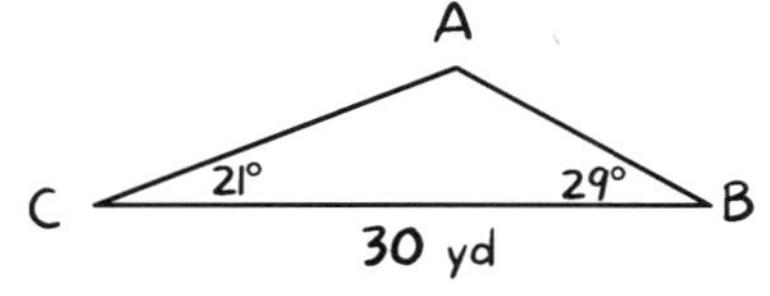

134. Find AB

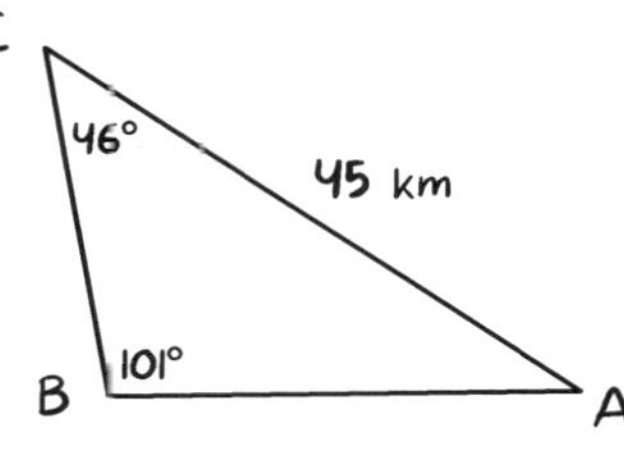

135. Find AC

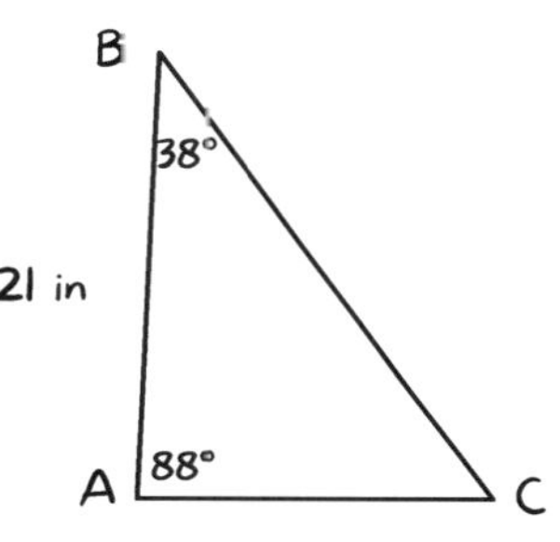

136. Find BC

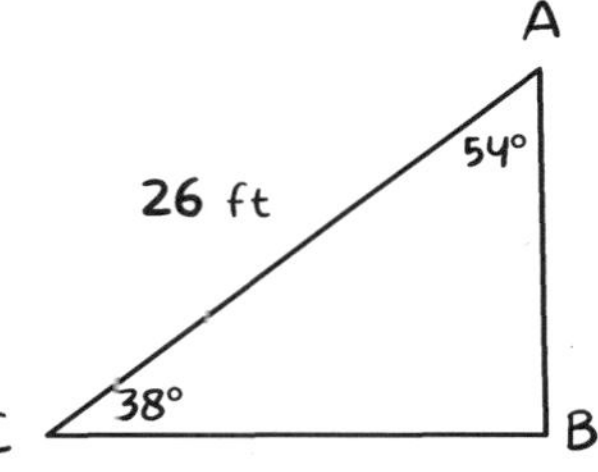

137. Find AC

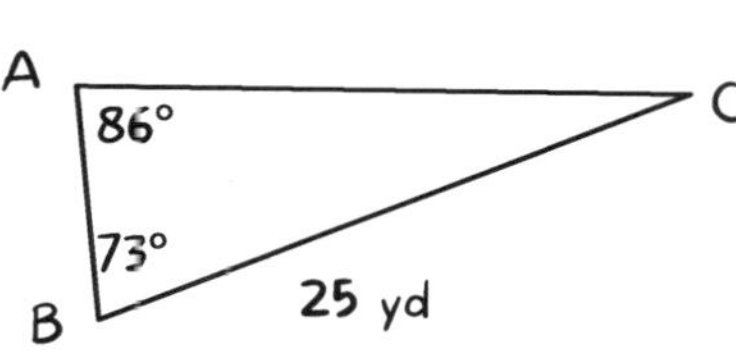

138. Find AB

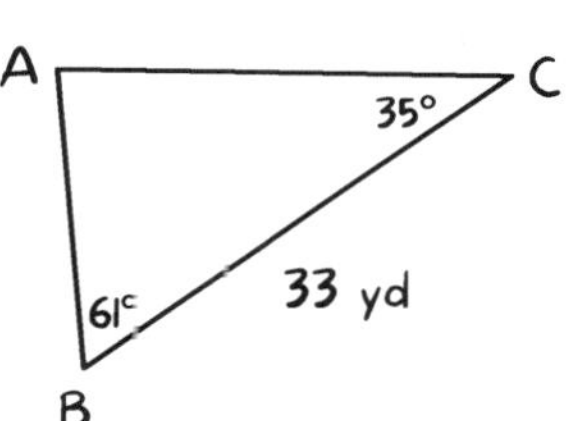

Section 6.1 Quiz

139. Find AC

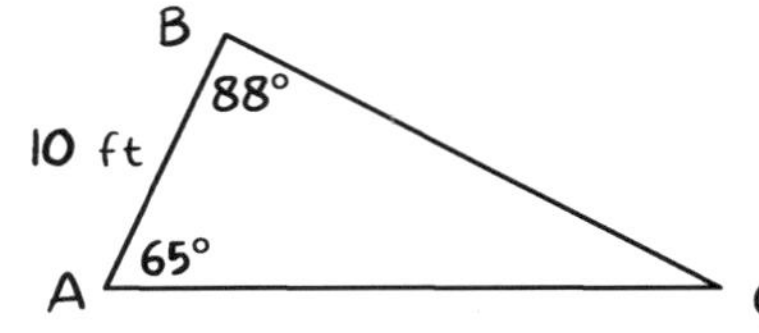

140. Find BC

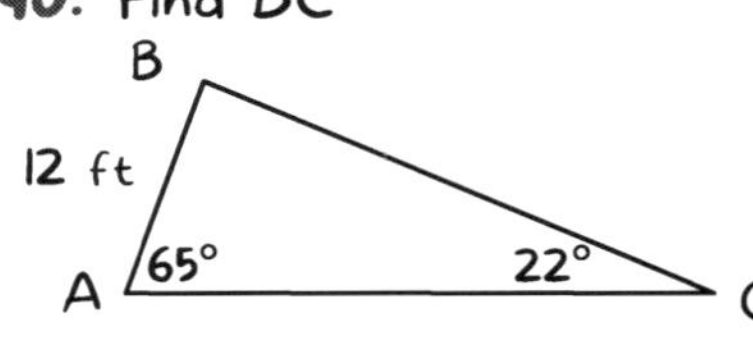

141. Find BC

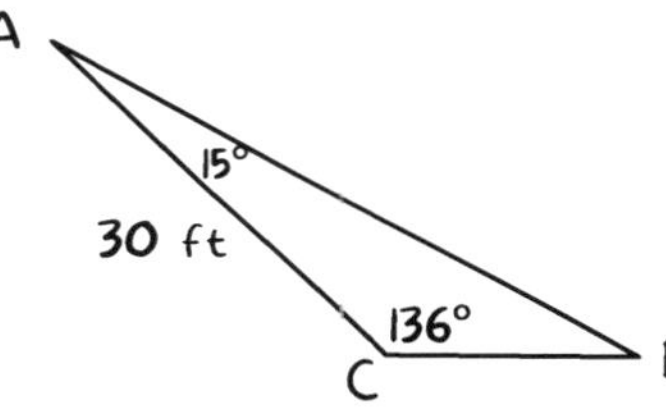

142. Find AB

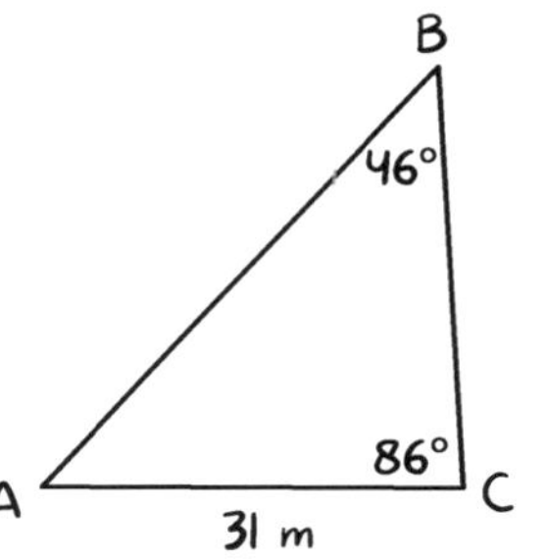

143. Find AC

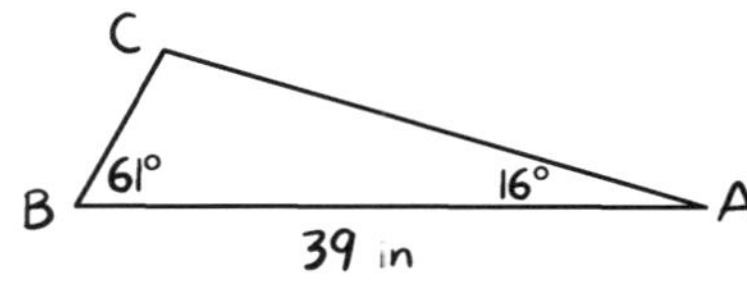

144. Find AC

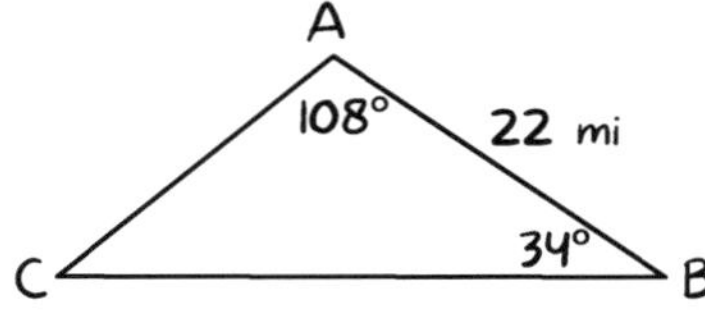

145. Find AC

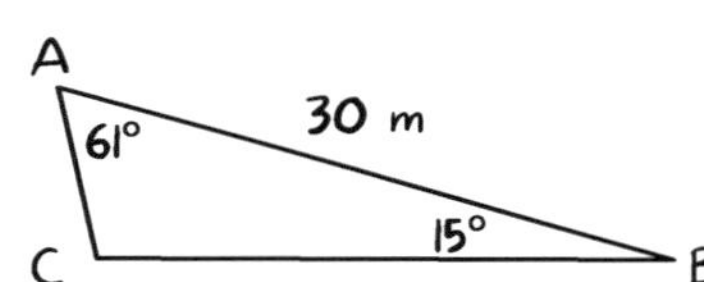

146. Find AC

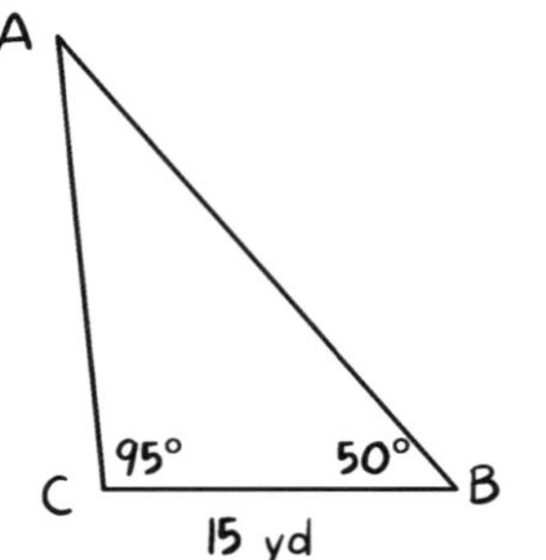

147. Find AB

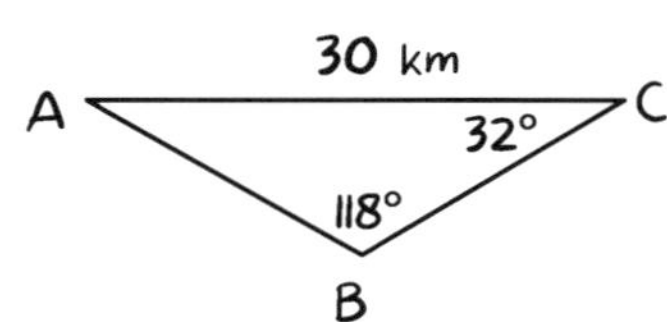

148. Find AB

149. Find BC

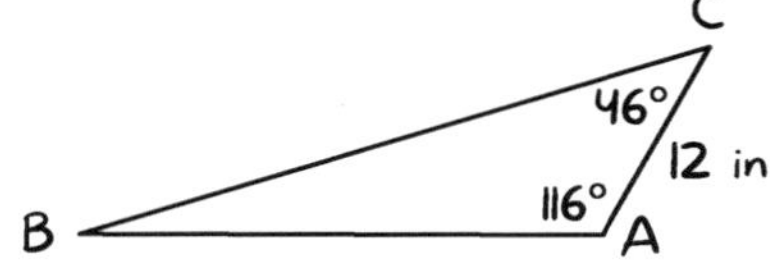

150. Find BC

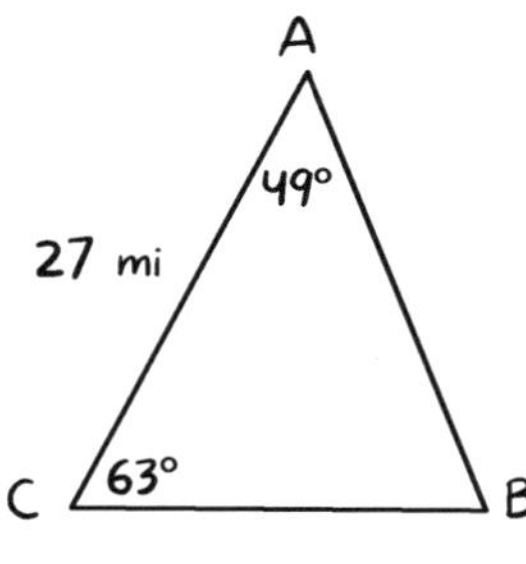

151. Find BC

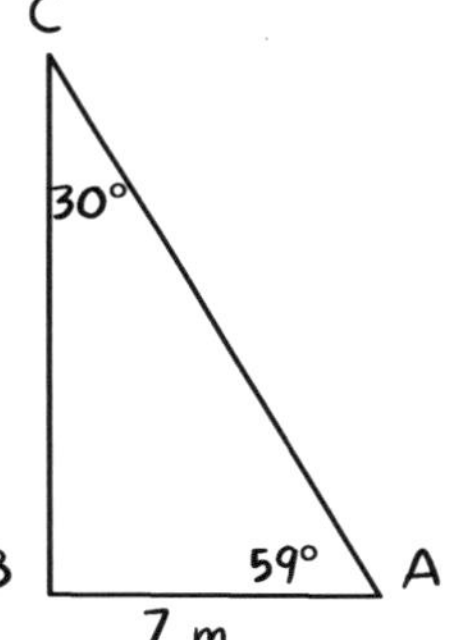

152. Find BC

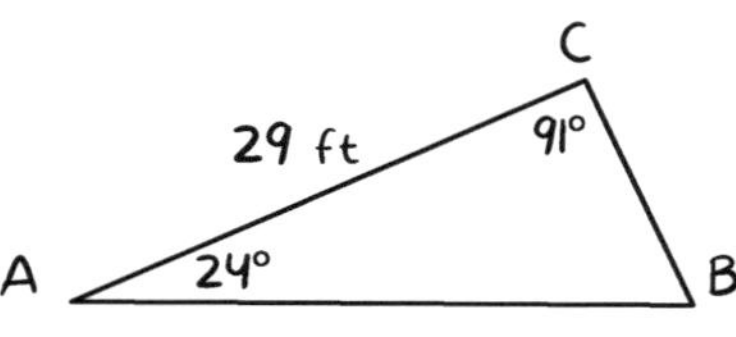

153. Find AC

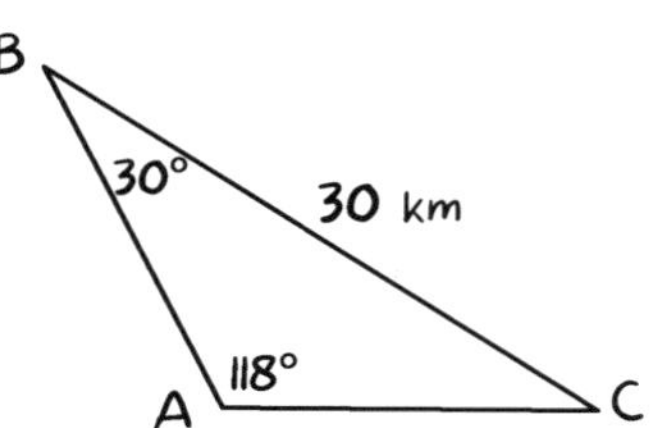

Section 6.1 Quiz

154. Find AC

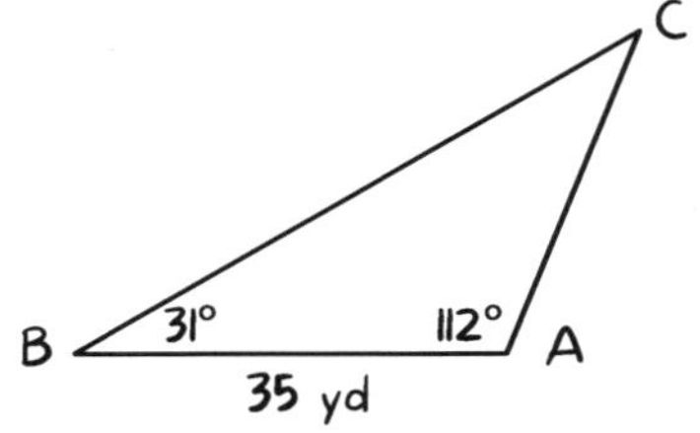

155. Find AB

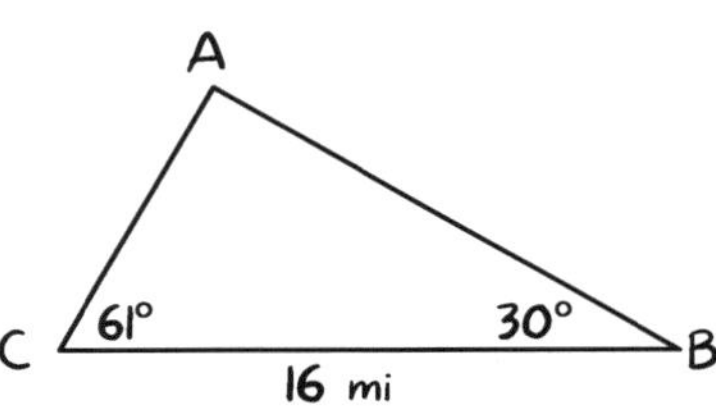

156. Find AB

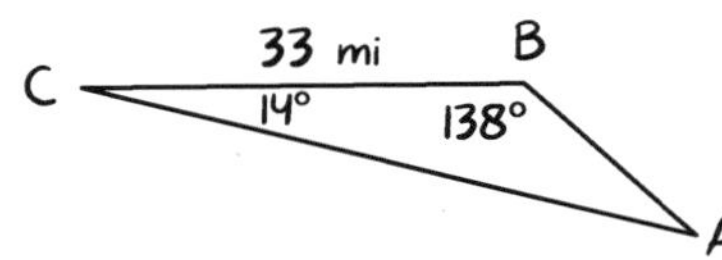

157. Find AC

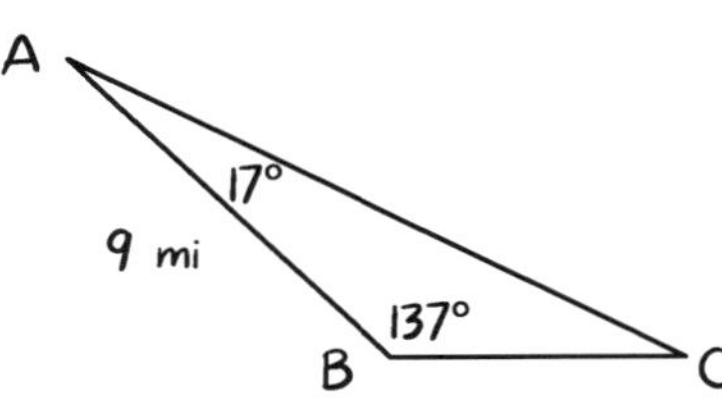

158. Find BC

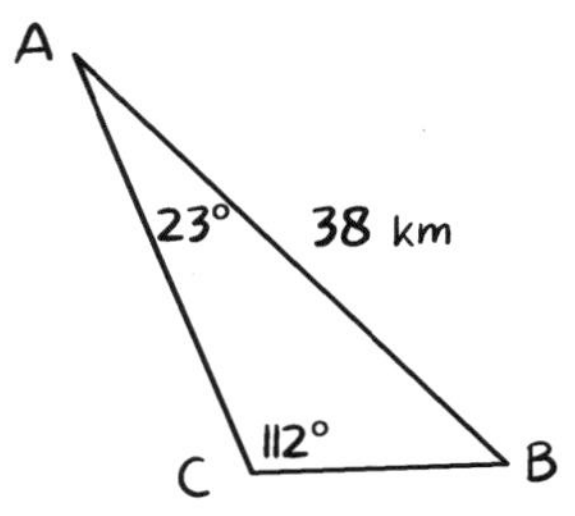

159. Find BC

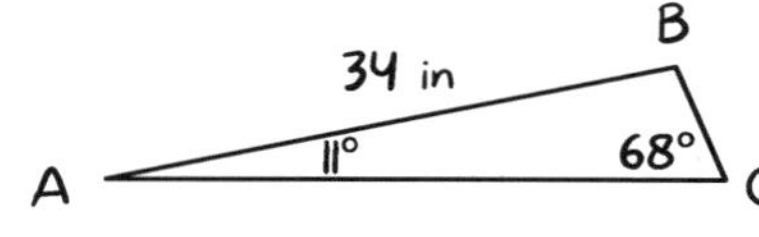

160. Find AB

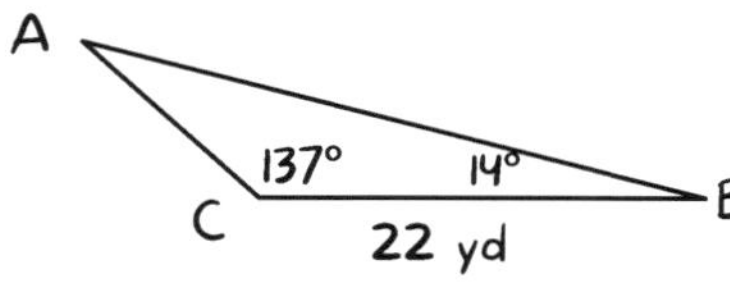

161. Find AB

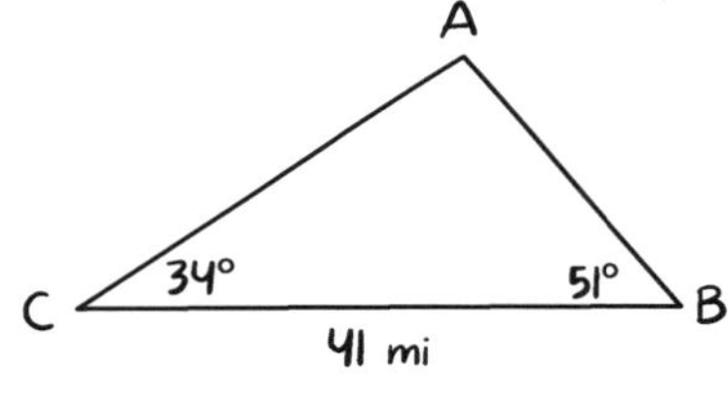

162. Find BC

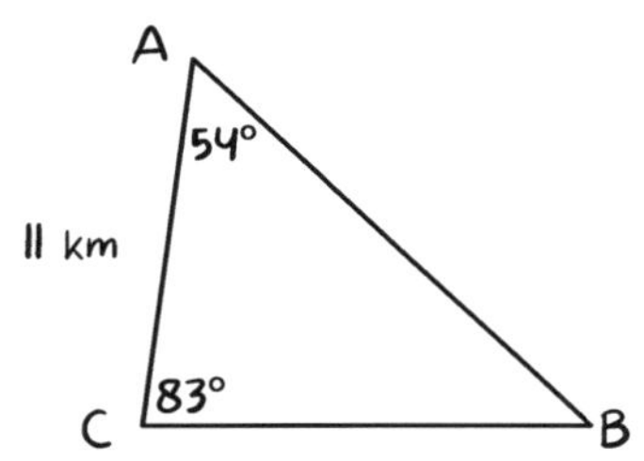

163. Find BC

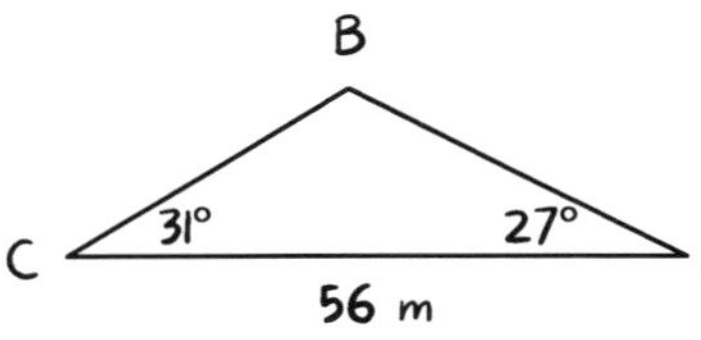

164. Find AB

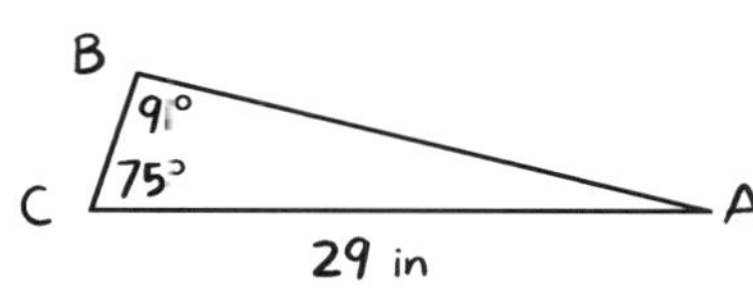

165. Find AB

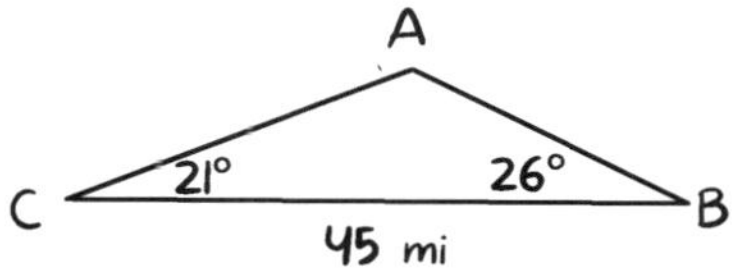

166. Find AC

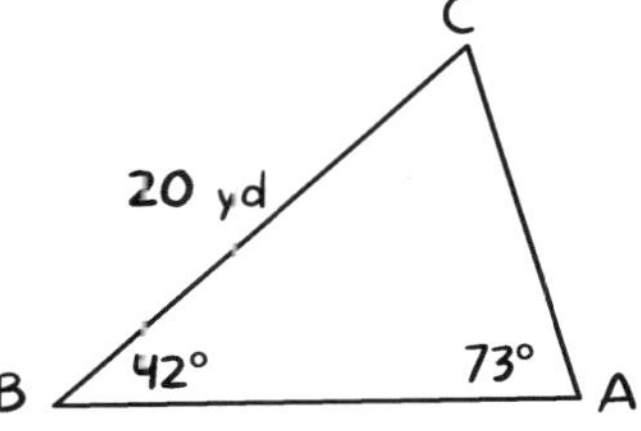

167. Find BC

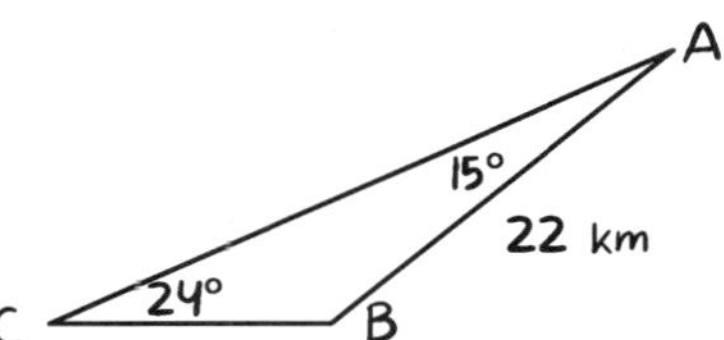

168. Find BC

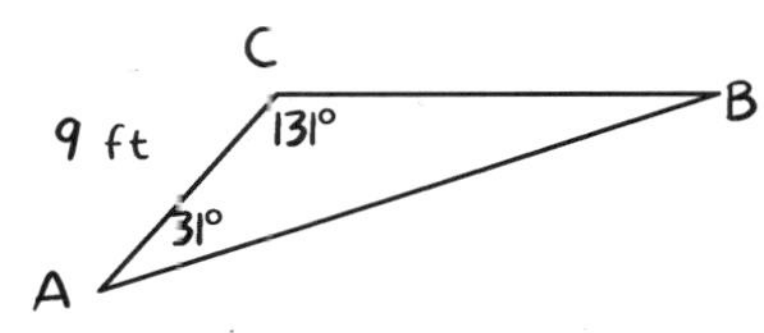

Section 6.1 Quiz

169. Find AC

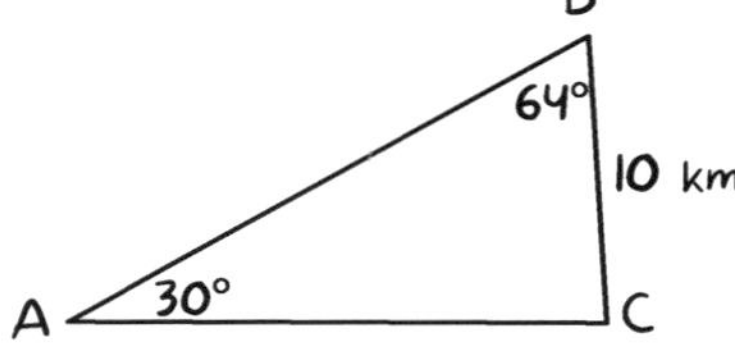

170. Find AC

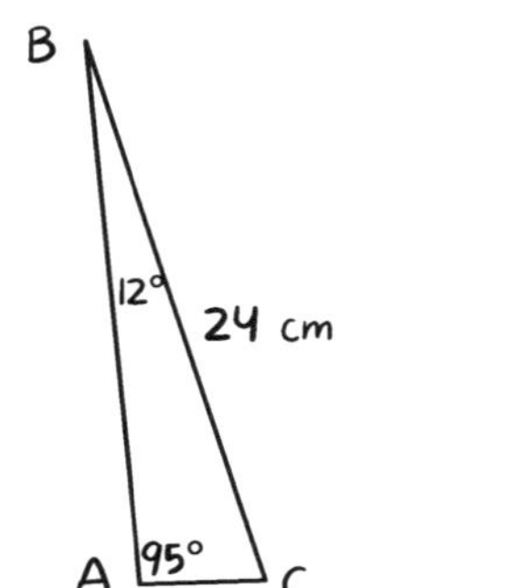

171. Find AB

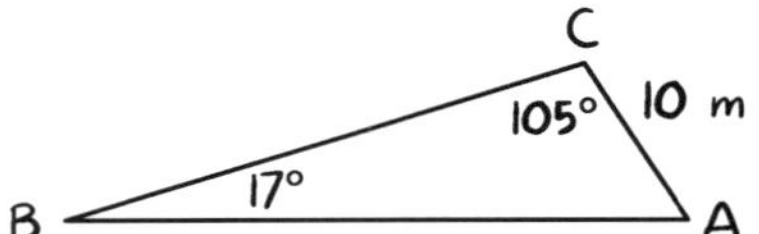

172. Find AC

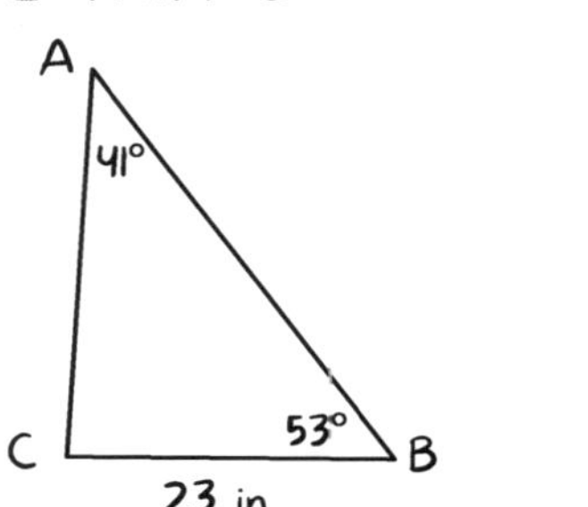

173. Find AC

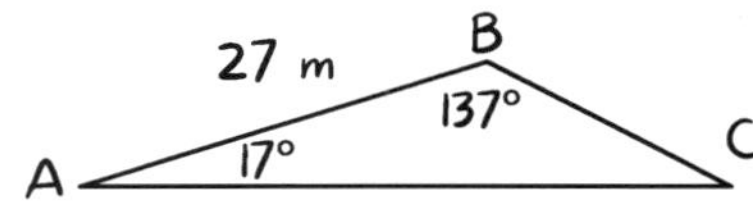

174. Find BC

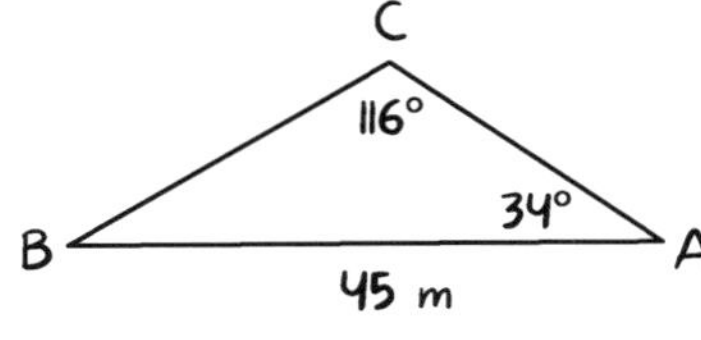

175. Find AC

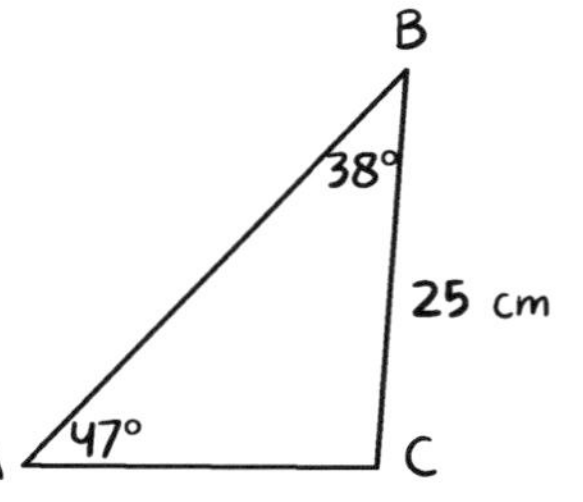

176. Find AB

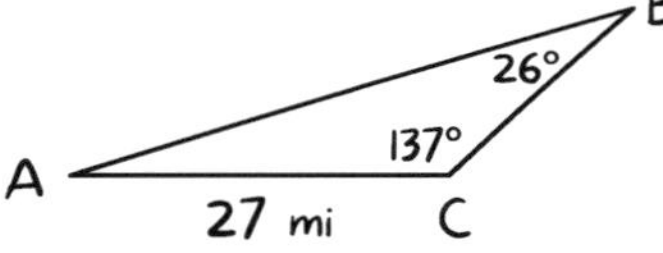

177. Find BC

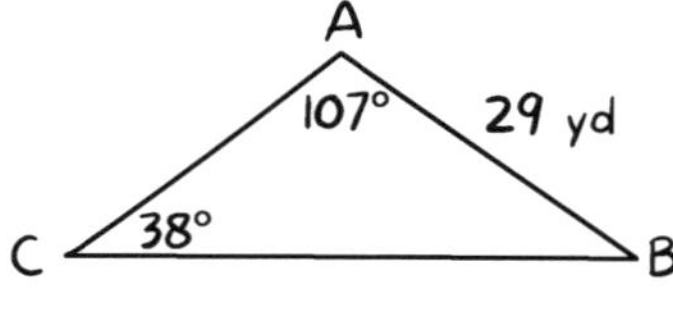

178. Find AC

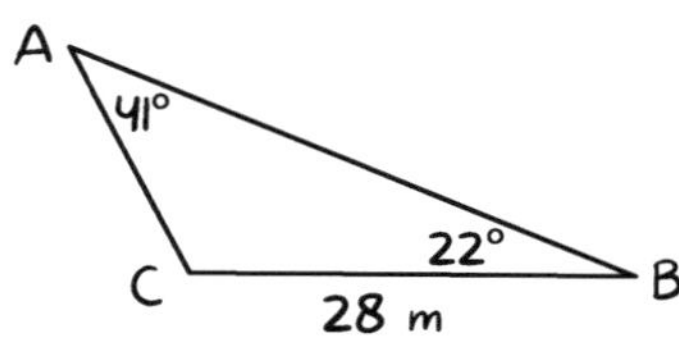

179. Find BC

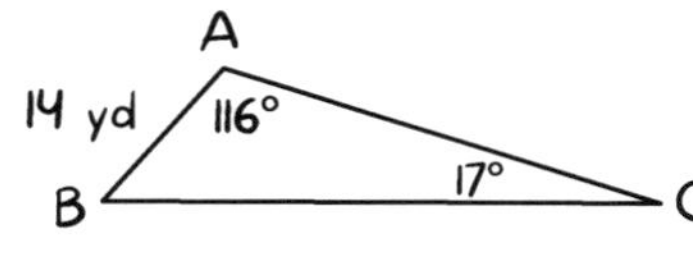

180. Find AC

181. Find AC

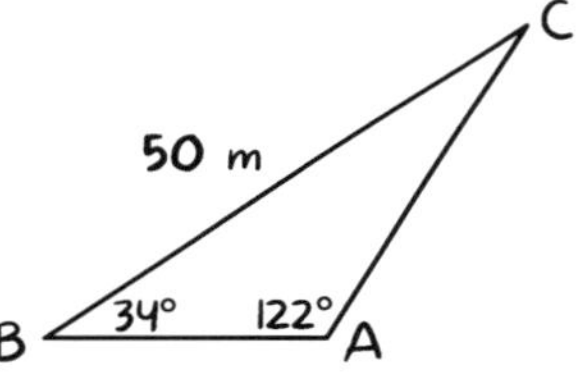

182. Find AB

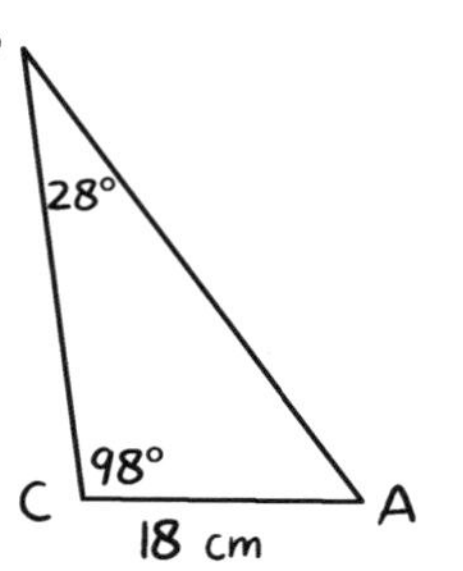

183. Find AC

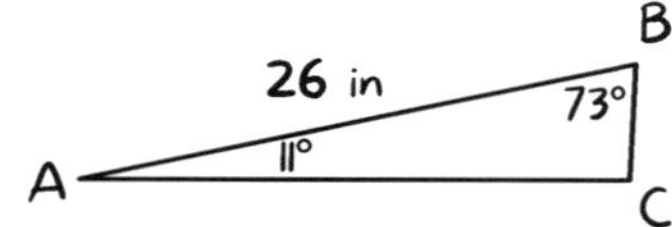

Section 6.1 Quiz

184. Find AB

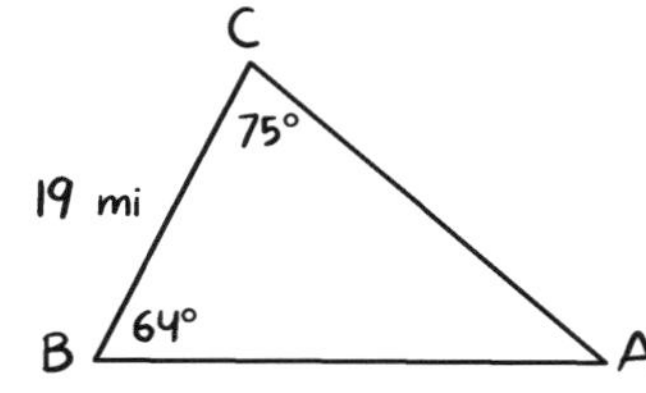

185. Find AB

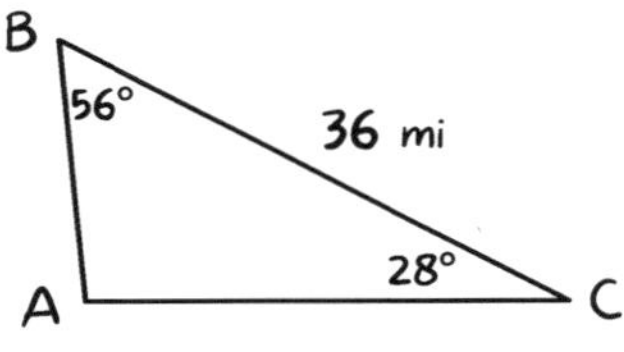

186. Find BC

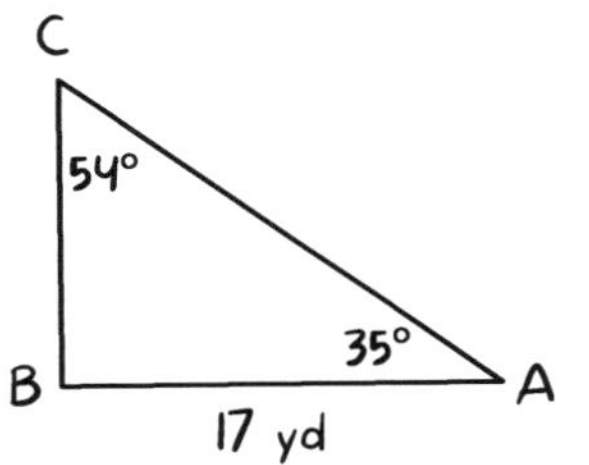

187. Find AB

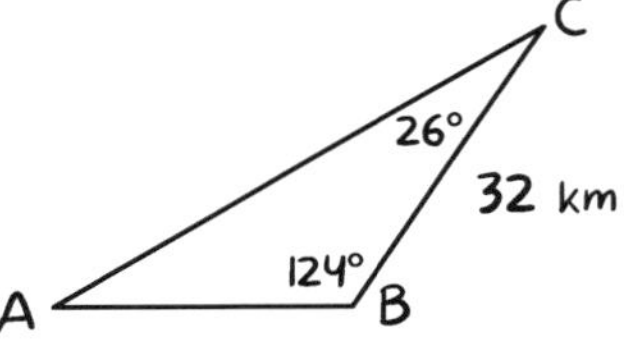

188. Find AC

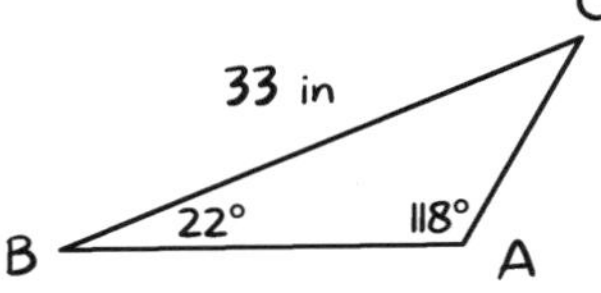

189. Find AB

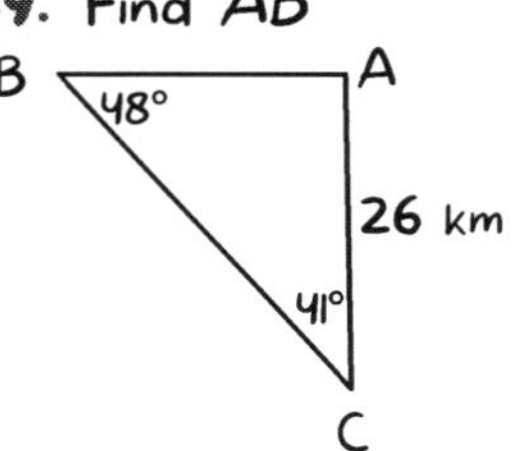

190. Find AC

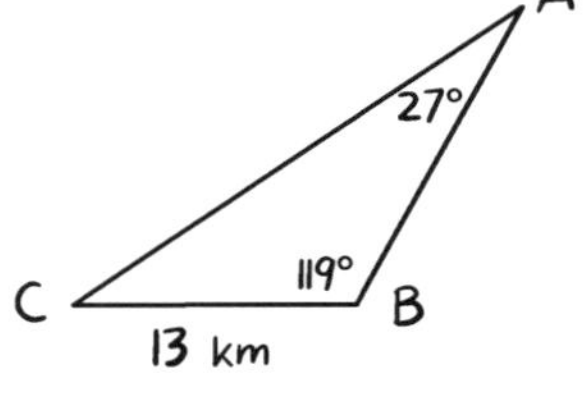

191. Find AC

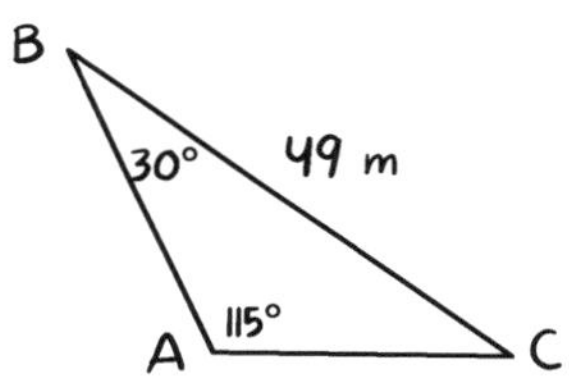

192. Find AB

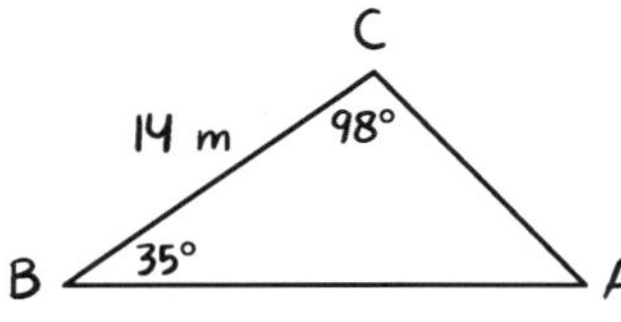

193. Find BC

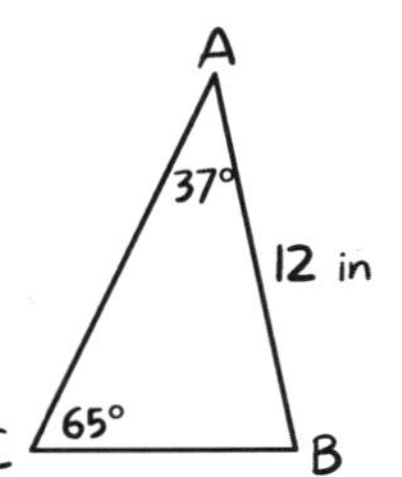

194. Find AC

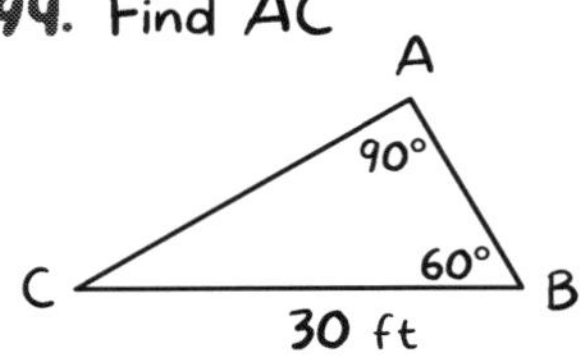

195. Find AC

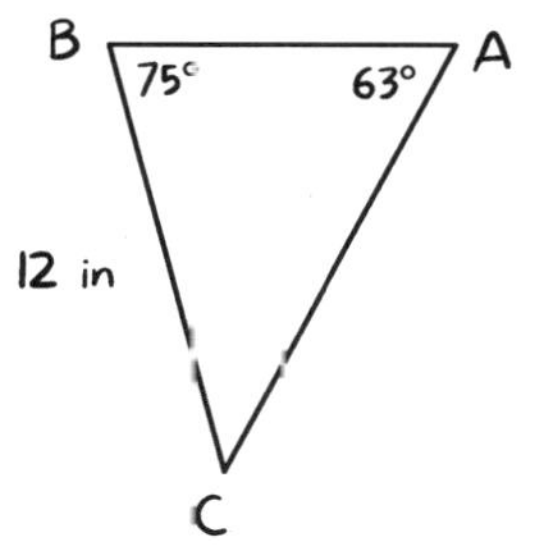

196. Find AB

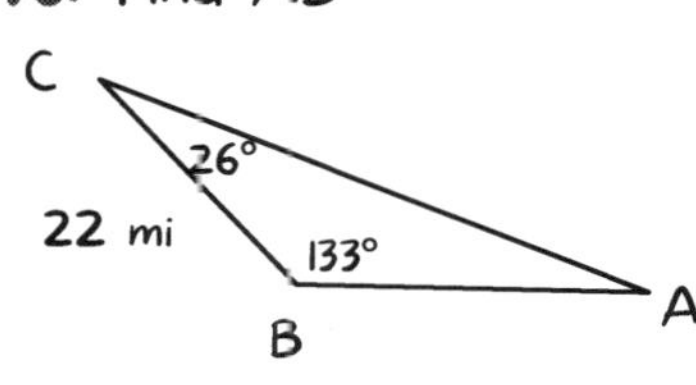

197. Find BC

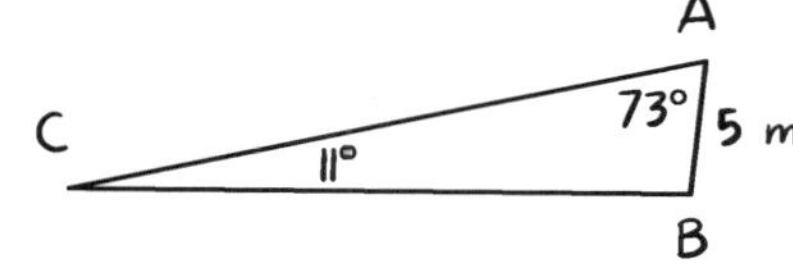

198. Find AC

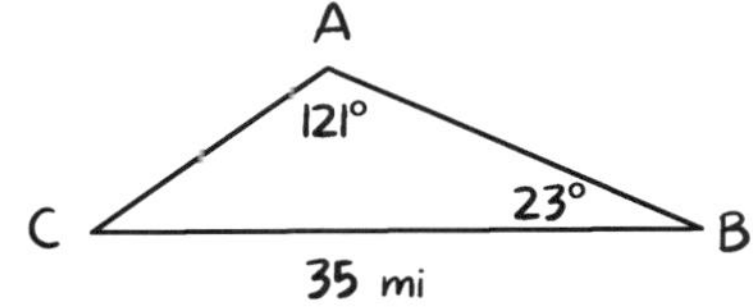

199. Find AC

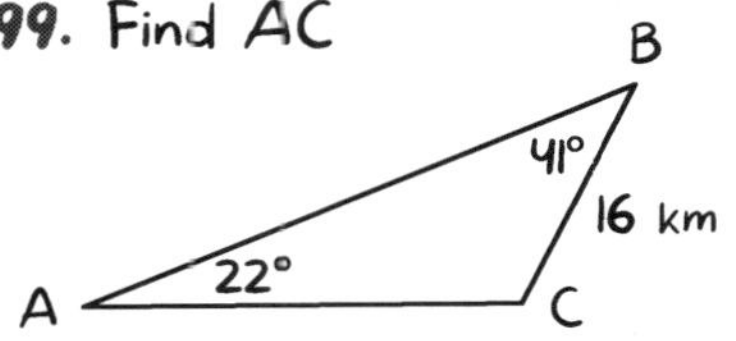

200. Find AC

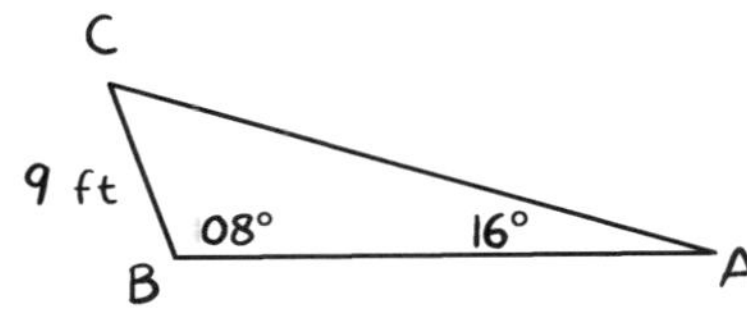

Section 6.2: The Law of Cosines

Law of Cosines:
Imagine you have an **oblique** triangle (a triangle with **no** right triangle) with sides of lengths a, b, and c, and the angles opposite these sides are A, B, and C respectively.

The Law of Cosines essentially relates one side of the triangle to the other two sides and the cosine of its included angle.

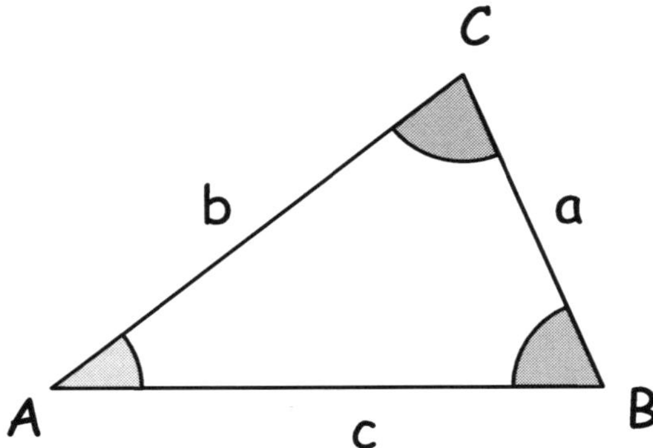

Mathematically:

$$c^2 = a^2 + b^2 - 2ab \cdot \cos(C)$$

This formula can also be written as $a^2 = b^2 + c^2 - 2bc\cos(A)$ **OR** $b^2 = a^2 + c^2 - 2ac\cos(B)$

You just need to remember one of these formulas since all three are the exact same.

You can use the Law of Cosines when you are given the lengths of two sides and the angle between them (SAS) **OR** when you are given the lengths of all three sides (SSS). In these situations, the Law of Sines won't work, as it doesn't provide a feasible ratio to solve.

Let's take a look at a few practice examples to understand how to use the Law of Cosines formula.

Example 1:

What is BC? Round to the nearest tenth.

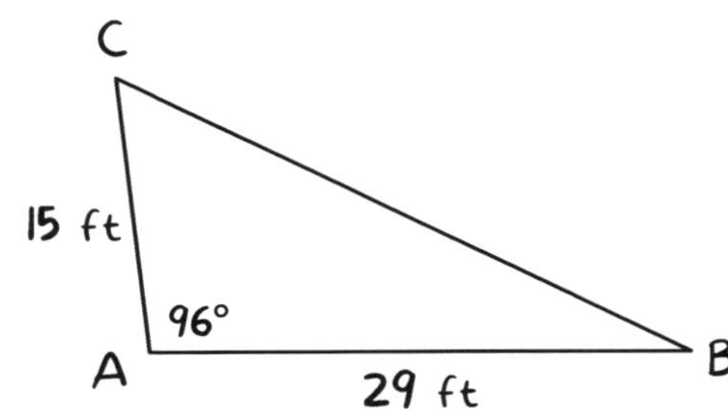

In this example, we are provided with **two sides** and the included angle (SAS). Let's use our formula to solve.

$$c^2 = a^2 + b^2 - 2ab \cdot \cos(C)$$

$$c = \sqrt{a^2 + b^2 - 2ab \cdot \cos(C)}$$

$$c = \sqrt{15^2 + 29^2 - 2(15)(29)(\cos 96^\circ)}$$

$$c = \sqrt{1066 - 870(\cos 96^\circ)}$$

$$c = \sqrt{1066 - (-90.9397)}$$

$$c = \sqrt{1156.9397}$$

$c = 34.01$ ft ⟵ The problem states to round to the nearest tenth so the answer is 34.0 ft, or just 34 ft.

Example 2:

What is BC? Round to the nearest tenth.

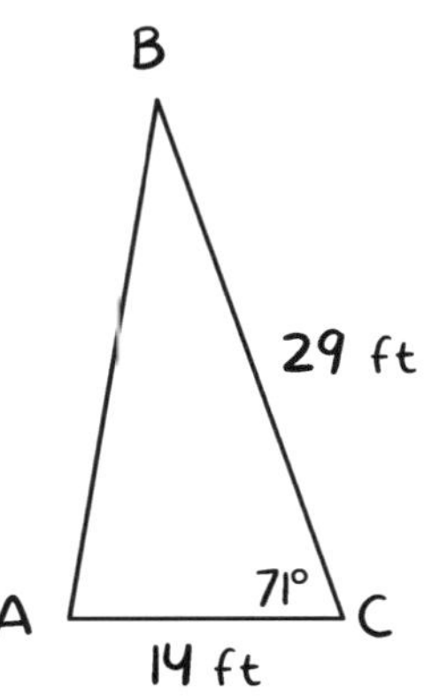

Just like on the example above, we are provided with **two sides** and the included angle (SAS). Let's use our formula to solve.

$$c^2 = a^2 + b^2 - 2ab \cdot \cos(C)$$

$$c = \sqrt{a^2 + b^2 - 2ab \cdot \cos(C)}$$

$$c = \sqrt{14^2 + 29^2 - 2(14)(29)(\cos 71^\circ)}$$

$$c = \sqrt{1037 - 812(\cos 71^\circ)}$$

$$c = \sqrt{1037 - 264.361}$$

$$c = \sqrt{772.639}$$

$c = 27.79$ ft ⟵ The problem states to round to the nearest tenth so the answer is 27.8 ft.

Example 3:

What is m∠A? Round to the nearest tenth.

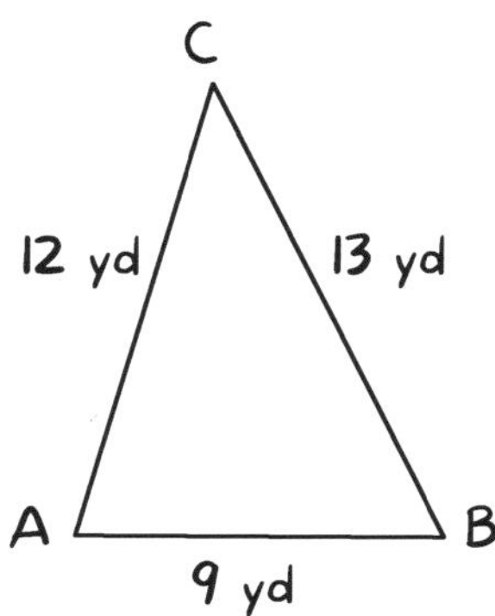

In this example, we are provided with the lengths of all three sides (SSS). We need to determine m∠A. We can use the Law of Cosines to determine the answer.

Notice that opposite of m∠A, we have the side length 13. This will be the value for **a in our formula for Law of Cosines.**

Since we are solving for an angle, it's easier to manipulate the formula where Cos A is isolated on one side of the equation.

$a^2 = b^2 + c^2 - 2bc\cos(A)$ ← We can subtract $b^2 + c^2$ from both sides.

$a^2 - b^2 - c^2 = -2bc\cos(A)$ ← We can divide both sides by $-2bc$

$\frac{a^2 - b^2 - c^2}{-2bc} = \cos(A)$ ← This is the formula we will use to find m∠A.

Simply plug in the known values.

$$\cos(A) = \frac{a^2 - b^2 - c^2}{-2bc} = \frac{13^2 - 12^2 - 9^2}{-2(12)(9)} = \frac{-56}{-216} = 0.2592$$

$\cos(A) = 0.2592$ ← We need to use our calculator and take the inverse cosine (arccosine).

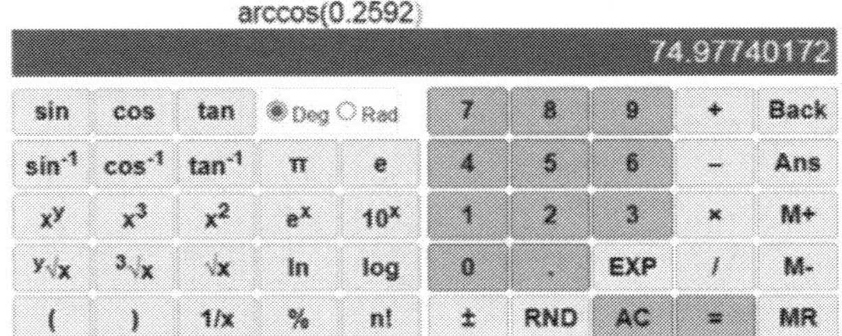

We get $m\angle A = 74.97°$. Round to the nearest tenth and we get our answer $m\angle A = 75°$.

Example 4:

What is $m\angle C$? Round to the nearest tenth.

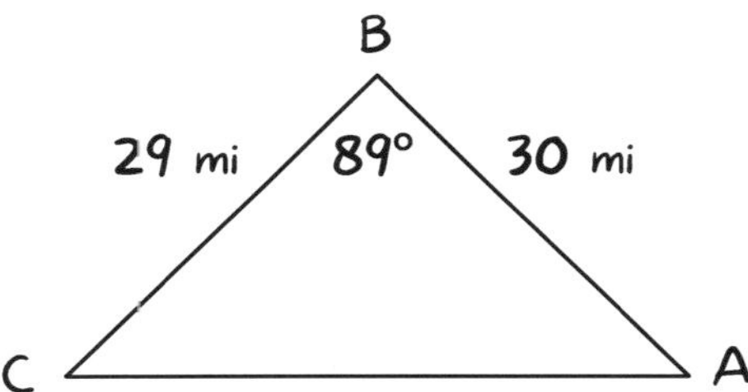

In this example, we are provided with a side, angle and side (SAS). We are asked to find angle C. We **cannot** solve this problem like we solved the previous ones. Notice if we try to use the formula $c^2 = a^2 + b^2 - 2ab\cos(C)$, we have **two unknown** variables. We don't know cos(C) which we are trying to solve for, but more importantly we do not know the value of b. Therefore, we cannot solve this problem until we know the value of b.

So, the first question we ask our self is what is the value or B or length of AC (they are the same thing).

We can use the formula $b^2 = a^2 + c^2 - 2ac\cos(B)$. Plug in the known values.

$$b^2 = 29^2 + 30^2 - 2(29)(30)\cos(89°)$$

$$b^2 = 29^2 + 30^2 - 2(29)(30)\cos(89°)$$

$$b^2 = 1741 - 1740\cos(89°)$$

$$b^2 = 1710.633 \leftarrow \text{Square root both sides}$$

$$b = 41.359 \text{ mi}$$

Let's add in the new information to our diagram. We can round to the nearest hundredths for more accuracy.

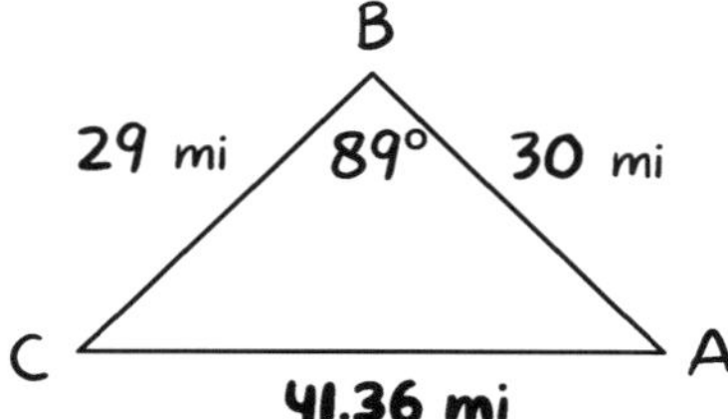

Now we can find $m\angle C$ by using the Law of Sines **or** Law of Cosines formula.

If we use the Law of Sines formula, remember $\frac{a}{\sin(A)} = \frac{b}{\sin(B)} = \frac{c}{\sin(C)}$

We can set up the proportional equation $\frac{41.36}{\sin(89°)} = \frac{30}{\sin(C)}$ ← Cross multiply

$41.36\sin(C) = 30\sin(89°)$

$41.36\sin(C) = 29.995$ ← divide both sides by 41.36

$\sin(C) = 0.725$

Use the inverse function (arcsin) on your calculator and we will get $m\angle C = 46.46°$. We need to round to the nearest tenth as requested in the original problem. **Therefore,** $m\angle C = 46.5°$

What if we used the Law of Cosines instead? Let's try it.

$c^2 = a^2 + b^2 - 2ab\cos(C)$ ← manipulate this equation so $\cos(C)$ is only on one side.

$\frac{c^2 - a^2 - b^2}{-2ab} = \cos(C)$ ← Plug in your known values

$$\cos(C) = \frac{c^2 - a^2 - b^2}{-2ab} = \frac{30^2 - 29^2 - 41.36^2}{-2(29)(41.36)} = \frac{-1651.649}{-2398.88} = 0.6885$$

$\cos(C) = 0.6885$ Use the inverse function (arccos) on your calculator and we will get $m\angle C = 46.5°$.

We got the same answer. Although, you probably noticed it is much **easier** to use the Law of Sines. **To avoid careless mistakes, please use Law of Sines when you can.**

Example 5:

Find all the missing angles and sides for the triangle below.

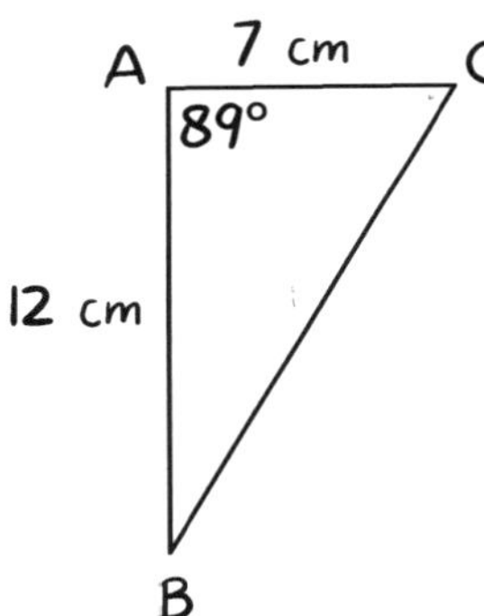

In order to solve this problem, we will need to use Law of Cosine, Law of Sine and our knowledge of triangles.

In this problem, we can first find the value of BC. Notice $m\angle A$ is opposite of BC so we will use the formula $a^2 = b^2 + c^2 - 2bc\cos(A)$.

$$a^2 = 7^2 + 12^2 - 2(7)(12)\cos(89°)$$

$$a^2 = 193 - 168\cos(89°)$$

$a^2 = 190.068 \leftarrow$ Square root both sides

$a = 13.8$ cm (rounded to the nearest tenth)

Great! We have solved for BC which is 13.8 cm.

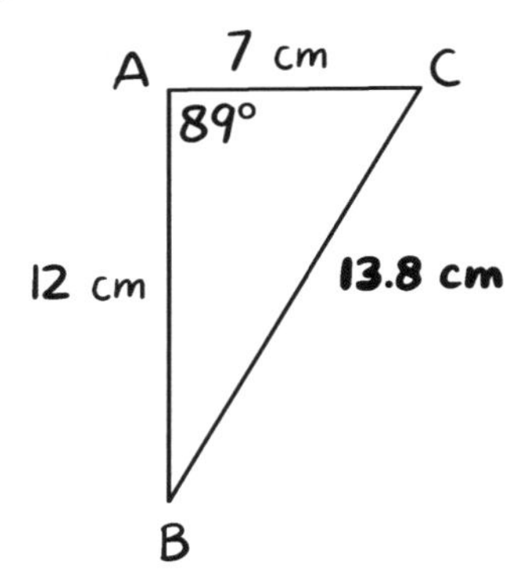

Now we can use Law of Sines and solve for $m\angle B$.

$$\frac{13.8 \text{ cm}}{\sin(89°)} = \frac{7 \text{ cm}}{\sin(B)}$$

$13.8 \sin(B) = 7 \sin(89°)$

$\sin(B) = 0.507$ ← Use the inverse function (arcsin) on your calculator and we will get $m\angle B = 30.5°$.

Finally, we are missing the last angle. That is the easiest to find out! We know all three angles in a triangle always add upto 180°. Since we know the other two angles, we can add the two known angles and subtract by 180.

$180° - (30.5° + 89°) = 60.5°$

A
7 cm
C
89°
60.5°
12 cm
13.8 cm
30.5°
B

You are now ready to try practice problems on your own. Double check your work as it is easy to make careless mistakes on these types of problems.

Section 6.2 Quiz

Directions: : Solve for the missing sides, angles or both! Show your work on a separate piece of paper. Round your final answers to the nearest tenth.

1. Find BC

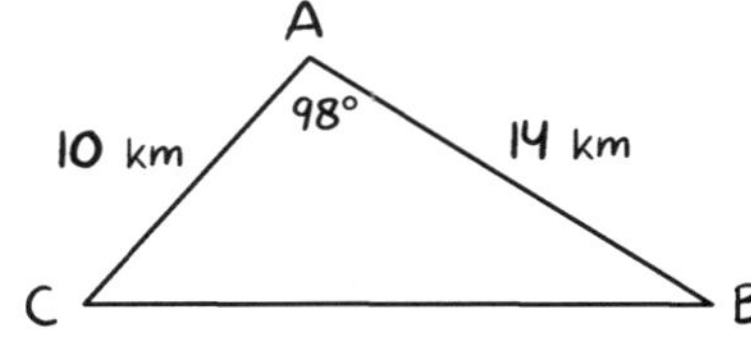

2. Find AB

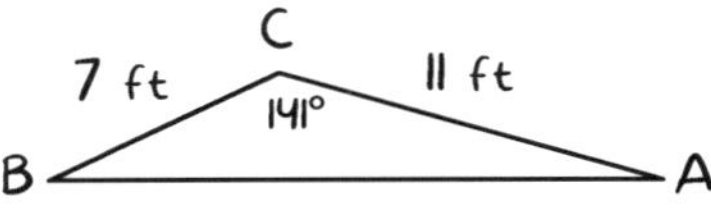

3. Find AC

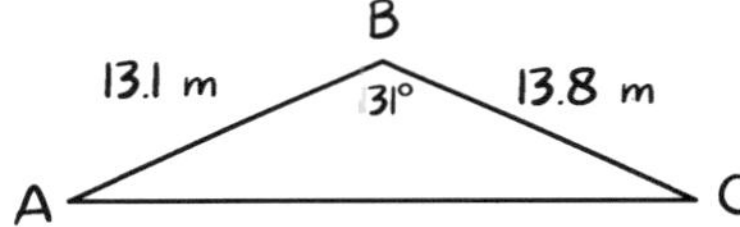

4. Find AC

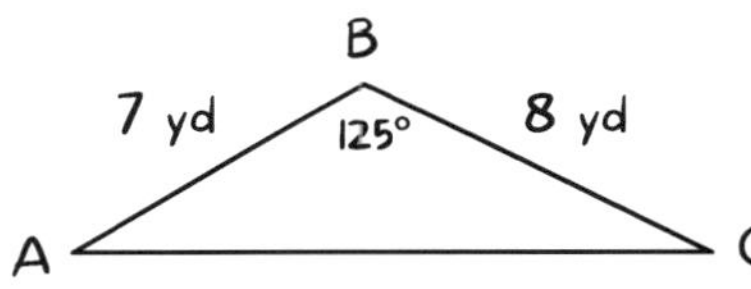

5. Find AC

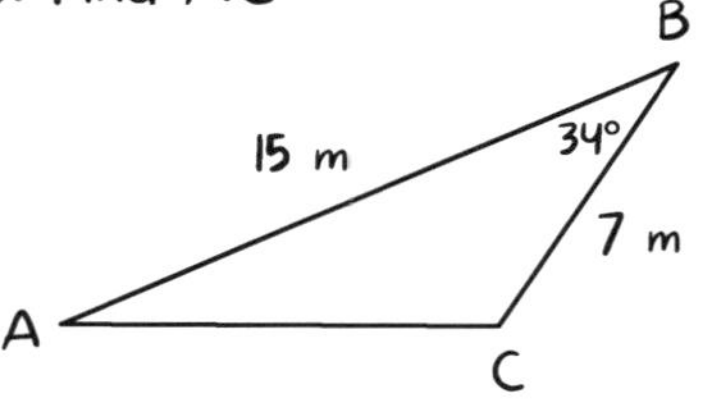

6. Find AB

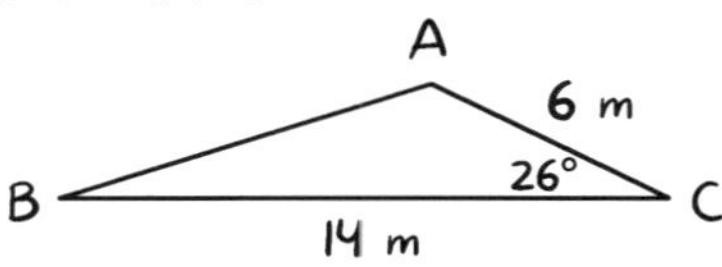

7. Find BC

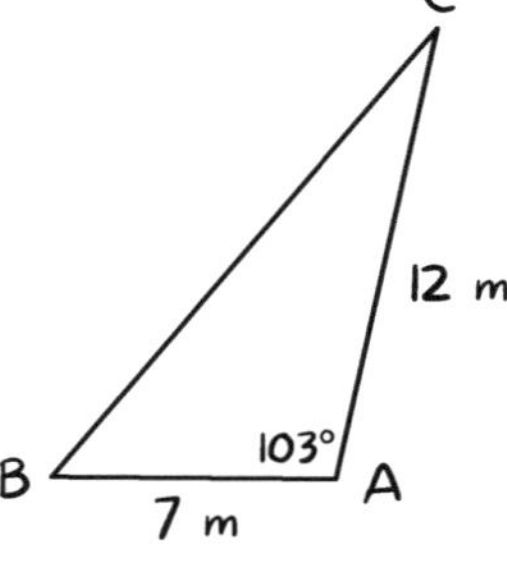

8. Find AC

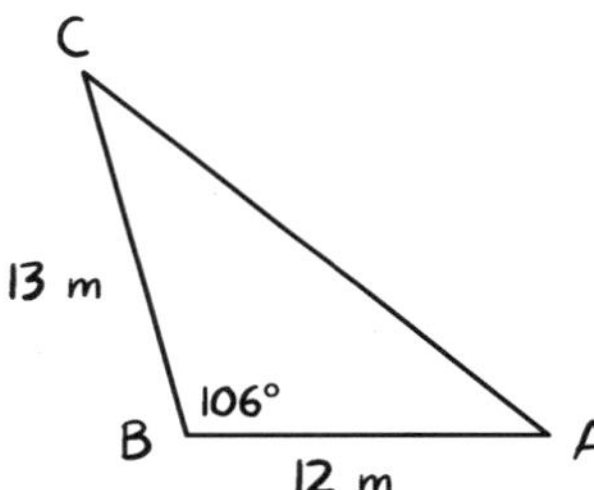

9. Find AB

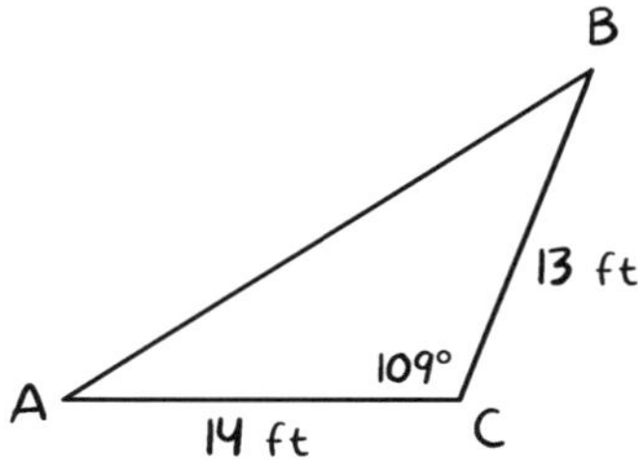

10. Find AC

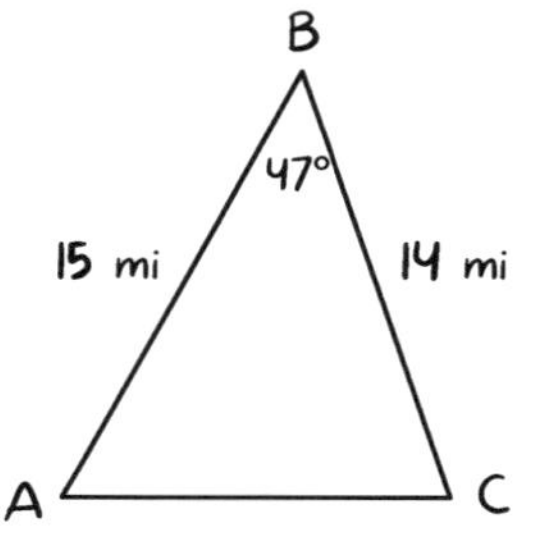

11. Find AB

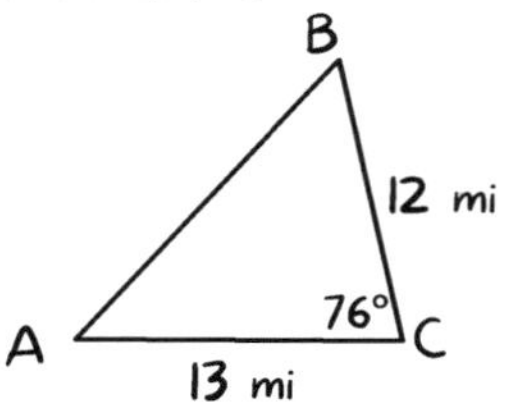

12. Find AB

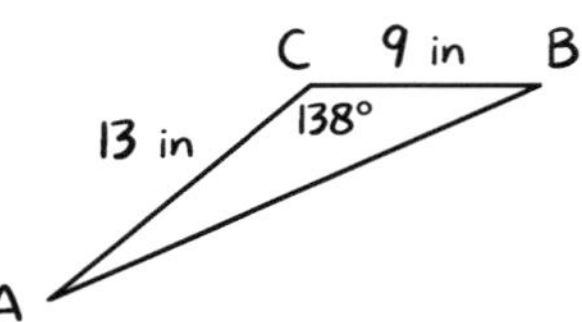

13. Find AC

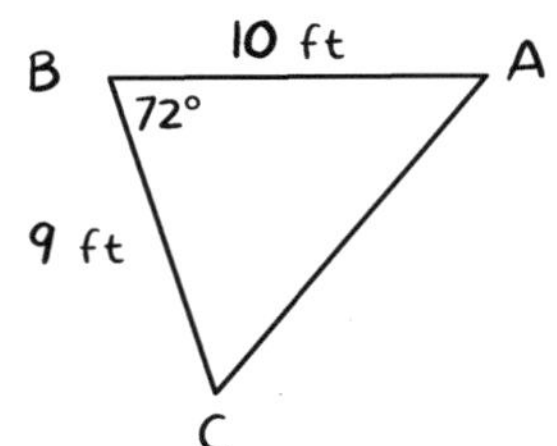

14. Find BC

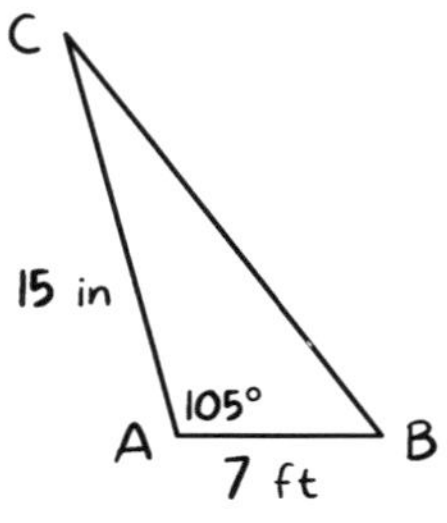

15. Find BC

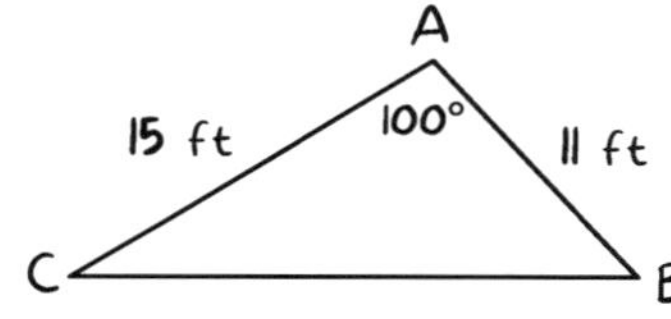

Section 6.2 Quiz

16. Find BC

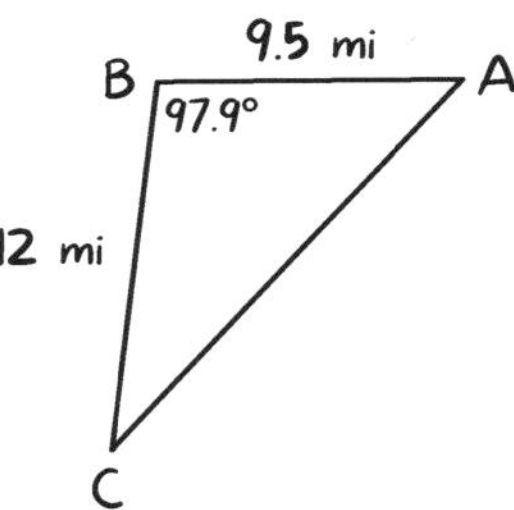

17. Find BC

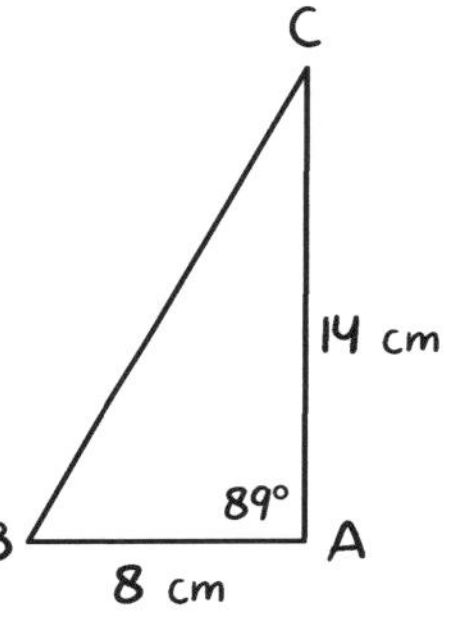

18. Find AC

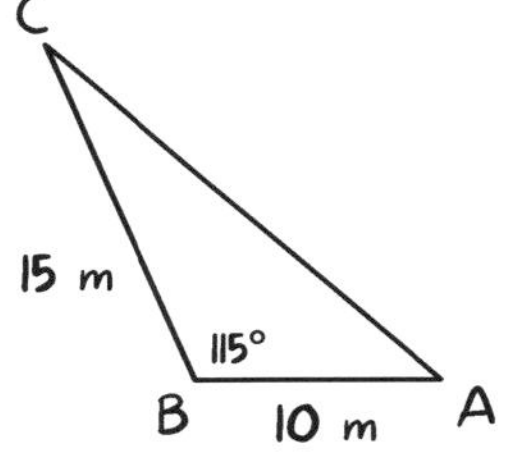

19. Find AC

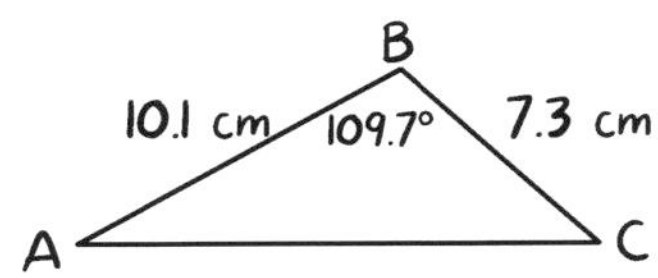

20. Find AB

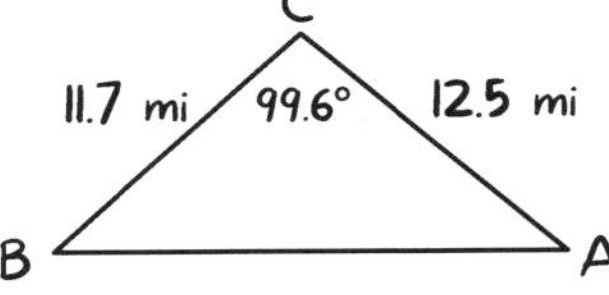

21. Find BC

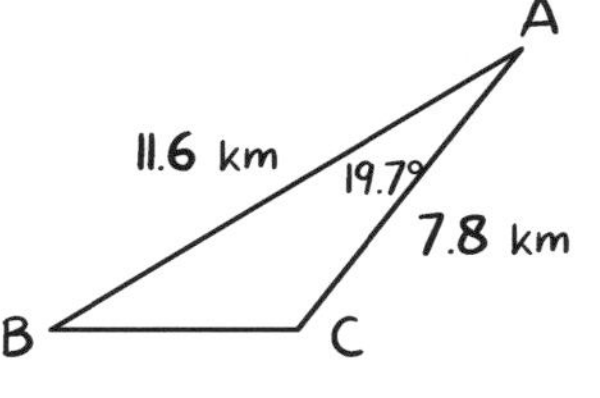

22. Find BC

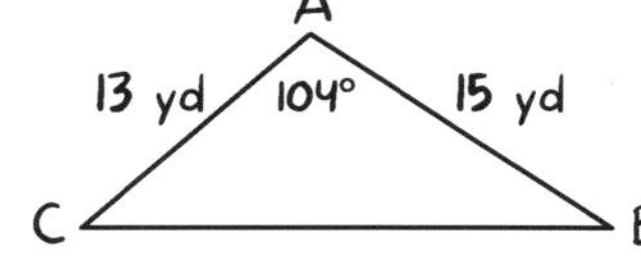

23. Find AB

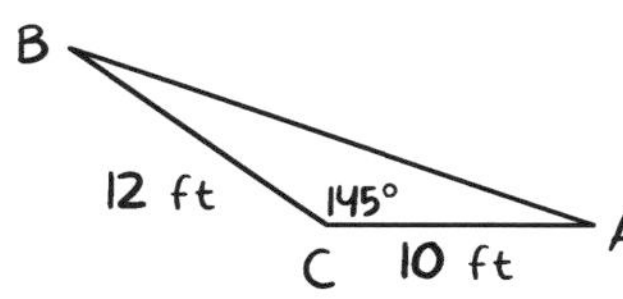

24. Find BC

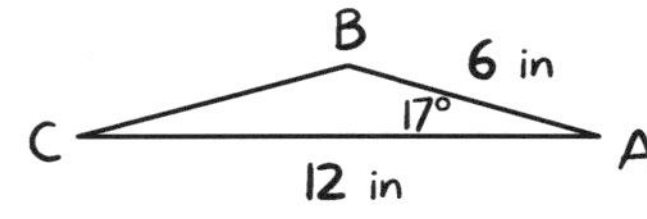

25. Find AB

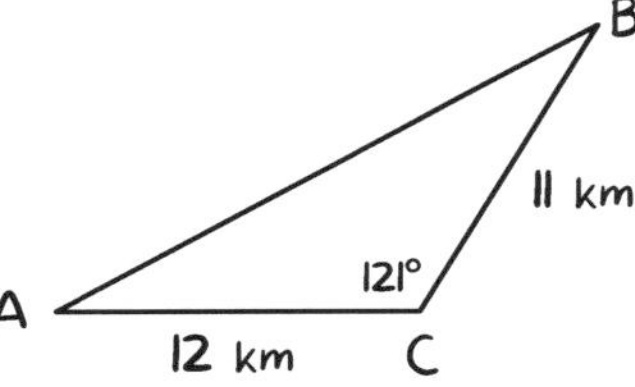

26. Find AC

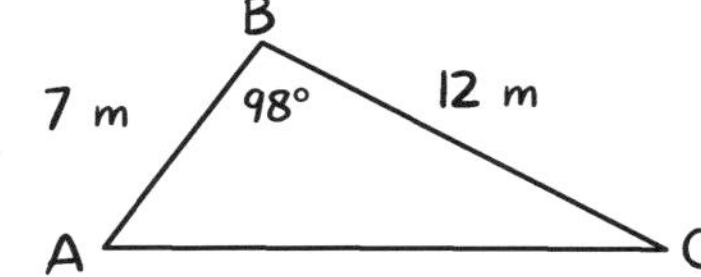

27. Find AB

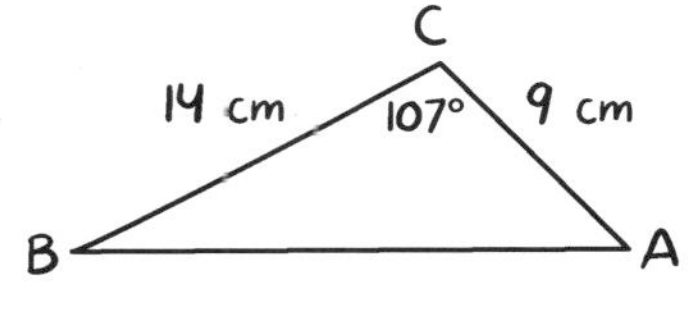

28. Find AC

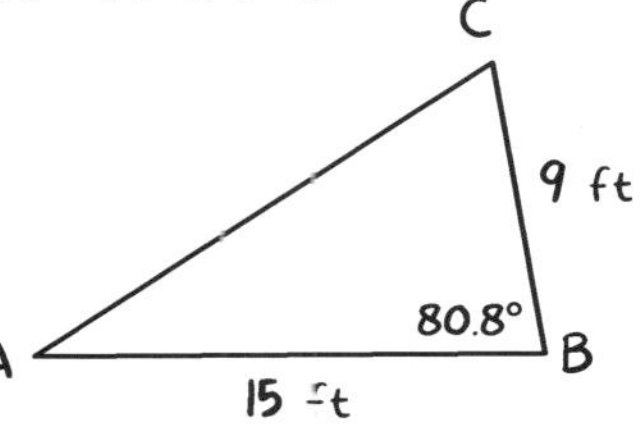

29. Find AC

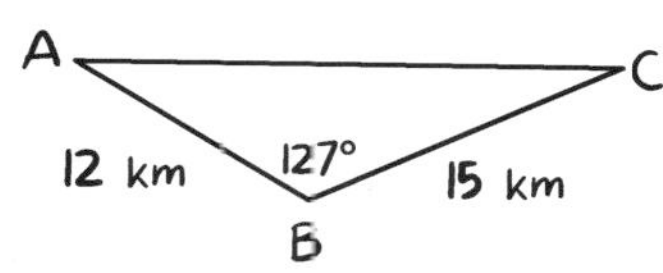

30. Find AC

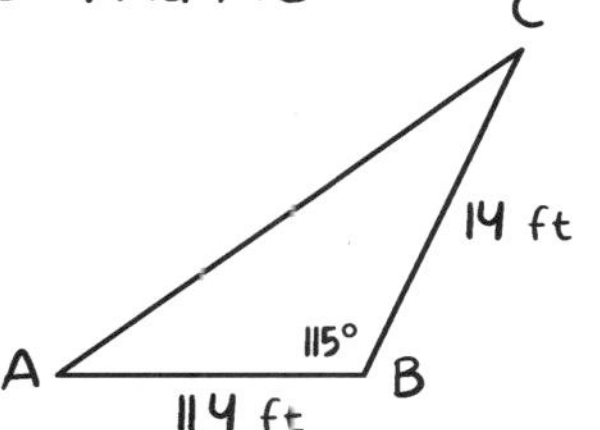

31. Find AC

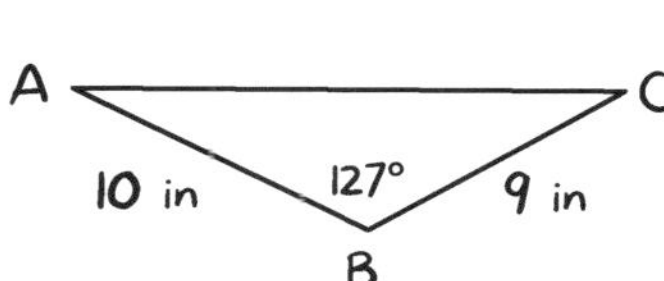

32. Find AC

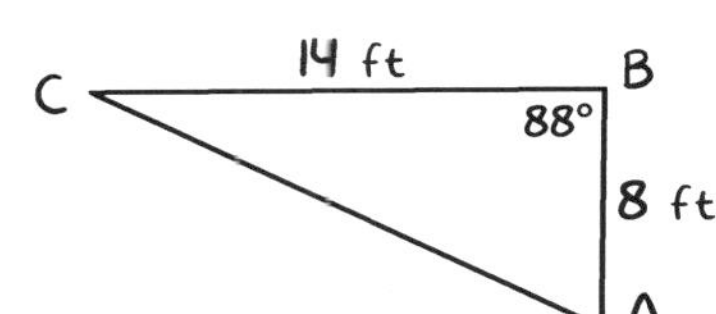

Section 6.2 Quiz

33. Find AB

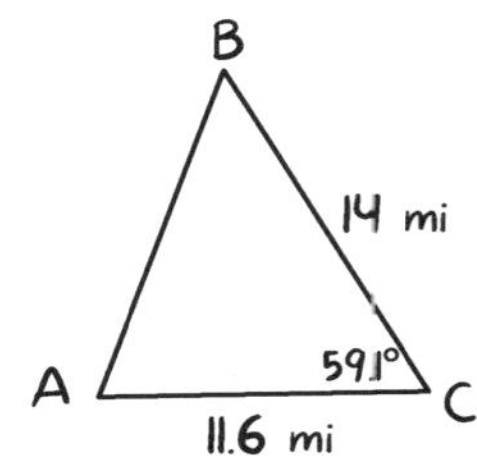

34. Find AB

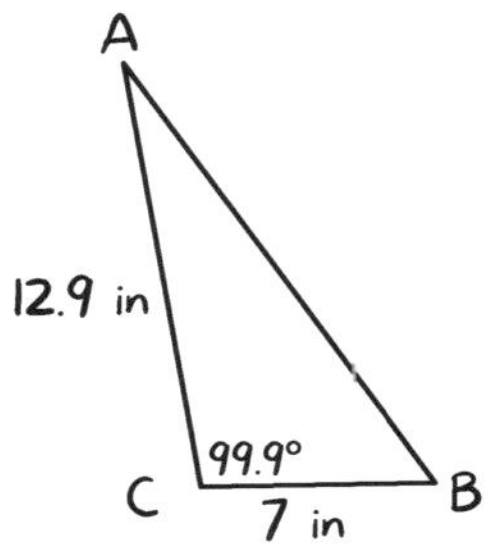

35. Find BC

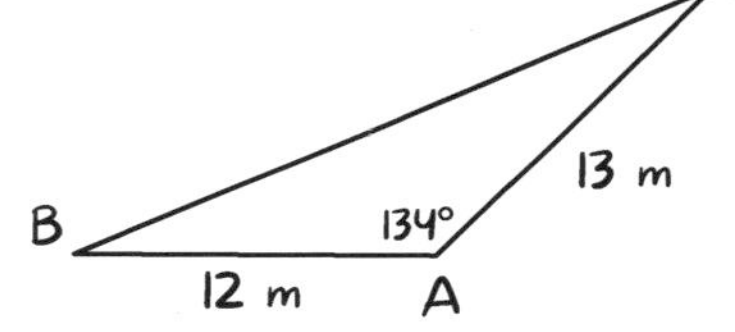

36. Find AB

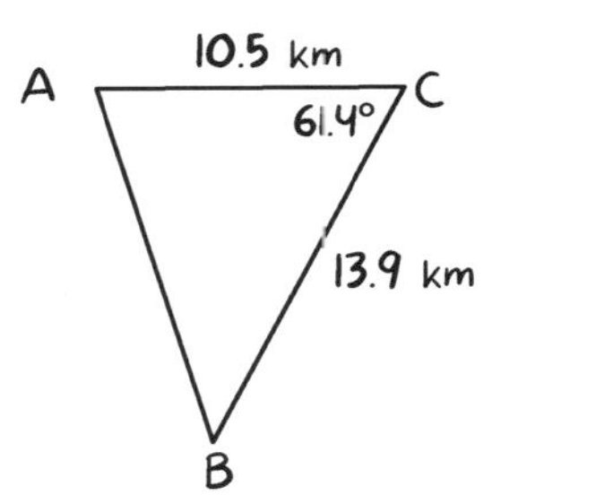

37. Find BC

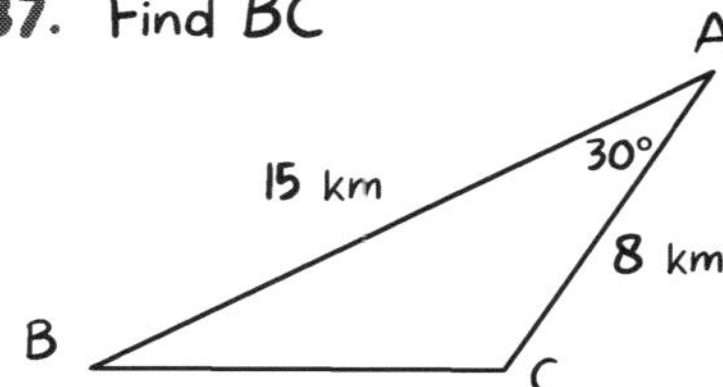

38. Find BC

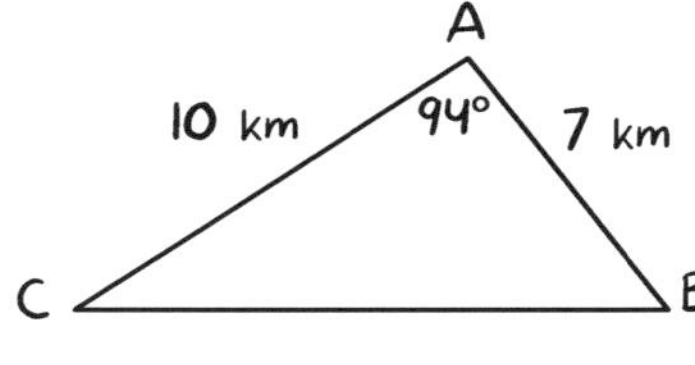

39. Find BC

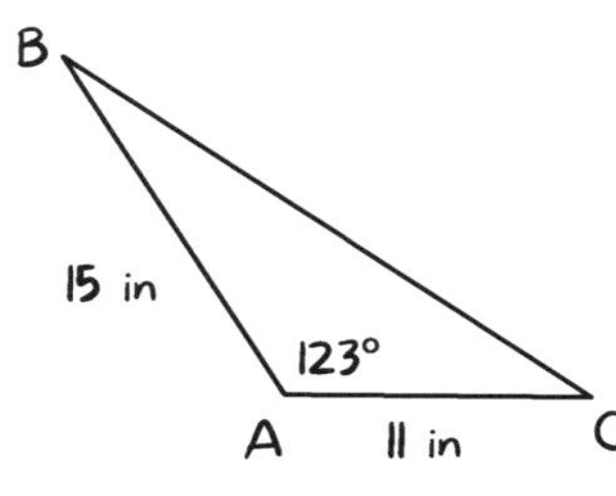

40. Find BC

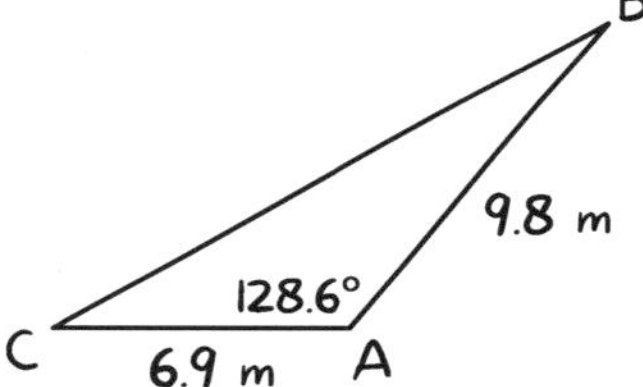

41. Find $m\angle C$

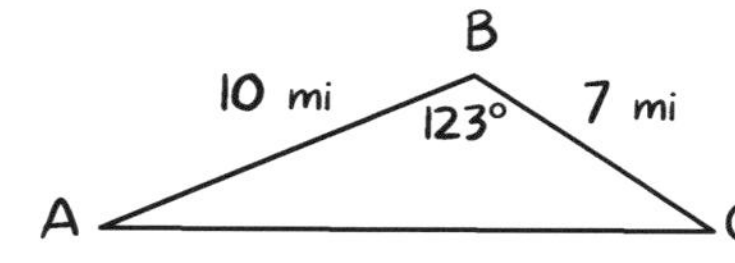

42. Find $m\angle A$

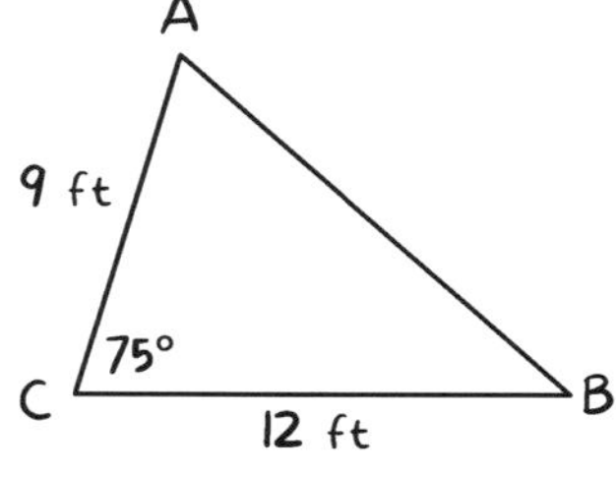

43. Find $m\angle A$

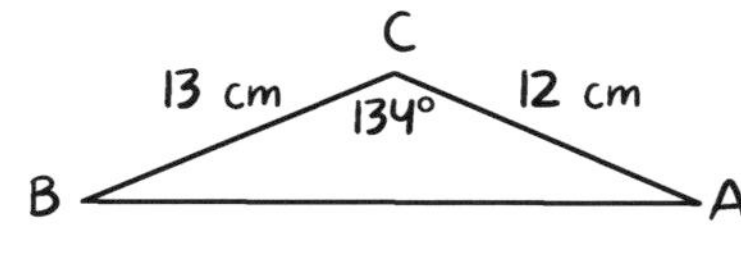

44. Find $m\angle A$

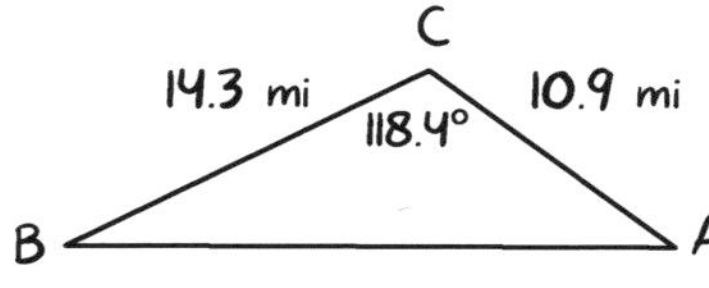

45. Find $m\angle A$

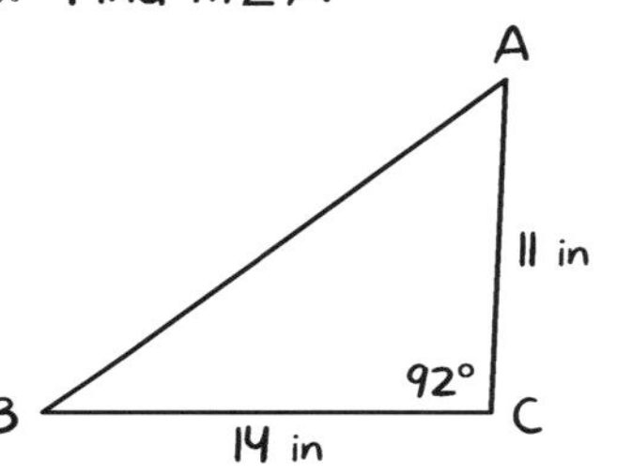

46. Find $m\angle B$

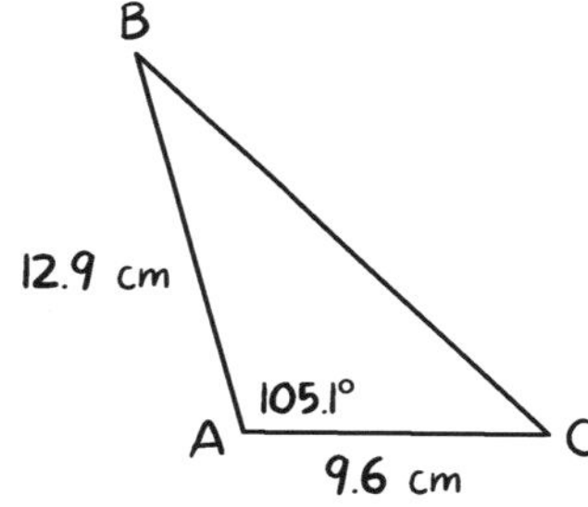

47. Find $m\angle B$

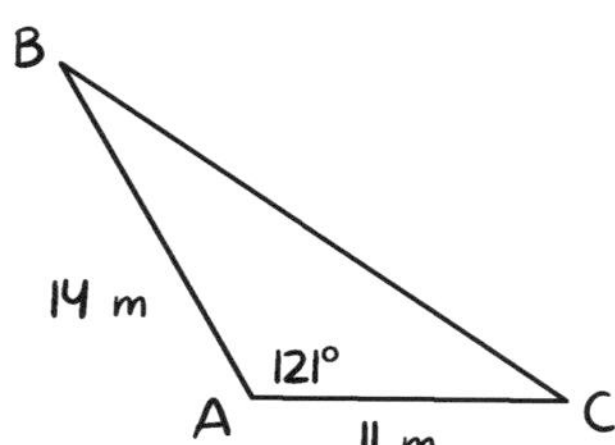

Section 6.2 Quiz

48. Find $m\angle B$

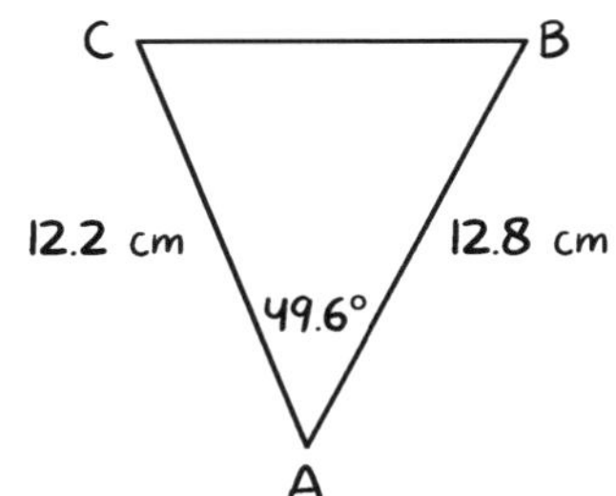

49. Find $m\angle C$

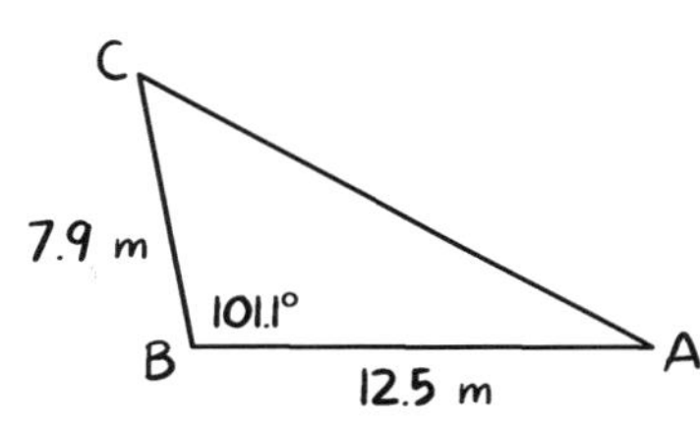

50. Find $m\angle B$

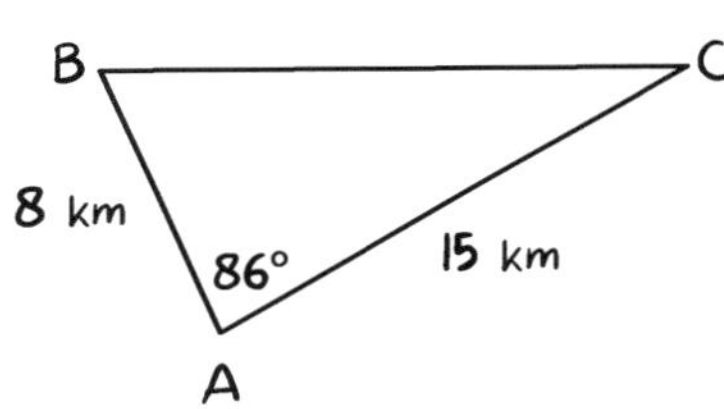

51. Find $m\angle B$

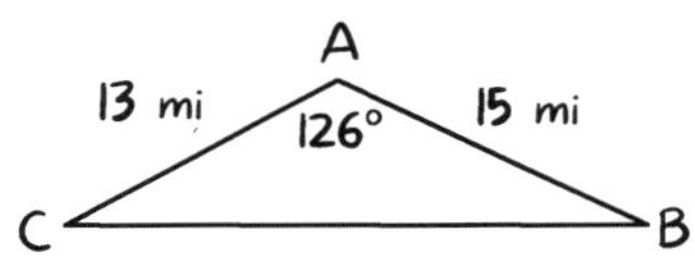

52. Find $m\angle C$

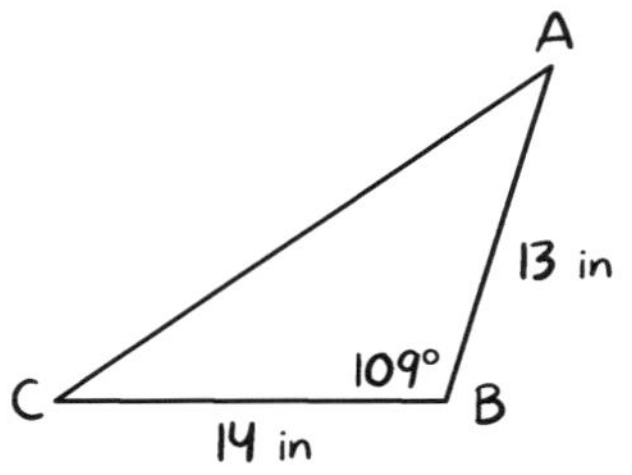

53. Find $m\angle A$

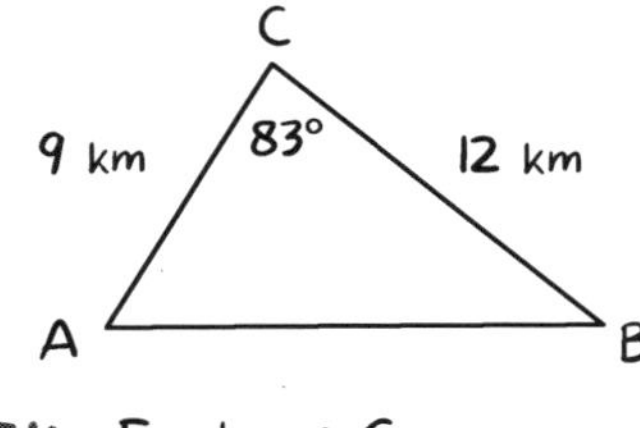

54. Find $m\angle C$

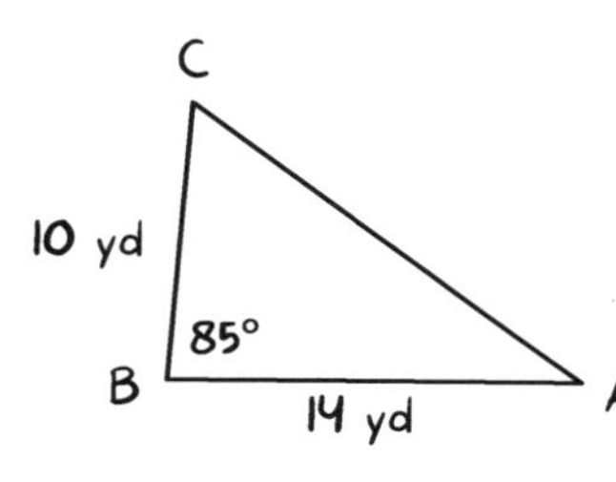

55. Find $m\angle A$

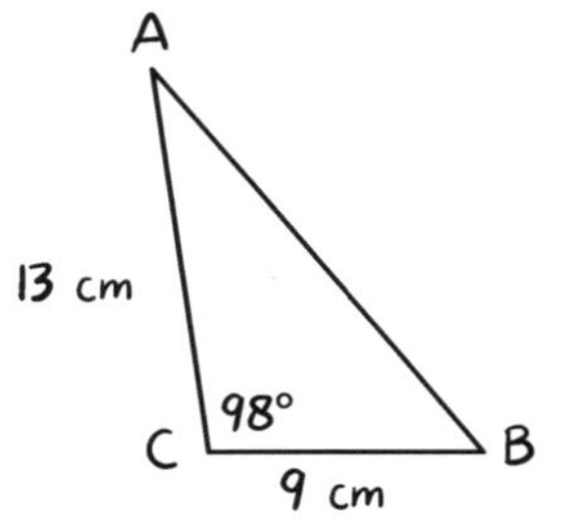

56. Find $m\angle C$

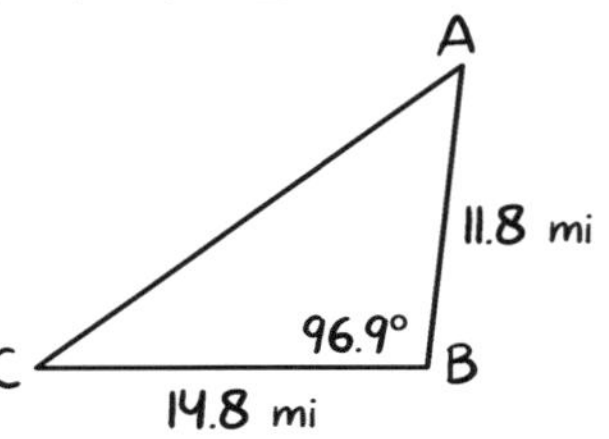

57. Find $m\angle C$

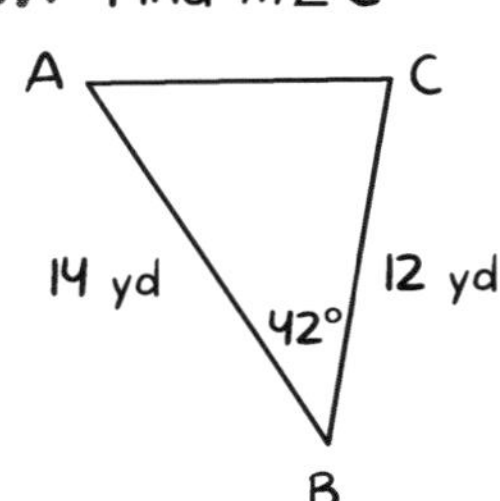

58. Find $m\angle B$

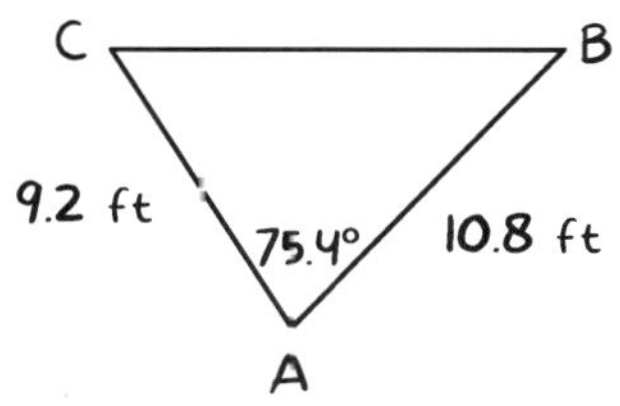

59. Find $m\angle B$

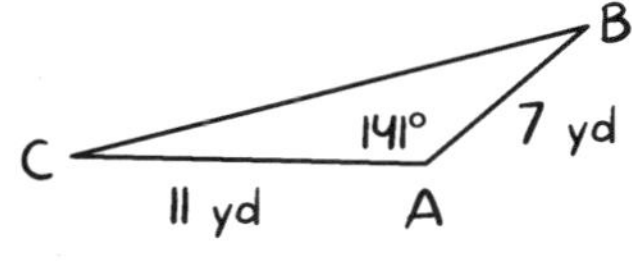

60. Find $m\angle C$

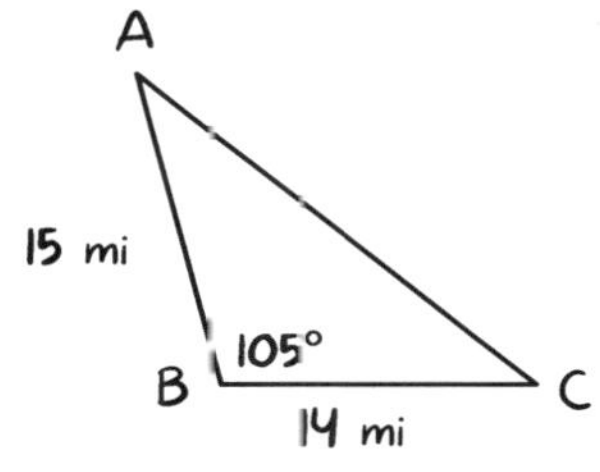

61. Find $m\angle B$

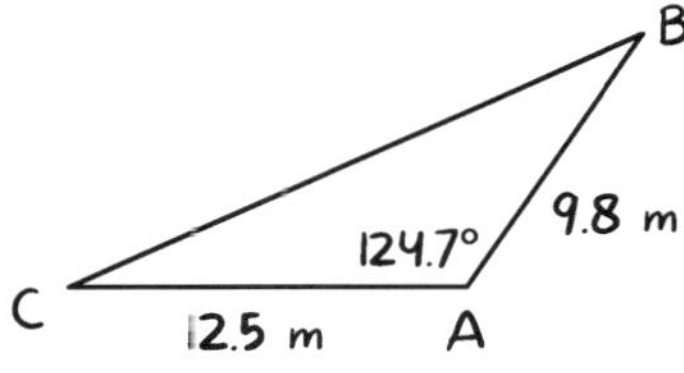

62. Find $m\angle B$

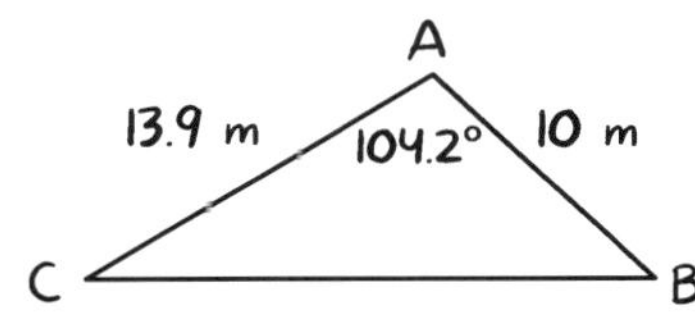

Section 6.2 Quiz

63. Find $m\angle B$

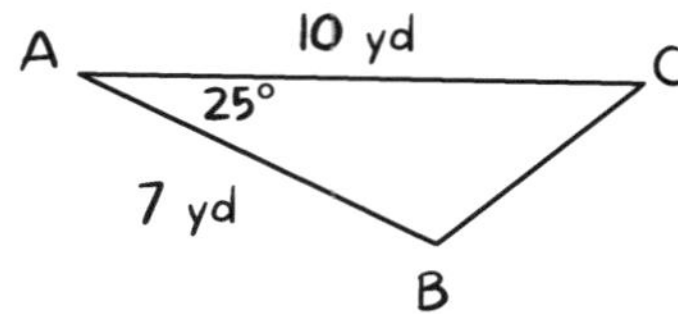

64. Find $m\angle B$

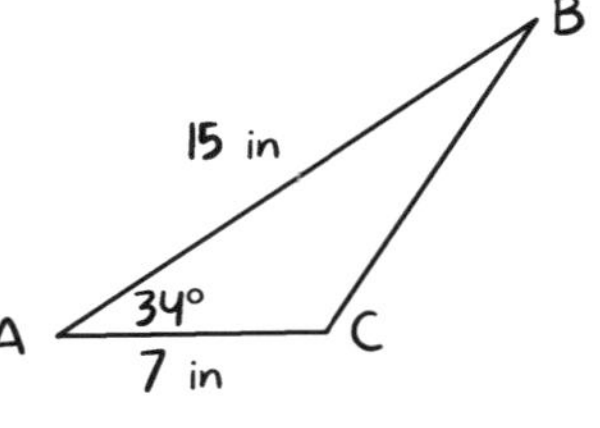

65. Find $m\angle C$

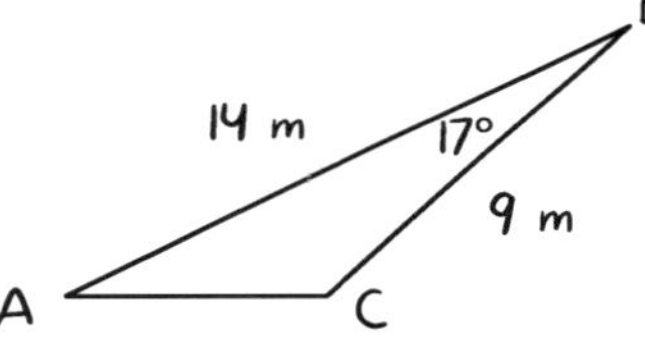

66. Find $m\angle B$

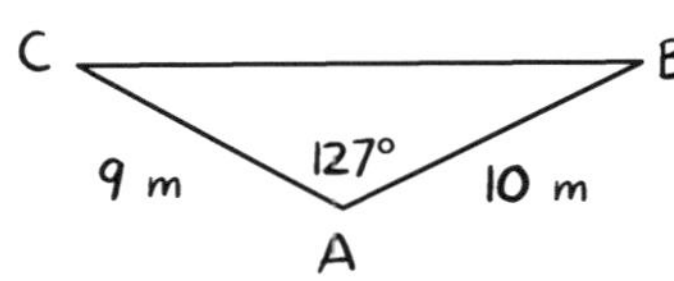

67. Find $m\angle B$

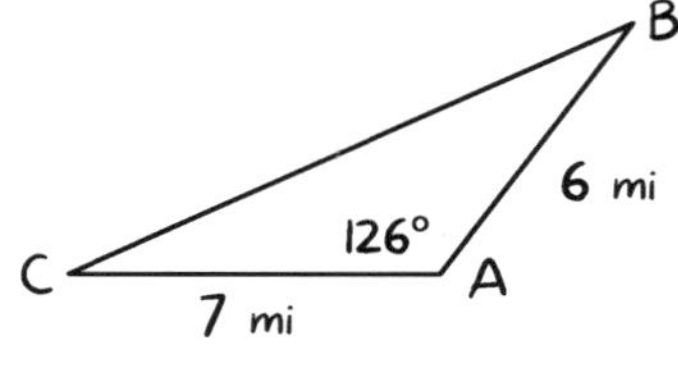

68. Find $m\angle A$

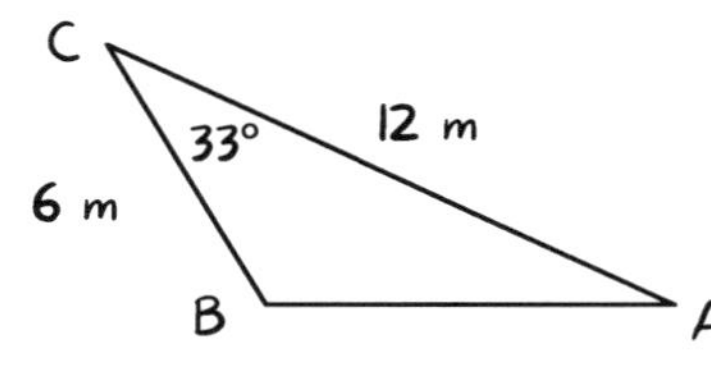

69. Find $m\angle C$

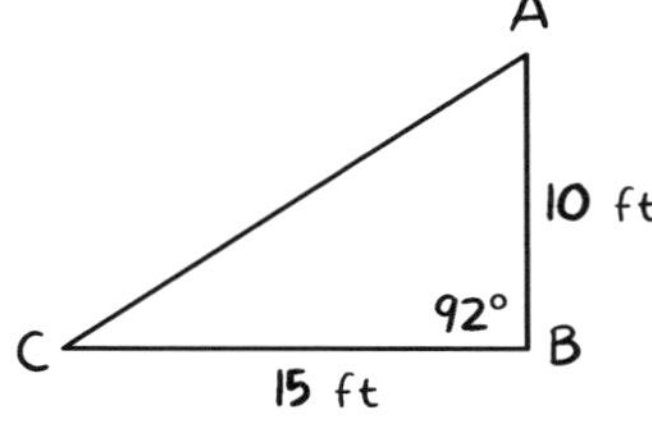

70. Find $m\angle C$

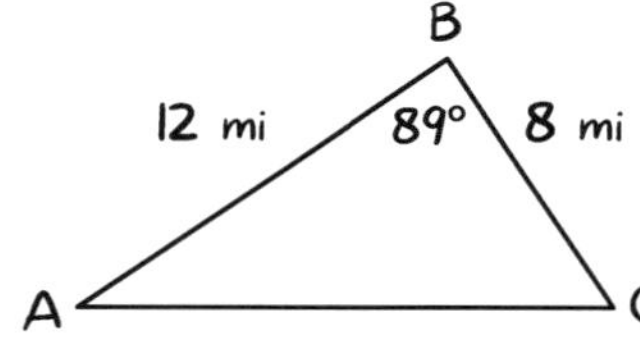

71. Find $m\angle A$

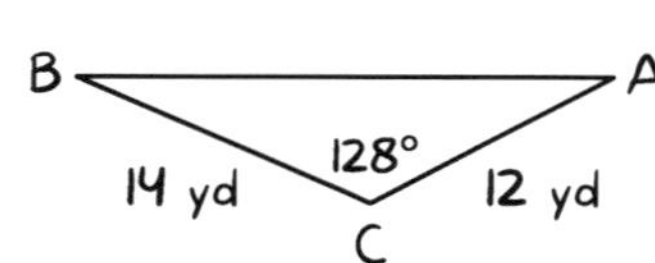

72. Find $m\angle A$

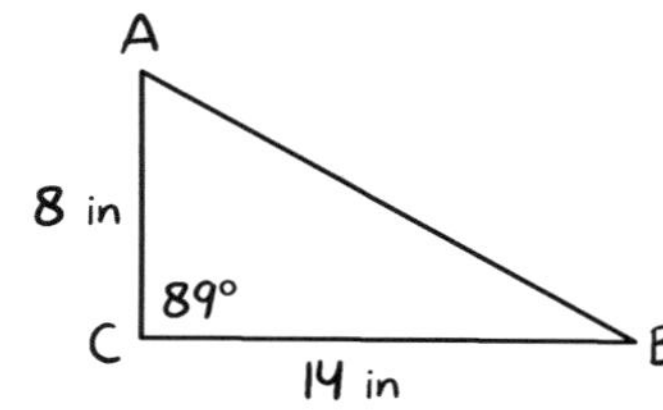

73. Find $m\angle C$

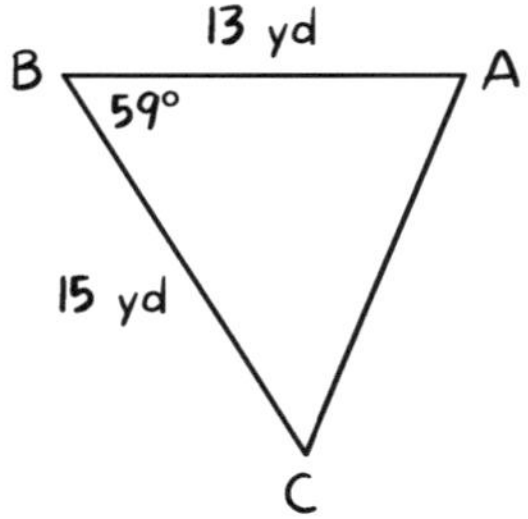

74. Find $m\angle C$

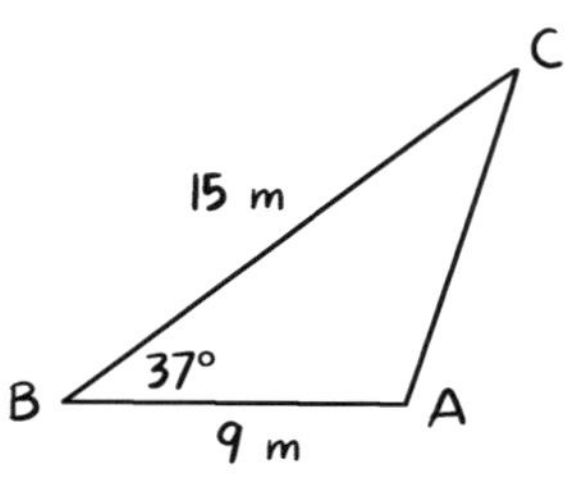

75. Find $m\angle A$

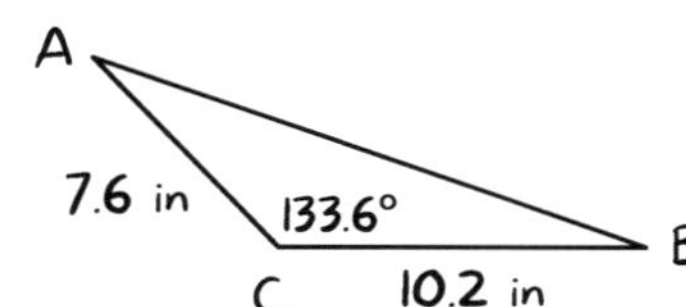

76. Find $m\angle A$

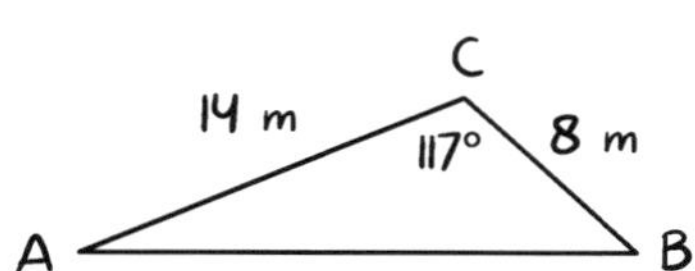

77. Find $m\angle A$

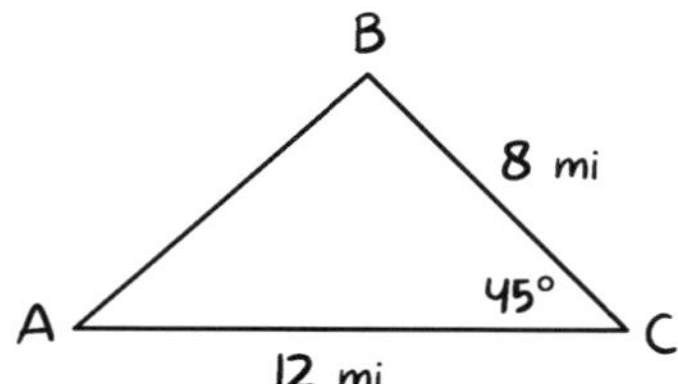

Section 6.2 Quiz

78. Find $m\angle B$

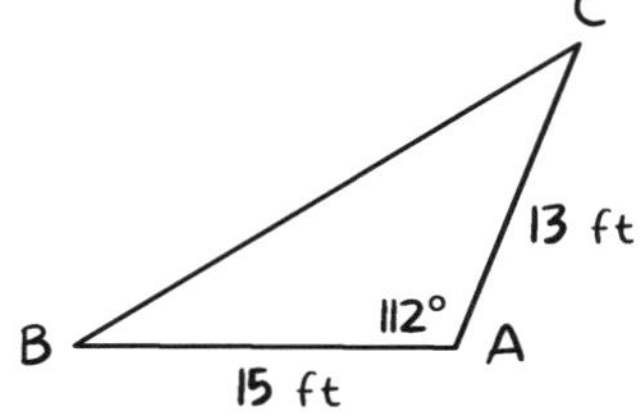

79. Find $m\angle A$

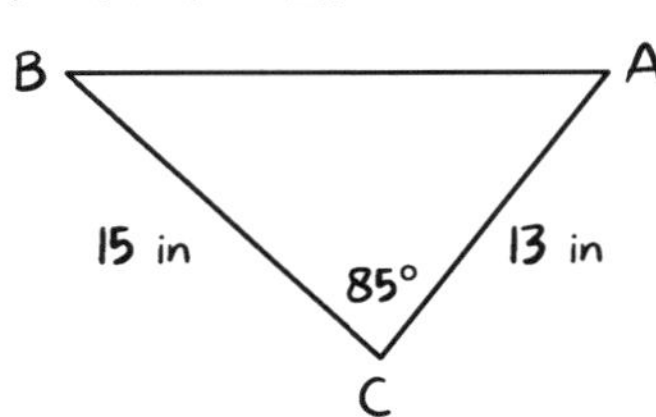

80. Find $m\angle A$

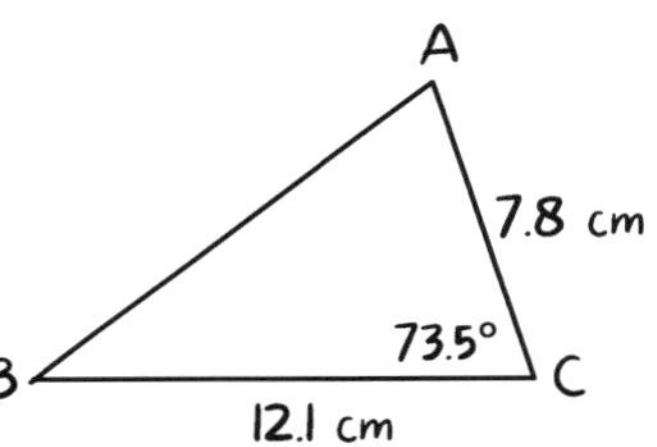

81. Find $m\angle B$

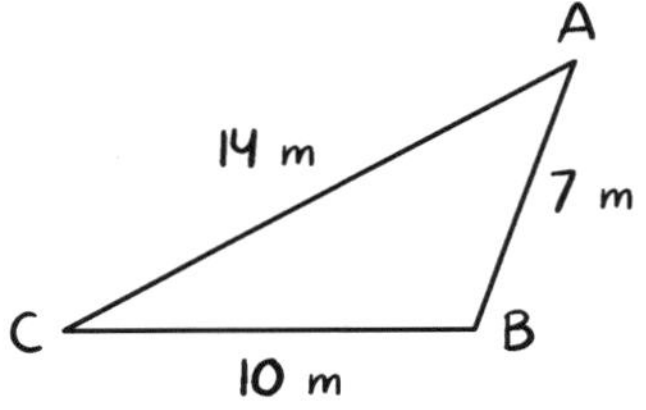

82. Find $m\angle A$

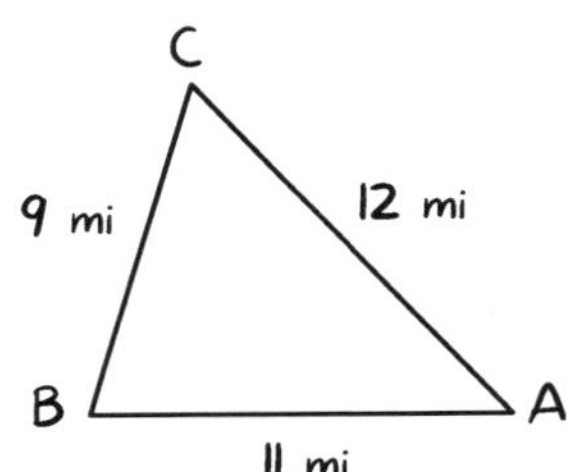

83. Find $m\angle B$

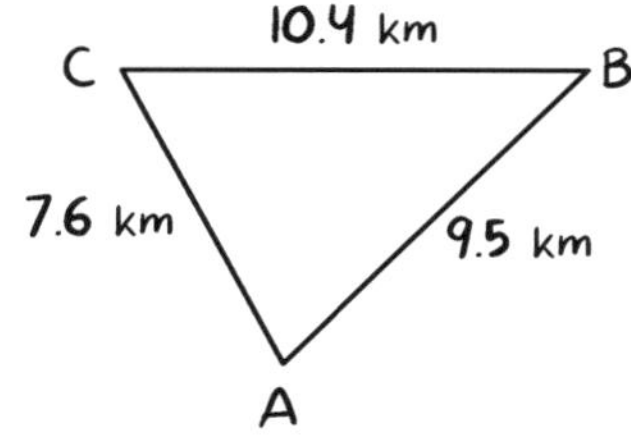

84. Find $m\angle C$

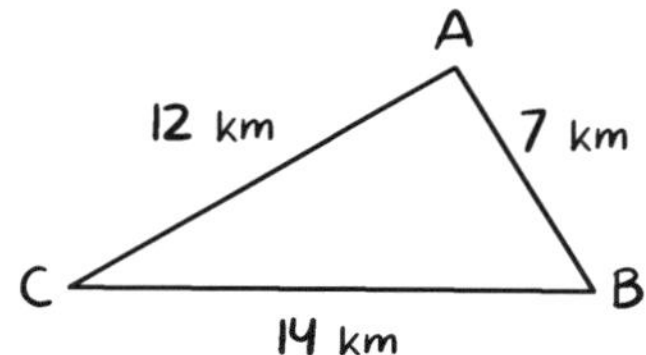

85. Find $m\angle C$

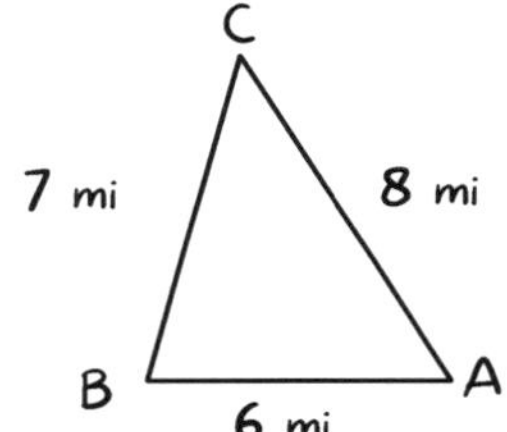

86. Find $m\angle A$

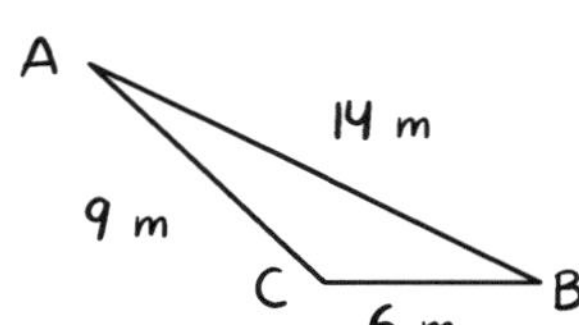

87. Find $m\angle C$

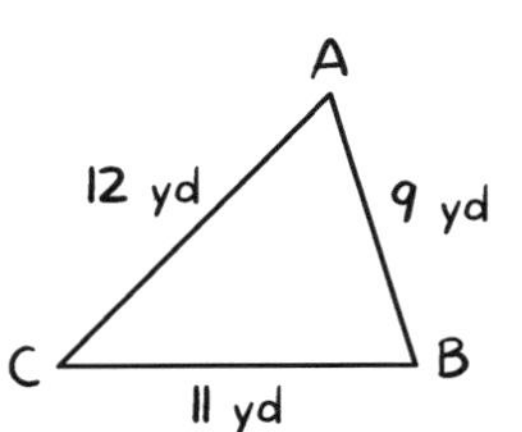

88. Find $m\angle A$

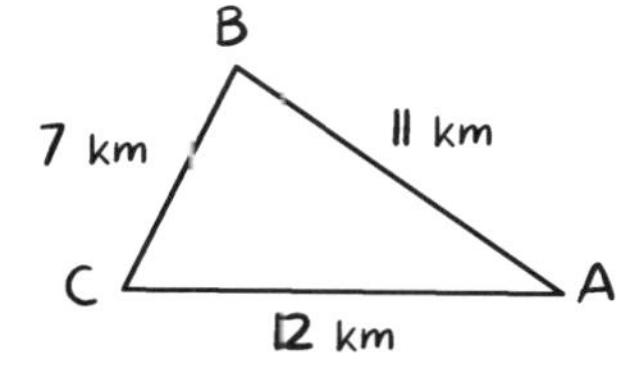

89. Find $m\angle C$

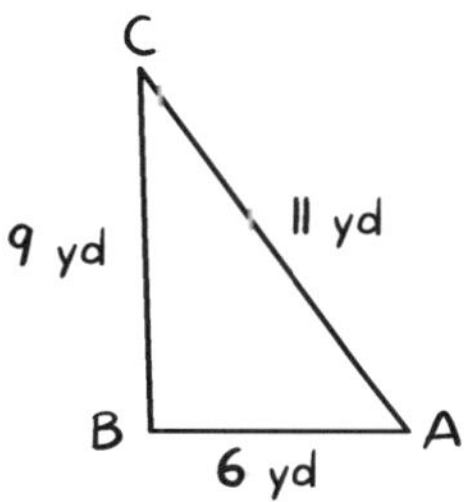

90. Find $m\angle A$

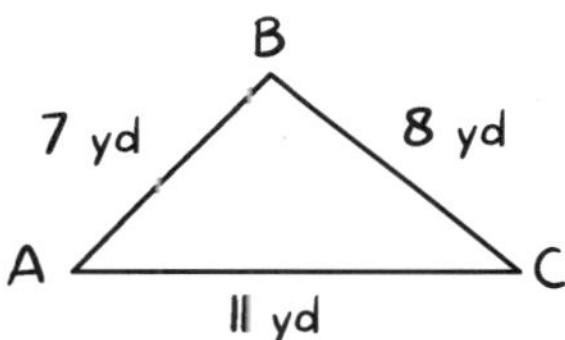

91. Find $m\angle A$

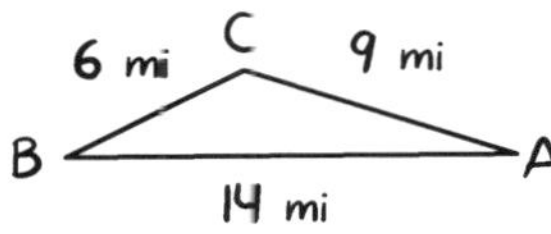

92. Find $m\angle A$

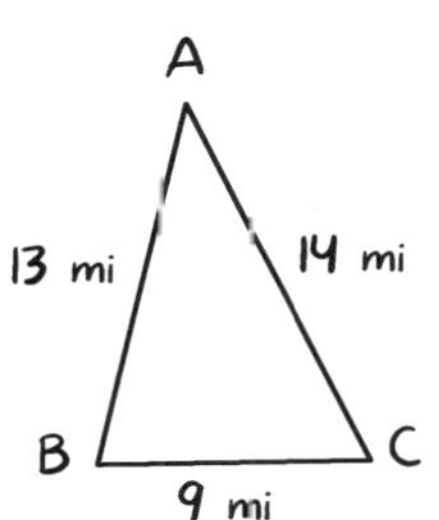

Section 6.2 Quiz

93. Find $m\angle A$

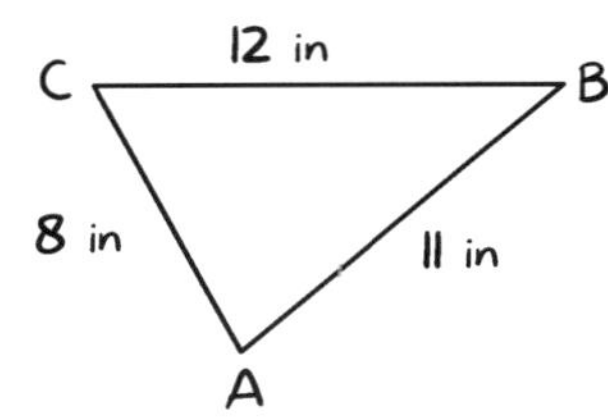

94. Find $m\angle C$

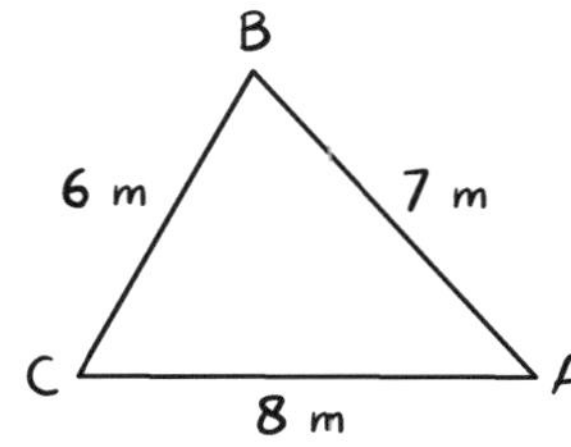

95. Find $m\angle A$

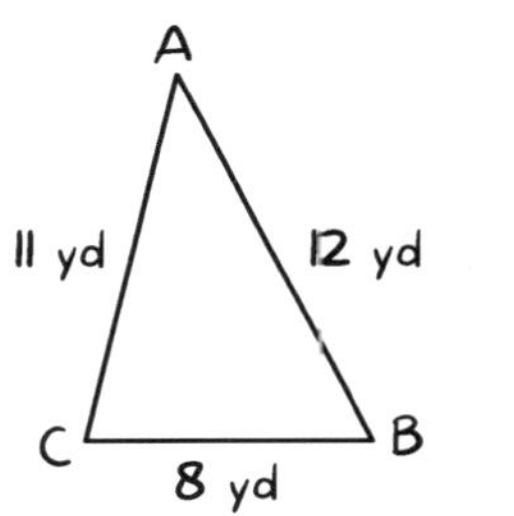

96. Find $m\angle C$

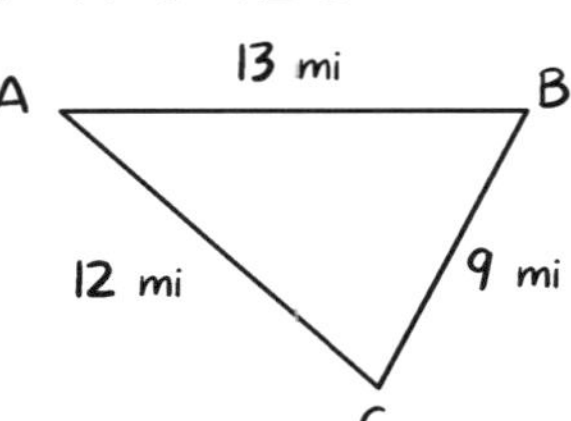

97. Find $m\angle B$

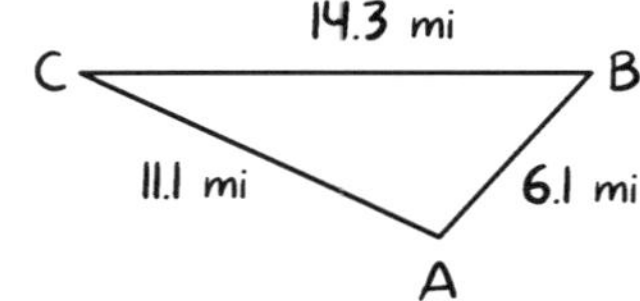

98. Find $m\angle A$

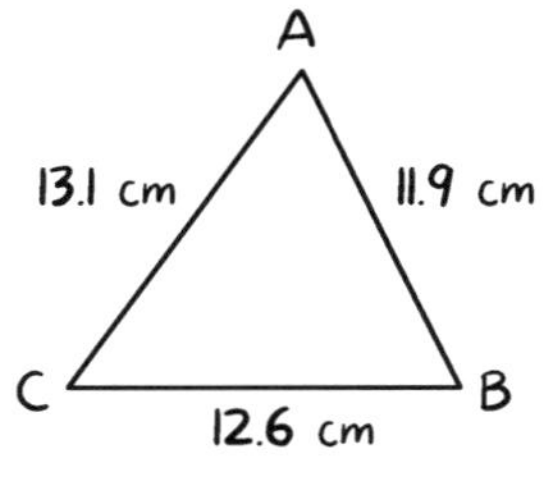

99. Find $m\angle B$

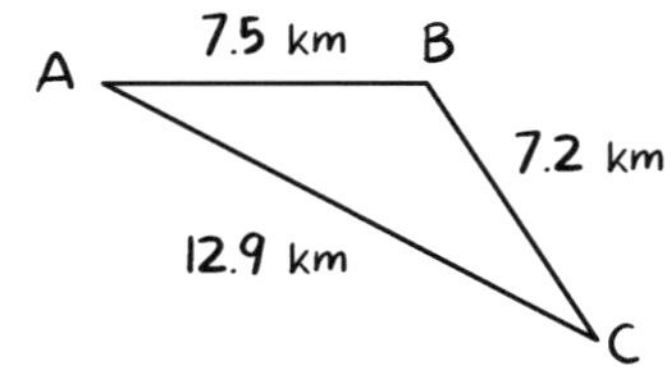

100. Find $m\angle B$

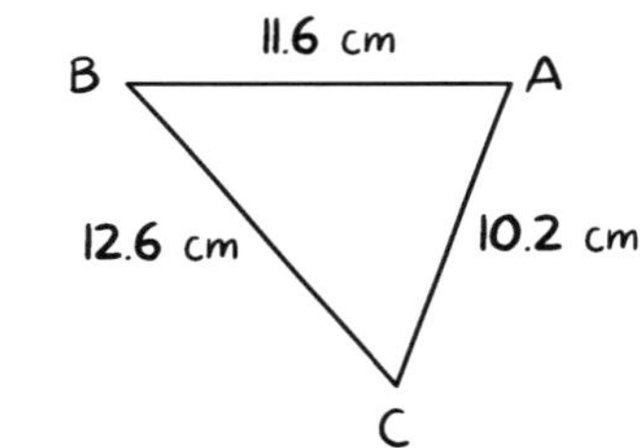

101. Find $m\angle A$

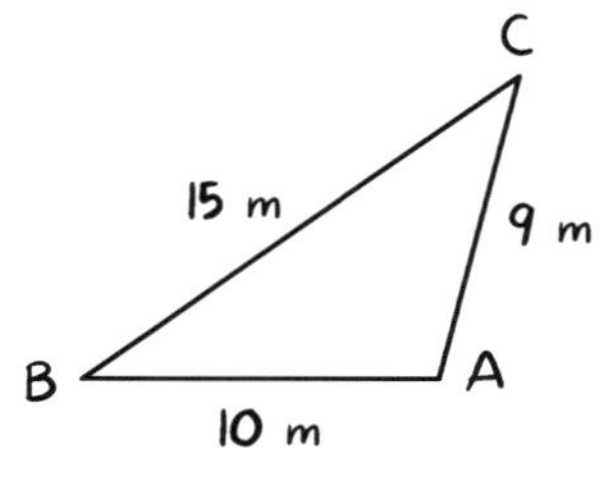

102. Find $m\angle C$

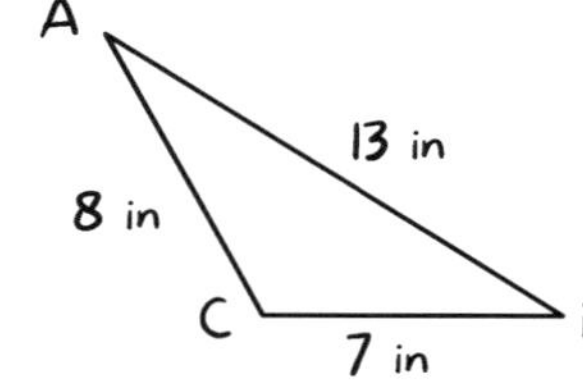

103. Find $m\angle C$

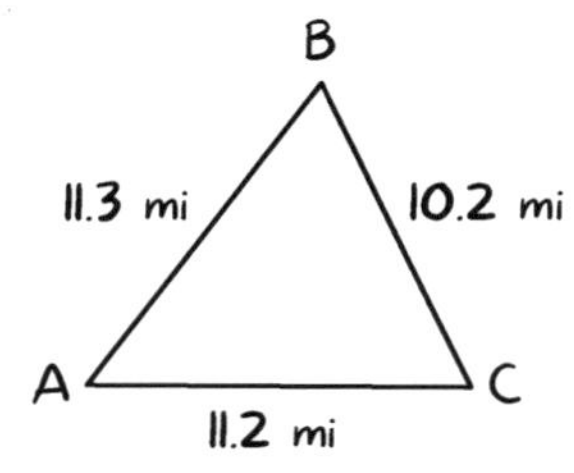

104. Find $m\angle C$

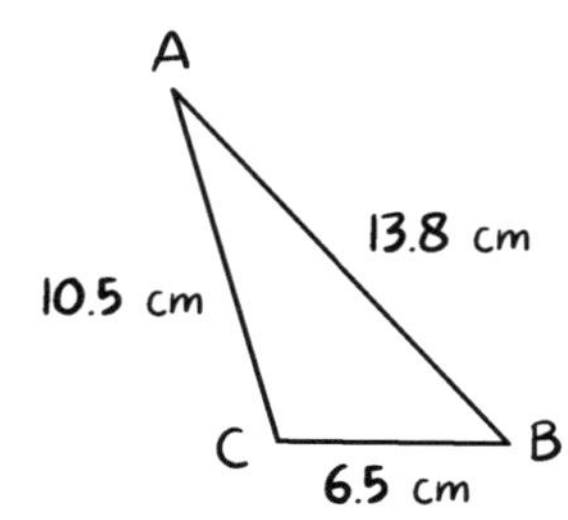

105. Find $m\angle C$

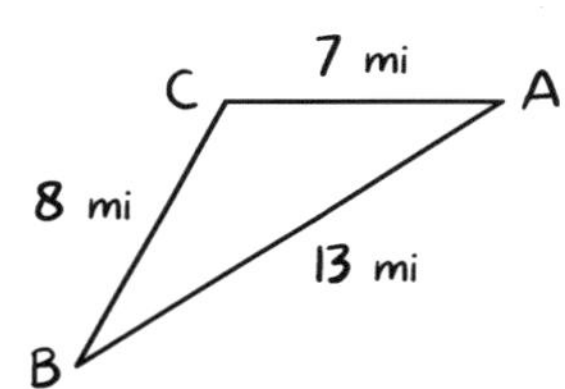

106. Find $m\angle B$

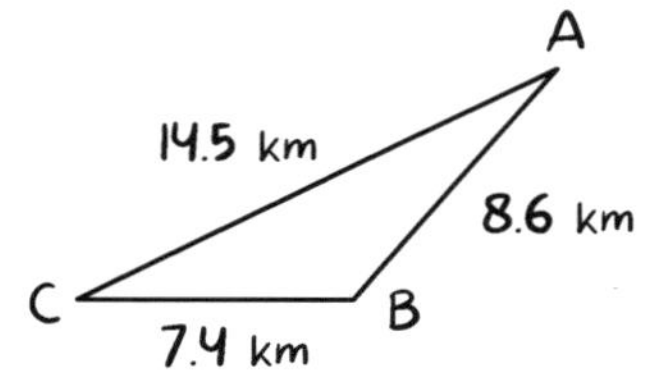

107. Find $m\angle B$

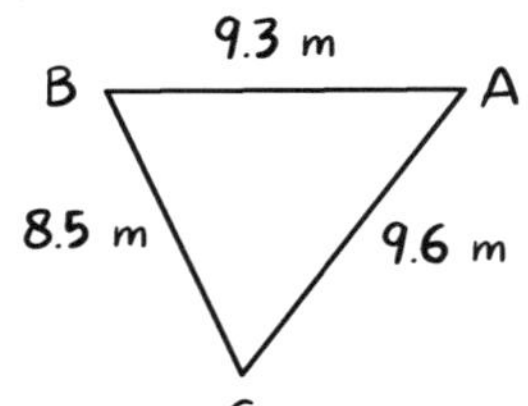

Section 6.2 Quiz

108. Find $m\angle B$

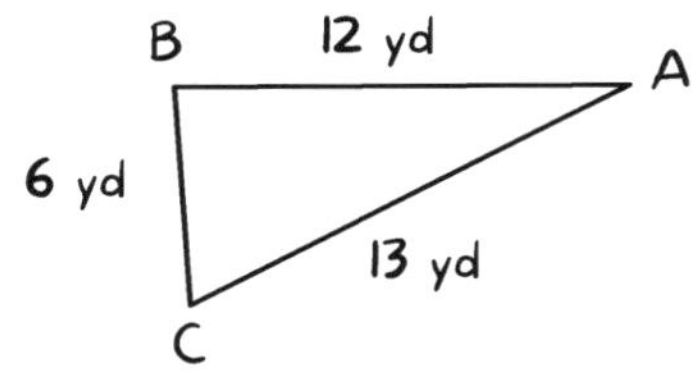

109. Find $m\angle C$

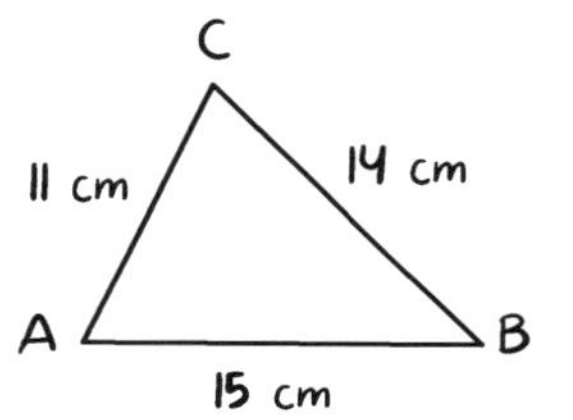

110. Find $m\angle B$

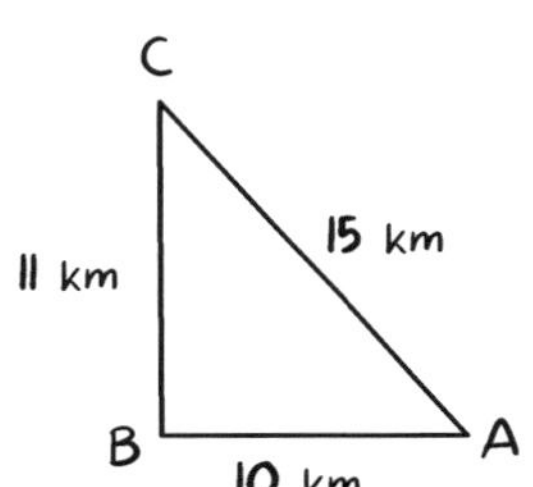

111. Find $m\angle B$

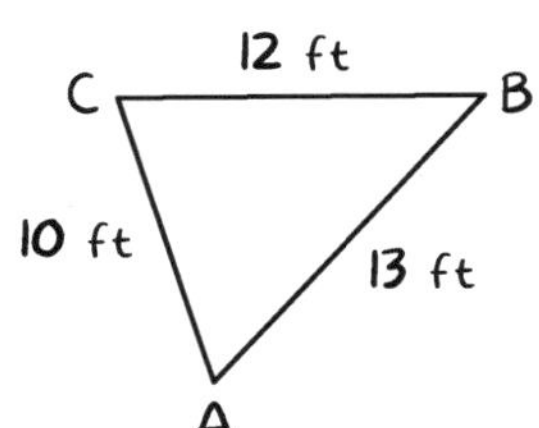

112. Find $m\angle A$

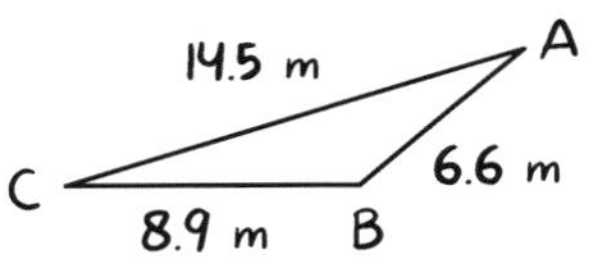

113. Find $m\angle A$

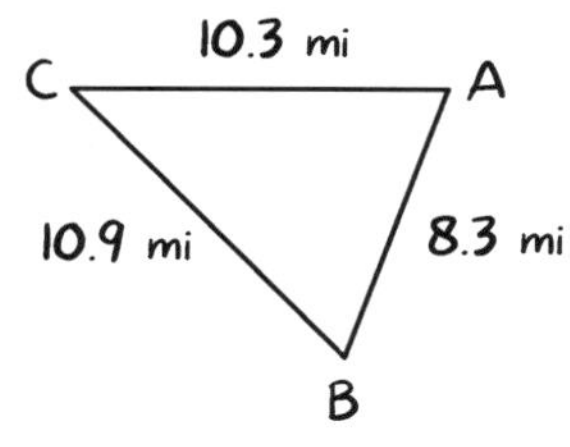

114. Find $m\angle C$

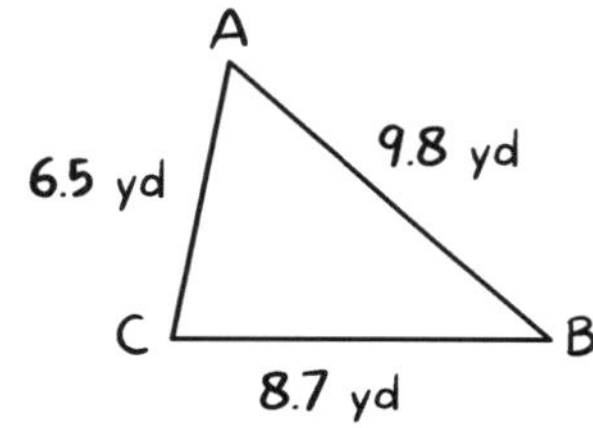

115. Find $m\angle B$

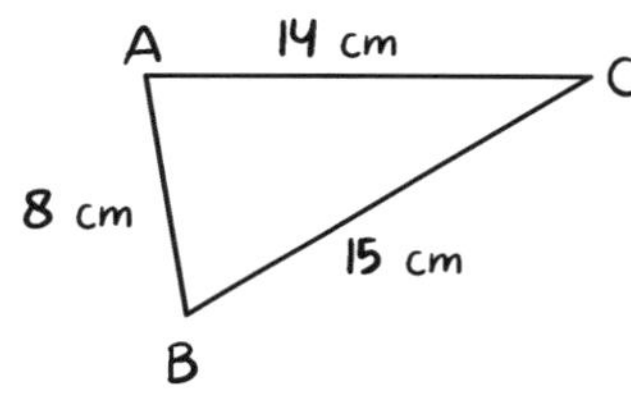

116. Find $m\angle A$

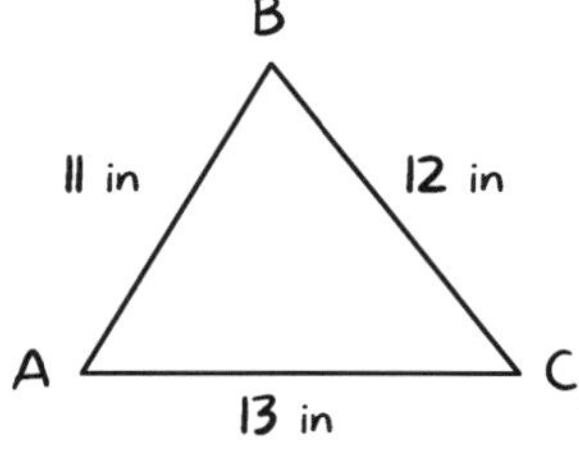

117. Find $m\angle B$

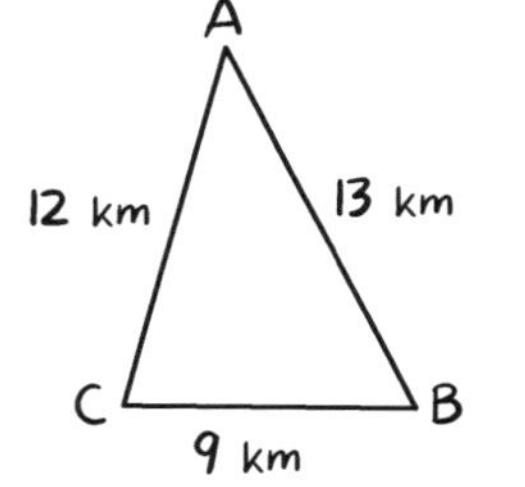

118. Find $m\angle B$

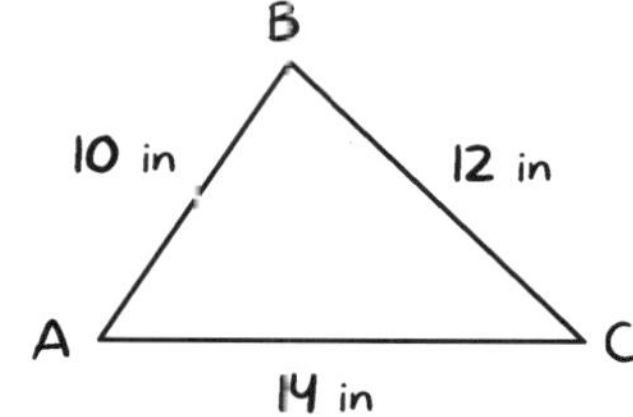

119. Find $m\angle B$

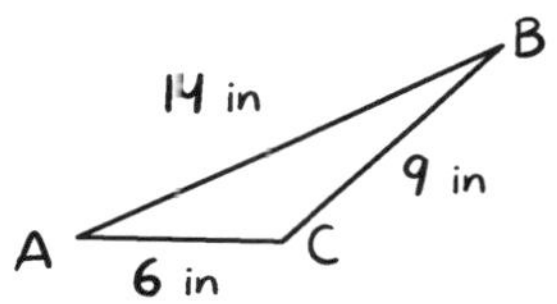

120. Find $m\angle A$

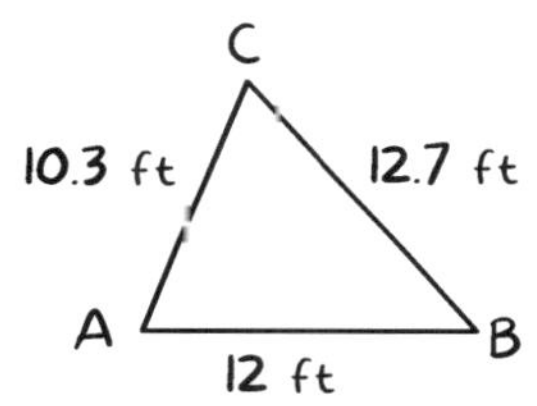

Section 6.2 Quiz

Directions: For questions 121 - 200, find all the missing sides and angles.

121.

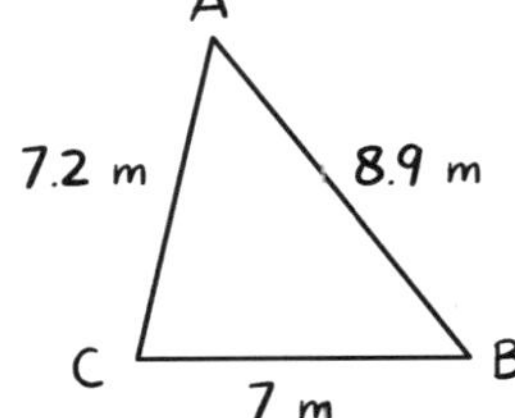

122.

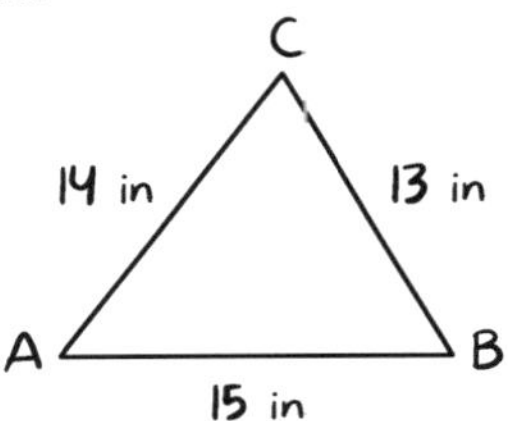

123.

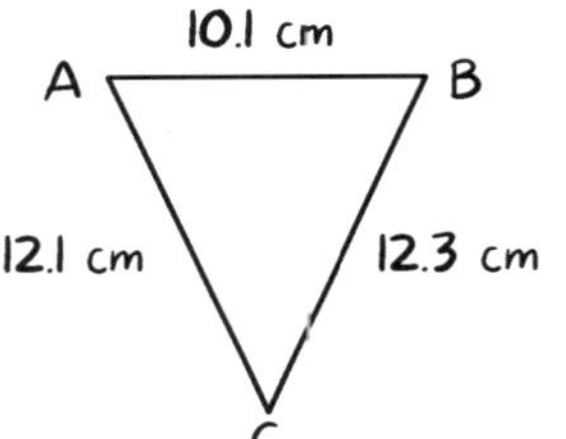

124.

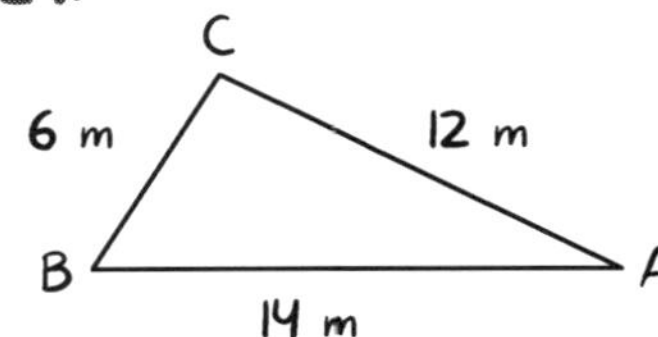

125.

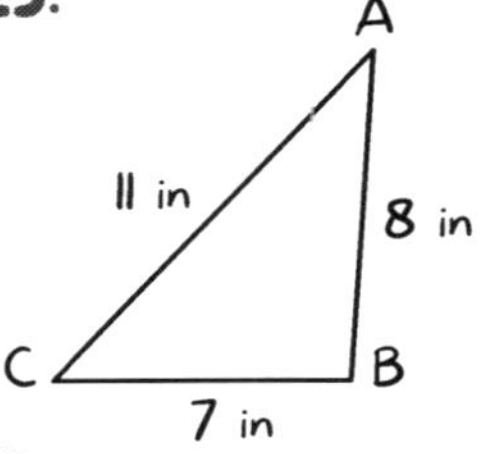

126.

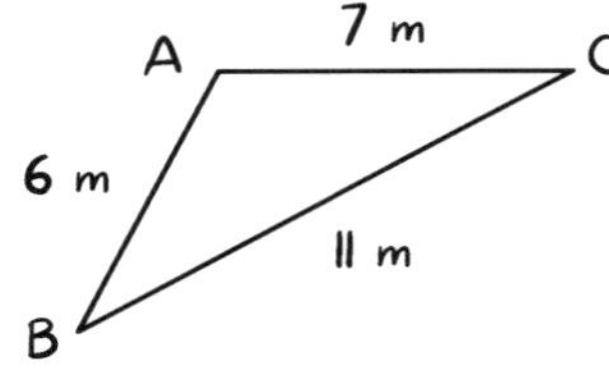

127.

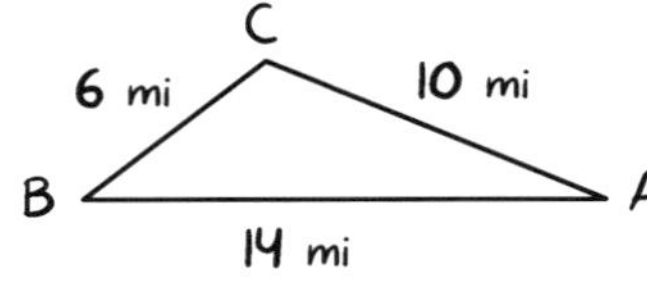

128.

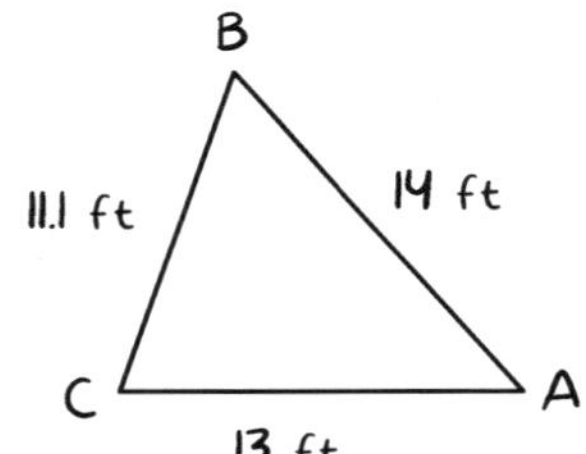

129.

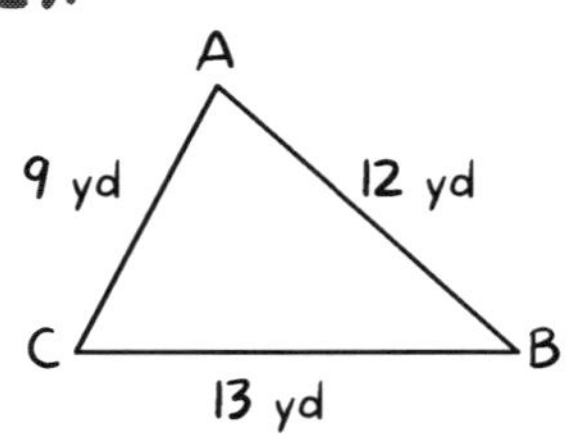

130.

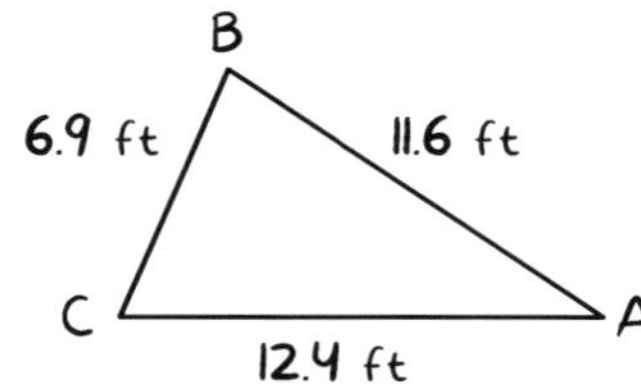

131.

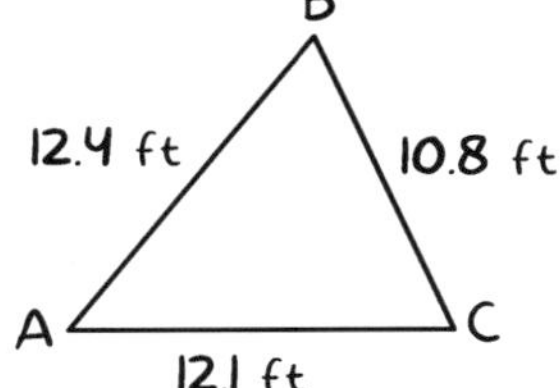

132.

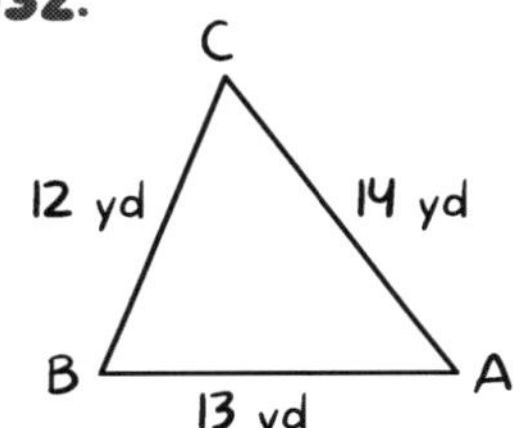

133.

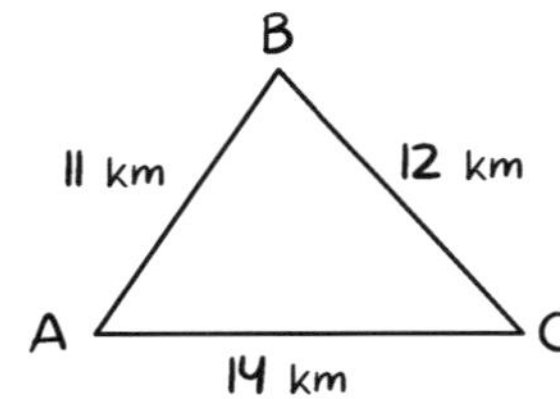

134.

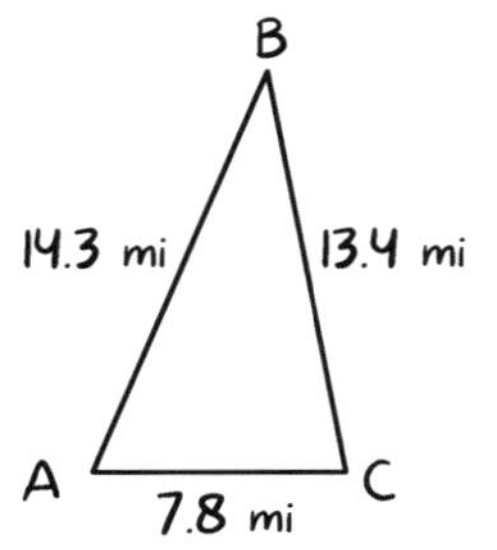

135.

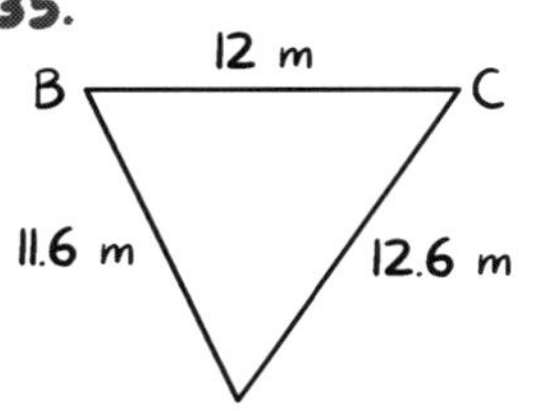

Section 6.2 Quiz

136.

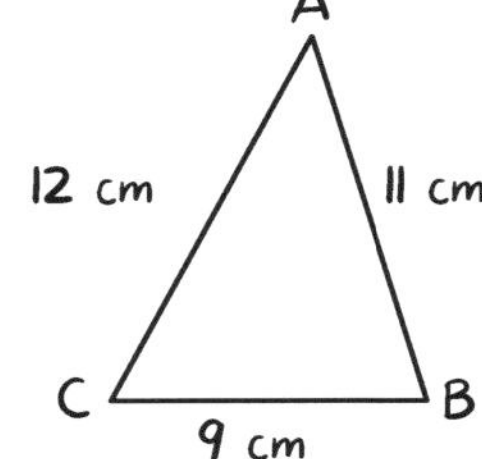

137.

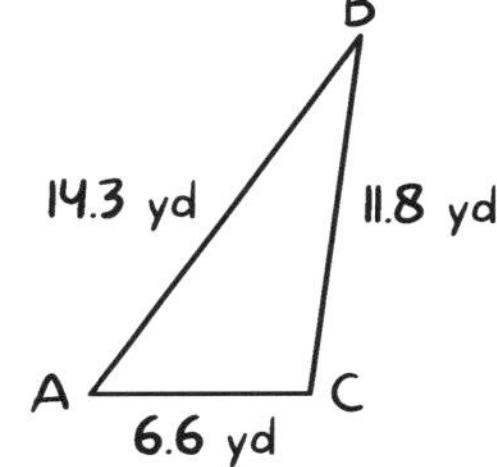

138.

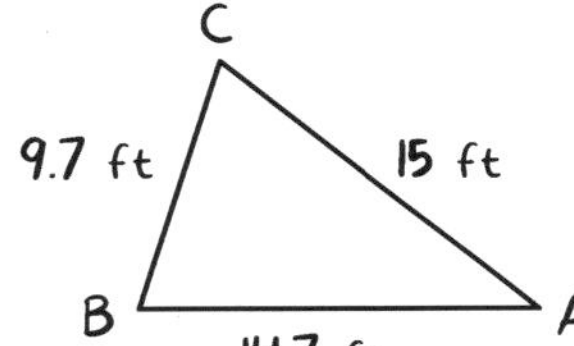

139.

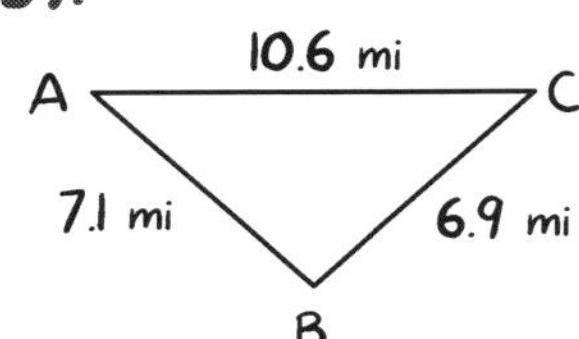

140.

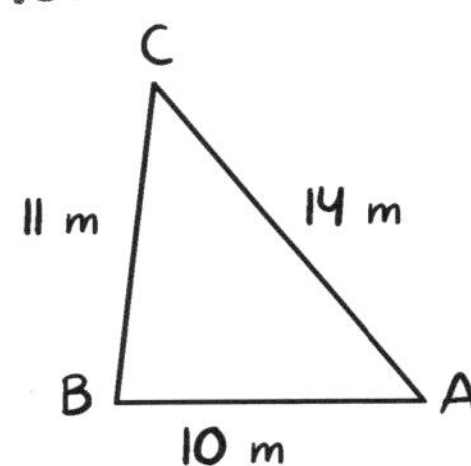

141.

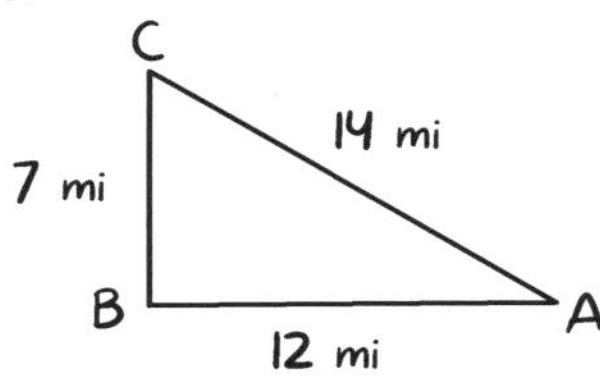

142.

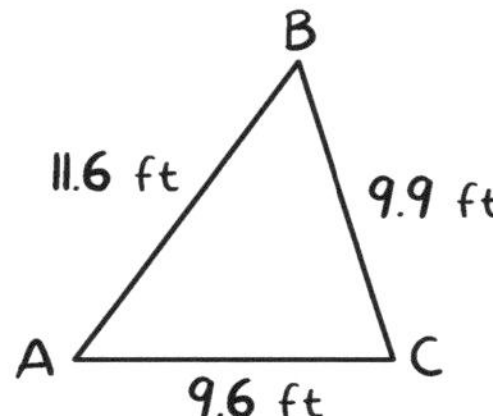

143.

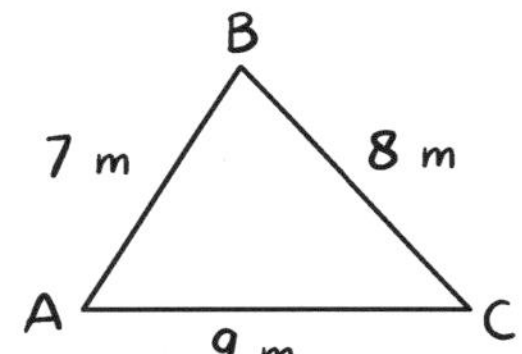

144.

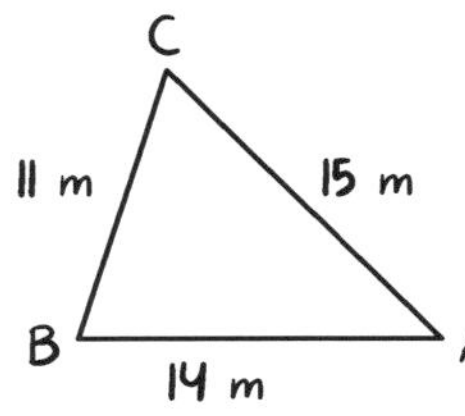

145.

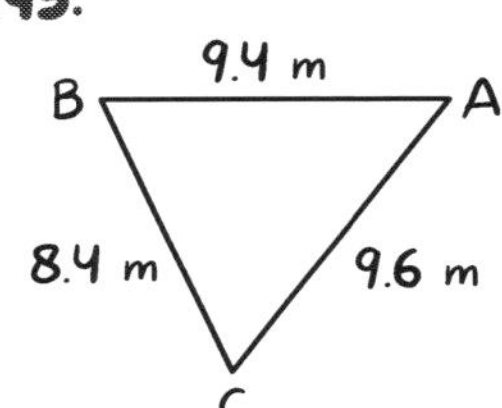

146.

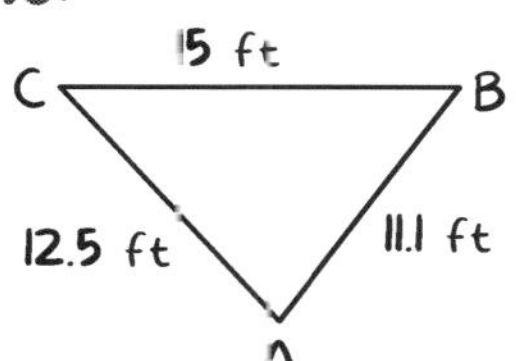

147.

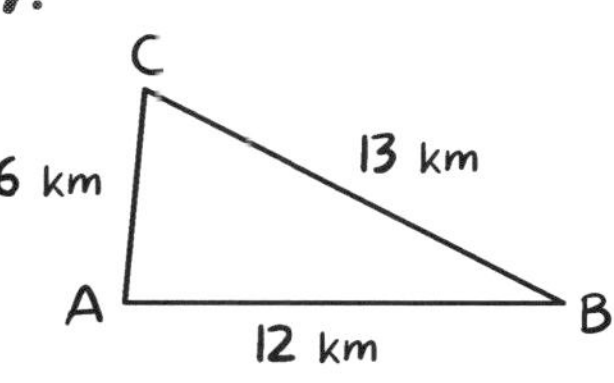

148.

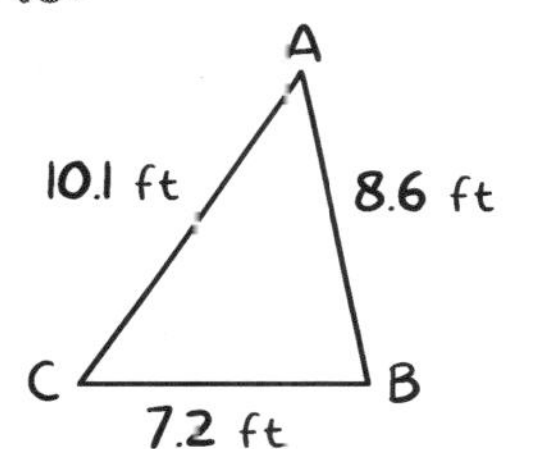

149.

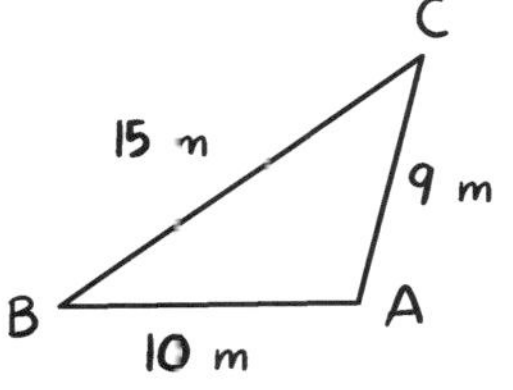

150.

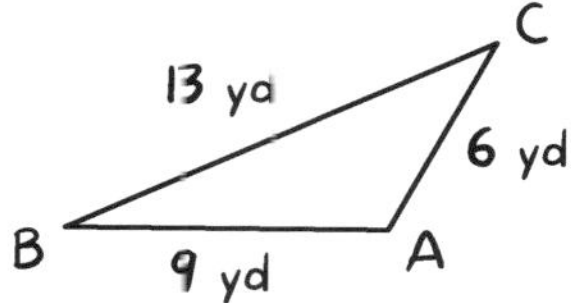

151.

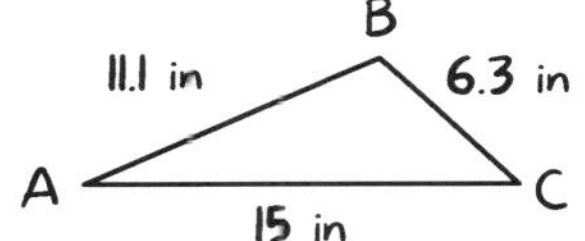

Section 6.2 Quiz

152.

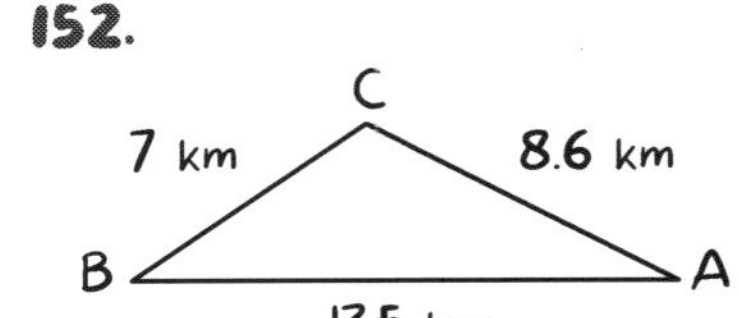

153.

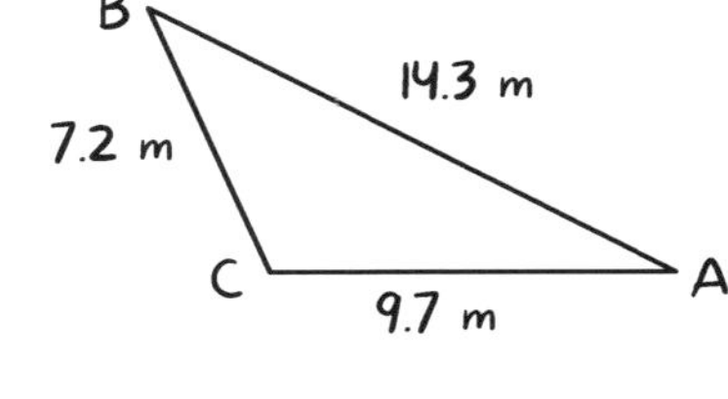

154.

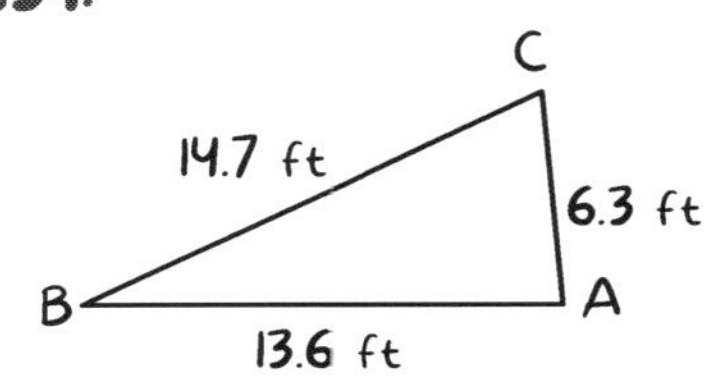

155.

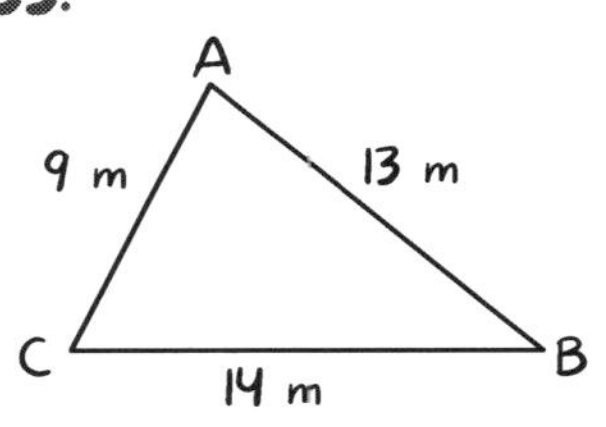

156.

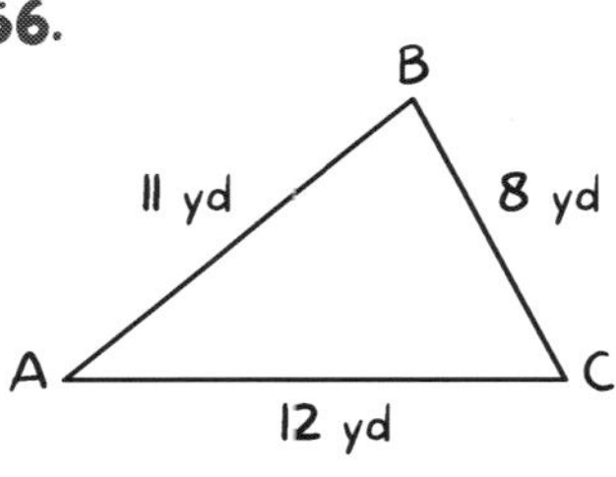

157.

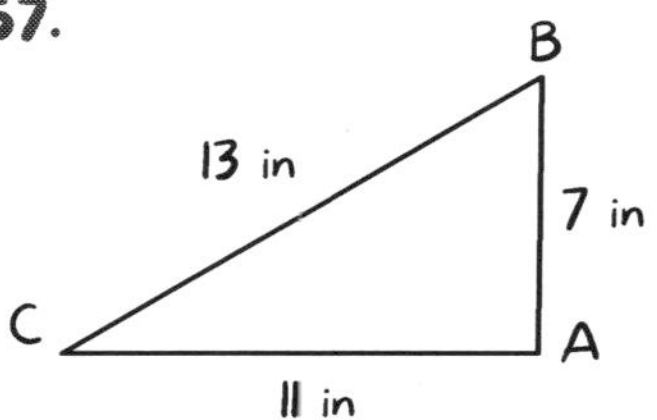

158.

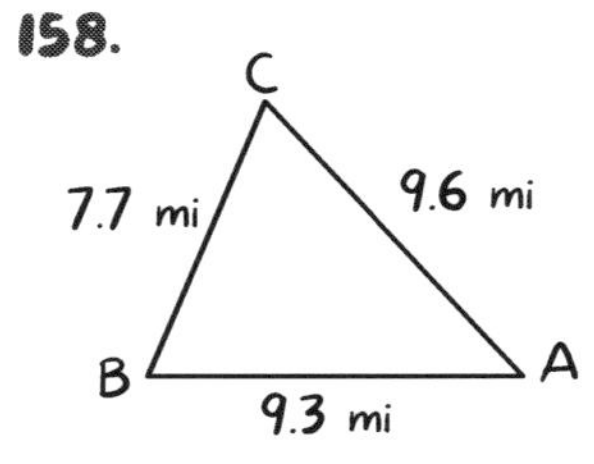

159.

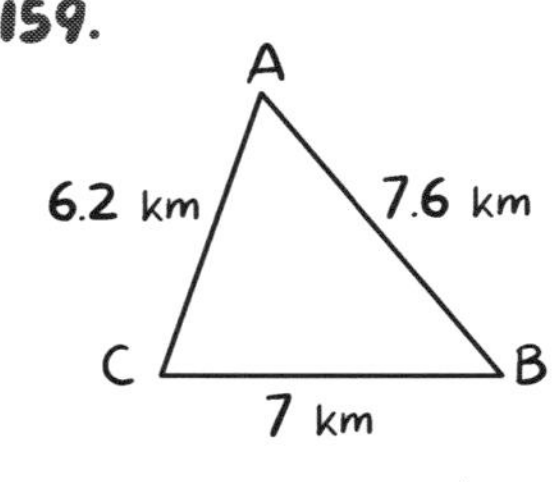

160.

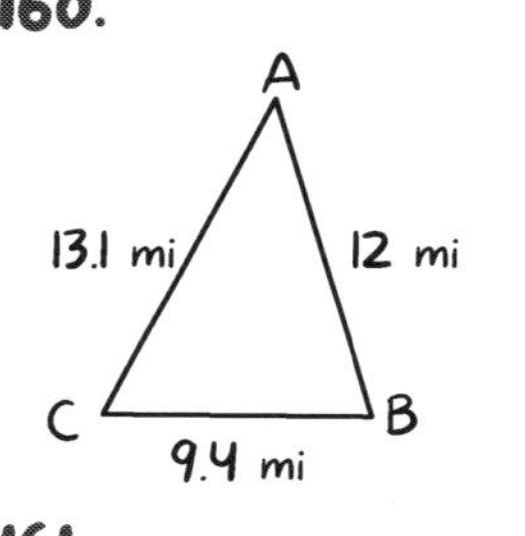

161.

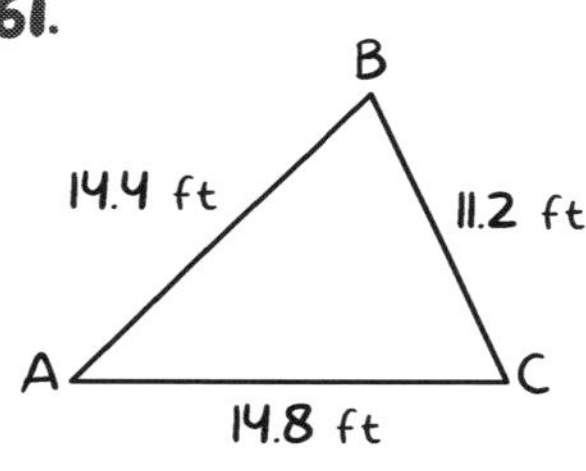

162.

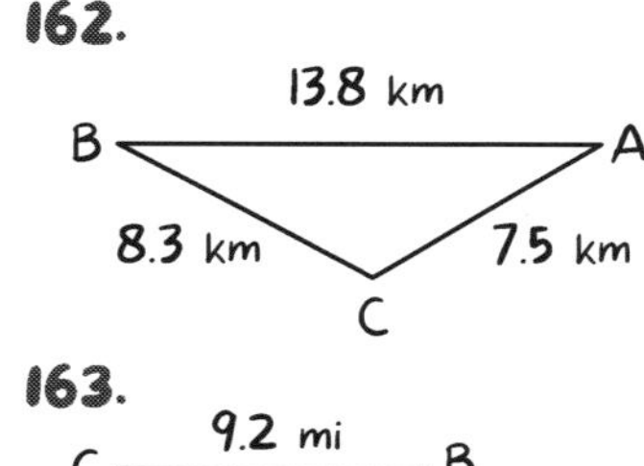

163.

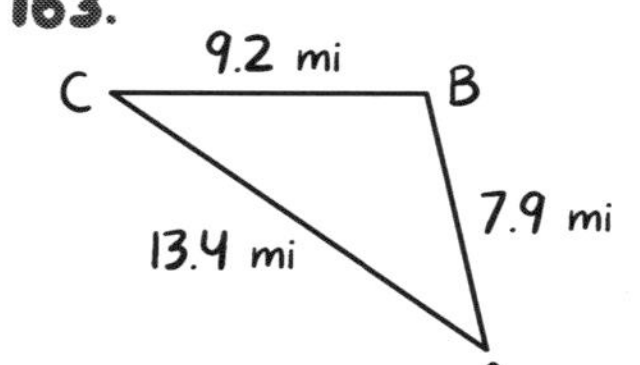

164.

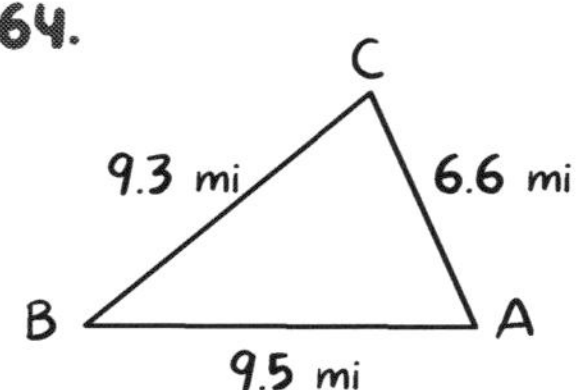

165.

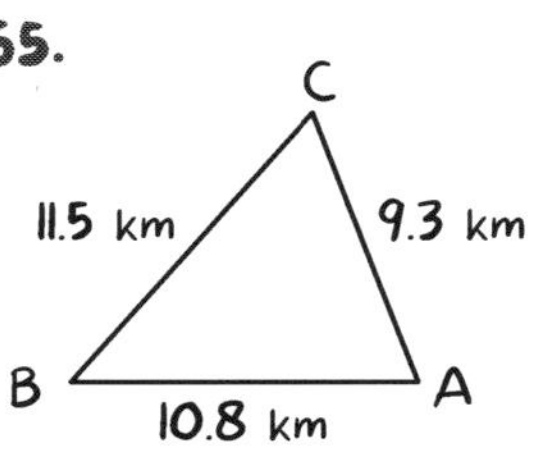

166.

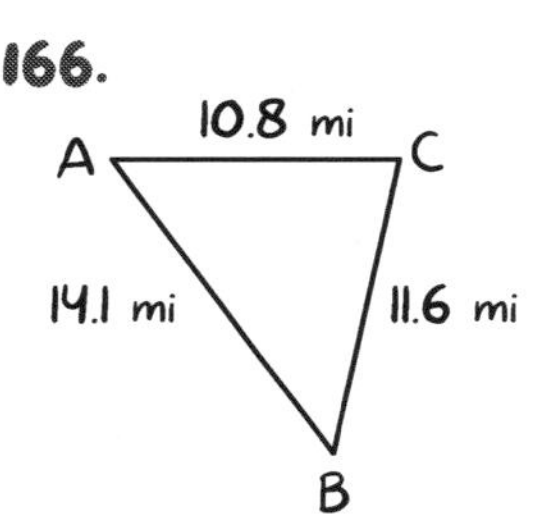

167.

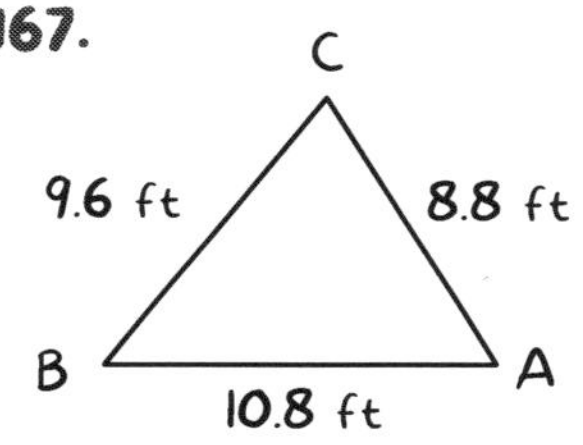

168.

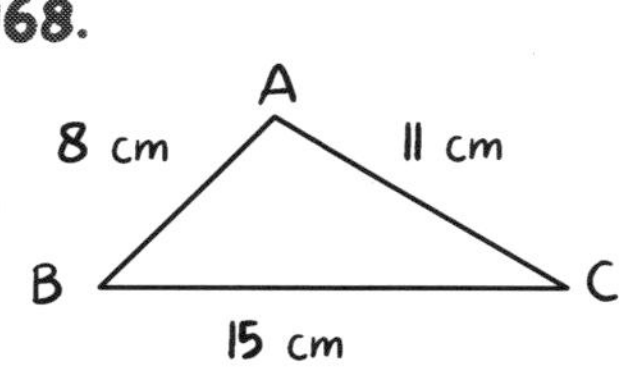

169.

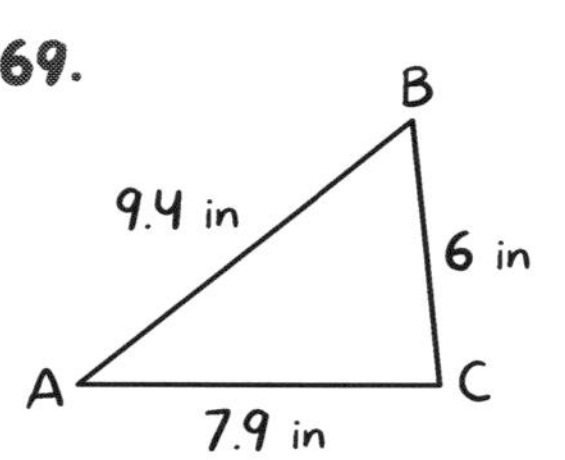

Section 6.2 Quiz

170.

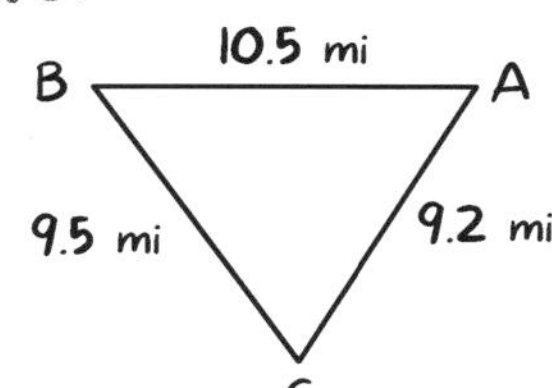

171.

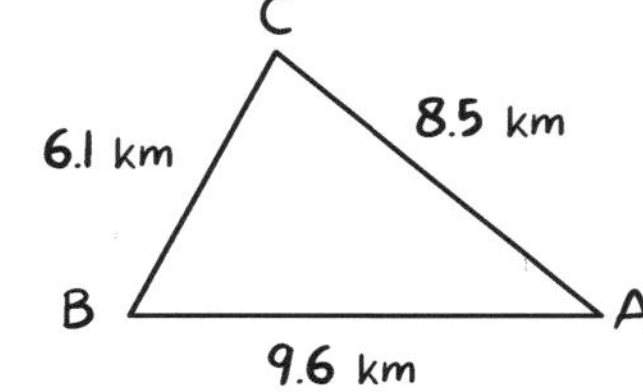

172.

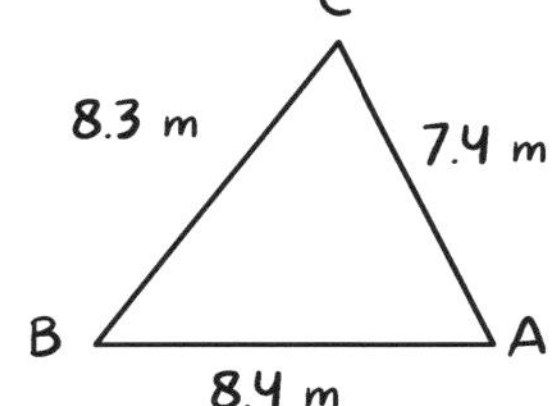

173.

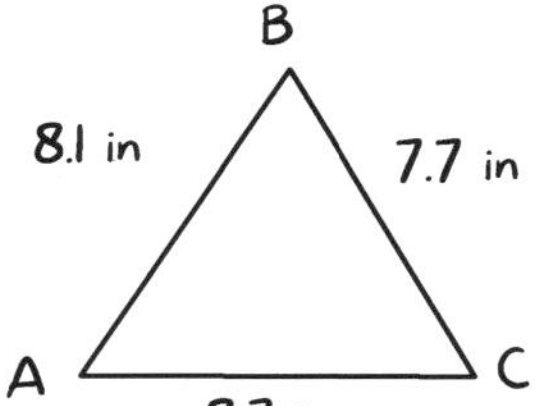

174.

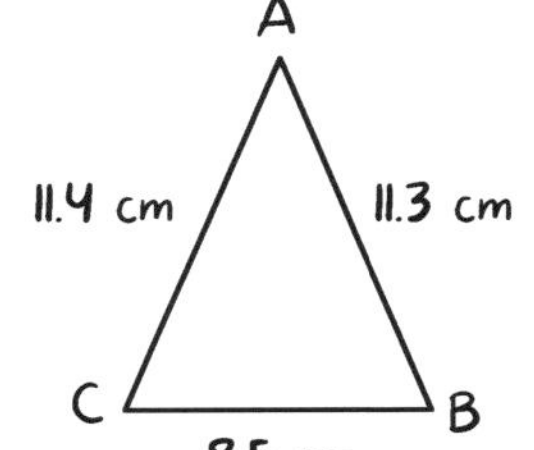

175.

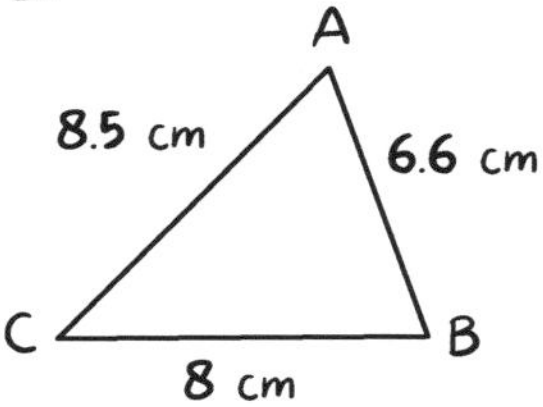

176.

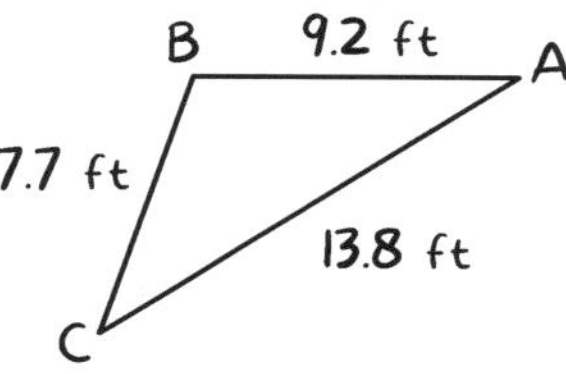

177.

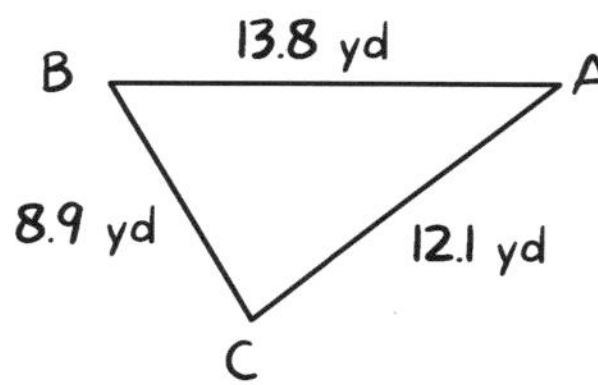

178.

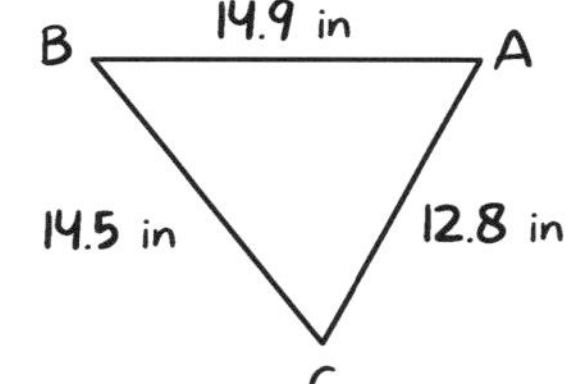

179.

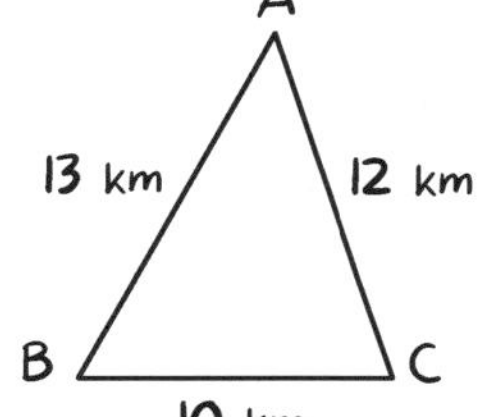

180.

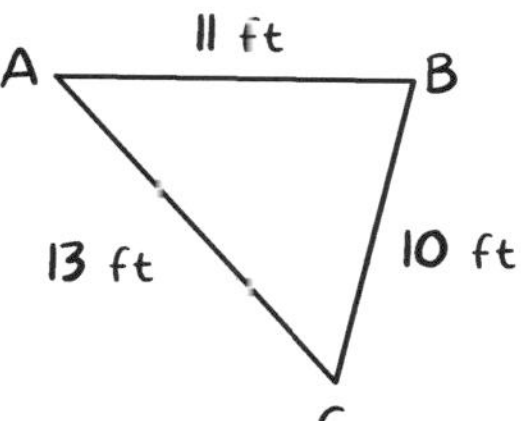

181.

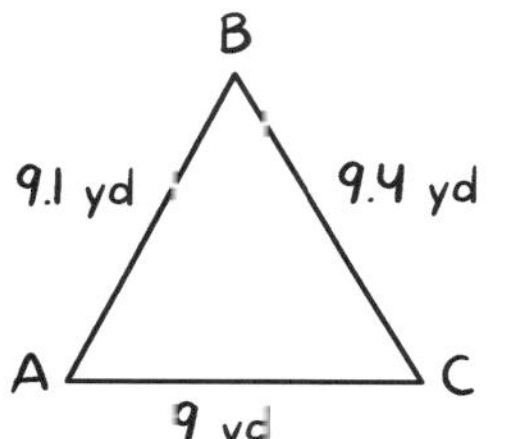

182.

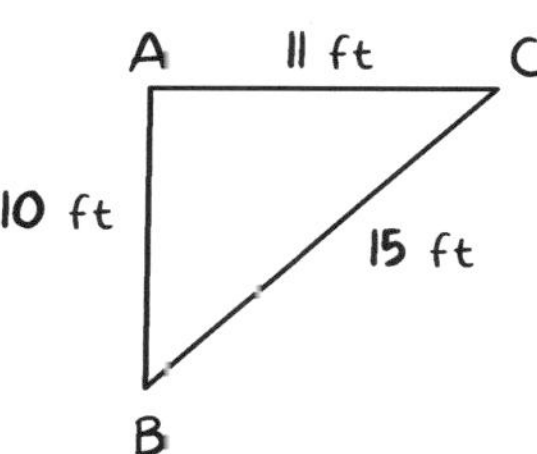

183.

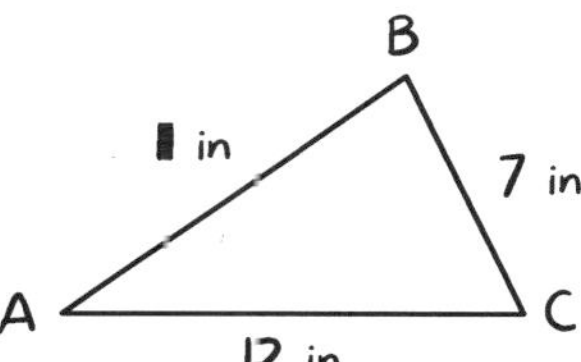

184.

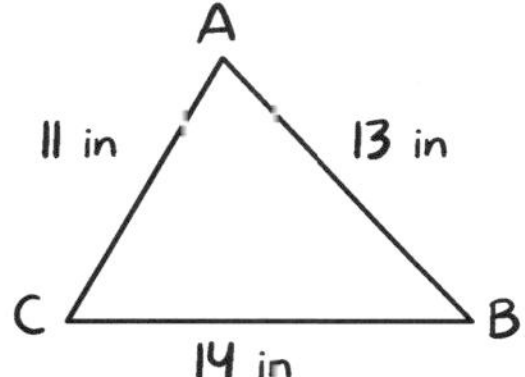

Section 6.2 Quiz

185.

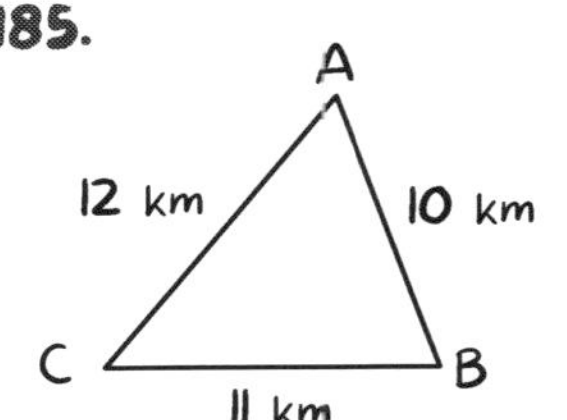

186.

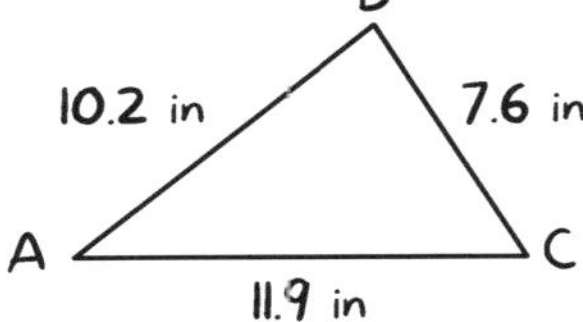

187.

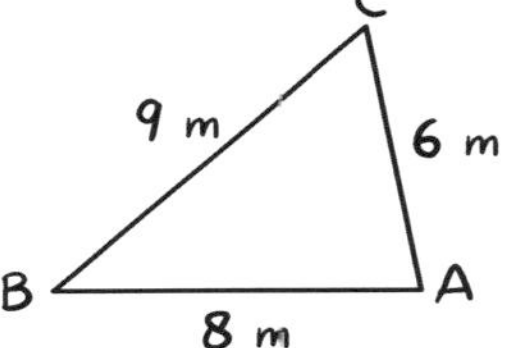

188.

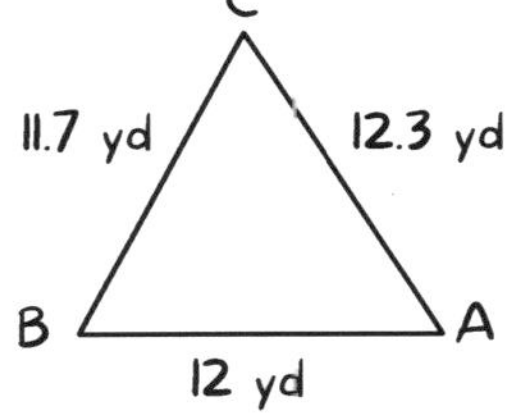

189.

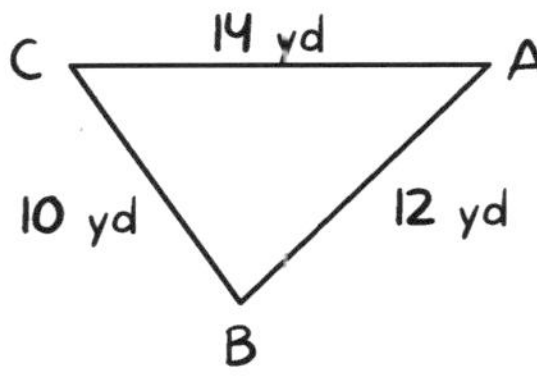

190.

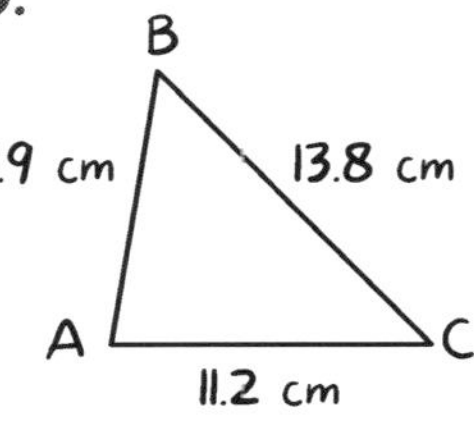

191.

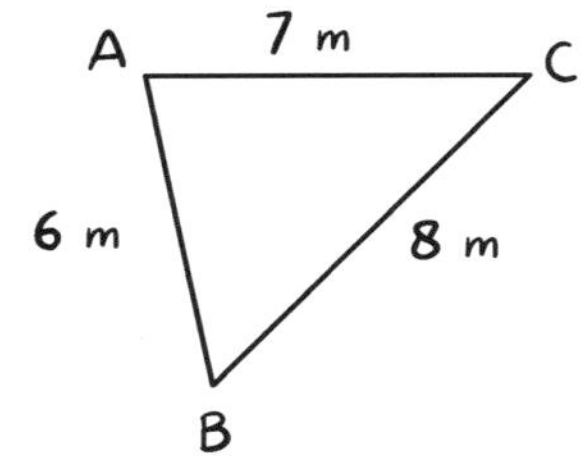

192.

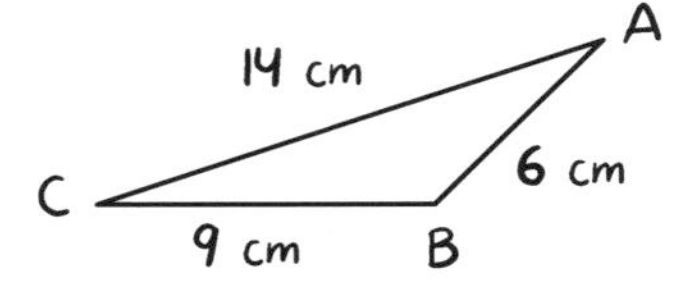

193.

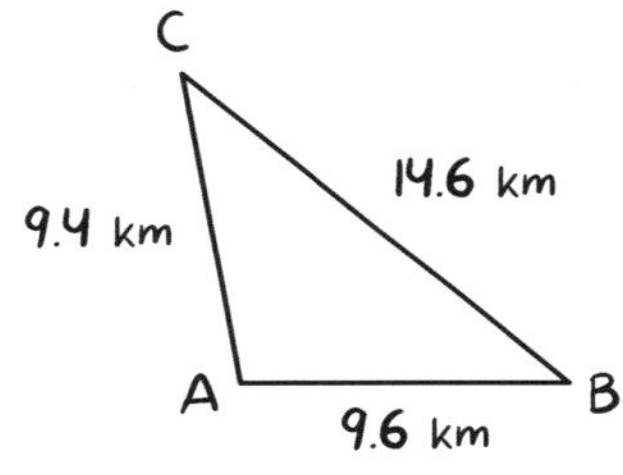

194.

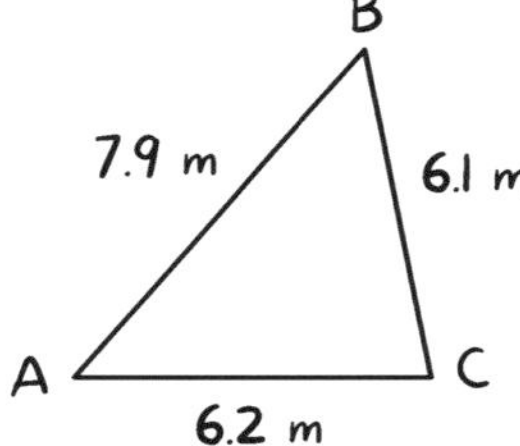

195.

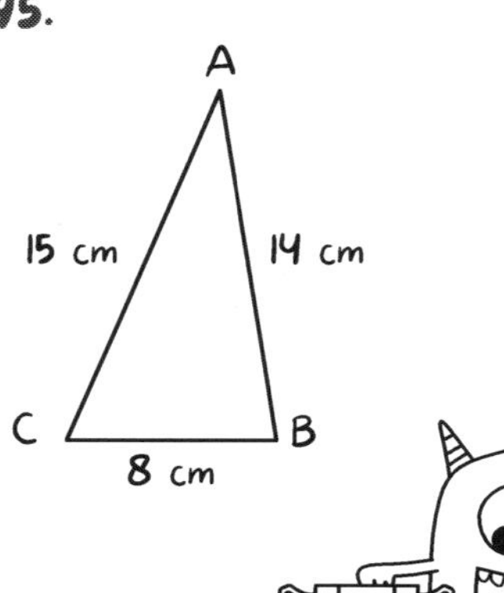

196.

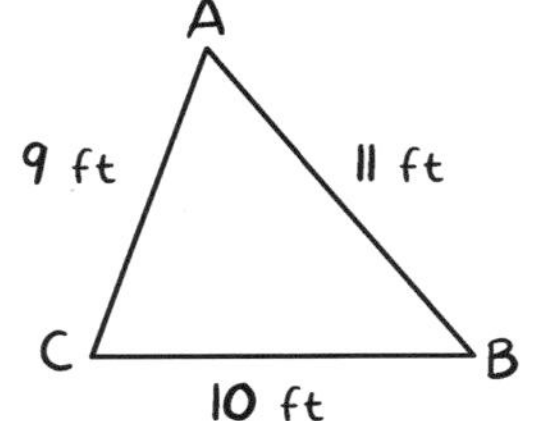

197.

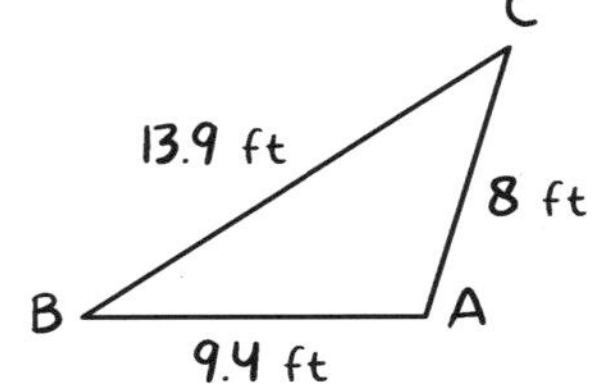

198.

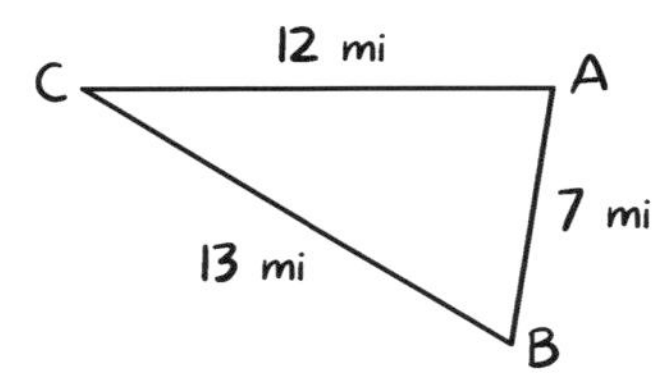

199.

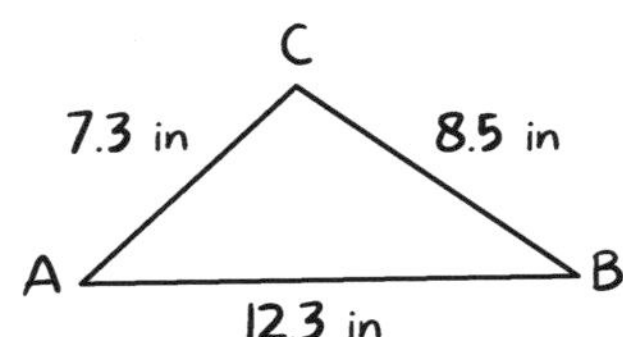

200.

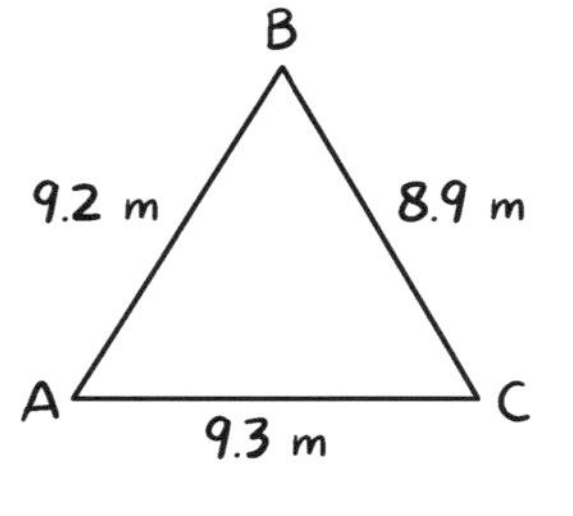

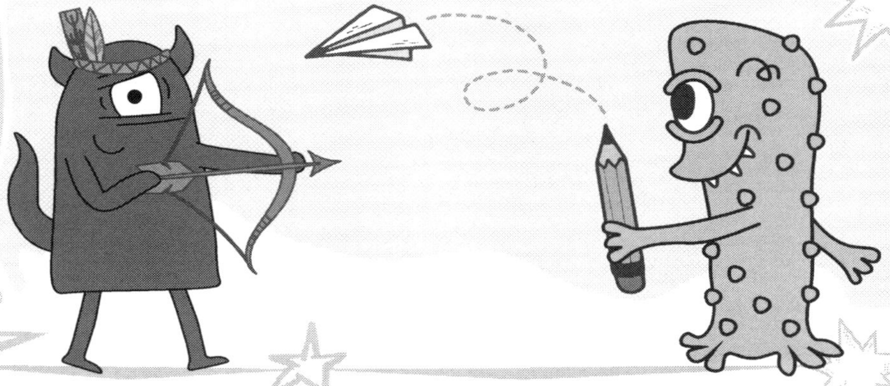

ANSWER SHEET

You can find detailed explanations of each problem in the book by visiting: ArgoPrep.com/trigonometry

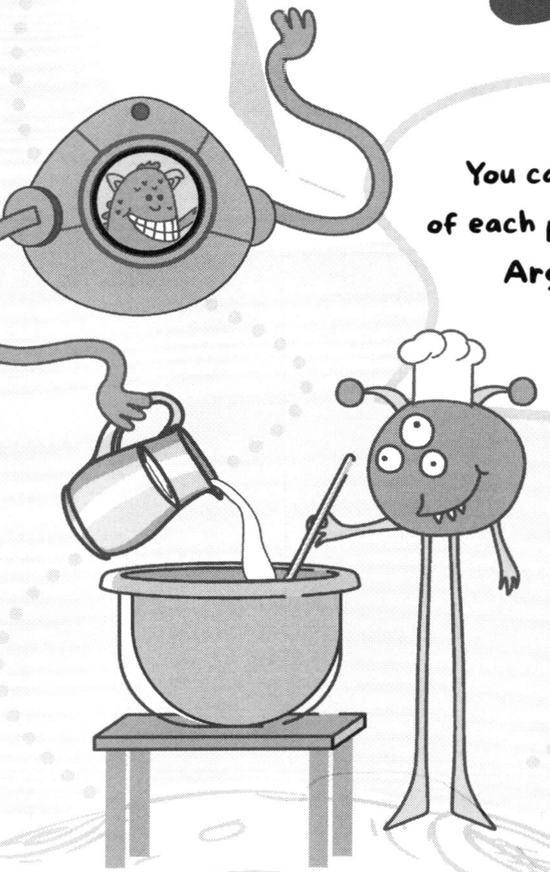

To see the answer explanations to the entire workbook, you can easily download the answer key from our website!

*Due to the high request from parents and teachers, we have removed the answer key from the workbook so you do not need to rip out the answer key while students work on the workbook.

All you need to do is:

Step 1 - Visit our website at: www.argoprep.com/trigonometry
Step 2 - You will see **DOWNLOAD ANSWER SHEETS** button.

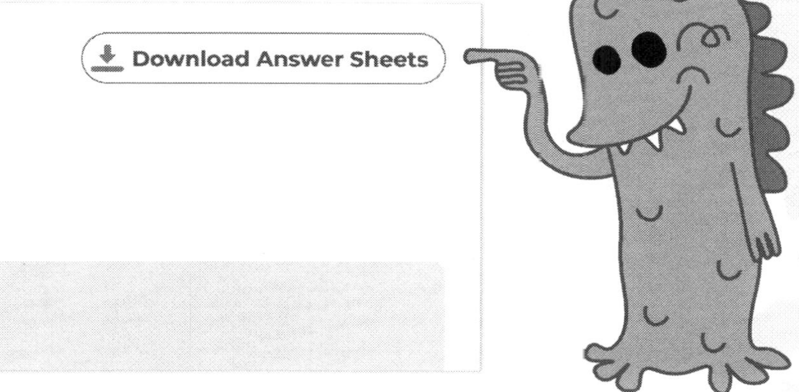

Or scan the QR Code below:

Made in the USA
Las Vegas, NV
30 January 2025

17222812R00090